# STATE OF THE
# WORLD
# 1992

Other Norton/Worldwatch Books

Lester R. Brown et al.

*State of the World 1984*

*State of the World 1985*

*State of the World 1986*

*State of the World 1987*

*State of the World 1988*

*State of the World 1989*

*State of the World 1990*

*State of the World 1991*

*The World Watch Reader*

*Saving the Planet*

# STATE OF THE WORLD
# 1992

*A Worldwatch Institute Report on Progress Toward a Sustainable Society*

PROJECT DIRECTOR
*Lester R. Brown*

ASSOCIATE PROJECT DIRECTORS
*Christopher Flavin*
*Sandra Postel*

EDITOR
*Linda Starke*

SENIOR RESEARCHERS
*Lester R. Brown*
*Alan Thein Durning*

*Christopher Flavin*
*Hilary F. French*
*Jodi Jacobson*
*Marcia D. Lowe*
*Sandra Postel*
*Michael Renner*

RESEARCH ASSOCIATES
*Holly B. Brough*
*Nicholas Lenssen*
*John C. Ryan*
*John E. Young*

W·W·NORTON & COMPANY

NEW YORK     LONDON

The text of this book is composed in Baskerville, with the display set in Caslon.
Composition and manufacturing by the Haddon Craftsmen, Inc.

First Edition

ISBN 0-393-03082-2 (cloth)
ISBN 0-393-30834-0 (paper)

W. W. Norton & Company, Inc., 500 Fifth Avenue, New York, N.Y. 10110
W. W. Norton & Company Ltd., 10 Coptic Street, London WC1A 1PU

1 2 3 4 5 6 7 8 9 0

 The book is printed on recycled paper.

# Acknowledgments

Last year, over four days in August, the world held its breath as one of the most dramatic scenes in recent decades unfolded on television screens. The swift takeover of the reins of government in Moscow, and its equally swift failure, reminded us all how rapidly the world situation can change these days. Being able to respond to such developments in an annual publication is both a pleasure and a headache. Thus we would like to begin by thanking our partners at W.W. Norton, especially Iva Ashner and Andy Marasia, for being so understanding about our need to rewrite, revise, and recast right up to the last minute. If the world ever stops changing so quickly, we promise them we will stick to a more routine publication schedule.

The authors' ability to focus on our ever changing world is in large part due to the superb research, administrative, and communications team now assembled at Worldwatch. Our thanks go to research assistants Erik Hagerman (for Chapters 8 and 10), Ann Misch (Chapters 6 and 9), Marnie Stetson (Chapters 1 and 3), and Peter Weber (Chapter 11). Worldwatch Librarian Heather Hanford contributed to research for the whole volume by organizing the vast amounts of information received at the Institute over the years, as well as assisting with the research for Chapter 1. The administrative backbone of Worldwatch, keeping us all on track and filling your orders, among other things, consists of Barbara Fallin, Gloria Grant, Blondeen Gravely, Joseph Gravely, Millicent Johnson, Reah Janise Kauffman, Steven Kaufman, James Porter, and Sarah Roberts.

Our ability to communicate the results of our research through Worldwatch Papers and *World Watch* magazine is in the capable hands of Ed Ayres, Carole Douglis, James Gorman, Denise Byers Thomma, and Howard Youth. The communication of the messages of *State of the World* itself is once again due to the red pen (actually, now a computer) and skills of independent editor Linda Starke. Our index this year was prepared by Julie Phillips.

The Worldwatch Board of Directors, under the chairmanship of Orville Freeman, continues to provide invaluable support, as do several foundations we have been pleased to deal with through the years. The Rockefeller Brothers Fund and the Winthrop Rockefeller Trust provide core funding for the *State of the World* series. Research funding comes from the Geraldine R. Dodge, George Gund, William and Flora Hewlett, W. Alton Jones, William D. and Catherine T. MacArthur, Andrew W. Mellon, Curtis and Edith Munson, Edward John Noble, Public Welfare, Surdna, and Frank Weeden foundations; from the United Nations Population Fund and the Lynn and Karl Prickett Fund; and from personal grants by Roy Young and Turki al Faisal.

Support for our work also comes from the many other people around the world who are working on the issues of concern to us all. We are most grateful for the reviews of chapter drafts by the following people, while noting that any errors remain of course the responsibility of the authors: Frank Baker, Elizabeth P. Barratt-Brown, Greg Bischak, Layne Coppock, Ward Cates, Robert Chen, Mark Cohen, Herman Daly, Diane D'Arrigo, Henry David, Elizabeth Deakin, Joan Dunlop, Jeffrey Dunoff, Holger Eisl, William L. Fisher, Beth Frederick, Mike Frisch, Adrienne Germaine, Robert Goodland, Carl Haub, Susanna Hecht, Robert A. Hefner III, Helmut Hirsch, Peter Hoffmann, Jeffrey Kenworthy, Lee Kimball, Eric D. Larson, Kenneth L. Lay, David Lowry, J.P. Maceda, Reed Noss, Joan M. Ogden, William R. Pace, Sara Parkin, David Pimentel, Lydia Popova, John Pucher, Walter Reid, Michael Replogle, Anita Glazer Sadun, Scott Saleska, Mycle Schneider, Laurel Shreck, Peter Skillern, Barry D. Solomon, Frederik van Bolhuis, Gary Vocke, Michael P. Walsh, Miranda S. Wecker, Michael Wells, Bryan D. Willson, Edward Wolf, and Garth Youngberg.

We are also indebted to many of the publishers of *State of the World* who promote the book vigorously—often beyond the level associated with the usual commercial arrangement—simply because of their commitment to these issues. For those who labor night and day, sometimes without compensation, to translate *State of the World* into various languages so that it can be published in numerous countries at the same time as the English edition, we are particularly grateful.

Although we often give special thanks in this space to an individual who has been particularly close to the Institute or especially inspirational in our work, this year it seems more appropriate to dedicate *State of the World* to a meeting—and a movement. Twenty years ago, the Stockholm conference launched the international environmental movement, and inspired many national groups to take up the cause. This June, the U.N. Conference on Environment and Development in Rio de Janeiro holds the promise of doing the same for sustainable development. If the revolution in the way the world works is to succeed, the gathering in Rio must itself be a success. To that hope we dedicate this year's *State of the World.*

*Lester R. Brown, Christopher Flavin,*
*and Sandra Postel*

# Contents

# List of Tables and Figures

## LIST OF TABLES

## LIST OF FIGURES

# Foreword

Twenty years have passed since the United Nations Conference on the Human Environment in Stockholm in 1972, the event that officially launched the international environmental era. The anniversary will be marked by the U.N. Conference on Environment and Development, to be held in Rio de Janeiro in early June. This "Earth Summit" will be concentrating on such central issues as the need to stabilize climate and preserve the biological diversity of the planet.

In an environmentally interdependent world, no country can separate its fate from that of the world as a whole. Failure to deal effectively with such issues as climate change, the loss of plant and animal species, stratospheric ozone depletion, and population growth means that all countries will suffer. That's the bad news. The good news is that interest in these issues continues to spread. One sign of this close to us is that this edition of *State of the World* is slated to appear in some 27 languages, including all the major ones—English, Spanish, Portuguese, Arabic, Hindi, Chinese, Korean, Japanese, Indonesian, German, French, Italian, Polish, Dutch, and Russian. Recent additions include Danish, Hungarian, Turkish, and Persian.

Both the English and Spanish editions of *State of the World* are now published in several different places. For example, the English edition is published in North America, the United Kingdom, India, and Australia. The Spanish edition is published in Spain, Mexico, and Argentina, with publishers in the latter two dividing the distribution in the Spanish-speaking Western Hemisphere.

Among these various editions, the North American English one is by far the largest, with a first printing of 100,000. In intensity of sales, tiny Norway with 9,000 copies for 4 million people continues to set the pace. The 1991 Finnish edition, the first in that language, bounced immediately to the top of the nonfiction best seller list, the first *State of the World* in any language to occupy that position.

As interest in this annual report escalates, more publishers are moving to publish simultaneously with the English edition. Among these are Norwegian, Swedish, Danish, Finnish, Italian, Dutch, French, and Korean. German and Japanese appear a few months after the English edition.

This past year also saw the organization of Worldwatch Institute Europe. The chairman of the board, Laurent Fabius, president of the French Assembly and former Prime Minister, hosted the launching at the French National Assembly in Paris in September. Among the founding board members are Colin Moynihan, U.K. Undersecretary of State for Energy; Jan Pronk, minister of international development from the Netherlands; Anita Roddick, founder and group managing director of The Body Shop; Federico Mayor, Secretary-General of UNESCO; Ernst von Weisacker, president of Wuppertal-Instit of Klima in Germany; Umberto Colombo of Italy; and Enrique Baron Crespo, president of the European Parliament. Like Worldwatch Institute Norden and Worldwatch Japan, Worldwatch Europe will facilitate the flow of information to the research team in Washington while working to broaden the distribution of Institute publications in Europe.

In addition to the commercial marketing of *State of the World* in various languages, the associated Worldwatch groups are also working on special distribution to national parliaments and leaders of the business community. For example, *State of the World 1991* was given to all members of the national parliaments in the four Nordic countries under the auspices of Worldwatch Institute Norden. Worldwatch Institute Europe is undertaking a similar effort in Europe, where *State of the World 1991* was distributed to all members of parliament in Belgium and France. It is a goal of the Institute to distribute copies of *State of the World* eventually to national legislators throughout the world, preferably in the local language.

Another key audience is the educational community. In the United States, 1,379 professors adopted *State of the World* for course use in 633 colleges and universities. The University of Michigan is the campus leader, using *State of the World* in some 17 courses, with a total of 1,399 students. It is followed closely by Michigan State University, the University of Colorado, Cornell University, and the University of California. In Canada, an estimated 50 or more universities have adopted *State of the World* as a text in at least one course. Other countries where *State of the World* is used in universities include Australia, Belgium, and Japan.

Another trend boosting environmental literacy emerged in 1991 as colleges started using *State of the World* for freshman orientation purposes. Slippery Rock State University in Pennsylvania used *State of the World* during orientation for its 2,300 incoming students in the fall of 1991. Similarly, Broome Community College in New York state incorporated it into an introductory program for all 2,000 freshman—a series of convocations and workshops organized around the theme of "Science and Technology for a Sustainable Society."

A project at Pennsylvania State University entitled "The Environmentalist's Bookshelf" is conducting a worldwide survey of environmental leaders, asking them to list the most influential environmental books they have read. Early returns indicate that *State of the World* is in the top three, after Aldo Leopold's *Sand County Almanac* (1949) and Rachel Carson's *Silent Spring* (1962). Needless to say, to be in such company is both humbling and encouraging.

Another new initiative in 1991 has come from Worldwatch Japan, which is working with a Japanese publisher to produce an edition of *State of the World* that could be used at the late elementary or secondary school level. Our French publisher, Economica, is working on a similar edition for use in French schools. Meanwhile, Worldwatch Norden is exploring a school version for both Norway and Sweden.

One of the sources of inspiration for us at Worldwatch is the extraordinary effort that many individuals are making to foster the distribution of *State of the World* in various languages. For example, the Norwegian edition is translated by a team of three, headed by Poul Henrik Poulsson, who is chief of information for Scandinavian Airline System (SAS). Poulsson spends evenings and weekends in November and December, not to mention Christmas Day, working on the translation to ensure that it is published simultaneously with the English edition. In Iran, Dr. H. Taravaty, a physician deeply concerned about the environmental deterioration of his country, has single-handedly translated *State of the World*, adding long hours to his demanding medical practice in order to produce a Persian edition.

The tradition of buying copies for distribution is continuing to spread. For several years Ted Turner, head of Turner Broadcasting, has been distributing copies to members of the U.S. Congress and to chief executive officers of the Fortune 500 corporations. Raymond Rooth, Norwegian business executive, purchases 900 copies for distribution in Norway. Bjorn Stigson, a director of ABB Fläkt AB, gives 500 copies to key policymakers in Sweden. They have now been joined by an Iranian physician who purchased 1,000 copies of the Persian edition for distribution to key people in Iran.

In 1991, the development assistance agencies of Norway, Sweden, and Denmark supported the Institute in an effort to raise environmental awareness and understanding in the countries to which they provide aid by funding the distribution of all Worldwatch publications, including *State of the World*, to key individuals in some 24 countries in Asia, Africa, and Latin America. They feel that a modest investment in information distribution in countries that are starved for environmental information can pay handsome dividends in policymaking.

As in the past, we welcome ideas and comments. We also like to hear about how the book is being used. The more feedback we get, the more useful *State of the World* can become.

Lester R. Brown
Christopher Flavin
Sandra Postel

Worldwatch Institute
1776 Massachusetts Ave., NW
Washington, DC 20036

*December 1991*

# STATE OF THE
# WORLD
# 1992

# 1

# Denial in the Decisive Decade

## *Sandra Postel*

Before August 1991, few people imagined that change so monumental could happen virtually overnight. In a remarkable series of events, the Soviet brand of communism crumbled irreparably, relegating the cold war to history. As striking and swift as these changes were, the remainder of this decade must give rise to transformations even more profound and pervasive if we are to hold on to realistic hopes for a better world. At issue is humanity's badly damaged relationship with its earthly home, and the urgency of repairing it before more lasting and tragic harm is done.

For better or worse, the nineties will be a decisive decade for the planet and its inhabitants. A glimpse at the environmental trends under way:

*The protective ozone shield in heavily populated latitudes of the northern hemisphere is thinning twice as fast as scientists thought just a few years ago.*

---

Chapter 1 this year is in the form of an opening essay.

Units of measure throughout this book are metric unless common usage dictates otherwise.

*A minimum of 140 plant and animal species are condemned to extinction each day.*

*Atmospheric levels of heat-trapping carbon dioxide are now 26 percent higher than the preindustrial concentration, and continue to climb.*

*The earth's surface was warmer in 1990 than in any year since recordkeeping began in the mid-nineteenth century; six of the seven warmest years on record have occurred since 1980.*

*Forests are vanishing at a rate of some 17 million hectares per year, an area about half the size of Finland.*

*World population is growing by 92 million people annually, roughly equal to adding another Mexico each year; of this total, 88 million are being added in the developing world.*[1]

Eliminating these threats to our future requires a fundamental restructuring of many elements of society—a shift from fossil fuels to efficient, solar-based energy systems, new transportation networks and city designs that lessen automobile use, redistribution of land and wealth, equality between the sexes in all cultures, and a rapid transition to smaller families. It demands reduced consumption of resources by the rich to make room for higher living standards for the poor. And with current notions of economic growth at the root of so much of the earth's ecological deterioration, it calls for a rethinking of our basic values and vision of progress.

Faced with this degree of change, we are tempted to deny the severity of environmental threats, and to assume we can get by with minor adjustments to business-as-usual. We elect politicians who validate our belief that the workings of the world are basically in order. And we tune out words like those spoken by José Lutzenberger, Brazil's Secretary of State for Environment, at a ceremony in Washington, D.C.: "It is impossible to give the whole planet the kind of lifestyle you have here, that the Germans have, that the Dutch have . . . and we must face this reality."[2]

Psychology as much as science will thus determine the planet's fate, because action depends on overcoming denial, among the most paralyzing of human responses. While it affects most of us to varying degrees, denial often runs particularly deep among those with heavy stakes in the status quo, including the political and business leaders with power to shape the global agenda.

This kind of denial can be as dangerous to society and the natural environment as an alcoholic's denial is to his or her own health and family. Because they fail to see their addiction as the principal threat to their well-being, alcoholics often end up destroying their lives. Rather than face the truth, denial's victims choose slow suicide. In a similar way, by pursuing life-styles and economic goals that ravage the environment, we sacrifice long-term health and well-being for immediate gratification—a trade-off that cannot yield a happy ending.

There is a practice in the treatment of alcoholism called intervention, in which family members and friends, aided by a counselor, attempt to shake the alcoholic out of denial. In a supportive but candid manner, they help the person grasp the gravity of the disease, the harm it is causing at home and at work, and the need for fundamental change if life for them all is to improve. A successful intervention results in the alcoholic finally acknowledging the problem, and deciding to embark upon the challenging path back to health.[3]

A similiar kind of "intervention" is needed to arrest the global disease of environmental degradation, and a uniquely suitable forum is already planned. For the first time in 20 years, people around the world—including heads of state, scientists, and activists—will gather in June 1992 to focus on environment and development. This U.N. Conference in Rio de Janeiro offers a historic opportunity to shake up our senses, to admit—individually as earth citizens, and collectively as a community of nations—that dramatic course corrections are required.

Building an environmentally secure world—one in which human needs and wants are met without destroying natural systems—requires a wholly new economic order, one grounded in the recognition that high levels of consumption, population growth, and poverty are driving the earth's environmental decline. Today, 85 percent of the world's income goes to 23 percent of its people—the affluent consumers. By contrast, more than 1 billion people, the absolute poor, survive on less than $1 a day.[4]

The rundown of environmental threats is thus matched by an equally sobering list of unmet human needs:

*One in three children is malnourished.*

*Some 1.2 billion people lack water safe to drink.*

*Nearly 3 million children die annually from diseases that could be averted by immunizations.*

*One million women die each year from preventable reproductive health problems.*

*About 1 billion adults cannot read or write.*

*More than 100 million children of primary school age are not in school.*[5]

Moreover, the developing world is dealing with these problems under greatly constrained conditions. Because of their staggering debt burdens, poor countries paid nearly as much to rich ones over the last decade as they received in new funds—including public and private loans, grants, and direct foreign investment. Besides sapping them of capital, large debt payments force developing countries to plunder forests, fisheries, and other natural resources to increase export earnings. Meanwhile, the international push for free trade may create competitive pressures for nations to adopt minimal environmental standards so as to attract investors.[6]

Put simply, the global economy is rigged against both poverty alleviation and environmental protection. Treating the earth's ecological ills as separate from issues of debt, trade, inequality, and consumption is like trying to treat heart disease without addressing a patient's obesity and high-cholesterol diet: there is no chance of lasting success.

Thus far, global environmental politics has been characterized more by foot-dragging and denial of problems than by cooperation. Few rich countries have acknowledged that they have caused the preponderance of environmental damage, and therefore have the responsibility to underwrite most of the transition to global sustainability. The United States has stonewalled even modest efforts, such as setting targets to reduce carbon emissions as part of ongoing negotiations to protect the global climate. Developing countries, on the other hand, harbor suspicions that multilateral environmental deliberations are disguised attempts to keep them economically disadvantaged. A recipe for stalemate could not be more foolproof.[7]

Applying old politics to new realities is a losing proposition for all. Just as a new set of relationships is taking shape between East and West, one that dismantles mutual threats and creates a climate of economic cooperation, so is there need for a new partnership between wealthier countries (the "North") and the developing world (the "South")—one that embraces the common goals of restoring the planet's health and promoting sustainable progress.

## Few rich countries have acknowledged that they have caused the preponderance of environmental damage.

The ending of the cold war offers an auspicious opportunity to set new priorities and to reallocate resources. Bloated military budgets represent an enormous source of additional funds for investments in energy efficiency, forest protection, infant and maternal health, education, family planning, safe drinking water, and other development work. At roughly $980 billion in 1990, or $185 for every person on the planet, global military spending is way out of line with the diminishing magnitude of military threats. Efforts to ward off far more pervasive environmental and social hazards, meanwhile, are grossly underfunded. Worldwide spending on family planning, for instance, totals about $4.5 billion annually.[8]

Estimates by the United Nations Development Programme (UNDP) suggest that additional investments equal to just over 2 percent of global military expenditures, or about $20 billion per year, would allow everyone in the world to receive primary education and health care, family planning services, safe drinking water, and adequate nutrition. Far larger shifts will be needed to deal with major environmental threats. Cleaning up nuclear weapons sites in the United States alone, for example, may cost upwards of $300 billion.[9]

Military expenditures anywhere represent an unfortunate drain on productive resources, but they are strikingly wasteful in developing countries racked by poverty. Many Third World governments spend twice as much on the military as on health or education, and a few—including Angola, Iran, and Pakistan—expend twice as much as on both combined. While in the industrial world there are 3.3 soldiers for every doctor, in the developing world soldiers outnumber doctors by 8.4 to 1.[10]

**A successful global partnership would include sizable transfers of capital and technology from North to South on preferential terms.**

To encourage shifts in public expenditures, Mahbub ul Haq, former Finance and Planning Minister of Pakistan and now an advisor to UNDP, advocates tying bilateral aid to reductions in military spending by recipient governments: "Unless external donors are willing to put a squeeze on powerful vested interests within the system, the squeeze will inevitably fall on the weakest and the most vulnerable groups in society. External assistance should be regarded as an alliance not with governments—which often change—but with people." Although developing countries often decry the imposition of conditions on bilateral aid, focusing on the people the funds are supposed to benefit puts the concept of development assistance in the proper perspective.[11]

Efforts to curb consumption of energy and other resources would save money in most cases, yet some of the worst offenders are unwilling to commit to even a cost-effective efficiency path. The United States would have spent $160 billion more on energy in 1990 had it not improved energy efficiency beyond 1973 levels. But these savings are only a beginning: the California Energy Commission estimates that cost-effective investments could reduce total U.S. electricity demand by 40–75 percent while improving the quality of life through cleaner air and lower energy costs.[12]

Nationwide installation of just one fixture—low-flow showerheads that conserve hot water—would save as much energy as oil drilling in Alaska's Arctic National Wildlife Refuge would be expected to produce, and at far lower economic and environmental cost. By insisting on drilling in the Arctic wilderness and other sensitive areas, the U.S. administration shows the degree to which its decisions are controlled by addiction to a destructive energy path and denial of the long-term consequences—a dependency nourished by the power of special interests.[13]

Along with an overhaul of domestic priorities within both industrial and developing societies, a successful global partnership would include sizable transfers of capital and technology from North to South on preferential terms. Ministers from 41 developing nations met in Beijing in June 1991 and called for the establishment of a new "Green Fund" to step up financial flows. The Beijing Declaration makes clear that for the developing world to sign on, a global bargain must include some such mechanism for the industrial countries to repay the ecological debt they incurred during decades of destructive economic practices.[14]

One noteworthy move in this direction is the new Global Environment Facility managed by the World Bank (in collaboration with UNDP and the United Nations Environment Programme) and slated to invest some $1.5 billion over three years. Given the World Bank's poor environmental record, however, and the industrial countries' dominance of Bank lending practices, this pilot financing scheme has many obstacles to overcome if it is to promote both a new North-South partnership and conservation projects that meet local people's needs.[15]

Additional financing could come from taxes on carbon emissions, the leading cause of global warming. Such levies would help bring the prices of fossil fuels into line with their true costs, including environmental damages, and thereby curb greenhouse gas emissions. The executive commission of the European Community (EC) has endorsed such a tax, and in mid-October 1991 the environment ministers of all 12 EC countries expressed support for it. Industrial countries could devote a share of the resulting revenues to energy efficiency improvements in poorer nations. An extra tax of $10 per ton of carbon emitted by the leading industrial nations, for instance, would initially generate some $30 billion per year for a global fund.[16]

Thus far, however, the United States and other key lenders remain opposed to the idea of greatly increasing investment aid to the developing world. Indeed, the foreign aid budgets of only a handful of countries—Denmark, the Netherlands, Norway, and Sweden—currently meet the internationally endorsed level of 0.7 percent of gross national product (GNP). The United States, near the bottom of the donors' list, gives 0.2 percent of its GNP in aid. And, as with many other countries' assistance, much U.S. aid serves strategic political purposes rather than development.[17]

At the heart of reshaping the global economy is the establishment of new goals centered on sustainability. "Economic growth," as measured by the GNP, continues to be our key indicator of "progress," even though it is steadily destroying the natural systems that are its foundation. Likewise, we persist in equating economic growth with "development," even when the poorest of the poor end up worse off. A revamping of economic rules and principles is essential to make them serve rather than subvert the fundamental aim of shaping a better future. National accounting that subtracts for the depletion or destruction of natural resources, decision-making techniques that value future costs and benefits more thoroughly, and investment criteria that stem the loss of natural capital are among the reforms vitally needed.[18]

Here and there, creative approaches are helping to redefine progress. The Grameen Bank of Bangladesh, for instance, has boosted income among the poor by making more than 800,000 loans, averaging $67 each, to women possessing an entrepreneurial spirit but little or no capital. Local communities in the Brazilian Amazon are attempting to manage tropical forests sustainably for rubber, nuts, and other products, and have succeeded in getting the government to set aside 3 million hectares as "extractive reserves" for their use.[19]

In the corporate world, Southern California Edison, an investor-owned energy utility with some 10 million ratepayers, plans to invest heavily enough in energy efficiency to reduce its carbon emissions by 19 percent over the next two decades. And among multilateral institutions, the U.N. International Fund for Agricultural Development has an impressive 14-year track record of more than 200 projects focused on helping poor people meet their needs as they perceive them. Working against the odds, initiatives like these advance the cause of global sustainability. But unless the odds are altered so as to favor such actions, they will remain too few in number and too small in scale.[20]

We can choose to downplay the dangers of the trends now unfolding, and muddle through awhile longer. But where will denial get us in the end? As Sara Parkin, spokesperson for the U.K. Green Party, observes: "Our numbness, our silence, our lack of outrage, could mean we end up the only species to have minutely monitored our own extinction. What a measly epitaph that would make:

'they saw it coming but hadn't the wit to stop it happening.' "[21]

Extraordinary change is possible when enough courageous people grasp the need for it and become willing to act. Five years ago, few envisaged that democratization could sweep so rapidly across so much of the world. Now the question is, who will lead an intervention against our collective denial of environmental threats? Who will be the Gorbachevs of the Environmental Revolution?

Building a sustainable world will ask a lot of ourselves and our leaders. But it is within our power, if we choose to take on the challenge. Once denial is stripped away, what other option do we have?

# 2

# Conserving Biological Diversity

*John C. Ryan*

Complex beyond understanding and valuable beyond measure, biological diversity is the total variety of life on earth. No one knows, even to the nearest order of magnitude, how many life forms humanity shares the planet with: roughly 1.4 million species have been identified, but scientists now believe the total number is between 10 million and 80 million. Most of these are small animals, such as insects and mollusks, in little-explored environments such as the tropical forest canopy or the ocean floor. But nature retains its mystery in familiar places as well. Even a handful of soil from the eastern United States is likely to contain many species unknown to science.[1]

Despite the vast gaps in knowledge, it is clear that biodiversity—the ecosystems, species, and genes that together make life on earth both pleasant and possible—is collapsing at nothing less than mind-boggling rates. Difficult as it is to accept, mass extinction has already begun, and the world is irrevocably committed to many further losses. Harvard biologist Edward O. Wilson estimates

that, at a minimum, 50,000 invertebrate species per year—nearly 140 each day—are condemned to extinction by the destruction of their tropical rain forest habitat. Large creatures as well as small are vanishing: deforestation condemns at least one species of bird, mammal, or plant to extinction daily.[2]

Moreover, biological impoverishment is occurring all over the globe. Ecosystems with fewer species than rain forests have, such as islands and freshwater lakes, are probably losing even greater proportions of their varied life forms. Genetic varieties within species and entire natural communities are also disappearing, likely at rates greater than the extinction of species themselves.[3]

Protection of wildlands will be the top priority of any meaningful strategy to safeguard the world's biological heritage. True protection of these ecosystems alone will require sweeping changes in the way humanity views and uses land and a commitment to limit the amount of the earth's bounty that society appropriates to itself. But in order to staunch the massive bleeding of life from the planet, humanity must learn not only to save diversity in remote corners of the world, but to maintain and restore it in the forests and waters that we use, and in the villages and cities where we live.

---

**Like every species, ours is intimately dependent on others for its well-being.**

---

Why should disappearing beetles, plants, or birds concern us? To biologists, and to many others, the question hardly needs asking: a species is the unique and irreplaceable product of millions of years of evolution, a thing of value for scientific study, for its beauty, and for itself. For many people, however, a more compelling reason to conserve biological diversity is likely to be pure self-interest: like every species, ours is intimately dependent on others for its well-being.

Time after time, creatures thought useless or harmful are found to play crucial roles in natural systems. Predators driven to extinction no longer keep populations of rodents or insects in check; earthworms or termites killed by pesticides no longer aerate soils; mangroves cut for firewood no longer protect coastlines from erosion. Diversity is of fundamental importance to all ecosystems and all economies.

Few would argue that every beetle or remaining patch of natural vegetation is crucial to planetary welfare. But the dismantling, piece by piece, of global life-support systems carries grave risks. No one has pleaded biodiversity's case better than American wildlife biologist Aldo Leopold nearly a half-century ago: "If the biota, in the course of aeons, has built something we like but do not understand, then who but a fool would dis-

card seemingly useless parts? To keep every cog and wheel is the first precaution of intelligent tinkering."[4]

## LIFE ON THE BRINK

Biodiversity is commonly analyzed at three levels: the variety of communities and ecosystems within which organisms live and evolve, the variety of species themselves, and the genetic variety within those species. The degradation of whole ecosystems, such as forests, wetlands, and coastal waters, is in itself a major loss of biodiversity and the single most important factor behind the current mass extinction of species.

Home to at least half the planet's species, tropical forests have been reduced by nearly half their original area, and in 1990 deforestation claimed 17 million hectares, an area about the size of Washington state. In Benin, Côte d'Ivoire, western Ecuador, El Salvador, Ghana, Haiti, Nigeria, and Togo, forests have all but disappeared. In most nations, forests occur increasingly in small fragments surrounded by degraded land, with their ability to sustain viable populations of wildlife and vital ecological processes impaired.[5]

Brazil has more tropical forest—and likely more species—than any other nation. (See Table 2–1.) Massive deforestation continues there, but has slowed appreciably since its 1987 peak, thanks to unusually rainy weather, changes in government policy, and a slowdown in the Brazilian economy. Moreover, with nearly 90 percent of its groves still standing, by national or international standards the Brazilian Amazon is relatively untouched. Brazil's most endangered ecosystems are its unique coastal forests. Logging and agricultural and urban expansion have destroyed more

## Table 2-1. Deforestation in the Megadiversity Countries, Eighties

| Country | Share of World's Land Area | Share of World's Flowering Plant Species[1] | Annual Deforestation Rate[2] | |
|---|---|---|---|---|
| | (percent) | | (square kilometers) | (percent) |
| Brazil | 6.3 | 22 | 13,820[3] | 0.4 |
| Colombia | 0.8 | 18 | 6,000 | 1.3 |
| China | 7.0 | 11 | n.a. | n.a. |
| Mexico | 1.4 | 10 | 7,000 | 1.5 |
| Australia | 5.7 | 9 | n.a. | n.a. |
| Indonesia | 1.4 | 8 | 10,000 | 0.9 |
| Peru | 1.0 | 8 | 2,700 | 0.4 |
| Malaysia | 0.2 | 6 | 3,100 | 1.5 |
| Ecuador | 0.2 | 6 | 3,400 | 2.4 |
| India | 2.2 | 6 | 10,000 | 2.7 |
| Zaire | 1.7 | 4 | 4,000 | 0.4 |
| Madagascar | 0.4 | 4 | 1,500 | 1.5 |

[1]Based on total of 250,000 known species; because of overlap between countries, figures cannot be added. [2]Closed forests only. [3]1990 figure.
SOURCES: Jeffrey A. McNeely et al., *Conserving the World's Biological Diversity* (Gland, Switzerland, and Washington, D.C.: International Union for Conservation of Nature and Natural Resources (IUCN) et al., 1989); World Resources Institute, *World Resources 1990–91* (New York: Oxford University Press, 1990); Ricardo Bonalume, "Amazonia: Deforestation Rate Is Falling," *Nature,* April 4, 1991; Walter V. Reid, "How Many Species Will There Be?" in J. Sayer and T. Whitmore, eds., *Tropical Deforestation and the Extinction of Species* (Gland, Switzerland: IUCN, forthcoming).

than 95 percent of the once-vast Atlantic coastal rain forests and the coniferous Araucaria forests of southern Brazil.[6]

Outside the tropics, a number of ecosystem types have been all but eliminated from the planet, including the tall grass prairies of North America, the great cedar groves of Lebanon, and the old-growth hardwood forests of Europe and North America. Less widespread than their tropical counterparts, temperate rain forests are probably the more endangered ecosystem. Of the 31 million hectares once found on earth, 56 percent have been logged or cleared. In the contiguous United States, less than 10 percent of old-growth rain forests survive, scattered in small fragments throughout the Pacific Northwest. In the rain forests of British Columbia, only one of 25 large coastal watersheds has wholly escaped logging.[7]

Wetlands, like forests, are important repositories of biological diversity. Among the world's most productive ecosystems, they help regulate water flows, remove sediments and pollutants, and provide essential habitat for waterfowl, fish, and numerous other species. They are threatened in many parts of the world by drainage for agriculture or urban expansion, conversion to aquaculture ponds, overgrazing, and, in forested wetlands, logging.

Damage to wetlands has been severe in industrial nations, with losses in Australia, New Zealand, and California exceeding 90 percent. Canada houses one fourth of the world's wetlands, and overall it has lost relatively few. But even here, major losses have occurred: Atlantic salt marshes, prairie wetlands, and Pacific estuarine marshes have all been reduced to a third of their original extent. Vast areas of bog and marsh remain in the country's sparsely populated northern regions.[8]

Mangroves, one of the most threatened and valuable types of wetlands, have suffered heavy losses in Asia, Latin America, and west Africa. Nearly half of these protective swamp forests in Ecuador, for example, have been cleared, mostly for shrimp ponds, and plans call for the conversion of a like proportion of the remaining areas. India, Pakistan, and Thailand have all lost at least three fourths of their mangroves. Indonesia seems determined to follow suit: in Kalimantan, its largest province, 95 percent of all mangroves are to be cleared for pulpwood production, even though the fisheries nursed by Indonesian mangroves earn roughly seven times as much in export revenue as all their wood and charcoal production combined.[9]

Mangroves and other coastal wetlands form part of an interdependent complex of coastal habitats, protecting those inland from the erosive force of the sea and those offshore from land-based pollution. Although coral reefs withstand the constant pounding of ocean waves, they are especially sensitive to changes in nutrients, water temperature, and light levels. When soil erosion, fertilizers, or sewage pollute the clear tropical waters where they thrive, these communities of slow-growing animals are often killed off, smothered or overgrown by fast-spreading algae.[10]

Direct monitoring is difficult for underwater communities, but it is likely that reefs are in worse condition than forests or wetlands. The most recent global survey, based on data from the early eighties, found problems such as sedimentation, water pollution, and direct damage from fishers and tourists degrading reefs off 90 of 109 countries. In a decade-old study, the Philippine government estimated that 71 percent of that nation's reefs—the most diverse in the world—were in "poor to fair" condition at best; only 6 percent were judged "excellent."[11]

Deforestation and coastal populations in the tropics have increased dramatically in the past decade, undoubtedly burdening reefs with greater sedimentation and pollution. In addition, corals are undergoing an entirely new category of degradation: massive bleaching. When corals are subjected to extreme stress, they jettison the colorful algae they live in symbiosis with, exposing the white skeleton of dead coral beneath a single layer of clear living tissue. If the stress persists, the coral dies. Now considered the worst threat to survival of coral reefs, worldwide bleaching occurred without warning in 1980, 1983, 1987, and 1990, affecting most seriously the corals of the Caribbean. Its causes are not known, but bleaching appears when ocean temperatures are abnormally high, leading some scientists to call it a harbinger of global warming.[12]

The most familiar type of biodiversity loss is the decline of species, a process now occurring at thousands of times its natural "background" rate. (See Table 2–2.) The majority of species—and of extinctions—are invertebrates of the tropical forest, too numerous to identify, let alone monitor the status of. Outside the tropics, the situation is somewhat easier to track. All 41 species of Hawaiian tree snail, for example, were listed as endangered by the U.S. government in 1981; today only two remain in substantial numbers, and they are declining rapidly.[13]

Little attention has been paid to conservation of such unbecoming creatures, but their loss can have profound consequences. Populations of American oysters, which were once so numerous in the Chesapeake Bay that they filtered all its water every three days, have fallen by 99 percent since 1870. Now, it takes a

**Table 2-2. Observed Declines in Selected Animal Species, Early Nineties**

| Species Type | Observation |
| --- | --- |
| Amphibians[1] | Worldwide decline observed in recent years. Wetland drainage and invading species have extinguished nearly half New Zealand's unique frog fauna. Biologists cite European demand for frogs' legs as a cause of the rapid nationwide decline of India's two most common bullfrogs. |
| Birds | Three fourths of the world's bird species are declining in population or threatened with extinction. |
| Fish | One third of North America's freshwater fish stocks are rare, threatened, or endangered; one third of U.S. coastal fish have declined in population since 1975. Introduction of the Nile perch has helped drive half the 400 species of Lake Victoria, Africa's largest lake, to or near extinction. |
| Invertebrates | On the order of 100 species lost to deforestation each day. Western Germany reports one fourth of its 40,000 known invertebrates to be threatened. Roughly half the freshwater snails of the southeastern United States are extinct or nearly so. |
| Mammals | Almost half of Australia's surviving mammals are threatened with extinction. France, western Germany, the Netherlands, and Portugal all report more than 40 percent of their mammals as threatened. |
| Carnivores | Virtually all species of wild cats and most bears are declining seriously in numbers. |
| Primates[2] | More than two thirds of the world's 150 species are threatened with extinction. |
| Reptiles | Of the world's 270 turtle species, 42 percent are rare or threatened with extinction. |

[1]Class that includes frogs, toads, and salamanders.    [2]Order that includes monkeys, lemurs, and humans.
SOURCE: Worldwatch Institute, based on sources documented in endnote 13.

year for oysters to filter the waters of the Chesapeake, one reason the bay is increasingly muddied and oxygen-poor.[14]

Reflecting the widespread degradation of aquatic habitats, freshwater fish are declining in many areas. In the main rivers and great seas (the Black, Caspian, Aral, and Azov) of the southern Soviet Union, more than 90 percent of major commercial fish species have been killed off. A recent four-year inventory in peninsular Malaysia found fewer than half the 266 fish species known to have inhabited the region's rivers before the advent of large-scale logging.[15]

Intensive fishing has mined many coastal and open-ocean fisheries. Catches of Atlantic cod and herring, Southern African pilchard, Pacific Ocean perch, King Crab, and Peruvian anchovies have all declined over the past two decades, according to the U.N. Environment Programme. Namibian fisheries are on the brink of collapse: in mid-1991 the fisheries department said that a fishing moratorium of at least five years was needed to allow anchovies, mackerel, and other species to recover from "potentially disastrous" levels.[16]

Scientists have discovered an apparent worldwide decline in amphibians (species such as frogs and salamanders) in recent years. Because amphibians divide their time between land and water habitats and their skin is permeable to airborne gases, they are especially sensitive indicators of environmental degradation. Habitat conversion and acid precipitation are likely causes of many species' decline, but they mysteriously appear to be diminishing in seemingly pristine nature reserves. Again, the unexpected consequences of extinction can be severe. An adult frog can eat its own weight in insects daily: in India, diminishing frog populations have been linked to higher rates of pest damage to crops in Maharashtra state and malaria in West Bengal.[17]

Paralleling patterns of animal diversity, two thirds of the world's plants are found in the tropics. Although prehistorical extinction spasms tended to claim mostly animals, plants are now threatened with extinction on a large scale. Peter Raven of the Missouri Botanical Garden estimates that one fourth of all tropical plants are likely to be wiped out in the next 30 years.[18]

Outside the tropics, the arid landscapes of southern Africa house the world's greatest concentration of threatened plants. Four fifths of the plants there are found nowhere else, and 13 percent of these—more than 2,300 species—are reportedly threatened. About 3,000 species in the United States, nearly one in every eight native plants, are considered in danger of extinction; more than 700 are likely to disappear in the next 10 years without strong efforts to save them.[19]

Some analysts believe that the greatest threat to human welfare comes from the loss of genetic diversity within species, most notably food crops and their wild relatives. Farmers have used and created genetic diversity for millennia to increase agricultural production; genetic engineering and other high-tech forms of crop breeding are equally dependent on it. Especially in developing nations, generations of farmers have developed a remarkable array of crops. The Ifugao people of the island of Luzon in the Philippines identify more than 200 varieties of sweet potato by name, while farmers in India have planted perhaps 30,000 different strains of rice over the past 50 years.[20]

The widespread introduction of a handful of high-yielding crop varieties has boosted food production over the past several decades but eliminated many traditional strains that were well adapted to local ecosystems and could have been used to develop higher-yielding, locally appropriate crops. At current planting rates, three quarters of India's rice fields may be sown in only 10 varieties by 2005. In Indonesia, 1,500 local varieties of rice have disappeared in the past 15 years, and nearly three fourths of the rice planted today descends from a single maternal plant. Similarly, 71 percent of U.S. corn fields are planted in just six varieties, while nine varieties of wheat occupy half of all U.S. wheatland.[21]

Such high levels of agricultural uniformity leave fields vulnerable to pest and disease outbreaks that, at worst, can rampage over entire countries, as in the Irish potato famine of 1846. In 1991, the genetic similarity of orange trees in Brazil provoked the nation's worst-ever outbreak of infections such as citrus cancer, severely reducing output. Fortunately, some farmers add new crops to their traditional menu without completely abandoning the old. Peasants in the Tulumayo Valley of eastern Peru, for example, raise nearly 180 different varieties of potato, even though nearly half their fields now grow improved potatoes.[22]

Genetic erosion is also a problem among wild life forms: through population reductions or intentional homogenization, many species have lost much of their internal diversity, and hence their ability to survive collectively. On the west coast of North America, at least 106 major populations of salmon and steelhead have been wiped out; another 214 types of anadromous fish (those that migrate between fresh water and the ocean) are at some risk. Just as monoculture plantations have largely replaced the region's forest wilderness, hatchery fish have supplanted their wild cousins—about 75 percent of the Columbia River basin's fish are now hatchery-produced.[23]

## PROTECTING ECOSYSTEMS

For the past century, nature conservation efforts have focused on the protection of habitats in parks and other reserves. This strategy has had an important role in preserving biological diversity. Today there are just under 7,000 nationally protected areas in the world, covering some 651 million hectares, 4.9 percent of the earth's land surface. (See Table 2–3.)

Several nations have, on paper at least, set impressive proportions of their territory off-limits to development: Bhutan, Botswana, Czechoslovakia, Panama, and Venezuela notably have over 15 percent of their lands designated as parks. National or global figures, however, mask great unevenness. Parks in Chile, for example, are concentrated high in the scenic Andes, and more than half of Chile's unique vegetation types are not protected at all. Globally, high-altitude

**Table 2-3. Nationally Protected Areas, Selected Countries and World, 1990**

| Country | Area of National Parks and of Equivalent Sites[1] | Share of Total Land Area |
|---|---|---|
| | (thousand hectares) | (percent) |
| Venezuela | 20,265 | 22.2 |
| Bhutan | 924 | 19.7 |
| Chile | 13,650 | 18.0 |
| Botswana | 10,025 | 17.2 |
| Panama | 1,326 | 17.2 |
| Czechoslovakia | 1,964 | 15.4 |
| Namibia | 10,346 | 12.6 |
| United States | 98,342 | 10.5 |
| Indonesia | 17,800 | 9.3 |
| Australia | 45,654 | 5.9 |
| Canada | 49,452 | 5.0 |
| Mexico | 9,420 | 4.8 |
| Brazil | 20,525 | 2.4 |
| Madagascar | 1,078 | 1.8 |
| Soviet Union | 24,073 | 1.1 |
| World | 651,468 | 4.9 |

[1]Includes protected areas over 1,000 hectares in IUCN's Categories 1–5 (Strict Nature Reserve, National Park, Natural Monument/Natural Landmark, Wildlife Sanctuary, and Protected Landscape or Seascape); does not include production-oriented areas such as timber reserves.
SOURCES: International Union for Conservation of Nature and Natural Resources, *1990 United Nations List of National Parks and Protected Areas* (Gland, Switzerland, and Cambridge: 1990); U.N. Food and Agriculture Organization, *Production Yearbook 1989* (Rome: 1990).

habitats have received a disproportionate share of protective efforts, while others of greater biological significance (such as lowland forests, wetlands, and most aquatic ecosystems) have been neglected. Belize, for instance, protects less than 2 kilometers of its 220-kilometer-long barrier reef, the longest in the western hemisphere. The natural systems most commonly found in the world's parks are deserts and tundra.[24]

Although most national parks have been established in the last two decades, societies have been consciously protecting ecosystems for thousands of years. South and Southeast Asian farmers have traditionally honored sacred groves, believed to be homes of powerful deities. The Kuna and Emberá-Chocó Indians of Panama leave patches of old-growth forest as supernatural parks, refuges for both wildlife and spirits. Waterways as well as forests are protected by the Tukano Indians of Brazil, whose taboos guard as much as 62 percent of nearby streams as fish sanctuaries.[25]

These traditional conservation methods, which include both protected areas and diversity-sustaining production systems, have probably been more effective than their modern counterparts. No global tallies of the land area under various indigenous conservation strategies are available. One reasonable surrogate is a 1989 Sierra Club survey of the world's large wilderness areas, defined as regions over 400,000 hectares free of roads or permanent settlements, where major habitat alteration is unlikely to occur. The study found that natural forces, rather than humans, are dominant over 4.8 billion hectares—one third of the earth's land surface. By and large, where these wildlands are habitable (the majority are desert and ice), they overlap with the traditional territories of indigenous groups. Although indigenous people have proved fully capable of abusing land and hunting wildlife to extinction, it is clear that the world's healthy ecosystems are found predominantly in areas under their control.[26]

Today, both modern and indigenous conservation systems are unraveling. In many areas, such as the Amazon basin, the often intimate knowledge of nature possessed by indigenous people is fading even faster than nature itself. On average, one Amazon tribe has disappeared each year since 1900. Especially for medicinal plants, traditional crops, and other life forms favored and used by native people, acculturation and the loss of traditional management systems are among the greatest threats to biological conservation.[27]

The relationship between cultural diversity and biological diversity is more ambiguous in the case of large animal species. But the indigenous practices that do conserve wildlife are also vanishing as native cultures and territories succumb to the expanding influence of the global commercial economy. Orangutans, for example, have been virtually wiped out in the Malaysian state of Sarawak by destruction of their rain forest habitat and hunting. Only along the upper reaches of the Batang Ai River in southern Sarawak do they thrive, in part because local Iban people believe it is taboo to kill them. But the Iban, constantly told that their culture is backward, are abandoning their traditional beliefs, and orangutan hunting is reportedly on the increase.[28]

Of the world's nationally protected areas, many, perhaps most, exist largely on paper. In the tropics, most parks have little or no staff or budget and are controlled by politically weak or corrupt departments. A 1988 survey by the Organization of American States found that only 16 out of 100 Caribbean marine parks (outside the United States) had management plans and adequate staff and funding. Similar problems exist in wealthy nations: Shiretoko National Park, Japan's wildest protected area, covers more than 37,000 hectares but has never had more than a single ranger.[29]

In addition, many parks encourage destructive but profitable activities. Logging, for example, occurs with government blessing in parks in Canada,

Czechoslovakia, and Indonesia. In Europe, Canada, and many of the world's marine areas, parks are oriented primarily toward recreation, with biological conservation a secondary or nonexistent mission. Because tourists part with their money more readily than cash-strapped governments, many parks rely on them to pay the bills, often at the price of serious crowding, pollution, and habitat degradation.[30]

The most common threats to parks originate outside their boundaries. Severe air pollution in Poland's Ojcow National Park has helped kill off 43 plant species there, and a third of the remaining plants are threatened. In just five years, explosives and cyanide used by local fishers have eliminated more than half the coral cover in the Philippines' Tubbataha Reef National Marine Park.[31]

While protection of whole ecosystems can offer sizable economic benefits, such as tourism revenues and clean and reliable water supplies for downstream communities, it also entails upfront costs. And few benefits reach the people at whose expense preserves are often created. Establishing parks in the tropics has often entailed evicting people or curtailing their customary uses of the area, without compensation. By disrupting traditional management and exacerbating the poverty that often drives environmental degradation, some parks have hastened the devastation of ecosystems they were designed to protect.[32]

Over the past decade, many park managers have come to realize that the survival of protected areas depends ultimately on the support of local people, rather than on fences, fines, and even armed force. A number of promising projects have been initiated by governments and nongovernmental organizations to reduce pressures for exploitation by alleviating poverty in communities in or near protected wildlands. These projects have typically focused on establish-

ing buffer zones around parks where limited exploitation of natural resources by local people is permitted; providing health care, water supplies, or other community services to compensate for lack of access to park resources; and supporting local economic development efforts such as tourism, wildlife ranching, or marketing of nontimber forest products.[33]

## The survival of protected areas depends ultimately on the support of local people.

The reasoning behind these efforts is sound: poverty alleviation is the only feasible or ethically tenable means of protecting natural areas in the long term. But the difficulty of this approach should not be underestimated. Many villagers are rightly suspicious of parks departments, which, in their view, have stolen resources from them often not for protective purposes but for wealthier bureaucrats to exploit. Park managers typically find calls for more participatory management a threat to their authority. And by no means are all local people, indigenous or otherwise, interested in conservation of natural areas. Villagers on the outskirts of Khao Yai National Park in Thailand, for example, are among the staunchest supporters of a proposal to build a large dam in the park.[34]

Given the opportunity, however, local communities can be powerful forces in the defense of protected areas. The Inter-Ethnic Association for the Development of the Peruvian Amazon, a coalition of 27 indigenous groups, has actively opposed the government's push to open the 2-million-hectare Pacaya-Samiria reserve to oil exploration. Along with Peruvian environmentalists, they insist that national law, which forbids such activities in protected zones, be upheld and that any drilling take place outside the 6 percent of the Peruvian Amazon ostensibly protected as parkland. The indigenous coalition is especially concerned about potential contamination of the waters and fisheries used by the 15,000 people who live along the rivers in the reserve, the nation's largest protected area.[35]

A recent survey of 23 projects aimed at improving park protection and local economic well-being in Africa, Asia, and Latin America concluded that they have had limited impact to date. Most are only a few years old, small-scale compared with the problems they seek to address, and unable to establish explicit linkages between conservation and development. For example, local people now receive the gate fees paid by butterfly-seeking tourists in Mexico's Monarch Overwintering Reserve. But this alternative source of income has not prevented them from logging in the area.[36]

Given the great difficulties in protecting whole ecosystems, many have called for solutions less demanding than the defense of wilderness, defined as very large, roadless, lightly managed, minimally polluted ecosystems. Scientists have come to realize that change and disturbance—from fire and windstorms to the ancient practices of indigenous peoples—play important roles in fostering biological diversity. And foresters, among others, are beginning to design production systems aimed at mimicking these processes. In addition, it can be argued that there are no truly natural areas on the planet, since the impacts of indigenous people and industrial pollutants have been found in even the remotest territories.[37]

So why maintain large areas with minimal human use? Quite simply, no other approach can protect biodiversity—at all its levels of organization—as well. Grizzly bear, harpy eagle, hornbill, spotted owl: species that roam over large areas, that require specialized habitats, or that do not get along well with humans need large wilderness reserves if they are to survive outside of zoos. In the Amazon, woolly monkeys (which play a key ecological role by dispersing seeds too large for other animals to eat) shy away from roads and clearings; they are severely threatened by hunters in any area occupied by either Indians or nontribal settlers. As American ecologist Reed Noss writes, "No matter how ecologically sophisticated our land management practices, how perfectly we think we can mimic natural processes, so long as there are roads and mechanized humans, some species will disappear."[38]

Because disturbance is essential to natural ecosystems but often inconvenient to humans, large areas of wildlands are needed to let fires and other large-scale natural phenomena play their course uninterrupted. Also, for protected areas to be functional over the long term, they have to be ample enough to ensure that only a fraction of the area is involved in any given disturbance. Habitats too small to weather the impacts of random variation in weather and wildlife populations will not be able to maintain their full complement of genes, species, and functions. Where smaller parcels of habitat are all that remain, more active (and costly) management will be required.[39]

If exploitation is minimal, areas of sustainable resource extraction can be nearly indistinguishable from wildlands. In these places, maintaining ecological integrity means continuing the traditional uses of the ecosystem. But this should not be confused with the more intensive commercial uses proposed as "sustainable" alternatives. For example, the widely hunted uacari monkeys of the Amazon basin have survived near Tukano Indian villages, which are one or two days' paddling apart, but among more closely spaced villages they are hunted close to extinction. Intensifying the use of minimally exploited areas will undoubtedly herald biological losses.[40]

In wilderness-rich nations such as Brazil or Papua New Guinea, it is inevitable that large areas of natural habitat will be converted as populations and economies grow. This is no excuse, however, for continued government-sponsored depredation of wildlands when there are large, often more suitable areas of degraded land available for the same purpose. In Latin America, for example, 1 percent of landowners commonly control over 40 percent of arable land, much of which stands idle on huge estates.[41]

In most nations, the opportunity to achieve a balance between wild and domesticated landscapes was lost long ago, and a necessary—if seemingly Draconian—goal is to cease "developing" any more relatively undamaged ecosystems. A first step toward this is determining where these areas are. In the United States, an Endangered Ecosystems Act has been proposed that would inventory and restrict development of any ecosystems reduced below a given percentage. On a global scale, Israeli landscape ecologist Ze'ev Naveh has proposed the compilation of a list of threatened landscapes.[42]

Because so many remaining areas of global importance to biodiversity are inhabited by indigenous people, who usually have the greatest knowledge of the ecosystem to be safeguarded, protection will need to be on their terms. A first step is the recognition of the inalienable rights of people to lands and resources they have used for generations. In the Amazon basin, where native people have full legal title to less than 30 percent of their lands, the Venezuelan government broke with regional tradition in mid-1991 by recognizing an Austria-sized patch of forest as the permanent home-

land of the beleaguered Yanomami tribe.[43]

Where current or desired practices are incompatible with biodiversity conservation, governments or conservation advocates can negotiate with traditional residents about the protection of ecosystems and compensation for any benefits they forgo. In South Africa, infamous for its racially skewed distribution of land and power, the parks department recently agreed with local herders to establish Richtersveld National Park, the nation's first "contractual" park. The Nama pastoralists of the area have agreed to herd their sheep and goats under new restrictions; in return, they get a healthy portion of all earnings from the park and are well represented on its management committee. Similar efforts are under way to establish cooperative protected areas in Papua New Guinea, American Samoa, and Western Samoa.[44]

Beyond allowing greater local control over the designation and management of protected areas, the root causes of degradation must be addressed. Usually agents rather than causes of destruction, the rural poor face complex forces pushing them to harmful short-term behavior; turning back these forces, and the equally serious vectors of degradation in industrial nations, will take far-reaching changes in government policies, corporate behavior, distribution of resources, and individual ethics. Fundamentally, it will require an embrace of diversity not just in the areas set aside from human dominance but in those we dominate as well.

# CONSERVATION BEYOND PARKS

Even if societies undertake radical efforts to curb their impacts on remaining natural areas, most of the world's landscapes will continue to be dominated by human beings, and most will fall outside the scope of strictly protected reserves. Seminatural areas—such as second-growth forests, waters whose fish are intensively harvested, and rangelands grazed by livestock—prevail around the globe. Unless society can learn to tolerate and maintain wildness in these civilized landscapes, biodiversity has a bleak future.

---

**Many species little known to science or industry are already used and managed by local communities.**

---

Nature has long been viewed as an obstacle to economic development, and ecological decline seen as the inevitable price of progress. The protection of ecosystems within parks has usually been predicated on the assumption that natural systems outside them were to be homogenized at will. Recently, however, both environmentalists and industrialists have espoused the idea that economic and environmental well-being are linked, not opposed, and have begun to seek ways to blend production and protection.

Nonprofit groups and green-minded businesses are bringing new foods, cosmetics, medicines, soaps, and other products from the world's tropical forests to stores in Europe and North America. The range of products hidden in forests, reefs, and other ecosystems is a powerful argument for their conservation. Less than 1 percent of the plants of Madagascar, for example, where medicinal plants are a major export as well as the basis of local health care, have been analyzed chemically. But it is frequently overlooked that many species little

known to science or industry are already used and managed by local communities.[45]

Tropical forests are critical to hundreds of millions of rural people as sources of nutrition, health care, raw materials, and cash income. Traditional medicine, based largely on tropical plants, nurtures four fifths of humanity, while rain forest plants provide key ingredients in pharmaceuticals worth tens of billions of dollars annually. International commerce in the most widely traded nontimber forest product, rattan (palm stems used for wicker furniture and baskets), is alone worth roughly $3 billion annually.[46]

As with rangelands, fisheries, and wildlife throughout the developing world, forests have long been managed as common property resources, often with few negative ecological impacts. Many communal management systems are unraveling as populations surge, traditional cultures erode, and national governments confiscate or privatize resources held by communities. In addition, when subsistence-level economies have adopted modern technologies or become commercialized, increasing levels of production have tended to strain local ecosystems without improving local welfare.[47]

From Southeast Asia's rattan to the fish and fruits of the Peruvian Amazon, the usual fate of species that gain long-term popularity in industrial markets is depletion. And the usual lot of their harvesters is continued poverty, as the profits from their work are siphoned off by powerful intermediaries and elites. Brazil nut gatherers, for example, receive about 4¢ a pound for their labors, just 2–3 percent of the New York wholesale price. Three fourths of the market is controlled by three companies, owned by three cousins.[48]

Brazil's rubber tappers are perhaps the most successful of the world's forest people in their efforts to break out of this cycle of human and environmental suffering. Though most are chronically in debt and under threat of violence or death from landowners, they have gained some government support for their claims against cattle ranchers and speculators who seek to clear the forest. Their vision of an alternative form of development has centered around extractive reserves: areas owned by the state but managed by local communities for uses compatible with the continued existence of the forest. Since 1987, the Brazilian government has recognized 14 extractive reserves covering 3 million hectares; the national rubber tappers' union hopes eventually to manage 100 million hectares (one fourth the Brazilian Amazon) in this way. These successes have inspired similar efforts in other countries, including the declaration of forest and lake reserves in Guatemala and Peru.[49]

But Brazil's forest extractors face serious economic, ecological, and political hurdles. Although they hope to diversify their economic base, they currently get most of their income from rubber and Brazil nuts, the economic viability of which is fragile at best. Until 1990, when they fell by two thirds, rubber prices in Brazil were propped up to three times the world price with heavy taxes on imports of cheap Asian rubber. Plantations of Brazil-nut trees have been started in Malaysia, and a decade-old stand near Manaus, Brazil, was expected to begin producing a commercial crop in 1991. As with other Amazonian plantations, disease will likely besiege the domesticated trees, but perhaps not before they have flooded the market with low-priced nuts.[50]

Tapping trees and gathering fruit are fairly benign activities, especially compared with the wholesale destruction usually wrought by cattle ranching or commercial logging in tropical forests.

But removing industrial quantities of any material from an ecosystem is likely to cause major changes. Although traditional people's knowledge of their local area usually outstrips that of biologists, neither group has much experience in sustainable commercial use of tropical ecosystems. Biologists know little or nothing about most of the species of the tropics; even the ecology of commercially important species remains little understood. No one knows, for example, if the pronounced absence of Brazil nut seedlings and saplings in many areas today is a result of overharvesting or simply a natural cycle.[51]

Rain forest trees form the base of a complex food chain. In turn, they rely on birds, insects, mammals, and even fish to disperse their pollen and seeds. According to ecologist Charles M. Peters of the New York Botanical Garden, "it is obvious that removing commercial quantities of fruits, nuts, and oil seeds will have an impact on local animal populations." The economic incentive to "enrich" forests with money-making species and cut down their competitors could also reduce the diversity of plant species (along with symbiotic animals) within extraction areas. Without careful management, losses at the genetic level are also likely: as the best fruits or leaves from a given population are continually harvested, the "inferior" plants may be the ones to survive over time.[52]

The dangers of market-oriented extractive economies can be minimized by carefully choosing species and ecosystems. Some tropical forest areas are naturally less diverse than others and thick with commercially promising species— such as the vitamin C–rich fruit of the *camu camu* that grows in dense stands throughout the floodplains of the Peruvian Amazon. Ancient yet seminatural forests also hold great promise. Anthropologist Christine Padoch of the New York Botanical Garden reports finding fruit-filled, remarkably diverse groves (44 tree species within 0.2 hectares) in Kalimantan, Indonesia, that had been created by generations of villagers casually planting, weeding, and even spitting out fruit seeds over their shoulders.[53]

In some cases, making the use of diversity rewarding to local people can be aided by developing markets for new or unknown products. But in all cases, this approach will only work if the fundamental concerns of the rural poor are addressed first. Political reforms will be required to secure rural people's rights to land and resources, reduce their vulnerability to exploitation and violence by outsiders, and ensure that the benefits of conservation stay within local communities.

---

## Village-based wildlife management in Zambia is more effective and 10–50 times cheaper than law enforcement.

---

In Africa, wildlife is typically considered state property, and benefits from hunting or viewing animals usually flow to national coffers and foreign tour operators. Local peasants have borne the costs of living with wildlife, such as trampled crops and attacks on livestock, with no recompense short of poaching for the black market.[54]

In several southern African nations, the state has ceded exclusive control over wildlife. Rural communities living in 10 of Zambia's 31 Game Management Areas have been granted rights to wildlife; poaching has fallen dramatically and wildlife populations appear to be rebounding as a result. Area youths, who know the wildlife and local bush better than anyone, are now trained as village scouts to keep out poachers; revenues

from safari hunting fees go into a revolving fund that supports both conservation activities and community development projects. Another state-community management program has quickly gained popularity in rural Zimbabwe: as of 1990, residents of communal lands covering nearly one eighth of the country had begun, or planned to begin, participatory wildlife management programs.[55]

Besides fulfilling the legitimate historical claims of local people, restoring some degree of local control over resources is probably the only way that vast areas in the tropics can be "managed" at all. Governments claim ownership of 80 percent of the remaining mature tropical forests but have little hope of controlling their usage. Each officer in Indonesia's Ministry of Forestry, which has a full-time field staff of 17,000, is responsible for more than 8,000 hectares of state forest. Meanwhile, more than 30 million Indonesians live on or near the 143 million hectares of state forestland. The nation also has the world's longest coastline and more than a million fishers, yet the government claims all responsibility for fisheries management. Cost as well as staffing constraints favor new approaches: village-based wildlife management in Zambia is more effective and 10–50 times cheaper than law enforcement.[56]

Full recognition of traditional resource rights, however, is not sufficient to ensure sustainable use of those resources. In Papua New Guinea, native people have full ownership of 97 percent of the country's largely forested land base. But predatory logging by Japanese and other firms is no less a problem here than in Malaysia, where the state (and closely allied timber companies) control forests. The Papuan state is too weak and corruption-ridden to prevent widespread abuses by multinationals, and local owners are easily swayed into selling their forests at discount rates.[57]

Reconciling diversity with development will require loosening the grip of industry on natural resources and accepting that production of any single commodity will be constrained if ecosystems are managed for diversity. The success of some U.S. foresters' efforts to develop a "new forestry," for example, depends on whether they can free forest management from its historical timber bias. Rather than homogenize ecosystems in order to maximize wood production, new forestry ostensibly aims to maintain and use the ecological complexity of natural forests. But because diversity conservation will require protecting the few scattered remnants of pristine forest and logging other areas less intensively, new forestry cannot succeed without major reductions in the timber harvest on national forests—a politically charged issue. (See Chapter 9.)[58]

While new forestry, extractive reserves, and other programs of sustainable commercial use of ecosystems are in their infancy, it is already clear that their success depends on programs of sustainable *nonuse*. Protecting large areas of undisturbed forest near logging or extraction areas is the only way to ensure the survival of animals that pollinate and disperse the seeds of commercially important tropical trees. Studies in the western United States have shown intact stands of native forest to harbor insect predators that safeguard plantations from pest outbreaks; the protection of coral reefs from fishing in Belize and the Philippines has revived local fishing economies by providing depleted fish stocks room to grow. Ultimately, only natural areas can tell us if our uses are in fact sustainable. As essayist Wendell Berry writes, "we cannot know what we are doing until we know what nature would be doing if we were doing nothing."[59]

## LIVING WITH DIVERSITY

Fishers' nets and loggers' saws may directly impoverish local ecosystems, but most biological losses have root causes far away, in long-settled farmlands and urban areas where diversity is seldom a concern. In general, these peopled landscapes have lost much of their biological wealth, but what remains is still important to their continued functioning and livability. Reconciling farms and cities with diversity will require stopping the damage they bring to remaining natural habitats, but also beginning to halt and reverse the homogenization of these unnatural environments.

Uniformity is not inherently undesirable. In fact, to some degree, homogenization is the basis of all agriculture: a given type of plant is favored and others suppressed or eliminated. But trends in recent decades—most notably the Green Revolution and the parallel intensification of farming systems in industrial nations—have pushed uniformity to dangerous levels.

The unsustainability of modern agriculture is in part a measure of its inability to tolerate diversity. Both genetic and ecological uniformity—the sameness of fields sown horizon to horizon without interruption—demand costly and often dangerous or futile reliance on chemicals to protect crops from pests or diseases that are rapidly spreading and evolving. The drive to leave no hectare unplowed worsens soil erosion, pushing tractors onto highly erodible hillsides and removing windbreaks and hedgerows.[60]

Some of agriculture's biological impacts are obvious—expanding farms that eat into forests and wetlands, for example. While the increasing reliance on chemical inputs and machinery has reduced these impacts in some cases by decreasing the area needed to produce a given amount of food, it has worsened others. Chemical runoff and soil erosion from farms on the Belize coast, for example, constitute one of the greatest threats to that nation's barrier reef; aquatic ecosystems in the United States and Europe suffer acutely from pollution from croplands. In the United Kingdom, many bird species have declined over the past 20–30 years, likely due to increased herbicide use and the elimination of hedgerows and unused lands from agricultural landscapes.[61]

**Protection of habitat is the single most effective means of conserving diversity.**

A fundamental transition away from today's wasteful and inequitable farming systems is needed to put the world's food supplies on a secure footing. Many of the reforms that will reduce farming's dependence on fossil fuel inputs and its misuse of soils and waters can also restore diversity to agricultural landscapes. Pesticides, for example, kill not only pests but other animals, such as pollinators and predators, that are beneficial to agriculture. Alternative pest control measures that lower pesticide use can also, ironically, reduce pest damage to crops by reviving the diversity of soil and insect communities, which play crucial roles in maintaining soil productivity and checking the spread of pest outbreaks.[62]

The likely reduction of agricultural subsidies in Europe under international trade agreements could cause large areas of farmland to fall out of production, including many traditional farms that have considerable value as wildlife habitat on a continent largely devoid of pristine nature. But proper planning could ensure that highly erodible cropland and ecologically sensitive areas

such as wetlands are retired first in order to reclaim vital habitats and protect waterways. The U.S. government spends billions of dollars each year to idle croplands for price-support or erosion-control reasons; these programs could easily encourage the planting of wildlife-supporting vegetation or the maintenance of biological corridors—crucial links between the nation's tattered remnants of natural habitat.[63]

Many off-site efforts, including gene banks, botanical gardens, and zoos, are necessary, but protection of habitat is the single most effective means of conserving diversity. This is no less true for traditional crop varieties, whose habitats are the world's small farms. Protecting these dynamic habitats means reversing the policies and forces that push farmers off the land or encourage them to abandon customary crops. Subsidies for pesticides and top-down agricultural research programs that scorn local knowledge are just two of the hidden forces that erode genetic diversity. Less hidden is the highly skewed ownership of fertile land in most developing countries that pushes peasants into urban slums or fragile ecosystems unsuited for cultivation.[64]

The lack of compensation for the knowledge and genetic resources of traditional people when used by plant breeders, biotechnology firms, or pharmaceutical companies has received more attention as a cause of genetic erosion; discussions are under way in several international fora to devise compensation mechanisms. How small farmers, medicinal healers, and others should be compensated for their knowledge (which is often held collectively rather than by individuals) is a controversial matter. The reluctance of northern nations to address these issues of intellectual property rights and the transfer of technology to genetically rich but technologically poor southern nations threatens to swamp current efforts to negotiate a global biodiversity convention.[65]

Traditional agroecosystems also contain the seeds of a sustainable, diversity-based mode of agriculture. At varying levels, diversity is the basis of production for many peasants. Farmers often mix strains of a given crop in their fields as a hedge against the vagaries of weather. They also tend to recognize the dependence of their farms on adjacent ecological systems and to tolerate wild plants (often crop relatives whose continued interbreeding with domestic descendants contributes to genetic variety) on the outskirts of their fields. More commonly, farmers mimic the species diversity of natural systems and grow varied crops together; such multiple cropping still accounts for as much as 20 percent of world food production.[66]

Population growth and the expansion of large commercial farms have made many ecologically sound practices not viable, and traditional agriculture badly needs infusions of money and research to increase its modest yields without abandoning its stability. Few generalizations can be made about the variety of sustainable approaches to agriculture. But to one degree or another, diversity and information replace energy and chemicals as the primary basis of such systems. Healthy soil biota, patches of natural vegetation for pollinators, polycultures, and many other types of diversity: as much as any gene bank or biotechnology firm, the small farms of the world contain the diversity and the locally relevant knowledge that will make sustainable agriculture possible.[67]

Urban areas, with good reason, are considered the antithesis of natural diversity. Only the most resilient creatures—those considered weeds and pests—thrive in them, and cities' ceaseless expansion, consumption of resources, and emissions of waste threaten both farmland and wilderness almost ev-

erywhere. As with agricultural lands, the first priority for urban areas is to halt their expansion onto other ecosystems and reduce the damage they export, such as the sewage poured onto coral reefs by burgeoning coastal cities throughout the tropics.

But even concrete jungles can support some diversity. Most urban areas have waterways running through them or corridors of unused land such as steep ravines; if their use as waste receptacles is reduced, these can be maintained or restored as wildlife habitat. A number of European and U.S. cities have moved to establish greenway corridors along rivers, old railroad tracks, and urban perimeters. (See Chapter 8.) Although created primarily for recreation, these greenways have great biological potential to help reconnect increasingly fragmented and dysfunctional enclaves of nature beyond city limits.[68]

Especially in developing nations, a surprising amount of agricultural production takes place within city limits, in home gardens. These hidden farmlands contain a great deal of genetic diversity and their expansion could help reduce the environmental impacts of commercial agriculture. In the United States, converting a quarter of the 13 million hectares of lawn to gardens would be equivalent to expanding the nation's cropland by 2 percent.[69]

One of the reasons biological diversity is so threatened is that urban dwellers have little experience of the natural and less understanding of its importance. Restoring nature where people live—reestablishing a personal link with the living world—is necessary if we are to save it. But the greatest benefits of making human settlements more hospitable to other organisms may be human, not biological. As naturalist Gary Nabhan writes, "something that has long kept our cultigens [crops] and even our peopled landscapes healthy and tolerable is now disappearing. That valuable entity is wildness. If it is lost from the world around us, we will lose something within ourselves as well."[70]

Infusing the world's peopled landscapes with wildness assumes even greater importance in the face of the ultimate threat to life on earth: global warming. In countless ways, a rapidly warming world will be hostile to life. Most notably, natural communities will be forced to migrate away from the equator, or up from sea level, if they are to maintain their usual climate. Even if reduced emissions of greenhouse gases slow global warming to a pace that migrating ecosystems can keep up with, habitats fragmented by roads, clearings, and human settlements will literally be pushed up against the wall. Only by making diversity a concern on all landscapes, from the wild to the urban, can the inevitable migrations of species and communities be accommodated, and the options to deal with unpredictable change be maintained.

Ironically, the most important reforms are those that seemingly have little to do with biodiversity. To intelligently limit the amount of the planet we dominate and to tolerate nature more in the places we do dominate will entail tackling two of the most intractable and fundamental forces in the modern world: galloping consumption and exponential population growth. No conservation strategy, however ingenious, can get around the fact that the more resources one species consumes, the fewer are available for all the rest.

Many of the changes needed for biodiversity's sake are a step beyond those considered in discussions of sustainable development. The human costs of a lost medicinal plant may never be known, and any economic deterioration that results from biological decline could take years or decades to appear. But the protection of biodiversity has to be considered a basic requirement of sustainability—passing on to future generations a world of undiminished options—and a fundamental moral responsibility as travelers on the only planet known to support life.

# 3

# Building a Bridge to Sustainable Energy

*Christopher Flavin*

Since mid-century, scientists and political leaders have tried to figure out what a post–fossil fuel economy might look like. Such long-range planning is notoriously difficult, in this case complicated by the economic and political power of today's energy industries and a tendency to assume that the future will be like the past. Even today, as the fossil fuel age brings us ever closer to ecological catastrophe, there is no consensus on our energy future. Now more than ever, the world desperately needs a vision of a sustainable energy economy—and a map of how to get there.

For a brief time in the fifties, an age of cheap nuclear energy and a way out of the fossil fuel era seemed to beckon. As recently as 1971, U.S. government scientists advised the nation's leaders that breeder reactors would make obsolete any energy source that cost more than the 1991 equivalent of $5 per barrel of oil. Eventually, it was believed, we would live in an electrified, nuclear-powered world. Even today, with nuclear power costing more than five times what it once

did and construction being abandoned worldwide, some scientists cling to the dream, and beguile politicians with their plans.[1]

An alternative vision is starting to emerge. At its center is a simple fact: the world is swept each day by an abundance of renewable energy, most of it derived from sunshine. Wind power, biomass energy, geothermal power, and solar energy itself could run a highly energy-efficient world economy many times over. But practical problems remain. Renewable energy sources are diverse, dispersed, and in most cases intermittent. The electricity they generate is hard to store—suitable for many applications but not for running an entire economy. While oil can be moved from remote areas by tanker, and coal can be transported by barge, sunshine is hard to carry to distant cities.

One option is to convert renewable power to a gaseous form that is easy to transport and store—such as hydrogen. Hydrogen is a simple gas composed of a single atom that can be substituted for most other energy carriers. It can be used to generate electricity, power industry, run home appliances, fuel automobiles, and even fly commercial aircraft. Burning it produces virtually no air pollution or greenhouse gases. And hydrogen can be produced easily by running an electric current through water—a process known as electrolysis. Solar, wind, or geothermal plants in remote regions can produce hydrogen that can be stored and then transported to cities with little energy loss.

Building the infrastructure of a solar-hydrogen economy will naturally take time. One of the first cornerstones that must be laid is to increase the overall energy efficiency of the economy. By lowering the amount of power needed to heat and light buildings, run a computer, or drive a car by 50–90 percent, the feasibility and economics of using solar hydrogen are greatly enhanced. In a truly sustainable energy economy, people would live in efficient solar homes, the need for traveling by automobile would be reduced through improved urban design, and factories would run on a fraction of today's voracious energy requirements.

Making the shift to sustainable energy will also require a transitional fuel. Petroleum products such as gasoline are unlikely ever to be made from renewable energy, and trying to electrify the entire economy would be expensive and impractical. The better course is to encourage the substitution of natural gas for oil, coal, and even electricity. New natural gas technologies make it possible to boost conversion efficiencies considerably, cutting air pollutants 90–99 percent and carbon dioxide ($CO_2$) emissions 30–65 percent from those typical of today's fossil-fuel-based engines and power plants.[2]

Although a decade ago many countries seemed to be running out of natural gas, geologists now believe that it is available in sufficient quantity to be the bridge fuel to a renewable energy economy. Natural gas is not only more abundant than oil, it is dispersed more widely around the world. In many countries, resources have barely begun to be tapped. And as concern about the environment mounts and new policy measures such as carbon taxes are enacted, the use of gas is likely to accelerate. If a more heavily gas-based economy does take hold, solar hydrogen can be added gradually to the mix of fuels, making a smooth shift to a sustainable energy economy.

## FUEL SHOCK

The energy news of the past two years sometimes seems like a great sound and fury signifying nothing. Although the Gulf War focused the attention of oil importers on their vulnerability, it yielded few convincing plans to reduce that dependence. In the United States, a new energy strategy announced in the last week of the war reopened debates over nuclear power and oil drilling in the Arctic while calling for even greater reliance on petroleum. Western Europe, meanwhile, is taking a quite different tack—considering major energy policy changes in response to the risk of global warming.[3]

Despite the emergence of new approaches in Europe, most experts still seem to believe that the world is firmly stuck in the fossil fuel age. From the Bush administration's National Energy Strategy to energy analyst Daniel Yergin's best-selling history of the oil industry—published in the midst of the Gulf crisis—few political leaders or "experts" seem willing to contemplate seriously a life after oil and coal. Yet the scale of the problems posed by today's energy economy suggests that a change in direction is essential—and that the best-laid plans may soon have to be shelved.[4]

Ever since the 1973 oil embargo, world energy trends have been on a seesaw course, driven first by economic constraints and later by ecological ones. Only by understanding the new dynamics of the fossil fuel economy can policymakers shape them to advantage.

The first reaction to skyrocketing oil prices was a sharp reversal of the consumption trend, which had been doubling each decade. In fact, world oil use actually dropped from 65 million barrels daily in 1979 to 59 million barrels in 1985. Although it rebounded to about 64 million barrels a day by 1991, this was only 12 percent more than in 1973. (World population grew almost 40 percent during the same period.) In North America, Europe, and Japan, oil use per dollar of gross national product—the best measure of vulnerability to oil shocks—is down by 30–50 percent. Poorer nations have been less successful in reducing their dependence, leaving them more vulnerable to oil price shocks. (See Table 3–1.) In fact, oil use continues to rise in Latin America and Asia, slowed only by mounting debts that have left many poor nations short of hard currency.[5]

The use of oil in electric power generation and home heating has been slashed in many nations. But petroleum is more central than ever to transportation. Some 540 million vehicles now travel the world's roads, a figure that seems destined to continue rising in the years ahead. In the Third World, car ownership has doubled since the late seventies, leaving cities from Santiago to Shanghai choked with vehicles and pollution. Even in the United States, where new-car fuel economy rose from 14 miles per gallon in 1974 to 28 in 1990, and where average fleet efficiency has reached 22 miles per gallon, increased driving has caused fuel use to rise.[6]

**Table 3-1. Oil Consumed Per Unit of National Output, Selected Countries, 1989/90[1]**

| Country | Oil Consumed (million barrels per day) | Oil Dependence (million barrels oil per billion dollars GNP) |
|---|---|---|
| United States | 16.20 | 1.11 |
| Japan | 5.25 | 0.66 |
| West Germany | 2.40 | 0.59 |
| China | 2.28 | 1.95 |
| India | 1.04 | 1.48 |
| South Korea | 0.81 | 1.41 |
| Brazil | 1.20 | 1.25 |

[1]Oil dependence figures for industrial and developing countries may not be comparable.
SOURCES: Industrial-country data for 1990 from British Petroleum, *BP Statistical Review of World Energy* (London: 1991), and from Organisation of Economic Co-operation and Development, *In Figures* (Paris: 1991); developing-country data for 1989 from United Nations, *Yearbook of Energy Statistics* (New York: 1991), and from Central Intelligence Agency, *Handbook of Economic Statistics* (Washington, D.C.: 1990).

The oil crises of the seventies also accelerated efforts to shift to other energy sources. One alternative, nuclear power, was already being expanded at a rapid pace. But in most countries construction of new reactors began to decline soon after the first oil crisis—slowed by rising costs and public concern that was later heightened by the Three Mile Island and Chernobyl accidents. Coal became the alternative of choice for many nations trying to reduce petroleum dependence. Worldwide, the use of coal is up more than 30 percent since the mid-seventies. (See Figure 3–1.) A few countries even followed the path of Japan: importing coal in order to replace imported oil.[7]

By the early eighties, however, the world began to focus on the extensive environmental damage that can result

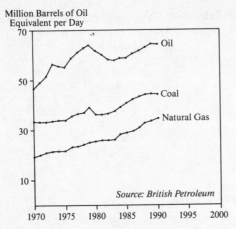

**Figure 3-1. World Oil, Coal, and Natural Gas Use, 1970–90**

from the heavy use of this fossil fuel—in particular, the acid rain that stems in part from the high sulfur content of many kinds of coal. In addition, because coal has a higher carbon content than the other fossil fuels, rising coal combustion accounted for more than half the increase in carbon emissions between 1975 and 1990. By then, coal was responsible for 42 percent of the world's carbon emissions from fossil fuels, almost exactly the same share as oil. In response to rising environmental concerns, including strengthened clean air laws, the coal boom has slowed since the mid-eighties.[8]

One of the most important developments in the past two years is a sudden decline in the use of highly polluting coal and lignite in Eastern Europe and the Soviet Union, as they begin to restructure both their economies and their environmental policies. Combined with a modest recession in the West, this was enough to drive world carbon emissions down in 1990 and 1991, the first yearly declines since the early eighties. (See Figure 3–2.) In all likelihood, Soviet carbon emissions will continue to fall in the next few years and then only slowly recover. The collapse of the inefficient

centrally planned economies is therefore a plus for the global environment.[9]

Third World fossil fuel use has expanded rapidly, limited only by recent financial problems, and now accounts for 28 percent of the world total, up from 18 percent in 1970. But large disparities exist among the developing countries, with the bulk of the energy growth occurring in a relatively small number of Asian, Middle Eastern, and Latin American countries. The outlook for the nineties is for most of the growth in world carbon emissions to come from the developing world, which could account for half the world total as early as 2010.[10]

China's energy economy deserves special attention for its global significance. The nation is trying to do something that is nearly unique today—fueling its rapid economic expansion almost entirely with coal. Indeed, coal now accounts for a remarkable 76 percent of the country's total commercial energy supply. Carbon emissions there have increased 60 percent in the past decade and account for 37 percent of the Third World total. China is already the world's third largest carbon emitter, and is likely to surpass the Soviet Union within the

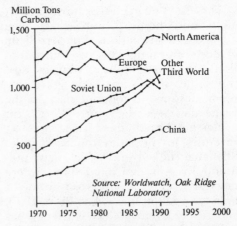

**Figure 3-2. Carbon Emissions from Fossil Fuels in Selected Regions, 1970–90**

decade. Redirecting China's energy economy is fast becoming as important to the global atmosphere as changing those of Europe and the United States.[11]

While growth in the use of oil and coal has slowed in most nations, natural gas has maintained a steady growth path—up 87 percent during the past two decades. Natural gas now represents one quarter of world fossil fuel use, but accounts for only 17 percent of carbon emissions due to its lower carbon content. Moreover, the use of gas may accelerate with the enactment of tighter clean air laws and with the consideration of new global warming policies such as carbon taxes. The growth in Europe is particularly dramatic, relying on supplies from the North Sea, North Africa, and the Soviet Union. And many developing countries are just starting to exploit their extensive gas resources.[12]

But as the nineties unfold, the ugly consequences of overdependence on oil threaten to reappear with little warning. The Gulf War showed the political fragility of the petroleum market and further undermined its remaining foundations. A *Financial Times* editorial that ran in the first days of the war summed up the conflict: "Not only is oil at the heart of this war, but the war is at the heart of the world's most significant reserves of oil." Roughly two thirds of the world's proven oil reserves are located in a narrow crescent running from Iran in the north to the United Arab Emirates in the south.[13]

Darkening the outlook is the decline of oil production in key countries. In the United States, the world's number two producer, daily output has declined from 10.6 million barrels in 1985 to 8.9 million barrels in 1990. Industry analysts expect further declines of 1.6 million barrels per day by the end of this decade. In addition, North Sea production, which only began in the seventies, has already plateaued. More alarming is the

decline of the world's number one producer: by mid-1991, Soviet oil production (three quarters of which is in the Russian Republic) was down to 10.4 million barrels a day, 17 percent below the peak achieved just three years earlier. The drop can be traced to a series of interlocking problems—depleted oil fields, abysmal management, outdated machinery, and shortages of spare parts.[14]

As the Soviet Union's economic crisis deepens and political fragmentation proceeds, oil production is likely to continue declining, putting more pressure on the world market. As a result, the Middle East's share of that market is expected to accelerate from 27 percent in 1990 to nearly 40 percent by the end of the decade, with the market becoming as dangerously tight as it was in the seventies. (See Figure 3–3.) Third World economies in particular were hurt badly by the Gulf crisis and are acutely vulnerable to another oil shock. By the mid-nineties, the world is likely to need at least 4–6 million additional barrels of Middle Eastern oil each day. Even if Iraq and Kuwait are able to return fully to their prewar production levels, that level of demand would require all-out production by most Persian Gulf countries.

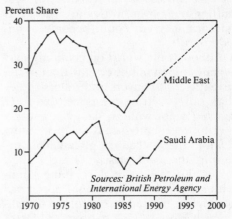

Figure 3-3. **Middle Eastern and Saudi Oil Production as Share of World Total, 1970–91, With Projection to 2000**

The last time that was needed, in 1979, a relatively modest disruption in Iranian output resulted in a near tripling of prices. Saudi Arabia, the traditional "swing" producer, may soon be stuck with the production accelerator on the floor—whether it wants to or not.[15]

The five countries with the bulk of the world's oil reserves are marked by huge wealth disparities, rapid social change, high rates of population growth, and autocratic political systems. Some face serious economic difficulties, and even Saudi Arabia was forced by the Gulf War to draw down its financial reserves. The war may also accelerate the erosion of the authority of the Gulf States' ruling families, as it has already deepened tensions between Arab haves and have-nots.

In the war's aftermath, Saudi Arabia has become a virtual U.S. protectorate. The United States has pledged to defend the Saudis from their poorer regional neighbors, while the Saudi rulers have at least implicitly agreed to seek stability in the world oil market. But it seems unlikely that bargains of this sort can provide more than short-term comfort, or that the United States can ultimately defend the Saudi ruling family from internal threats. Indeed, if it is used by industrial countries as an excuse for not putting their own houses in order, this tidy arrangement could become a suicide pact.[16]

Although the world oil economy may seem to function better now than in the seventies, with buyers and sellers rather than cartels setting the price, this freer market is not without dangers: witness the unprecedented daily oil price fluctuations that rocked the global economy during the Gulf crisis. These caused major disruptions in developing countries such as India that could not afford the higher price and were forced to temporarily close service stations and factories. Unlike the seventies—when economic rationality was at least one consideration in the oil cartel's decision making—the irrationality of politics is now often the driving force. Oil is clearly not a firm footing on which any nation can base its economic future—now less than ever.[17]

# THE CLEAN ENERGY REVOLUTION

While oil dependence remains a problem, many societies are now even more concerned about the environmental implications of fossil fuels. The basic question is simple: does it make sense for our generation's energy systems to impair the health of our children or to risk altering the global climate on which future generations depend? Answering that question is pushing many nations toward greater energy efficiency and a new mix of energy sources.

Traditionally viewed as an urban, rich-country problem, air pollution has spread to the countryside—even rural Maine now sometimes experiences unhealthful levels of ozone—and to cities and rural areas worldwide. Some of the most debilitating air pollution occurs in areas of Eastern Europe that depend on brown coal. In Prague, for example, sulfur dioxide concentrations average more than twice the World Health Organization standard. While Europe, North America, and Japan make progress in cleaning up their air, Third World air quality continues to worsen at an alarming pace. Breathing in Bombay is now equivalent to smoking 10 cigarettes a day. In Mexico City, female diplomats are urged to return home during pregnancy, and in Bangkok, where a million city residents were treated for respiratory problems in 1990, lung cancer is three times as common as in the rest of the country.[18]

In many parts of the world, air pollution and acid rain are also damaging crops and forests. Most of Europe's forests are deteriorating, and in some cases are already dead. In the northeastern United States, the prized sugar maple is experiencing stunted growth, and foresters report that many stands are declining rapidly. Extensive forest damage has also been identified in China, which recently passed the United States as the world's leading burner of coal—much of it containing high concentrations of acid-producing sulfur.[19]

Although pollution controls can greatly reduce air pollution, growing numbers of automobiles, factories, and power plants have overwhelmed even the most ambitious programs. In response, many societies are now investing in improved energy efficiency and switching to cleaner fuels. In the United States, 1990 amendments to the Clean Air Act allow power companies that emit sulfur dioxide to choose their own reduction strategies. Those that find cost-effective ways to improve efficiency or switch to less polluting energy sources are able to go beyond the minimal reductions and sell "emission allowances" to other companies. Even more dramatic reductions are likely in Eastern Europe, where much of the existing industrial infrastructure may be replaced by more-efficient technologies and less polluting fuels.[20]

Carbon dioxide, the leading greenhouse gas and therefore a contributor to global warming, is a more basic challenge to the fossil fuel economy. Carbon is a basic component of all fossil fuels that is released whenever they are burned. Ignored by policymakers as recently as 1988, the risk of climate change, and the enormous damage to agriculture and the rest of the environment it could bring, is now a force that drives energy policy in many nations. Not only did carbon dioxide concentrations in the atmosphere reach 354 parts per million in 1990, global average temperatures reached the highest levels of the past century. By 1991, some 23 countries had announced intentions to limit their carbon emissions. Although some are planning just to slow the rate of growth, others, such as Germany, are aiming at reductions of up to 25 percent. Meanwhile, negotiations on a climate treaty are under way, with the hope that an agreement will be signed by heads of state at the U.N. Conference on Environment and Development in Brazil in June 1992.[21]

## Many societies are now investing in improved energy efficiency and switching to cleaner fuels.

The main responses to global warming so far are programs to improve energy efficiency. By cutting the amount of gasoline needed to run a car or the electricity needed to light a home, the use of oil and coal can be reduced—while at the same time saving money. This is the approach being followed by European governments. And two U.S. electric utilities—the investor-owned Southern California Edison Company and the Los Angeles Department of Water and Power, a municipal utility—plan to rely on investments in improved energy efficiency in their customers' buildings and factories to reduce carbon emissions from power plants by 19 percent over the next 20 years.[22]

For societies eventually to achieve the 60–80 percent reduction in global carbon emissions needed to stabilize climate, however, they cannot afford to ignore the choice of fuels. Renewable energy sources are best, since they cause no net additions to the carbon dioxide level. Technologies such as wind power, geothermal energy, and solar power are now approaching competitiveness with fossil-fuel-based power generation, and are poised for rapid growth in the years ahead. But even among the fossil fuels there are wide variations in environmental impact. One key distinction is that oil contains 17 percent less carbon per unit of energy than coal, while natural gas has 43 percent less. Coal is far and away the most environmentally damaging of the fossil fuels, both from an air pollution and a climate standpoint.[23]

Natural gas, on the other hand, is the simplest of the hydrocarbons. Its main ingredient—methane—is one of the most basic organic molecules, made up of a carbon atom surrounded by four hydrogen atoms. The methane generally is accompanied by varying amounts of $CO_2$ as well as flammable gases such as ethane and propane. The simplicity of natural gas, particularly the fact that it is usually low in sulfur, is one reason it causes less air pollution than other hydrocarbons do.

---

**Heating with natural gas is in most circumstances less polluting than heating with electricity produced from coal or oil.**

---

The main uses of natural gas today are as an industrial energy source and as a heating fuel in residential and commercial buildings. These applications can both be expanded and made more efficient—thanks to a new generation of gas furnaces, water heaters, and air-conditioning systems. Heating with natural gas is in most circumstances less polluting—and contributes less to global warming—than heating with electricity produced from coal or oil. In addition,

two major elements of the global energy economy stand out for their potential to use large additional amounts of natural gas: the electric power industry and transportation. Together, they are responsible for more than half the carbon emissions from fossil fuels. Rapid increases in electricity use are a major reason for rising carbon emissions and acid rain, particularly since coal-fired power plants have dominated the construction plans of many nations in recent years.[24]

Throughout most of the eighties, the United States and the European Community were so worried about shortages of natural gas that they prohibited the building of gas-fired power plants. More recently, falling gas prices and rising concern about air pollution have thrust gas-fired power plants to the forefront of the power industry. About half the plants now being built in the United States are gas-fired, a sharp reversal from a decade earlier when the vast majority were nuclear or coal-fired.[25]

One reason for the shift in direction is a new generation of more-efficient gas turbines—similar to the engines used to power today's jet aircraft. Some 39 companies, ranging from Rolls Royce to Mitsubishi and Westinghouse, now manufacture gas turbines, which are being used in Europe, Mexico, Pakistan, Thailand, and other countries. Burning gases are used directly to spin a turbine connected to a power generator. This contrasts with conventional power plants, which heat water that is used to drive a steam turbine. Steam power plants improved steadily in the early part of the century, but since 1960 have had a nearly static conversion efficiency of about 36 percent—falling slightly with the advent of pollution control technologies in the seventies.[26]

Gas turbine systems, in contrast, have evolved rapidly as a result of extensive aerospace-related research. They also lend themselves to combined cycle applications: the excess heat from the gas turbine is used to produce steam that either can be reinjected into the turbine or can power a second steam turbine. Combined cycle systems have achieved conversion efficiencies of 45 percent, and engineers believe that 55 percent can be reached by the mid-nineties. Such systems have only been on the market for a few years, but already they have spurred a major shift: their higher efficiency means that natural gas can compete with coal for steady, "baseload" generating capacity. In fact, at today's fuel prices, producing power with a combined cycle gas plant costs 25 percent less than a coal plant does. (See Figure 3–4.) This is because a gas plant costs only about half as much to build as a coal plant equipped with the latest pollution control devices.[27]

Gas-fired combined cycle systems also have environmental advantages. Since natural gas contains little or no sulfur or particulates, these two major pollutants from coal-fired plants are virtually eliminated. Nitrogen oxide ($NO_x$) emissions are more problematic since they form readily in the hot flame that comes from burning methane. However, steam-injected gas-turbines and an even newer

technology, the chemically recuperated gas turbine, greatly reduce nitrogen oxide emissions—by 85 percent compared with the most advanced coal plants yet built. Moreover, the more-efficient combined cycle plants emit 65 percent less $CO_2$ than coal plants in use today do. (See Table 3–2.)[28]

Although economics alone may make gas turbines the largest new generating source in the nineties, a commitment to slow global warming would justify a more aggressive effort—shutting down the least efficient and most polluting oil- and coal-fired plants and replacing them with renewable energy and natural gas. Wind power and geothermal energy, for example, are already competitive, though they cannot entirely replace baseload plants. To fill that niche while reducing fossil fuel emissions, gas turbine combined cycle systems can be installed at older, inefficient coal, oil, or gas plants. Calculations for the United States show that an effort, say over 20 years, to replace half the existing coal capacity with gas turbines would by itself cut the country's carbon emissions by 16 percent and greatly reduce acid rain. Moreover, this would require only a 30-percent increase in U.S. gas supplies. (Naturally, such an effort should be accompanied by major investments in energy efficiency—an even more cost-effective way to reduce carbon emissions.)[29]

Natural gas is also gaining notice as a vehicle fuel. Compared with other new fuels being considered—including ethanol and methanol—natural gas has environmental as well as economic advantages. Its chemical simplicity is again a plus, reducing emissions and allowing for less engine maintenance. The main problem is that methane gas requires changes in vehicle fueling and storage systems, including a means to compress the gas and a special pressurized tank for carrying it aboard motor vehicles.[30]

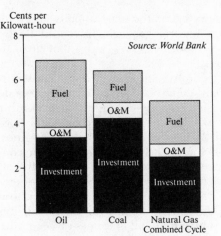

Cents per
Kilowatt-hour

Source: World Bank

**Figure 3-4. Costs of Power Generation by Fuel, 1990**

**Table 3-2. Air Pollutants from Various Electricity-Generating Technologies[1]**

| Technology | Conversion Efficiency | Emissions | | |
|---|---|---|---|---|
| | | NO$_x$ | SO$_2$ | CO$_2$ |
| | (percent) | (grams per kilowatt hour) | | |
| High-Sulfur Coal-Fired Steam Plant (without scrubbers)[2] | 36 | 4.3 | 21.1 | 889 |
| High-Sulfur Coal-Fired Steam Plant (with scrubbers)[2] | 36 | 4.3 | 2.1 | 889 |
| Low-Sulfur Coal-Fired Fluidized Bed Plant | 32 | 0.3 | 1.2 | 975 |
| Oil-Fired Steam Plant (uncontrolled) | 33 | 1.4 | 1.6 | 794 |
| Integrated Gasification Combined Cycle Plant (coal gasification) | 38 | 0.2 | 0.3 | 747 |
| Gas Turbine Combined Cycle Plant (current)[3] | 43 | 0.3 | 0 | 416 |
| Gas Turbine Combined Cycle Plant (advanced)[4] | 55 | 0.03 | 0 | 331 |

[1]The figures in this table are for particular plants that are representative of ones in operation or under development.  [2]Burning coal with 2.5 percent sulfur content.  [3]Using steam-injected gas turbines. [4]Using intercooled chemically recuperated gas turbine with reheat to improve the efficiency of converting exhaust steam into fuel energy.
SOURCES: Richard L. Ottinger et al., *Environmental Costs of Electricity* (New York: Oceana Publications, 1990); Jennifer Lowry, Applied Energy Systems, Arlington, Va., private communication, September 18, 1991; Meridian Corporation, "Energy System Emissions and Materiel Requirements," prepared for Deputy Assistant Secretary for Renewable Energy, Department of Energy, Alexandria, Va., February 1989; Edwin Moore and Enrique Crousillat, "Prospects for Gas-Fueled Combined Cycle Power Generation in the Developing Countries," Energy Series Paper No. 35, World Bank, Washington, D.C., 1991; California Energy Commission, *Fuels Report 1989* (Sacramento, Calif.: 1989).

Until recently, compressed-gas vehicles were confined to just a few countries: nearly 300,000 natural gas vehicles are on Italy's roads, and more than 100,-000 are found in New Zealand. Interest has blossomed in the past few years, however, as cities struggle to cope with intractable air pollution. In the United States, for example, methanol lost ground to natural gas in 1991 as its environmental drawbacks became better known. Several states, led by California, are now encouraging the use of gas vehicles. It will not take too much persuasion, since the wholesale price of natural gas is now less than one third that of gasoline. A study by the natural gas industry estimates that as many as 4 million natural gas vehicles could be on U.S. roads by 2005 as a result of clean air laws.[31]

Definitive figures on air emissions from compressed-gas vehicles remain elusive because the only vehicles on the road so far are converted ones not optimized for the use of this fuel. Engines, fuel injection systems, and catalytic converters must be redesigned if the full efficiency and pollution reduction potential is to be realized. But even without optimization, today's methane engines produce minimal amounts of key pollutants such as carbon monoxide, reactive hydrocarbons, and particulates. Moreover, natural gas can be burned in a high-compression engine, which allows efficiency to improve 15–20 percent and $CO_2$ emissions to be cut 30 percent.[32]

As with power plants, the main problem with hot-burning natural gas engines is nitrogen oxide emissions. Since natural gas produces a much smaller range of emissions than gasoline engines do, they will require a different, though ultimately simpler and probably more effective kind of catalyst. Engineers believe that a special catalytic converter can be designed that will nearly eliminate $NO_x$ emissions and at the same time keep hydrocarbon emissions low. Several major manufacturers are already working on this problem. Overall, the main advantages of natural gas vehicles lie in their ability to displace oil and reduce air pollution. Greenhouse gains are less impressive, particularly compared with what is possible by switching to natural gas in power plants.[33]

The main challenge in switching to natural gas as a major vehicle fuel lies in fuel distribution and storage systems. Such cars will, for example, need to be fitted with a cylindrical pressurized tank big enough to travel extended distances between refills, without sacrificing trunk space. Engineers believe that this is feasible even for small passenger vehicles, but that it will require extensive redesign. Most trucks, vans, and buses, however, can be fitted with such tanks with only minimal modification. The initial market for gas vehicles will likely be bus systems, delivery trucks, and the fleet vehicles owned by many government agencies and private companies. The United Parcel Service in the United States, for example, is testing natural gas in its vehicles and considering a conversion effort.[34]

Converting service stations to provide natural gas presents no insurmountable challenges, and several oil companies have already begun to do so in California. In Europe and North America, virtually all cities and many rural areas have natural gas available, and simply need to provide service stations with compressors for putting the gas into pressurized tanks. And it may well be possible for residential buildings, millions of which are already hooked up to gas lines, to be fitted with compressors, allowing drivers to reduce their trips to a service station.[35]

The efficiency of natural gas use may be boosted further by another new technology—fuel cells. These chemically combine methane or hydrogen with oxygen to generate electricity efficiently and cleanly on a small scale—particularly in city buildings. But fuel cells can also be used to run an electric motor in a car. Since they are likely to be at least twice as efficient as internal combustion engines, cars will not need to carry as much gas, making storage easier and reducing fuel costs. Although several prototypes are in use, an economical, compact version for use in light vehicles is not yet ready. The best bet is that fuel-cell-powered cars and trucks will begin to make an appearance between 2000 and 2010.[36]

The biggest environmental objection to increasing the use of natural gas is that methane is a powerful heat-trapping gas that is building in the atmosphere and exacerbating the greenhouse effect. If increased use of natural gas were to lead to large leakages of methane, global warming would be exacerbated and the benefits of reduced carbon emissions partly offset. Methane is one of the least-understood contributors to climate change, but scientists now believe that many activities are adding to its concentration in the atmosphere, including rice cultivation, sewage treatment, landfills, and livestock. Fossil fuels account for one fifth of the total, of which coal min-

ing accounts for at least half; oil processing and gas-venting in connection with
oil production are other important contributors. The remaining 5 percent
share of total methane emissions that is
believed to be related to natural gas is
largely a product of the notoriously
leaky Soviet pipelines and older local
distribution systems in Europe and
North America.[37]

Methane emissions would only have to
be reduced 10 percent, however, to
achieve an atmospheric balance. And
methane on average lasts just 10 years in
the atmosphere; further emission reductions could lead to an actual decline in
atmospheric concentrations in a decade
or two—something that would take
more than a century for carbon dioxide.
Landfills, livestock feeding practices,
and coal mining are the readiest sources
of such reductions. Lowering natural gas
leaks also deserves priority as a means of
slowing global warming. It should be
possible to cut methane emissions from
Soviet pipelines and older gas distribution systems.[38]

The most recently developed pipelines, compressors, power plants, and
vehicles are unlikely to contribute significantly to global methane concentrations, however. Beyond the built-in incentive to restrict emissions of a valuable
fuel, safety demands it. Since methane
can cause fires, any vehicle that is to
meet standards for indoor parking, as
some already do, cannot be leaky. Moreover, regulatory authorities, including
the U.S. Environmental Protection
Agency, are already setting standards for
total hydrocarbon emissions—a major
source of which is unburned methane
that escapes from the tailpipes of natural
gas vehicles. Engineers believe that
these emissions can be largely eliminated by catalysts now under development. And tighter seals can prevent
leaks from the fuel injection system.[39]

## THE GAS RESOURCE BASE

Natural gas cannot be a viable transition
fuel, of course, unless the resource base
is adequate to support it. Many countries
have just come through a period when
natural gas was thought to be more limited than oil, and equally vulnerable to
price shocks. This largely excluded it
from consideration as a major future energy source. But conditions have
changed dramatically in recent years.
Extensive natural gas resources have
been discovered, and geological evidence suggests that many of the assump-
tions on which current priorities are
based need to be reconsidered.

The Chinese were the first to use geo-
logically occurring methane gas, approximately 2,000 years ago. Gas was
then ignored until the early twentieth
century, when it reappeared as a by-
product of oil extraction that was often
vented. It was not until the United States
built up an infrastructure to transport,
store, and use this gaseous hydrocarbon
in the fifties that its potential became
clear. Even today, heavy reliance on gas
is confined mainly to the industrial countries, although, ironically, China is the
world's leading user of biologically
derived methane gas—produced mainly
from agricultural wastes.[40]

Natural gas geology is a surprisingly
immature science. As recently as the late
seventies, extensive reserves had been
found in few areas, and some of the largest—in the Netherlands, for example—
appeared to be running out. But experts
were missing a key point: most of what
was then known about natural gas geology was a by-product of oil exploration.
Little effort had been made to identify
gas in areas unlikely to contain oil.[41]

The U.S. experience provides insights, since it has a very large natural
gas industry and its resources are the
most heavily exploited. While the use of
gas soared in the fifties and sixties, by

the seventies the nation was experiencing shortages—a phenomenon of particular concern during a period of harsh winters and rising oil prices. Both industry and government sought to limit the use of natural gas, including introducing a federal ban on the construction of gas-fired power plants. Congress also started to abolish price controls that had been in place for decades and that had helped create the shortages of the seventies.[42]

U.S. reliance on natural gas declined steadily from 1972 until 1986 as higher prices and new technologies spurred conservation, both in industries and homes. The resulting decline in production reinforced the notion that the country was running out of this fuel, though throughout most of the eighties available supplies far exceeded demand. The price of gas peaked in 1984 and has since fallen more than 40 percent—to an oil equivalent of just $9 per barrel. The gas market is now almost entirely insulated from the oil market; witness the fact that prices were barely affected by the Gulf crisis. Although lower prices reduced the incentive to find gas, production began to increase in 1986 and was up 16 percent by mid-1991. (See Figure 3–5.) Natural gas is now the fastest growing major energy source in the United States, and domestically produced gas supplies 17 percent more energy than domestic oil does.[43]

The sharp turnaround in production was accompanied by a reevaluation of the geological resource base. A 1991 National Research Council study of official estimates made by the U.S. Geological Survey found that "after a detailed examination of [U.S.G.S.'s] data bases, geological methods, and statistical methods, the committee judged that there may have been a systematic bias toward overly conservative estimates." The same conclusion would apply to other leading industry and government studies of the gas resource base.[44]

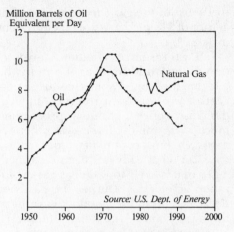

Million Barrels of Oil Equivalent per Day

*Source: U.S. Dept. of Energy*

**Figure 3-5. Natural Gas and Oil Production in Continental United States, 1950–91**

These studies are in question in part because they are based on limited data. Relatively few areas have been explored for natural gas, and extrapolations based on accidental discoveries that occurred during oil exploration tend to be conservative. Oil only exists at relatively modest temperatures and pressures, limiting it mainly to shallow deposits. Methane, on the other hand, does not readily break down and can be found at extreme depths. In fact, the pressure found at such depths allows large quantities of gas to be squeezed into a small space. In addition, much gas is found in small, tight formations that new technology is making easier to locate. New techniques of horizontal drilling make it much cheaper to tap these resources. Natural gas is also being found in abundance in many coal seams.[45]

Although total recoverable gas resources are still hard to assess, the lower bounds of U.S. resources are now estimated by several studies to be at least 50 percent higher than a decade ago—approximately 1,000–1,300 trillion cubic feet. This is enough to last the country 60 years at current rates of use. While the price is likely to rise from today's extraordinarily low level, it is estimated that most of the gas can be exploited at a price of $15 per barrel of oil equivalent or less.[46]

U.S. gas resources are only a tiny fraction of the world total, as shown by the fact that the United States has just 5 percent of world proven reserves. Indeed, gas discoveries are now proceeding much more rapidly in several other regions. On most continents, more natural gas than oil already has been identified, a gap that is likely to widen as gas exploration accelerates. During the past two decades, enormous amounts have been discovered in Argentina, Indonesia, Mexico, North Africa, the North Sea, and central Russia. Each region either is or could become a major exporter of natural gas. Indeed, Russia's proven natural gas reserves more than match Saudi Arabia's oil. With its reserves, this Soviet republic could supply both Europe and Japan with gas via pipeline for at least 50 years.[47]

Dozens of other countries have proven natural gas reserves that are minor on a global scale, but sufficient to fuel their economies for decades. (See Table 3–3.) However, most developing nations have barely begun to look for this resource. One reason is that the large oil companies with the capital and technical know-how to find it are less interested in gas since it is not easily sold for hard currency. Moreover, few developing countries have made the investments in pipelines and distribution systems needed for widespread use of gas. And the World Bank has been stingy in its support of such projects compared with electric power systems, which traditionally command nearly a fifth of its loans.[48]

China, which according to official statistics has less than 1 percent of the world's proven natural gas reserves, may be an example of hidden potential. The nation's energy planners, who in the fifties and sixties overtapped and badly

**Table 3-3. Proven Natural Gas Reserves, by Country, 1990**

| Country | Natural Gas Reserves | Gas Reserves Remaining at Current Rates of Oil Use |
|---|---|---|
| | (billion cubic meters) | (years) |
| Soviet Union | 52,000 | 95 |
| Iran | 17,000 | 437 |
| Canada | 7,578 | 100 |
| Argentina | 7,154 | 282 |
| United Arab Emirates | 5,492 | 659 |
| Saudi Arabia | 5,135 | 906 |
| United States | 4,930 | 7 |
| Qatar | 4,621 | 2,080 |
| Algeria | 3,250 | 132 |
| Iraq | 3,115 | 117 |
| Venezuela | 2,993 | 56 |
| Indonesia | 2,423 | 64 |
| Norway | 2,295 | 207 |
| Australia | 2,170 | 75 |
| Mexico | 2,060 | 29 |
| Malaysia | 1,485 | 176 |
| Kuwait | 1,370 | 69 |
| Libya | 1,218 | 84 |
| India | 1,100 | 19 |
| China | 1,000 | 9 |

SOURCES: Edwin Moore and Enrique Crousillat, "Prospects for Gas-Fueled Combined Cycle Power Generation in the Developing Countries," Energy Series Paper No. 35, World Bank, Washington, D.C., 1991; United Nations, *Yearbook of Energy Statistics* (New York: 1991).

damaged some of their shallow gas reserves, are so convinced of its limited potential that they have based the country's development on coal. Yet geologists who have examined China's geological structures believe that they contain gas resources at least equal to the United States, which now produces nearly 40 times as much. If so, China has enough natural gas to do everything it is planning to do with coal over the next few decades, with far less air pollution and lower carbon emissions. Some of the largest deposits may be located in the Ordos and Szechuan basins, within easy reach of most of the country's industrial and population centers. Although the costs of building a gas transmission system are considerable, they could be offset by reduced investments in coal mines, rail lines, and power plants, as well as by avoided ecological damage.[49]

**Worldwide natural gas resources are sufficient to at least double world use of gas during the next 20–30 years.**

Increased reliance on natural gas raises other environmental concerns, however, in particular the impact of exploration and extraction. Natural gas development is far less damaging than coal development, and somewhat less risky than petroleum, as gaseous methane dissipates rather than contaminating land or water, the way oil does. But gas development often involves hazardous drilling fluids, and, at least for a time, mars the landscape with drilling rigs, pipelines, and other equipment. Of particular concern is the potential for gas development in scenic areas, including national forests and parks. In fact, disputes have already arisen in the Canadian province of Alberta, where a gold rush–like interest in coalbed methane threatens wilderness areas with new roads and vehicle traffic.[50]

Such conflicts are relatively infrequent, and could be largely avoided with strict regulation. Many areas should be kept off-limits for gas exploration; where drilling does occur, it needs to be controlled—for example, mandating the reinjection of excess liquids, as is already required in many countries. The main environmental constraints on natural gas are similar to those that arise with some renewable energy sources: questions of land use. Just as it makes little sense to flood vast areas of farmland with a hydro project or to permit wind farming in a national park, so should gas drilling be prohibited in sensitive areas. Because natural gas development is not particularly land-intensive, and resources are much more dispersed than oil, even strict limits would not greatly reduce the natural gas potential.[51]

Estimating the ultimate scale of the worldwide natural gas resource base is still difficult, but available data suggest that resources are sufficient to at least double world use of gas during the next 20–30 years and then to sustain that level for at least a couple of decades. Since world oil production is likely to grow only modestly from the current level, and could well begin to decline soon after the turn of the century, natural gas will almost certainly soon become the most important fossil fuel—available in sufficient quantity to replace many existing uses of oil and coal.[52]

## THE BRIDGE TO SUSTAINABLE ENERGY

Increased use of natural gas is by no means a solution to the world's energy problems—but rather a stepping stone to a sustainable energy system. Relying on this energy source as a substitute for oil and coal will allow a rapid reduction in air pollution and greenhouse gas emissions during the next two decades. But it cannot, by itself, remove the specter of global warming. For that to happen, the long-term transition to an energy-efficient economy based on renewable resources must be achieved.

The year 2010 can be viewed as a midpoint in the energy transition. It is far enough off to allow extensive change, but near enough to be anticipated with some reliability, since the world is unlikely to be relying on any completely new energy source or technology within a mere two decades. Although renewable energy can play a much larger role by then, it cannot by itself displace sufficient coal or oil to achieve the desired cuts in carbon emissions.

With modest encouragement, it now appears that the use of natural gas may double by the year 2010—and not begin to decline until at least 2030 as resources are depleted. If combined with a 25-percent cut in oil use in 2010 (driven largely by rising oil prices), a 75-percent cut in coal use (dictated by ecological constraints, carbon taxes, and an effort to replace coal-fired power plants), and a doubling in renewables, the result would be a 20-percent decline in global carbon emissions. World primary energy use would fall slightly under this scenario, but delivered energy services could be increased more than 50 percent as a result of improved energy efficiency.[53]

At some point, natural gas will itself be phased out, either due to resource exhaustion or the need to eliminate carbon emissions entirely. But societies cannot afford simply to wait 20 years before beginning the shift to renewable energy. In fact, large-scale wind, geothermal, and solar power plants are already in operation in some parts of the world, and are increasingly competitive even with the most efficient combined cycle plants. In 1991, for example, major new wind farm projects similar to those already developed in California were announced in northern Germany and in Iowa. Although most of these renewable energy sources are not suited to the 24-hour-a-day baseload operation of today's coal and nuclear plants, utility engineers believe that they can be an effective complement to the current mix of large power plants.[54]

Still, electric power from renewables is unlikely to provide all the energy needed for twenty-first century economies. Today's batteries are expensive, heavy, and must be recharged frequently. Better batteries are being developed, but even these are likely to have drawbacks. Long-distance power lines are also costly, relatively inefficient energy carriers, and they generate potentially dangerous electromagnetic fields. Although electricity is likely to play important roles in a sustainable energy economy—powering computers and efficient light bulbs, for example—hydrogen gas is more likely to be the main energy carrier, replacing many existing uses of oil, natural gas, and even electricity.[55]

Hydrogen can be produced using electricity from any source, through a process known as electrolysis. And it is more readily stored than electricity—in a pressurized tank, as a cryogenic (very cold) liquid, or in metal hydrides, a new technology based on metal powders that absorb gaseous hydrogen and release it when heated. Several years' worth of hydrogen could be stocked in depleted oil or gas reservoirs in regions such as the U.S. Gulf Coast, and it can be carried by pipeline for thousands of kilometers with minimal energy losses. In fact, small industrial hydrogen pipelines have been in operation for decades, including one running some 200 kilometers along the Rhine River in Germany. Over long distances, moving large amounts of energy in gaseous form costs much less than sending electricity through a wire. Gases are also much less risky to move than oil, today's most heavily traded fuel, which is often spilled during routine transportation as well as in tanker accidents.[56]

Hydrogen can provide the concentrated energy needed by factories, motor vehicles, and homes. Indeed, it is already used to power some rockets, and is being studied both in Europe and the Soviet Union as an aviation fuel. It can run an automobile, for example, using either an internal combustion engine or, more efficiently, with a fuel cell. And new catalytic hydrogen-powered space heaters, stoves, and water heaters can be developed that will be much more efficient than today's appliances. The gas can also be used to produce electricity in small combined heat-and-power generators or fuel cells located in buildings—with virtually no pollution.[57]

The cost of electrolytically produced hydrogen—whether from renewable energy or any other new power source—is at least five times today's natural gas price. Closing this gap will be a slow process, dependent on progress in renewable energy as well as increases in gas prices. A hefty carbon tax (from which hydrogen would be exempt) would also help. As a vehicle fuel, however, hydrogen's market gap is smaller. Solar, geothermal, or wind-derived electricity at 4¢ per kilowatt-hour—achievable by the end of this decade—could produce hydrogen that sells at the pump for about the equivalent of a $3.00 gallon of gasoline, similar to current prices in Europe.[58]

The exhaust from a hydrogen-powered car contains only water vapor and small amounts of nitrogen oxides. Such cars have been built, with only modestly redesigned engines, but storage remains a problem. Because of its low density, hydrogen occupies even more space than natural gas. Tanks that contain compressed hydrogen are bulky and heavy; hydride storage systems are also heavy, as well as expensive. Improvements in storage technology are needed,

but in addition, major efficiency gains are critical, so as to reduce the amount of fuel that must be carried. Fuel cells are the most obvious alternative, since they allow the efficient production of electricity from hydrogen fuel—which can then be used to run an electric engine with an overall efficiency about twice that of today's engines.[59]

## In a sustainable energy economy, hydrogen gas is likely to be the main energy carrier, replacing many uses of oil, natural gas, and even electricity.

The transition to hydrogen may be made easier by the fact that it can be manufactured directly from natural gas as well as derived from a broad range of renewable energy sources. In addition, hydrogen can be mixed with methane in limited quantities without altering today's gas pipelines, furnaces, and burners. As natural gas resources are gradually depleted and prices rise, hydrogen can be eased into the mix bit by bit. Just as renewable electricity is quietly fed into today's electric grids, so could solar hydrogen gradually supplant natural gas. A one-to-seven hydrogen-natural gas mixture, dubbed "hythane" by Denver engineer Frank Lynch, cut auto emissions of hydrocarbons at least in half and of nitrogen oxides by 75 percent compared with natural gas. Although carbon monoxide levels increased, they still complied with California's ultra-low 1997 emission standards, the toughest in the world.[60]

Solar hydrogen could eventually become the foundation of a new global energy economy. All the world's major population centers are near sunny and wind-rich areas. Moreover, land constraints are not likely to affect the potential. Most hydropower projects require at least 20 times as much land per kilowatt-hour as solar power does. Calculations for the United States show that one quarter of today's electricity could be supplied by deploying solar generators on an area of 15,000 square kilometers—equivalent to 8 percent of the land used by the U.S. military.[61]

The U.S. Southwest could supply much of the country with either electricity or hydrogen. The pipeline routes that now link the gas fields in Oklahoma or Wyoming with the industrial Midwest and Northeast could one day carry hydrogen. (The pipelines themselves will need to be modified or rebuilt, since hydrogen is more chemically active than natural gas and leaks much more easily.) Although renewable energy sources are somewhat regionally concentrated, they are far less so than oil. From the windy high plains of North America, hydrogen could flow to the eastern seaboard; from the deserts of western China, it could move to the populous coastal plain; and from the Australian outback, hydrogen could power that nation's southern cities.

---

**Government policymakers would be better off setting overall goals rather than trying to micro-manage the details.**

---

For Europe, solar-hydrogen plants could be built in southern Spain or North Africa. From the latter, hydrogen would be transported along existing pipeline routes into Spain via Gibraltar or into Italy via Sicily. Within Europe, today's pipelines and electrical networks would make it relatively easy to distribute solar energy. To the east, Kazakhstan and the other semiarid Asian republics might supply much of the Soviet

Union's energy. In India, the sun-drenched northwestern Thar Desert is within 1,000 miles of more than a half-billion people. Electricity for China's expanding economy could be generated in the country's vast central and northwestern desert regions.

The path to a sustainable energy economy now appears clearer than ever before. Sufficient renewable energy resources have been identified, and the needed technologies are within reach. But the route is still a steep one, made more difficult by a lack of vision and by the powerful lobbying of today's energy industries. The key challenge, then, is political: how to reshape energy policy to encourage a sweeping energy transition in the decades ahead.

Governments have a long history of clumsy or counterproductive energy reform efforts. Certainly, the aggressive and monolithic attempt to jumpstart the nuclear industry in the sixties is not a model. Government policymakers would be better off setting the overall goals and policy context rather than trying to micro-manage the details. For example, national targets for greenhouse gas emissions or oil consumption can help focus governmental and private planning efforts. Japan's goals for lowering petroleum dependence led to far-reaching improvements in energy efficiency in the eighties, and Europe's recently enacted carbon targets may have a similar effect.[62]

Beyond that, specific policies regulating emissions of some pollutants and taxing those of others will tend to shift the world toward improved efficiency and more environmentally sustainable energy sources. The 1990 Clean Air Act Amendments in the United States, for example, may tilt the electric power industry away from coal by placing constraints on sulphur dioxide emissions. Some state air pollution laws may do the same. Legislatures and parliaments around the world are now considering a bold new approach—taxing a range of pollutants, including carbon, so as to discourage their production. Several European countries have already enacted taxes on carbon, and the European Commission has proposed a Community-wide combination energy-carbon tax equivalent to $10 per barrel of oil. Such levies could push the world into a new era in which the drive for sustainable energy is vastly accelerated.[63]

Research and development is another field in which governments have a large role to play, both directly and in concert with industry. Some of the bloated research budget that currently goes to military hardware could be redirected to wind turbines, solar photovoltaics, improved auto engines, hydrogen storage systems, fuel cells, and so on. But only if the funds are channeled on a competitive basis to various companies, including innovative smaller ones, will real progress be made. If budgets are tight, massive engineering projects such as supercolliders and fusion could be trimmed in favor of more decentralized technologies. Germany has already organized a joint government-industry hydrogen program, with a federal budget of $58 million in 1991. Among its results are solar electrolysis projects in Germany and Saudi Arabia, and prototype hydrogen-powered cars built by BMW and Mercedes-Benz.[64]

Electric and gas utilities may also help bridge the way to a sustainable energy economy. Although they have lost their monopoly in power plant construction—having been joined by independent power companies—they can be reinvigorated as suppliers of efficient energy services, investing in improved light bulbs, electric motors, home insulation, efficient gas furnaces, and so on. In the United States, an estimated $2 billion worth of low-interest capital was invested by utility companies in end-use efficiency in 1991. In some Californian utilities, such investments now outstrip those in new power plants. And as environmental costs are incorporated in utility decision making, these institutions could even help customers invest in more-efficient homes or less polluting cars.[65]

The road to sustainable energy is a long one, but a key gap may soon be crossed: a picture of a new energy economy is beginning to emerge, one that may bridge the political divisions that have stymied progress so far. The solar-hydrogen economy is compellingly simple in design, economically practical, and ecologically necessary. Moreover, it does not require any radical scientific breakthroughs or the discovery of entirely new resources. This vision of the possible may finally spark an energy revolution. If so, the pace of change could surprise us all.

# 4

# Confronting Nuclear Waste

*Nicholas Lenssen*

In December 1942, humanity's relationship with nature changed for all time. Working in a secret underground military laboratory in Chicago, an emigré Italian physicist named Enrico Fermi assembled enough uranium to cause a nuclear fission reaction. He split the atom, releasing the inherent energy that binds all matter together. Fermi's discovery almost immediately transformed warfare, eventually revolutionized medicine, and created hopes of electricity "too cheap to meter." But his experiment also generated a small packet of radioactive waste materials that will persist in a form hazardous to human health for hundreds of thousands of years.[1]

Fifty years later, scientists have yet to find a permanent and safe way to dispose of Fermi's radioactive waste—nor of any of the 80,000-odd tons of irradiated fuel and hundreds of thousands of tons of other radioactive waste accumulated so

An expanded version of this chapter appeared as Worldwatch Paper 106, *Nuclear Waste: The Problem That Won't Go Away.*

far from the commercial generation of electricity from nuclear power. Regardless of human actions, the waste of the nuclear age that Fermi inaugurated will be among our generation's longest lasting legacy.[2]

Only the natural decay process, which takes hundreds of thousands or even millions of years, diminishes the radioactivity of nuclear waste. No one suspected radioactivity was dangerous following its discovery in the late nineteenth century. As time passed, though, scientists found that radiation harms human health, even at low levels of exposure. And radioactive materials, carried by wind and water, can spread quickly through the environment. Burying the wastes deep in the earth, as most governments are now planning, does not guarantee they will remain sealed off from the earth's biosphere.

Though Fermi's crude experiment was aimed at building bombs, civilian nuclear reactors have created most of the radioactivity emanating from the world's nuclear wastes—nearly 95 percent of the radioactivity in wastes in the United States is from this source. And civilian waste has been growing in quantity faster than military waste: the cumulative output of irradiated fuel from nuclear electric plants around the world is now three times what it was in 1980 and 20 times what it was in 1970. Other uses of nuclear materials, especially medical ones, add little to the waste stream.[3]

From the beginning of the nuclear age, governments neglected wastes as best they could. Working with radioactive waste was "not glamorous; there were no careers; it was messy, nobody got brownie points for caring about nuclear waste," according to Carroll Wilson, first general manager of the U.S. Atomic Energy Commission (AEC). Meanwhile, governments promised fledgling commercial nuclear industries that they would handle waste problems.[4]

---

**The cumulative output of irradiated fuel from nuclear plants is now 20 times what it was in 1970.**

---

But even today, "solutions" do not seem to be close at hand. Like mirages in the desert, safe, permanent methods of isolating radioactive materials disappear under scrutiny as quickly as scientists propose them. Nor have past efforts worked as planned; old burial and storage sites have proved leaky, and the sordid condition of nuclear weapons facilities shows the potential legacy of radioactive wastes.

As the world seeks to redirect its energy future in order to reduce emissions of carbon dioxide and other greenhouse gases, efforts are being made to get stalled nuclear power construction programs on the move again. Government officials and executives in the nuclear industry believe that this will require a fast

resolution of the nuclear waste problem. But just as earlier nuclear power plants were built without a full understanding of the technological and societal requirements, a rushed job to bury wastes may turn out to be an irreversible mistake.[5]

## HEALTH AND RADIATION

In 1904, just nine years after Wilhelm Röntgen's discovery of X rays, the first technicians started dying from exposure to the mysterious beams. Although some radiologists expressed concern about their colleagues and themselves, most resisted the notion of radiation safety guidelines. Only in 1928 did the Second International Congress of Radiology succeed in setting standards to limit exposure. More than 60 years later, after tightening the standards several times, scientists are still struggling to understand just how dangerous radiation really is.[6]

The early X-ray technicians were most concerned about radiation burns and skin ulcers. Since then, however, scientists have found that ionizing radiation can lead to cancer, leukemia, degenerative diseases (such as cataracts), mental retardation, chromosome aberrations, and genetic disorders such as neural tube defects. Radiation also weakens the immune system, allowing other diseases to run their course unchallenged. Damage from radiation occurs at the atomic level within individual cells. The energy embodied in ionizing radiation can be transferred to the affected atom, leading to damage, mutations, or even death of individual cells in the body. The cumulative effect of cellular change is what leads to health problems. Children and fetuses are particularly susceptible to radiation exposure, because their rapidly dividing cells are more sensitive to damage.[7]

The timing and severity of health effects are closely related to the level of exposure. A single dose over 400 centisieverts usually results in painful death within a few weeks. (A centisievert measures the biological effect on the body of different types of radiation). Doses in the range of 100–400 centisieverts often lead to cancer. The health effects of lower doses, particularly those cumulatively received over a period of years, are still debated. However, most scientists believe "there is sufficient evidence that all radiation—however small—presents a risk. There is no threshold" dose of no consequence, according to Dan Benison of Argentina's Atomic Energy Agency and chairman of the International Commission on Radiological Protection (ICRP), a self-appointed body of radiological and nuclear professionals.[8]

Human beings live in a world full of "background" radiation that comes from radon gas seeping from uranium and thorium in the earth's surface and from cosmic rays arriving from outer space. The annual average total is between 0.25 and 0.36 centisieverts. Humans and other life forms evolved over millions of years adapting to these natural levels of radiation, though scientists believe these too have an impact on human health.[9]

Additional radiation exposure comes from human activity such as medical X rays, fallout from the testing of atomic bombs, and nuclear power and its wastes. For the average person, exposure from these sources is far lower than from background radiation, though not for some individuals working in or living near nuclear installations.[10]

The most extensive data on radiation's health effects come from Hiroshima and Nagasaki, where scientists have been following the health of atomic bomb survivors since 1950. By comparing the causes of death of those who survived the original blasts and their estimated exposure to radiation, scientists were once confident that lower doses of radiation had an insignificant health effect. In 1986, however, a reassessment of the original doses these people received found that they had been exposed to far less radiation than previously assumed, meaning that the cancer and other health effects attributable to radiation are higher. Using these new data, a 1989 U.S. National Research Council (NRC) committee concluded that an acute dose of radiation is three times likelier to cause cancerous tumors and four times likelier to induce leukemia than was thought 10 years ago.[11]

This information prompted the ICRP in 1990 to lower standards again for permissible levels of radiation exposure for nuclear workers. Indeed, such standards have been lowered several times since the first recommendations, from 30 centisieverts per year in 1934 to 2 centisieverts in 1990. Some scientists say the permissible level should be even lower.[12]

A 1991 study of employees at the U.S. Oak Ridge National Laboratory in Tennessee suggested that the NRC's estimates may be too low by as much as a factor of 10. Leukemia rates were 63 percent higher for nuclear workers exposed over long periods to small doses of radiation than for non-nuclear workers. Likewise, a 1990 report on families of workers at the Sellafield nuclear reprocessing facility in England found that children are seven to eight times as likely to develop leukemia if their fathers received legal low-level doses of radiation. Perhaps the children of Japanese victims have not experienced similar increases because they were exposed to a single, larger dose rather than the chronic exposure to lower levels of radiation received by nuclear workers, hypothesizes the report's author, Dr. Martin Gardner of Britain's University of Southampton.[13]

Other recent studies have neither confirmed nor disproved a connection between radiation from nuclear facilities and cancer. One found no radiation-induced health effects in nearby residents six years following the 1979 Three Mile Island accident. (At Oak Ridge, however, it took 26 years for the cancer rate to increase.) A U.S. National Cancer Institute report found no association between cancer and nuclear facilities. The data, however, were collected at the county level, which the authors admit could not spot radiation-induced cancer clusters.[14]

The greatest human experiment with radiation exposure is taking place in the Ukraine and Byelorussia, where much of the 50 million curies the Soviet government says were released by the 1986 accident at Chernobyl is being felt. (A curie measures the intensity of radiation and is equal to 37 billion disintegrations per second; as a reference point, the Hiroshima and Nagasaki bombs released an estimated 1 million curies.) Chernobyl's legacy could include hundreds of thousands of additional cancer deaths, yet the Soviet government made no systematic effort to track citizens' cumulative exposure to radiation, nor to log health effects. A secret Soviet decree prohibited doctors from diagnosing illnesses as radiation-induced. Current estimates predict anything from 14,000 to 475,500 cancer deaths worldwide from Chernobyl. No one will ever know for certain.[15]

The expanding use of radioactive materials in developing countries is particularly worrisome. In 1987, a Brazilian junk dealer opened a discarded X-ray machine and extracted a brilliant blue powder—which turned out to be radio-active cesium-137—and distributed it to his family and friends. By the time doctors determined what had happened, four people were fatally contaminated by radiation exposure and had to be buried in lead-lined coffins. An additional 44 people were hospitalized, suffering from hair loss, vomiting, and other symptoms of serious radiation sickness. Earlier mishandlings of radioactive wastes led to deaths in Algeria, Mexico, and Morocco. Third World institutions often are not well prepared to prevent accidental exposures even from the relatively small amounts of radioactive waste generated from research and medical activities that predominate in their countries.[16]

## Chernobyl's legacy could include hundreds of thousands of additional cancer deaths.

As intentional and accidental releases have shown, radiation can quickly spread through the environment, carried by wind and water. Radioactive wastes from Soviet and U.S. weapons facilities have turned up hundreds of kilometers from their sources, contaminating wildlife, foodstuffs, and people. The fallout from atmospheric atomic bomb testing has spread around the globe and will eventually cause an estimated 2.4 million cancer deaths, according to a 1991 study commissioned by the International Physicians for the Prevention of Nuclear War.[17]

Nuclear waste and its vast store of radioactivity presents a similar threat to future generations. A large, prolonged release of radioactive materials from nuclear wastes could affect human beings and other life over a broad area—indeed, even over much of the planet.

## PERMANENT HAZARD

The term radioactive waste covers everything from piping-hot irradiated (used) fuel to mildly radioactive clothes worn by operators. Each type of waste contains its own unique blend of hundreds of distinct unstable atomic structures called radioisotopes. And each radioisotope has its own life span and potency for giving off alpha and beta particles and gamma rays, which cause harm to living tissue. Radioisotope half-lives can vary from a fraction of a second to millions of years. (The half-life is the amount of time it takes for 50 percent of the original activity to decay; after 10 half-lives, one one-thousandth of the original radioactivity would remain, an amount that can still be dangerous.) This means that the radioisotope plutonium-239, for example, with a half-life of 24,400 years, is dangerous for a quarter of a million years, or 12,000 human generations. And as it decays it becomes uranium-235, its radioactive "daughter," which has a half-life of its own of 710,000 years.[18]

Irradiated uranium fuel from commercial nuclear power plants is among the most dangerous radioactive waste. It accounts for less than 1 percent of the volume of all radioactive wastes in the United States but for 95 percent of the radioactivity. The typical commercial nuclear reactor discharges about 30 tons of irradiated fuel annually, with each ton emanating nearly 180 million curies of radioactivity and generating 1.6 megawatts of heat. Since many of the radioisotopes in irradiated fuel decay quickly, its output of radioactivity falls to 693,000 curies per ton in a year's time. After 10,000 years, just 470 curies exist in each ton. (See Table 4-1.)[19]

The world's 413 commercial nuclear reactors, producing about 5 percent of the world's energy, created some 9,500 tons of irradiated fuel in 1990, bringing the world's waste accumulation of used fuel to 84,000 tons—twice as much as in 1985. (See Figure 4-1.) The United States is home to a quarter of this, with a radioactivity of over 20 billion curies. (See Table 4-2.) Within eight years, the global figure could pass 190,000 tons. Total waste generation from all the nuclear reactors now operating or under construction worldwide will exceed 450,000 tons before the plants have all closed down in the middle of the next century, projects the U.N. International Atomic Energy Agency (IAEA).[20]

Most of the existing irradiated fuel is

**Table 4-1. Radioactivity and Thermal Output Per Metric Ton of Irradiated Fuel from a Light-Water Reactor**

| Age | Radioactivity | Thermal Output |
|---|---|---|
| (years) | (curies) | (watts) |
| At Discharge | 177,242,000 | 1,595,375 |
| 1 | 693,000 | 12,509 |
| 10 | 405,600 | 1,268 |
| 100 | 41,960 | 299 |
| 1,000 | 1,752 | 55 |
| 10,000 | 470 | 14 |
| 100,000 | 56 | 1 |

SOURCES: Ronnie B. Lipschutz, *Radioactive Waste: Politics, Technology and Risk* (Cambridge, Mass: Ballinger Publishing Company, 1980); J.O. Blomeke et al., Oak Ridge National Laboratory, "Projections of Radioactive Wastes to be Generated by the U.S. Nuclear Power Industry," National Technical Information Service, Springfield, Va., February 1974.

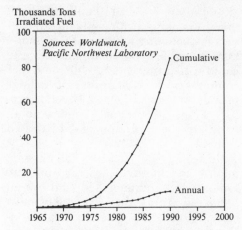

**Figure 4-1. World Generation of Irradiated Fuel from Commercial Nuclear Plants, 1965–90**

stored in large pools of cooling water alongside nuclear reactors. Originally designed to hold only a few years' worth of waste, space constraints have led to packing the spent fuel closer together and to the use of air-cooled vessels, including dry casks, to hold older, cooler irradiated fuel. Some countries have also opted to build large central storage facilities separate from nuclear power stations. To store older irradiated fuel, dry casks that rely on passive cooling are considered safer for preventing the fuel from overheating than water-based systems, which need electric-powered pumps to circulate the water.[21]

Some countries, such as France and the United Kingdom, reprocess their irradiated fuel. Originally developed to extract the fission by-product plutonium for atomic bomb production, reprocessing involves chemical procedures that also remove uranium not consumed in the reactor. This can then be enriched and again used as fuel. But reprocessing leaves behind radioisotopes created by splitting uranium atoms, including cesium, iodine, strontium, and technetium, which add up to 97 percent of the radioactivity of used reactor fuel. This refuse is called high-level waste. Other remainders include the products of the intense neutron bombardment of nuclear fission—elements such as americium and neptunium, known as transuranics because they are heavier than

**Table 4-2. Accumulation of Irradiated Fuel from Commercial Nuclear Plants, 1985 and 1990, With Official Projections for 2000**

| Country | 1985 | 1990 | 2000 |
|---|---|---|---|
| | (metric tons) | | |
| United States | 12,601 | 21,800 | 40,400 |
| Canada[1] | 9,121 | 17,700 | 33,900 |
| Soviet Union | 3,700 | 9,000 | 30,000 |
| France[2] | 2,900 | 7,300 | 20,000 |
| Japan | 3,600 | 7,500 | 18,000 |
| Germany | 1,800 | 3,800 | 8,950 |
| Sweden | 1,330 | 2,360 | 5,100 |
| Other[2] | 5,939 | 14,540 | 36,715 |
| Total[2] | 40,991 | 84,000 | 193,065 |

[1]Canadian total is proportionately higher due to its use of natural uranium instead of enriched uranium in its CANDU reactor technology. [2]France and United Kingdom (listed in "other" category) totals do not include 16,500 tons and 25,000 tons respectively produced by dual-use military and civilian reactors. Nor does the total include these additional 41,500 tons.
SOURCE: Worldwatch Institute, based on sources documented in endnote 20.

uranium. Many of these isotopes have extremely long half-lives. Thus reprocessing's net effect is to increase the volume of radioactive wastes, including that of long-lived wastes.[22]

Irradiated fuel is only part of the problem still piling up. Less intense though still dangerous "low-level" waste accounts for a far greater volume. Low-level waste is often portrayed as simply being radioactive materials with a half-life of 30 years or less. But debris classified as low-level can also contain longer-lived materials such as plutonium, technetium, and iodine. Technetium-99 and iodine-129, for example, have half-lives of 210,000 and 15.8 million years respectively.[23]

More than 76,000 cubic meters of weapons-related low-level waste and 46,000 cubic meters of civilian low-level waste were buried in shallow trenches in the United States in 1989 alone. Of the latter, nearly 95 percent of the radioactivity and more than 73 percent of its volume is from the nuclear power industry, including used resins, filter sludge, and discarded equipment. Medical radioisotopes account for less than 1 percent of the radioactivity and 2 percent of the volume of civilian low-level waste. Because of the wide range of types of low-level wastes, most countries other than the United States classify the longer-lived or more intense varieties as intermediate- or medium-level.[24]

The most voluminous though least concentrated waste comes from uranium mines and mills. Milling removes most uranium from the mined ore, but leaves about 85 percent of the radioactivity in the leftover tailings. A daughter of uranium, thorium-230, with a half-life of 77,000 years, predominates in tailings. As it decays, it turns into radium-226, and then radon-222, both potent carcinogens. In the former East Germany, just three of the Wismut uranium mines along the Czechoslovakian border have

a total of more than 150 million tons of uranium tailings, with contaminated liquids contributing millions of tons more. Stabilizing these vast mountains of waste could cost as much as $23 billion. Other countries with uranium mining tailings include Australia, Canada, Czechoslovakia, France, Namibia, Niger, South Africa, the Soviet Union, and the United States.[25]

Nuclear power reactors, along with mining and fuel facilities, also become radioactively contaminated, and like all industrial plants they eventually must close. Already, 58 generally small commercial nuclear reactors have shut worldwide, and 60 larger power plants could close by the end of this decade. Dismantling these facilities can produce a greater volume of wastes than operating them: a typical commercial reactor produces 6,200 cubic meters of low-level waste over a 40-year lifetime; demolishing it creates an additional 15,480 cubic meters of low-level waste.[26]

The most notorious failure of governments to control nuclear wastes has occurred at U.S. and Soviet military facilities. Weapons manufacturing over the past 50 years at roughly 100 U.S. military sites has led to extreme environmental pollution. According to the U.S. Office of Technology Assessment (OTA), there is "evidence that air, groundwater, surface water, sediments, and soil, as well as vegetation and wildlife, have been contaminated at most, if not all, of the Department of Energy nuclear weapons sites." Indeed, the bomb builders have contaminated everything from tumbleweeds and turtles to coyotes, frogs, and geese with radioactive wastes.[27]

U.S. weapons plant operators often vented waste directly into the air or dumped it into the ground, where it found its way into the groundwater. Some radioactive wastes ended up in the Columbia River, contaminating shellfish hundreds of kilometers away in the

Pacific Ocean. The facilities alone had some 379,000 cubic meters of liquid high-level waste from reprocessing, consisting of 1.1 billion curies of radioactivity, stored in steel tanks awaiting solidification at the end of 1989. These tanks, found at the Hanford Reservation in Washington State and at the Savannah River Plant in South Carolina, have a history of leaking and an internal buildup of explosive hydrogen gas—problems the U.S. Department of Energy (DOE) has turned a blind eye to in pursuit of producing more weapons.[28]

The situation in the Soviet Union is even worse, according to Thomas Cochran, director of the Natural Resources Defense Council's nuclear project. For the Soviet authorities, managing waste once meant dumping it in the nearest body of water. In the case of the Chelyabinsk-40 weapons facility, that was the nearby Techa River. In 1951, the Soviet government detected radioactivity in the Arctic Ocean, 1,500 kilometers from this weapons plant in the southern Ural Mountains. Weapons builders next sent waste into Lake Karachay, which Cochran now calls "the most polluted spot on the planet." Lake Karachay became so radioactive that even today standing at its shore for an hour would be lethal. In 1967, a hot, windy summer dried the lake and blew radioactive dust some 75 kilometers away, spreading contamination to 41,000 people.[29]

By 1953, the Soviet atomic industry put into operation steel tanks for storing reprocessing wastes, although discharges into Lake Karachay did not end until the sixties. The tanks at Chelyabinsk-40 proved to be even worse than those in use in the United States. In September 1957, one overheated and exploded, spewing a radioactive cloud that contaminated thousands of hectares and required the eventual evacuation of 11,000 people.[30]

The history of military facilities provides an example of the high costs of mishandling nuclear waste. Estimates for cleaning up the U.S. nuclear weapons plants run to more than $300 billion. But even such a vast sum may not be enough. According to OTA, "many sites may never be returned to a 'contaminant-free' condition or a condition suitable for unrestricted public access." Nuclear wastes have already created permanent sacrifice zones.[31]

## THEY CALL IT DISPOSAL

Since the beginning of the nuclear age, there has been no shortage of ideas on how to isolate radioactive waste from the biosphere. Scientists have proposed burying it under Antarctic ice sheets, injecting it into the seabed, and shooting it into outer space, allowing governments to continue to ignore the problem. But with each proposal came an array of objections. (See Table 4–3.) Scientists have increasingly fallen back on the idea of burying radioactive waste hundreds of meters deep in the earth's crust, arguing as does the U.S. National Research Council that geological burial is the "best, safest long-term option."[32]

All the countries using nuclear power are pursuing geologic burial as the solution to their waste, yet by their own timelines most programs have fallen way behind schedule. In 1975, the United States planned on having a high-level waste burial site operating by 1985. The date was moved to 1989, then to 1998, 2003, and now 2010—a goal that still appears unrealistic. Likewise, Germany expected in the mid-eighties to open its deep burial facility by 1998, though the government waste agency now cites 2008 as the year of operation. Most other countries currently plan deep geologic burial no sooner than 2020, with a

**Table 4-3. Technical Options for Dealing with Irradiated Fuel**

| Method | Process | Problems | Status |
|---|---|---|---|
| Antarctica Ice Burial | Bury waste in ice cap | Prohibited by international law; low recovery potential, and concern over catastrophic failure | Abandoned |
| Geologic Burial | Bury waste in mined repository hundreds of meters deep | Difficulty predicting geology, groundwater flows, and human intrusion over long time period | Under active study by all nuclear countries as favored strategy |
| Long-term Storage | Store waste indefinitely in specially constructed buildings | Dependent on human institutions to monitor and control access to waste for long time period | Not actively being studied by gov'ts, though proposed by nongovernmental groups |
| Reprocessing | Chemically separate uranium and plutonium from fission products in irradiated fuel; decreases radioactivity by 3 percent | Increases volume of waste by 160-fold; poor economics; increases risk of nuclear weapons proliferation | Commercially under way in four countries; total of 16 countries have reprocessed or plan to reprocess irradiated fuel |
| Seabed Burial | Bury waste in deep ocean sediments | Possibly prohibited by international law; transport concerns; nonretrievable | Under active study by consortium of 10 countries |
| Space Disposal | Send waste into solar orbit beyond earth's gravity | Potential launch failure could contaminate whole planet; very expensive | Abandoned |
| Transmutation | Convert waste to shorter-lived isotopes through neutron bombardment | Technically uncertain whether waste stream would be reduced; very expensive | Under active study by United States, Japan, Soviet Union, and France |

SOURCE: Worldwatch Institute, based on sources documented in endnote 32.

few aiming for even further in the future. (See Table 4–4.)[33]

The nuclear industry consistently suggests that burying radioactive wastes half a kilometer underground would mark a technical solution to the problem. According to Jacques de la Ferté, head of external relations and public information at the Nuclear Energy Agency of the Organisation for Economic Co-operation and Development, the industry has "both the knowledge and the technical resources to dispose of all forms of radioactive waste in satisfactorily safe conditions."[34]

Such blandishments notwithstanding, geological disposal is nothing more than a calculated risk. Future changes in geology, land use, settlement patterns, and climate will affect the ability to isolate nuclear waste safely. As Stanford University geologist Konrad Krauskopf wrote in *Science* in 1990, "No scientist or engineer can give an absolute guarantee that radioactive waste will not someday leak in dangerous quantities from even the best of repositories."[35]

The concept of geologic burial is fairly straightforward. Engineers would begin by mining a repository below the earth's surface; it would be made up of a broadly dispersed series of rooms from which thermally hot waste would be placed in holes drilled in the rock. Waste would be transported to the burial site in trucks, trains, or ships. Technicians would package it in specially constructed containers, made of stainless steel or other metal. Once placed in the rock, the waste containers would be surrounded by an impermeable material such as clay to retard groundwater movement. When the repository was full it would be sealed off from the surface. Finally, workers would erect some everlasting sign-post to the future—in one DOE proposal, a colossal nuclear stonehenge—warning generations millennia hence of the deadly radioactive waste entombed below.[36]

The cost of building such mausoleums is uncertain at best. In keeping with the tradition of nuclear construction projects, estimates of needed expenditures keep rising. In the United States, the expected cost of burying each ton of irradiated fuel has risen 80 percent just since 1983, with the bill for a single site holding 96,000 tons of irradiated fuel and high-level waste running upwards of $36 billion.[37]

Knowledge about deep geology comes principally from mining, an activity that seeks to extract valuable mineral resources in a short period. With deep burial of nuclear waste, problems arise in proving that such a system can provide adequate isolation for the thousands of years necessary. "The technical problem is not of digging a hole in the ground; it's of forecasting the unknown," according to Scott Saleska, staff scientist at the Institute for Energy and Environmental Research in Maryland.[38]

The scientific uncertainties surrounding radioactive waste burial are enormous. According to a 1990 NRC report on radioactive waste disposal, the needed long-term quantitative predictions stretch the limits of human understanding in several areas of geology and groundwater movement and chemistry. The report also notes that: "Studies done over the past two decades have led to the realization that the phenomena are more complicated than had been thought. Rather than decreasing our uncertainty, this line of research has increased the number of ways in which we know that we are uncertain."[39]

Experience at three sites in the United States and Germany, where government scientists are assessing and preparing specific sites for housing buried nuclear waste, has so far provided more questions than answers about the nature of geologic repositories. DOE is focusing on two locations: Nevada's Yucca Mountain for high-level waste and the Waste

### Table 4-4. Selected Country Programs on High-Level Waste Burial

| Country | Earliest Planned Year | Status of Program |
|---|---|---|
| Argentina | 2040 | Granite site at Gastre, Chubut, selected. |
| Belgium | 2020 | Underground laboratory in clay at Mol. |
| Canada | 2020 | Independent commission conducting four-year study of government plan to bury irradiated fuel in granite at yet-to-be-identified site. |
| China | none announced | Irradiated fuel to be reprocessed; Gobi desert sites under investigation. |
| Finland | 2020 | Field studies being conducted; final site selection due in 2000. |
| France | 2010 | Three sites to be selected and studied; final site not to be selected until 2006. |
| Germany | 2008 | Gorleben salt dome sole site to be studied. |
| India | 2010 | Irradiated fuel to be reprocessed; waste stored for 20 years, then buried in yet-to-be-identified granite site. |
| Italy | 2040 | Irradiated fuel to be reprocessed and waste stored for 50–60 years before burial in clay or granite. |

Isolation Pilot Plant (WIPP) in southeastern New Mexico, where construction of some burial rooms has already been completed. WIPP will have become the world's first deep repository for nuclear waste in late 1991 if DOE continued with plans to place long-lived transuranic waste from the U.S. nuclear weapons program in it. Meanwhile, German nuclear planners have targeted Gorleben salt dome to house the country's high-level waste from reprocessed irradiated fuel by 2008.[40]

The big problem with deep burial is water. In Germany, groundwater from neighboring sand and gravel layers is eroding the salt that makes up the Gorleben dome. Meanwhile, WIPP's burial rooms, more than 600 meters deep in a salt formation, are above a reservoir of brine—a saline liquid—and below a circulating groundwater system that feeds a tributary of the Rio Grande.[41]

The salt formation at WIPP has surprised government scientists again and again. Its rooms were expected to be dry, but brine is constantly seeping through the walls. Brine and corrosive groundwater could easily eat away steel waste drums and create a radioactive slurry. Sixty percent of the transuranic waste that nuclear planners intend to bury at WIPP also contains hazardous chemicals such as flammable solvents. This "mixed waste" gives off gases, including explosive hydrogen, that could send the radioactive slurry in a plume into the aquifer above it.[42]

**Table 4-4.** (*Continued*)

| Country | Earliest Planned Year | Status of Program |
|---------|------------------------|-------------------|
| Japan | 2020 | Limited site studies; cooperative program with China to build underground research facility. |
| Netherlands | 2040 | Interim storage of reprocessing waste for 50–100 years before eventual burial, possibly in the seabed or in another country. |
| Soviet Union | none announced | Eight sites being studied for deep geologic disposal. |
| Spain | 2020 | Burial in unidentified clay, granite, or salt formation. |
| Sweden | 2020 | Granite site to be selected in 1997; evaluation studies under way at Äspö site near Oskarshamn nuclear complex. |
| Switzerland | 2020 | Burial in granite or sedimentary formation at yet-to-be-identified site. |
| United States | 2010 | Yucca Mountain, Nevada, site to be studied and, if approved, receive 70,000 tons of waste. |
| United Kingdom | 2030 | Fifty-year storage approved in 1982; explore options including seabed burial. |

SOURCE: Worldwatch Institute, based on sources documented in endnote 33.

Groundwater conditions at the U.S. site at Yucca Mountain, a barren, flat-topped ridge about 160 kilometers north of Las Vegas, are also raising concerns. In theory, the waste in Yucca Mountain's volcanic tuff bedrock would stay dry since the storerooms would be located more than 300 meters above the current water table, and since percolation from the surface under current climatic conditions is minimal. But critics, led by DOE geologist Jerry Szymanski, believe that an earthquake at Yucca Mountain, which is crisscrossed with more than 30 seismic faults, could dramatically raise the water table. If water came in contact with hot radioactive wastes, the resulting steam explosions could burst open the containers and rapidly spread their radioactive contents. "You flood that thing and you could blow the top off the mountain. At the very least, the radioactive material would go into the groundwater and spread to Death Valley, where there are hot springs all over the place," says University of Colorado geophysicist Charles Archambeau.[43]

Human actions could also disrupt the planned repositories. At Yucca Mountain, there is evidence of gold and silver deposits nearby, and natural gas and potash deposits dot the area around New Mexico's WIPP. Salt domes like Gorleben are also prime targets for drillers seeking natural gas. Future efforts to tap these resources could disturb the buried nuclear waste.[44]

Humanity's vast body of scientific knowledge pales before the challenge of isolating nuclear waste until it is harmless eons hence. In 1990, scientists discovered that a volcano 20 kilometers from Yucca Mountain erupted within the last 20,000 years—not 270,000 years ago, as they had earlier surmised. Volcanic activity could easily resume in the area before Yucca Mountain's intended lethal stockpile is inert. It is worth remembering that less than 10,000 years ago volcanoes were erupting in what is now central France, that the English Channel did not exist 7,000 years ago, and that much of the Sahara was fertile just 5,000 years ago. Only a clairvoyant could choose a inviolable, permanent hiding place for the twentieth century's nuclear legacy.[45]

## THE POLITICS OF NUCLEAR WASTE

Both government and industry have long ignored warnings about radioactive wastes. In 1951, Harvard University President and former Manhattan Project administrator James B. Conant warned of wastes that would last for generations. A U.S. National Academy of Sciences (NAS) panel cautioned in 1957 that "unlike the disposal of any other type of waste, the hazard related to radioactive wastes is so great that no element of doubt should be allowed to exist regarding safety." In 1960, another Academy committee urged that the waste issue be resolved before licensing new nuclear facilities.[46]

Yet such recommendations fell on deaf ears, and one country after another plunged ahead with building nuclear power plants. Government bureaucrats and industry spokespeople assured the public that nuclear waste could be dealt with. Early failures of waste storage and burial practices resulted in growing mistrust of secretive government nuclear agencies, however. Three of the six shallow burial sites for commercial low-level radioactive waste in the United States, for example, have leaked and been closed. Trust also faded as the public viewed government agencies as being more interested in encouraging the growth of nuclear power than in resolving the waste problem. The result has been public opposition to nearly any attempt to develop radioactive waste facilities.[47]

The United States has perhaps the sorriest history of handling waste issues. Over 100 reactors now have operating licenses, accounting for about one fifth of the country's electricity, yet from the fifties onward nuclear waste problems were swept under the rug by the Atomic Energy Commission. A 1969 accident at the U.S. government's bomb-making facility at Rocky Flats, Colorado, and a stinging critique by the NAS in 1966 of the AEC's waste policy (which the AEC suppressed until Congress demanded its release in 1970) led to a speedy attempt to solve the problem: bury nuclear waste in a salt formation at Lyons, Kansas. By 1973 the AEC was forced to cancel the project because in its haste it had overlooked serious technical problems with the site that Kansas state scientists discovered. The Lyons failure set off a decade of wandering from one potential site to another, and of growing opposition from increasingly apprehensive states.[48]

In 1976, the California legislature approved a moratorium on building new nuclear power plants until "the federal government . . . approved . . . a demonstrated technology or means for the disposal of high-level nuclear waste." Seven states soon passed similar legislation that tied future nuclear power development to the solution of waste problems. The future growth of nuclear power seemed threatened, and the nuclear industry pushed AEC's successor, the Department of Energy, to bury waste quickly.[49]

DOE, however, had no better luck in finding a state amenable to housing the nation's waste. The department's repeated failures prompted the Congress to pass the Nuclear Waste Policy Act of 1982. A product of byzantine political bargaining, the law required DOE to develop two high-level repositories, one in the west of the country and the other in the east. The department was hampered, however, by an unrealistic timetable and its own insistence on pursuing sites that were clearly unacceptable. In the case of Hanford, Washington, where some of DOE's existing weapons facilities are located, the agency ignored findings by government scientists that a repository there could leak in short order. As DOE failed to gain public confidence, the whole process again became quickly embroiled in political conflicts at the state level. Finally, when eastern states forced the cancellation of a second repository in 1986, the glue that held the legislation together melted. With the whole program in jeopardy, and over the objections of Nevada's delegation, Congress ordered the DOE to study just one site: Yucca Mountain.[50]

Criticism of Yucca Mountain's selection has been widespread. Former Nuclear Regulatory Commissioner Victor Gilinsky describes it as a "political dead-end" as the federal government appears determined to saddle Nevada with the country's waste despite the state's growing opposition. The state has actively sought the disqualification of the site, and it challenges DOE's ability to conduct research objectively, given that Yucca Mountain is the only site being investigated. So strong are the feelings that the state legislature approved a bill

in 1989 prohibiting anyone from storing high-level waste there.[51]

Delays, which DOE blames on Nevada, have led to postponing waste burial in Yucca Mountain until 2010. The U.S. General Accounting Office, however, faults DOE's own ineptness for the delays. Nonetheless, the department is strongly supporting efforts in Congress to reduce Nevada's participation in the review process. DOE's program has also been criticized by Federal judge Reginald Gibson, who remarked that there was a strong suggestion of possible "impropriety and influence" in DOE's awarding of a $1-billion repository design contract for Yucca Mountain. In addition, Yucca Mountain is in a region claimed by the Western Shoshone Indians. Faced with a long list of technical difficulties and firm political opposition, Yucca Mountain has a very long way to go before becoming the country's burial site for high-level waste.[52]

---

**The United States has perhaps the sorriest history of handling waste issues.**

---

France is second only to the United States in production of nuclear electricity, the result of an ambitious construction program over the past 15 years. Since 1987, however, only one order has been placed for a new reactor, and the program has faced serious challenges over safety, economics, and waste management. In 1987, the French waste agency, ANDRA, announced four potential sites for burying high-level radioactive wastes. Local government officials, disturbed that they had not been consulted or forewarned, joined with farmers and environmentalists to organize an effective campaign to stop the research program. Blockades obstructed government technicians, and geologic survey work proceeded only with police protection. In January 1990, in one of the country's largest anti-nuclear demonstration since the late seventies, 15,000 people marched in Angers against the Maine-et-Loire site in west central France. By February, Prime Minister Rocard imposed a nationwide moratorium on further work at the four sites, providing the government a cooling-off period to reevaluate its waste program and try again to win public support.[53]

In an attempt to get the waste program back on track, the French Parliament approved a new plan in June 1991. ANDRA, which Parliament made autonomous from the country's Atomic Energy Commission, will reduce the number of sites to be investigated from four to two. Still, no sites have been named, and while the government says the selection process will be more open than the previous one, it is unclear how it will work. The government hopes to convince local communities to accept site investigations by paying local treasuries up to $9 million a year for "the psychological inconvenience" of being studied, according to then–Industry Minister Roger Fauroux. Any decision on a final burial site would be delayed for 15 years, and then Parliament would make the final decision. With its new plan, France is accepting a delay of at least another decade, a time during which the country's high-level waste inventory will nearly triple.[54]

In Germany, the controversy over radioactive waste mirrors that surrounding nuclear reactor construction, which has come to a standstill with 21 plants built. Local opposition to any nuclear project and an inability of the major political parties to agree on nuclear policy appear to be permanent fixtures. Strong public opinion led to the permanent closure of a new nuclear reactor, the Kalkar breeder plant, in 1991, as well as stymied

plans to build new plants in the former East Germany. The waste program has become caught up in a similar debate, with the Lower Saxony government joining local people who vigorously oppose federal plans to build nuclear waste burial sites at Konrad and Gorleben.[55]

Since the sixties, German policy has been to bury deeply all wastes, but the early failure to gain public confidence has led to conflicts. The western part of the country's low-level burial site at Asse was closed in 1978 due to local opposition and stability problems of the former mine's building. Since then, low-level wastes have been piling up, with some 50,000 cubic meters currently stored at temporary facilities and reactor sites, as public opposition and technical uncertainties delayed work at the replacement site, the abandoned iron ore mine at Schacht Konrad. Recently, work on Konrad continued only following judicial rulings against Lower Saxony. Hopes that the low-level waste dump at Morsleben in the former East Germany could handle the country's waste were dampened when the facility was closed by German officials in early 1991.[56]

Public opposition has also frustrated the government's attempt to develop a high-level waste burial site. In 1976, the federal government's first three investigation sites in Lower Saxony created such an uproar among local farmers and students that the state government rejected them. The following year, the federal government selected a salt dome at Gorleben, in Lower Saxony, along the East German border. Large protests erupted even before the official announcement; 2,500 people took over the drilling site for three months before police hauled them off and set up a secure camp from which scientific work could be undertaken. Although the federal government has put all its bets on Gorleben, continuing technical problems and protests threaten plans to bury waste by 2008. Critics have warned that the site's geology is unstable, but the government waste agency continues its work, even though a 1987 drilling accident caused by the geology's instability killed one worker, further eroding public confidence.[57]

Nuclear issues have torn at the social fabric of Sweden since the early seventies; two governments were thrown out of office over nuclear energy during that decade. In 1977, Parliament passed the Stipulation Act, requiring utilities to demonstrate the technical feasibility of safe high-level waste disposal. Only following a national referendum in 1980 and Parliament's decision to limit the number of reactors in the country to 12 and to phase them out by 2010 was the country able to focus on the waste issue. An immediate dividend from the agreed phaseout was a clarification of how much waste must eventually be dealt with: 7,750 tons of irradiated fuel, 90,000 cubic meters of low- and intermediate-level waste, and 115,000 cubic meters of decommissioning waste.[58]

Sweden's high-level waste program has won international praise for relying not simply on deep burial but on a theoretical system based on redundant engineering barriers, starting with a corrosion-resistant copper waste canister with four-inch thick walls that has a reported lifetime of 100,000 years or longer. The country has also avoided major siting problems by locating both its operating waste facilities next to power plants. Low-level wastes have been placed in a mined cavern 50 meters below the Baltic Sea near the Forsmark nuclear power plant since 1988, while irradiated fuel is being temporarily stored 30 meters underground at the CLAB facility alongside the Oskarshamn nuclear power plant. To reduce transportation controversies, irradiated fuel is shipped to CLAB from reactors by a special boat rather than by truck or rail.[59]

Public support for burying irradiated fuel in Sweden has not come as easy as with low-level waste, however. Protests halted efforts to site a permanent high-level burial facility 10 years ago, and efforts to explore other sites have met determined local opposition since then, even though opinion polls indicate that most Swedes would in principle accept a disposal site in their community. The government is likely to focus once again on a reactor site for its final irradiated fuel repository.[60]

Japan has the world's most ambitious nuclear construction program, with work progressing on some 11 new reactors to add to the existing 41. But public opposition to nuclear facilities has grown over the past decade, particularly since the Chernobyl accident and a spate of local mishaps. As a consequence of the Japanese tradition of not siting industrial facilities without local government support, no new reactor sites have been approved since 1986, and attempts to locate waste facilities have proved equally controversial.[61]

---

**In Japan, public opposition to nuclear facilities has grown over the past decade.**

---

Long-term efforts to handle waste did not begin in earnest until the early eighties, about when Japan started switching on a large number of nuclear reactors ordered in the seventies and waste began piling up. The nuclear industry selected the village of Rokkasho on the northern tip of Honshu Island to house a complex for reprocessing, high-level waste storage, and low-level waste burial. Local opposition to the project has been strong, with candidates opposing the facility winning mayoral and legislative elections in 1989 and 1990, and jeopardizing the whole project.[62]

Yet huge amounts of money "melted down" opposition to Rokkasho. In return for accepting the project, the government offered $120 million in subsidies to the village, equivalent to about $10,000 for each resident. An additional $120 million was offered to surrounding villages. The amounts are small when compared with the project's price tag of $9 billion, but Rokkasho is located in Japan's second poorest prefecture, and the offer appears to have had its intended effect. In February 1991, the incumbent governor, a supporter of the nuclear project, won reelection over two antinuclear candidates with 44 percent of the vote.[63]

While Rokkasho is planned to be the temporary home for high-level waste being returned from reprocessors in Europe as early as 1993, attempts to locate a final burial site have so far been thwarted by public opposition. Planners again looked to a poor region of the country, selecting an amenable village, Horonobe, near the northern tip of Hokkaido Island in 1984. But opposition from the Hokkaido Prefecture governor and diet and from nearby villages and farmers has stalled federal plans to construct a waste storage and underground research facility in Horonobe. Meanwhile, attempts to undertake exploratory drilling in other parts of the country have also faced protests.[64]

There are signs that Japan is looking beyond its borders for a high-level waste disposal site. China has shown interest since 1984 in importing irradiated fuel or waste for a fee or in return for assistance with its own fledgling nuclear program. In November 1990, China and Japan agreed to build an underground facility in China's Shanxi province where research would be undertaken on high-level waste disposal.[65]

Since the Chernobyl accident, antinu-clear grassroots groups have proliferated in the Soviet Union, bringing to a halt the country's nuclear construction program and attempts to deal with nuclear wastes. Trust between the public and nuclear authorities is at a low point as the Soviet press has been inundated with reports of "radiation disaster zones" unrelated to Chernobyl.[66]

The Soviet Ministry of Atomic Power and Industry reports that it is looking for burial sites near the Chelyabinsk site in the southern Urals, home to the country's main reprocessing facility, but is encountering opposition from local people. Also, efforts to build a major reprocessing plant at Krasnoyarsk in Siberia have been postponed, partially due to a petition delivered to local authorities in June 1989 that was signed by 60,-000 people protesting reprocessing and waste disposal plans. Further complicating the picture is a 1990 law passed by the Russian parliament that prohibits the burial of radioactive wastes from other Soviet republics or foreign countries. The Soviets have also faced criticism from Norway and Finland over waste storage facilities in the western part of the country.[67]

Bulgaria, Czechoslovakia, and Hungary have in the past returned irradiated fuel to the Soviet Union for reprocessing, without having to take back the waste. Since the late eighties, however, the Soviets have insisted on charging for a service they previously provided for free, and shipments from Eastern Europe have ceased. Irradiated fuel is now building up in temporary storage facilities that will be full in two to five years. The three countries are planning to expand storage capabilities, but eventually they will need to decide what is to become of the waste. Furthermore, public confidence is fast disappearing as past burial of low-level radioactive wastes is already coming back to haunt the new democracies.[68]

Elsewhere, radioactive waste also presents serious political problems. In South Korea, for example, the 1988 discovery of illegally dumped radioactive wastes in Changan Village near the Kori nuclear power plant spawned the country's antinuclear movement. Since then, protests—some of them violent—stopped government workers from developing low-level waste sites on two islands. The government now hopes to bury radioactive waste on uninhabited islands by 1995. No firm plans beyond temporary above-ground storage have been revealed for high-level wastes. Public pressure in Argentina also forced the government to renounce plans to quickly build a deep repository for high-level waste from the country's two operating reactors. And in Taiwan, government efforts to handle irradiated fuel from its six nuclear plants have advanced marginally: a research program, including geologic studies, has been initiated in the past five years, but no sites have been chosen yet. Meanwhile, public concern over radioactive waste is contributing to the opposition to more reactors in Taiwan.[69]

---

**Waste cannot be destroyed, nor can scientists prove that it will stay out of the biosphere if buried.**

---

India has the developing world's most ambitious construction program, with 13 reactors planned or under construction to add to the seven already built. A budding antinuclear movement confronts an entrenched bureaucracy accustomed to secrecy, but some successes have occurred in frustrating the country's nuclear planners. Citizen opposition stalled plans to build two reactors near Hyderabad. Efforts to site a nuclear waste repository, not yet commenced, could be hindered by the country's high population density. Meanwhile, the government devotes less than 1 percent of its substantial nuclear power budget to waste management.[70]

## MOVING FORWARD

In the words of François Chenevier, director of the French nuclear waste agency ANDRA, "it would be irresponsible for us to benefit from nuclear power and leave it to later generations to deal with the waste." Yet that has already occurred. While nuclear reactors generate electricity for 25–40 years, their radioactive legacy will remain for hundreds of thousands of years. Compensating future generations stricken with health effects from the current stockpile of radioactive materials is impossible. Resolving the waste problem is thus a moral obligation.[71]

Unfortunately, the problem of radioactive wastes cannot be "solved" in the normal fashion. Waste cannot be destroyed, nor can scientists prove that it will stay out of the biosphere if buried. Proof, via the scientific method, requires experimentation to confirm a hypothesis. Yet with radioactive waste, such an experiment would require gambling with people's lives over hundreds of human generations.

Sensing the inadequacy of geologic burial in 1972, nuclear pioneer Alvin Weinberg, former director of the Oak Ridge National Laboratory, suggested a startling alternative: indefinite storage in surface facilities that would be guarded and tended by a "nuclear priesthood." Such an endeavor, however, would have to overcome the fragility of human institutions. Waste will in some cases remain dangerous for far longer than the record of human history. A further weakness of above-ground storage is the potential for breaching of a storage facility, whether accidental or intentional.[72]

Yet due to the scientific and political difficulties with burial programs, above-ground storage may be the only option well into the twenty-first century. The very frailty of this course is apparent at weapons facilities in both the Soviet Union and the United States. Governments are under pressure to stabilize swiftly both liquid waste stored in dangerous, leaky tanks and contaminated soil and groundwater to prevent their further spread into the environment.

**Credibility problems plague government nuclear agencies, including those in France, the Soviet Union, and the United States.**

Less of an emergency exists with irradiated fuel from civilian nuclear power plants. Both governments and independent analysts believe that technologies such as dry casks are capable of safely containing materials for more than a century, though potential problems remain regarding institutional control of the wastes and accidents. One step toward a solution, proposed by some environmentalists in Europe and the United States, is to temporarily maintain nuclear waste at the site of its generation. Retired reactors could provide a decades-long home to irradiated fuel and other wastes, thereby reducing the number of radioactive waste sites, and limiting the handling and transportation of waste. Building storage facilities away from existing reactors immediately need only be considered in those cases where reactors are located in seismically active areas or other sites where there is justification for its rapid removal.[73]

Although most countries still expect to dismantle reactors shortly after they close, high cost estimates (from $200 million to $1 billion per reactor), technical difficulties posed by high levels of radiation found in recently closed reactors, the need to limit worker radiation exposure, and the potential lack of facilities to receive the vast volume of radioactive wastes will impede their efforts. Indeed, old reactors could soon be seen as permanent fixtures on the horizon of many countries; the United Kingdom, where commercial nuclear power first started in 1956, is the first to give up on the notion of dismantling its reactors and is now looking toward entombing them for at least 130 years. Short-term storage does not solve the problem of nuclear waste, but it could allow time for more careful consideration of longer-term options, including geologic burial, seabed burial, and longer-term storage.[74]

But moving forward on the waste issue demands much more than scientific research and reduced technical uncertainties. It also requires a fundamental change in emphasis in current operating programs and efforts to gain the public support. Reordering priorities can only take place once the threat from different types of waste is reevaluated. In the United States, for example, the classification system for wastes requires standards based not on the source, as is done now, but on the wastes' actual radioactivity and lifetime. Likewise, reactor vessel components of the Canadian CANDU reactors will be more radioactively dangerous than irradiated fuel from the plants 130 years after they are shut down, according to Marvin Resnikoff, a physicist and director of Radioactive Waste Management Associates in New York. Despite this, Canada currently plans on shallow burial of the reactor core upon dismantling. A reclassification of waste types should address the long-term threat posed by long-lived, low-level waste.[75]

Regaining public trust will require institutional changes, and closer scrutiny of radioactive waste programs. Credibility problems plague government nuclear agencies, including those in France, Japan, the Soviet Union, the United Kingdom, and the United States. Public distrust is rooted, in most cases, in the fact that the institutions in charge also promote nuclear power and weapons production, and have a long history of outright lies, misinformation, and secrecy associated with nuclear facilities. The same problem exists regarding the IAEA, which could play a far more constructive part in handling radioactive waste, particularly in developing countries, once it no longer had the conflicting roles of both promoter and controller of nuclear technology.[76]

For more than a decade several reports, including those by the U.S. Office of Technology Assessment and the National Research Council's Board of Radioactive Waste Management, have called for an independent organization to take over the task of managing the country's nuclear wastes. So far, Congress has responded by requiring more oversight of the Department of Energy, while neglecting to tackle the root problem of separating the organization responsible for weapons production and nuclear power promotion from the one that manages waste. Forming autonomous and publicly accountable organizations to handle nuclear waste will go a long way in regaining public support.[77]

In the end, the nuclear waste issue is a hostage to the overall debate on nuclear power, a debate that tears at nations. From Sweden and Germany to the Soviet Union and Italy, countries have found their political systems embroiled over the future of the atom. Due to the intense political controversy surrounding nuclear power, true progress on the waste issue may only come about once society turns away from nuclear power. Sweden, which has perhaps the broadest (though not universal) support for its nuclear waste program, made a national decision to phase out nuclear power by 2010. Without such a decision, public skepticism toward nuclear technologies and institutions only grows stronger. "If industry insists on generating more waste, there will always be confrontation. People just won't accept it," believes British environmental consultant David Lowry.[78]

A world with six times the current number of reactors, as called for by some nuclear advocates, would require opening a new burial site every two years or so to handle the long-lived wastes generated. Yet nuclear power proponents discount or even ignore the problem of wastes when calling for vast construction programs. For example, President Bush's 1991 National Energy Strategy proposed a doubling in the number of nuclear power plants in the next 40 years, but did not discuss the need for future waste sites. As experience with nuclear power plants has demonstrated, it will not become any easier to site and construct future geologic burial facilities once the first one is opened.[79]

Even if no more nuclear waste were created, addressing that which already exists will require attention and investments for a period that defies our usual notion of time. The challenge before human societies is to keep nuclear wastes in isolation for the millennia that make up the hazardous life of these materials. In this light, no matter what becomes of nuclear power, the nuclear age will continue for a long, long time.

# 5

# Reforming the Livestock Economy

## *Alan Thein Durning and Holly B. Brough*

Rings of barren earth spread out from wells on the grasslands of Botswana. Heather wilts in the nature preserves of the southern Netherlands. Forests teeming with rare forms of life explode in flame in Costa Rica. Water tables fall in the United States. Each of these cases of environmental decline springs from a single source: the global livestock industry.

During the past 50 years, livestock industries have surged in one country after another as soaring grain yields made feeding animals on corn and barley relatively inexpensive and as intensive, specialized meat, egg, and dairy farms proliferated. In much of the world, meat consumption is climbing steadily; domesticated animals now outnumber humans three to one.[1]

An expanded version of this chapter appeared as Worldwatch Paper 103, *Taking Stock: Animal Farming and the Environment*.

Factory-style livestock industries, now firmly entrenched in industrial countries, have environmental side effects that stretch along the production line—from growing vast quantities of feedgrain to disposing of mountains of manure. In developing nations, most livestock are still raised as a sideline to crops. Yet complex economic and social forces lead to mismanagement of herds, causing extensive degradation of drylands and destruction of forests. Worldwide, livestock emit the potent greenhouse gas methane into the atmosphere, contributing to climate change.

High levels of meat consumption and production translate into human losses as well. Meat-rich diets contribute to heart disease, stroke, and certain types of cancer that are leading causes of death in industrial countries. Furthermore, rising meat consumption among the fortunate few in developing societies sometimes puts pressure on food production for the poor and boosts imports of feed-grains.

Many governments—including China and the United States and those of the European Community (EC)—subsidize ecologically harmful methods of growing feed crops and raising animals. In Africa, expanding croplands and misguided development plans have reduced herding peoples' traditional range. In many Latin American countries, economic upheaval and ill-conceived development policies have channeled private investment into clearing rain forests for pasture. Livestock thus create an array of problems not because cows, pigs, and chickens are hazards in themselves, but because human institutions have forced some forms of animal farming out of alignment with their ecosystems.

## LIVESTOCK ECONOMY

Domesticated animals have played a prominent and largely beneficial role in the human economy for thousands of years, providing food, fuel, fertilizer, transport, and clothing. But in this century, the numbers and impacts of livestock have swelled apace with human population and affluence. Since mid-century, human numbers have doubled to 5.4 billion, while the number of cattle, pigs, sheep, goats, horses, buffalo, and camels has grown from 2.3 billion to 4 billion. At the same time, the fowl population multiplied from about 3 billion to nearly 11 billion.[2]

The world's most populous countries are also the livestock titans. China is home to 350 million pigs—two out of every five in the world—while India is browsed by an estimated 107 million goats, 196 million head of cattle, and 74 million water buffalo. These figures do not reflect meat production, however: with 40 percent of the world's livestock herd, for example, the rich countries produce 61 percent of the world's meat, 55 percent of the eggs, and 72 percent of the milk.[3]

And animals provide more than just food. Cattle were originally domesticated as beasts of burden, and throughout Asia and Africa 80–90 percent of agricultural land is still plowed by draft animals. Their manure is also a precious fertilizer and fuel in developing countries, supplying an estimated 30 percent of fuel energy in rural India. On farms that raise animals with crops, selling livestock products helps shield farmers' incomes from the vagaries of the market and the weather.[4]

Livestock largely define the lives of "pastoralists," the 30–43 million nomadic herders scattered on the world's drylands. Pastoralists migrate with their herds between wet- and dry-season range, a practice finely tuned to difficult environments. One study comparing pastoralism in the Sahel to ranches in Australia and the United States found that the stocking strategies of pastoralists can annually produce 8–10 times more protein per hectare than ranchers do. However, adverse economic conditions over the last decades have compelled many pastoralists to combine farming with herding.[5]

Goats and sheep, often disparaged as lowly and environmentally destructive, are actually critical to the poor's survival. Mahatma Gandhi even dubbed the goat the "poor man's cow." On meager rations, goats provide meat, milk, fiber, hides, and manure, and are readily traded for goods or cash. In sub-Saharan Africa, goats and sheep supply nearly 30 percent of the meat and 16 percent of the milk. The poor man's cow is often a poor woman's source of income.[6]

Still, at a global level the primary goal of raising livestock is to produce meat, milk, and eggs. Meat has always been popular among those able to afford it, and over the centuries that group has swelled. More than a billion people now consume at least a kilogram a week. In the case of the world's premier meat-eating country, the United States, per capita consumption is more than 2 kilograms a week. Around the world, meat consumption per person ranges from a high of 112 kilograms a year in the United States to a low of 2 kilograms in India.[7] (See Table 5-1.)

**Table 5-1. Meat Consumption Per Capita, Selected Countries, 1990**

| Country | Meat[1] |
|---|---|
| | (kilograms) |
| United States | 112 |
| Hungary | 108 |
| Australia | 104 |
| Czechoslovakia | 102 |
| France | 91 |
| Germany | 89 |
| Argentina | 82 |
| Italy | 77 |
| United Kingdom | 71 |
| Soviet Union | 70 |
| Brazil | 47 |
| Japan | 41 |
| Mexico | 40 |
| China | 24 |
| South Korea | 19 |
| Turkey | 16 |
| Philippines | 16 |
| Egypt | 14 |
| Thailand | 8 |
| India | 2 |

[1]Includes beef, pork, mutton, lamb, and poultry; based on carcass weights. Poultry figures are for 1989.
SOURCES: U.S. Department of Agriculture (USDA), Foreign Agricultural Service, "World Livestock Situation," Washington, D.C., April 1991; Linda Bailey, agricultural economist, USDA, Washington, D.C., private communication, September 11, 1990.

With the ascent of the meat-eating class worldwide, global meat production has soared, nearly quadrupling since 1950. (See Figure 5-1.) In 1990, the world produced 170 million tons—32 kilograms per person. Among meats, pork is the world leader, and China its leading consumer. Chinese pigs yield 35 percent of the world's pork. The European Community accounts for another 20 percent. Beef production—dominated by vast countries such as the United States, the Soviet Union, and Brazil—has risen slowly since 1976, when health-conscious North Americans began to cut back on beef in favor of less expensive poultry. Economic turmoil in Brazil and Argentina has also slowed the rise.[8]

Poultry is the fastest-growing part of the global meat market, with chicken accounting for 68 percent of the total. Forty years ago, the advent of abundant feedgrains, drugs to prevent poultry diseases, and improved breeds allowed U.S. farmers to start raising chickens on a massive scale. American-style chicken farming passed quickly to Europe, Japan, the Soviet Union, and other regions. The United States still leads the world in fowl, producing nearly 30 percent of poultry meat.[9]

The modern demand for meat can no

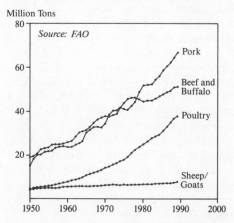

**Figure 5-1. World Meat Production, 1950–89**

longer be met by traditional livestock production systems, which integrated animals with crops. Outside of the world's grasslands, most ruminant (cud-chewing) animals such as cattle and sheep traditionally ate grass and crop wastes on farms. Pigs and fowl, which cannot digest grass, subsisted on crop wastes and kitchen scraps. In either case, domestic animals turned things that people could not eat into things people could.

To raise meat output, livestock producers adopted new, intensive rearing techniques relying on grains and legumes to feed some animals. Virtually all the pigs and poultry in industrial countries are now raised in gigantic indoor feeding facilities, for example. There, they eat carefully measured rations of energy-rich grain and protein-rich soybean meal. In contrast, cattle everywhere still spend most of their lives dining outdoors on grass, although beef producers—particularly in the United States—supplement that roughage with grain in the months before slaughter.[10]

Large areas of the world's cropland now produce grain for animals. Roughly 38 percent of the world's grain—especially corn, barley, sorghum, and oats—is fed to livestock. In the United States, animals account for 70 percent of domestic grain consumption, while India and sub-Saharan Africa offer just 2 percent of their cereal harvest to livestock. (See Table 5–2.) The crucial dietary complement to energy-rich grains is a protein-rich meal composed mostly of soybeans. The area worldwide planted in this crop is a good gauge of the rising importance of livestock production: during the past four decades, it has risen from 15 million to 55 million hectares, with the fastest growth in Brazil and Argentina.[11]

The expansion of the livestock economy has been the most dramatic change in world agriculture in recent decades.

**Table 5-2. Grain Consumed by Livestock, Selected Countries and Regions, 1990**

| Country/Region | Share of Grain Consumed |
| --- | --- |
| | (percent of grain use) |
| United States | 70 |
| Eastern Europe | 64 |
| European Community | 57 |
| Soviet Union | 56 |
| Brazil | 55 |
| | |
| Japan | 48 |
| Middle East | 33 |
| China | 20 |
| Southeast Asia | 12 |
| Sub-Saharan Africa | 2 |
| India | 2 |

SOURCE: U.S. Department of Agriculture, Foreign Agricultural Service, "World Cereals Used for Feed" (unpublished printout), Washington, D.C., April 1991.

Worldwide, the focus of livestock production has shifted from the multiple benefits of manure, draft power, milk, and eggs toward meat production. Along the way, factory-style production facilities have sprung up in much of the world, capitalizing on grain surpluses, advanced production technologies, and a growing global class of consumers rich enough to eat meat regularly. But abundance in the world's butcher shops has its costs—many of which are currently billed to the earth.

## LIVESTOCK ECOLOGY

"An alien ecologist observing . . . earth might conclude that cattle is the dominant animal species in our biosphere," writes University of Georgia biologist David Hamilton Wright. Cattle and other ruminant livestock graze half the planet's total land area. Along with pigs and poultry, they also eat feed and fodder raised on one fourth the cropland. Ubiquitous and familiar, livestock have a huge and largely unrecognized impact on the global environment.[12]

For hundreds of years, and even today in some areas, livestock rearing served as a critical counterpart to crop production in agriculture, keeping farms ecologically balanced. Growing hay, legumes, and other fodder for farm animals calls for environmentally sound crop rotation. Pastures and fodder fields suffer less soil erosion and absorb more water than row-crop fields, and nitrogen-fixing fodder plants such as alfalfa improve soil fertility.[13]

Yet ecological burdens arise both from modern, intensive livestock production methods—such as chicken and pig feeding houses and beef feedlots—and from extensive forms such as ranching and pastoralism. The environmental effects of intensive livestock operations run from grain fields to manure piles. And unsustainable grazing and ranching patterns sacrifice forests, drylands, and wild species. Multiple forces have disturbed traditional pastoralists' ecologically sound livestock systems, leaving herders to crowd with their animals in areas where the land is quickly laid to waste.

The concentrated feeding facilities of industrial and newly industrializing countries use vast quantities of grain and soy, along with the energy, water, and agricultural chemicals that farmers use to grow these crops. Pork production absorbs more grain worldwide than any other meat industry. Together with poultry production, it accounts for at least two thirds of feedgrain consumption. Dairy and beef cattle eat much of the remaining third.[14]

The efficiency with which livestock industries turn feed into meat, milk, and eggs varies by animal and by country. The United States, one of the more efficient producers, uses 6.9 kilograms of corn and soy to put one kilogram of pork on the table. (See Table 5–3.) U.S. beef cattle consume less grain and soybeans than pigs do, gaining about three fourths of their weight from grass, hay, and other fodder. Farmers in other countries, notably the Soviet Union, are less efficient. In the case of chicken, they use twice as much grain for each unit of meat.[15]

Other resources add to the livestock and feed industry's environmental tab, such as the fossil fuels used to supply feedgrain. Including fuel for powering farm machinery and for manufacturing fertilizers and pesticides, feedgrain turns out to be an energy-intensive product. Cornell University's David Pimentel, a specialist in agricultural energy, estimates that 30,000 kilocalories of fossil fuel energy are burned to produce a kilogram of pork in the United States—equivalent to the energy in almost four liters of gasoline. All told, almost half

**Table 5-3. United States: Inputs Used to Produce One Kilogram of Meat, Eggs, or Cheese, 1991**

| Product | Grain[1] | Energy |
|---------|----------|--------|
|         | (kilograms) | (thousand kilocalories) |
| Pork    | 6.9      | 30     |
| Beef    | 4.8      | 17     |
| Chicken | 2.8      | 13     |
| Cheese  | 3.0      | 10     |
| Eggs    | 2.6      | 10     |

[1]Includes soybean meal.
SOURCES: Cattle-Fax, Inc., "Grain Utilization in the Livestock and Poultry Industries," Englewood, Colo., December 8, 1989; U.S. Department of Agriculture, Economic Research Service, Washington, D.C., private communications; David Pimentel et al., "The Potential for Grass-Fed Livestock: Resource Constraints," *Science*, February 22, 1980; David Pimentel, Cornell University, Ithaca, N.Y., private communications.

the energy used in U.S. agriculture goes into the livestock sector. Producing all the meat eaten each year by a typical American takes the equivalent of 190 liters of gasoline.[16]

Feedgrain farming guzzles water, too. In California, now the leading U.S. dairy state, livestock agriculture requires nearly one third of all irrigation water. The beef feedlot center of the nation—Colorado, Kansas, Nebraska, and the Texas panhandle—relies on crops raised with water pumped out of the Ogallala aquifer, portions of which have been severely depleted. As half the grain and hay fed to U.S. beef cattle is grown on irrigated land, more than 3,000 liters of water are used to produce a kilogram of beef. The water used to supply a typical American with meat, milk, and eggs each day probably matches that person's daily water use at home, about 380 liters.[17]

Meat production in other wealthy countries rings up similar resource costs. Energy requirements for grain-fed pork and poultry production in Europe are higher than in the United States because of Europe's liberal application of fertilizers. Japanese beef cattle producers typically feed their animals twice as much grain as Americans do, aiming to produce the butter-soft beef Japanese consumers covet. In New Zealand, by contrast, sheep and cattle are raised purely on grass; energy use per kilogram of mutton or beef there is one fourth the level in the United Kingdom.[18]

Breaking the nutrient loop that once connected crops and livestock has left agriculture with problems at each end: high fertilizer bills and high waste disposal costs. Manure is a valuable organic fertilizer and soil-builder in modest quantities but a dangerous pollutant in excess. The nutrients in wasted manure from American enclosed feeding operations could replace an estimated 12 percent of the nitrogen, 32 percent of the phosphorus, and 30 percent of the po-tassium that U.S. farmers apply to their land in chemical fertilizers.[19]

The millions of tons of animal waste that accumulate at modern production facilities can pollute rivers and groundwater. Nitrogen and phosphorus in manure overfertilize algae, which grow rapidly, deplete oxygen supplies, and suffocate aquatic ecosystems. From the hundreds of algae-choked Italian lakes to the murky Chesapeake Bay, animal wastes add to the nutrient loads from fertilizer runoff, human sewage, and urban and industrial pollution.

## Almost half the energy used in U.S. agriculture goes into the livestock sector.

In the Netherlands, the pork-producing center of Western Europe, manure is a major ecological threat. The 14 million animals in feeding houses in the south excrete so much manure that nitrate and phosphate have saturated surface layers of soil and contaminated water in many areas. The European Community now terms the Netherlands, Belgium, and parts of France "manure-surplus" regions: they produce more than the land can absorb. Nitrogen from manure also escapes into the air as gaseous ammonia, a pollutant that causes acid rain and deposition. Ammonia from the livestock industry is the single largest source of acid deposited on Dutch soils—doing more damage than the country's cars or factories, according to the country's National Institute of Public Health and Environmental Protection.[20]

The danger is not just to ecosystems. Nitrates from manure nitrogen that percolate into groundwater can cause nervous system impairments, cancer, and methemoglobinemia or "blue baby" syndrome, a rare but deadly malady afflicting infants. Nitrate contamination is pervasive in Western Europe, and an official Czechoslovakian report speaks of a "nitrate cloud" contaminating groundwater under agricultural land.[21]

Livestock production outside modern intensive facilities also has environmental side effects. Many of the world's rangelands, one third of the earth's land surface, bear the scars: proliferating weeds, depleted soils, and eroded landscapes. In Africa, swelling human populations, shrinking rangeland, and misdirected development policies have conspired to concentrate cattle around water sources, degrading the land. Elsewhere, rangelands suffer from overstocking, while ranching in tropical Latin America—fostered by subsidies and land speculation—depletes forests and soils.

Cattle play a prominent role in global desertification—the deterioration of dryland's ecological health. Initially, cattle overgraze perennial grasses, allowing annual weeds and tougher shrubs to spread. This shift in species is the most prevalent form of range degradation. The new weeds anchor the topsoil poorly, leaving it vulnerable to trampling hooves and the erosive power of wind and rain. Under persistent grazing, the bare ground becomes impermeable to rainwater, which then courses off the surface, carrying away topsoil and scouring stream beds into deep gullies. Upstream, water tables are not replenished; downstream, flooding increases and sediment clogs waterways, dams, and estuaries. In drier climates, wind sweeps away the destabilized soil.[22]

Estimates by the United Nations Environment Programme indicate that 73 percent of the world's 3.3 billion hectares of dry rangeland is at least moderately desertified, having lost more than 25 percent of its carrying capacity. Some observers caution, however, that calculations of the number of livestock a region can support are a poor indicator of deg-

radation on Africa's drought-prone rangelands because drought destroys the vegetation with or without cattle. Still, where rainfall is more regular, native perennial plants are easily disrupted by cattle; clay soils are easily compacted; and rains often arrive in strong, sudden downpours, sluicing away unstable soils.[23]

Pastoralists have been accused wrongly of overstocking and destroying range because it was common land. But traditionally they have expanded their herds during rainy years so that a few animals might survive when drought returned. Moreover, they have systems to control rangeland use. The Zaghawa of Niger, for instance, move their animals north to wet-season Saharan pastures in separate, parallel paths, leaving ungrazed strips for their return treks. More commonly, pastoralists restrict access to dry-season range so its fodder is available when most needed.[24]

In truth, pastoralists are victims, not culprits of environmental degradation. Human population growth is a chief cause. In the southern Sahel, the number of people has more than doubled since 1960 and cropland has expanded by a third. Much of this expansion has spread over dry-season range formerly used by pastoralists. In Tanzania, the Barabaig herders have lost more than 40,000 hectares of their dry-season range to a mechanized wheat farm. Private ranches have also subsumed traditional rangeland. Forced onto poorer soil, herders and their animals have increased land degradation.[25]

Unfortunately, well-intentioned development plans often worsened environmental conditions. Starting in the fifties, for example, the World Bank and other organizations supported borehole, or deep-well, drilling in dry areas previously inaccessible to cattle. In Botswana, boreholes extended grazing land by two-and-a-half times. With uncontrolled access to the wells, cattle stripped the surrounding lands of vegetation and crushed them to moonscapes. Rings of windswept sand extend more than 10 kilometers from boreholes in the Kgalagadi district of Botswana.[26]

Outside of Africa, rangeland deterioration is more often directly attributable to mismanagement and overstocking. Though the savannas and open shrubland of South America yield poor-quality forage, ranchers commonly overstock their land, leading to weed invasion and erosion. In the temperate rangelands of Argentina, Paraguay, and Bolivia, the loss of plant cover has intensified surface evaporation and led to soil salinization.[27]

Wealthy nations are not immune from the effects of overgrazing on rangeland. Spain and Portugal still bear the scars of pro-sheep land policies that began hundreds of years ago. The western United States is likewise left with a sad legacy: the great cattle boom of the last century annihilated native mixed-grass ecosystems. Overstocking and grazing cattle for too long in the same place continue on much of the 110 million hectares of public land the federal government leases to ranchers.[28]

The U.S. Bureau of Land Management (BLM), which along with the U.S. Forest Service is responsible for overseeing public grazing land, reported in 1990 that only 23 million hectares—33 percent of its holdings in the west—were in good or excellent condition. Other studies indicate that half of U.S. rangeland is severely degraded, with its carrying capacity reduced by at least 50 percent, and that the narrow streambank habitats crucial to arid-land ecology are in the worst condition in history.[29]

In Australia, as in the western United States, the worst overgrazing occurred a century ago in uncontrolled cattle drives, but the damage remains and overgrazing continues. On the dry plains, some 56 percent of the area has suffered from a shift in vegetation; 13 percent of it is severely degraded. And in the drylands of South Africa, the invasion of woody plants following overgrazing has rendered 3 million hectares useless for cattle.[30]

Damage to rangeland is only one measure of the destructiveness of current grazing practices. Forests also suffer from livestock production, as branches are cut for fodder or entire stands are leveled to make way for pastures. Critical watersheds decline, plant and animal species are lost, and carbon dioxide is released into the atmosphere, contributing to global warming.

---

**Forests also suffer from livestock production, as branches are cut for fodder or entire stands are leveled to make way for pastures.**

---

In India, the loss of forest to cattle stems from the lack of grazing land. The nation's 12 million hectares of permanent pasture are vastly inadequate to the needs of its 196 million head of cattle. (By comparison, the cattle country of Uruguay has 13 million hectares for 10 million beasts.) Moreover, India's common land, crucial to the animals of the poor, has shrunk by about one fourth over the past 40 years. State forests, roadsides, and fallow lands make up the fodder deficit, but most cows still go hungry, and the pressure on forests grows.[31]

Latin America has suffered the most dramatic forest loss due to inappropriate livestock production. Since 1970, farmers and ranchers have converted more than 20 million hectares of the region's moist tropical forests to cattle pasture. In the Brazilian Amazon, about 10 million hectares have been cleared for cattle, while the Colombian Amazon has sacrificed 1.5 million hectares and Peru has lost a half-million. In Mexico, roughly 18 million hectares of pasture were originally forest, and an estimated 5.5 million of that was tropical.[32]

According to the U.N. Food and Agriculture Organization (FAO), Central America has lost more than a third of its forests since the early sixties; pastureland, meanwhile, has climbed by at least 50 percent. Nearly 70 percent of deforested land in Panama and Costa Rica is now pasture. Ranchers in Darién state, Panama, pay peasants to clear forests and plant grasses, while in Costa Rica ranchers practice "fence creeping"—literally edging their fences beyond their property lines into national parks.[33]

Eradicating tree cover sets the wheels of land degradation in motion. Shallow, acidic, and nutrient-poor, tropical soils rapidly lose critical nutrients when the forest is converted to pasture. Weeds and shrubs quickly invade, and most pasture is abandoned within a decade for land newly carved from the forest. Where forests recede before advancing ranches, so too does the diversity of life. (See Chapter 2.)[34]

Finally, livestock contribute to climate change by emitting methane, the second most important greenhouse gas. Ruminant animals release perhaps 80 million tons of this gas each year in belches and flatulence, while animal wastes at feedlots and factory-style farms emit another 35 million tons. This occurs when the wastes are stored in the oxygen-short environments of sewage lagoons and manure piles, where methane forms during decomposition. Livestock account for 15–20 percent of global methane emissions—about 3 percent of global warming from all gases.[35]

From the most immediate impacts—nitrogen contamination and retreating grasses—to the most far-reaching—loss of species and climate change—current methods of rearing animals around the world take a large toll on nature. Overgrown and resource-intensive, animal agriculture is out of alignment with the earth's ecosystems.

## FEED AND FOOD

High meat consumption and the expanding use of grain as feed can cause damage for humans too. The adverse health impacts of excessive meat-eating stem in large part from what nutritionists call the "great protein fiasco"—a mistaken belief of many westerners that they need to consume large quantities of protein. This myth has led Americans and others in industrial societies to ingest twice as much protein as they need. The danger lies in the saturated fats that accompany concentrated protein in meat and dairy products. These fats are associated with most of the diseases of affluence that are among the leading causes of death in industrial countries: heart disease, stroke, and breast and colon cancer.[36]

The U.S. National Research Council, the U.S. Surgeon General, the American Heart Association, and the World Health Organization are among the organizations now recommending low-fat diets. From the current U.S. norm of 37 percent of calories from fats—typical for western nations—they recommend lowering fat consumption to no more than 30 percent of calories.[37]

Recent scientific findings indicate even that may be too high. A landmark study of diet, life-style, and health in China—the largest such survey ever conducted—suggests that lowering fat consumption to 15 percent of calories prevents most diseases of affluence. Known as the China Project, this joint effort of Chinese, British, and American institutions tracked thousands of Chinese in dozens of counties. It showed that as fat consumption, protein consumption, and blood cholesterol levels rise, so does the incidence of heart disease, diabetes, and certain cancers.[38]

Surprisingly, Chinese villagers on low-fat, low-meat diets suffered less anemia (iron deficiency) and osteoporosis (a bone disease associated with calcium deficiency) than their urban compatriots eating more meat. Both conditions are commonly attributed to a diet too low in animal products. Study co-leader Colin Campbell of Cornell University told the *New York Times*: "We're basically a vegetarian species and should be eating a wide variety of plant foods and minimizing our intake of animal foods."[39]

If a diet rich in animal products is not an appropriate goal of public health policy, neither is it a wise development strategy. It creates dependence on imports for food and can widen the gap between rich and poor. Yet dozens of middle-income countries import livestock feed.

---

**Soviet livestock now eat three times as much grain as Soviet citizens do.**

---

For a poor country where people eat few animal products, reaching self-sufficiency in food grains requires just 200 kilograms of cereals per person per year. But that number quickly rises when people switch to a meat-based diet. Rapidly industrializing Taiwan, for instance, increased per capita consumption of meat and eggs sixfold from 1950 to 1990. To produce those animal products required raising annual per capita grain use in the country from 170 kilograms to 390. Despite steadily growing harvests, Taiwan could only keep up with the demand for feed by turning to imports. In 1950, Taiwan was a grain exporter; in 1990 it imported, mostly for feed, 74 percent of the grain it used.[40]

In the Soviet Union, rising meat consumption has created economic problems. Since 1950, meat consumption has tripled and feed consumption quadrupled. Use of grain for feed surpassed direct human consumption in 1964 and has been rising ever since. Soviet livestock now eat three times as much grain as Soviet citizens do. Grain imports have soared, going from near zero in 1970 to 24 million tons in 1990, and the nation is now the world's second-largest grain importer.[41]

On balance, the Third World exported grains until the early sixties; by the late seventies, it was consistently importing them. The change came not just from growing populations but also from exploding livestock industries. FAO reports that 75 percent of Third World imports of corn, barley, sorghum, and oats fed animals in 1981. Little has changed since.[42]

Higher meat consumption among the affluent frequently hurts the poor, as the share of farmland devoted to feed expands and reduces production of food staples. In Egypt, for example, over the past quarter-century corn for animal feed has taken over cropland from wheat, rice, sorghum, and millet—all staple grains. The share of grain fed to livestock rose from 10 to 36 percent.[43]

Likewise, the area in Mexico planted to corn, rice, wheat, and beans, the staples of the Mexican poor, has declined steadily since 1965, while that planted to sorghum has grown phenomenally. Sorghum, used to raise chicken and pork for urban consumers, is now Mexico's second-ranking crop by area. The share of cropland growing animal feed and fodder in Mexico went from 5 percent in 1960 to 23 percent in 1980. Mexico feeds 30 percent of its grain to livestock, although 22 percent of the country's people suffer from malnutrition.[44]

David Barkin of the Autonomous Metropolitan University in Mexico City and two U.S. colleagues examined agricultural developments in 24 developing countries. They found clear evidence in 13 of them that farmers were switching from food crops to feed crops; in eight, farmers had shifted more than 10 percent of grainland out of food crops in the past 25 years. Barkin and his colleagues concluded that, where data were available—Brazil, Colombia, Egypt, Mexico, Peru, the Philippines, South Africa, Thailand, and Venezuela—the demand for meat among the rich was squeezing out staple production for the poor.[45]

Ranch-based animal production fosters inequality between agriculturalists in Latin America. Ranchers in Central America, for example, have expanded onto fertile land more appropriate for crops. In 1950, 35 percent of Costa Rica's arable farmland was in pasture; in early 1991, the figure was 54 percent. As much as two thirds of the rich farmland along the Pacific coastal strip of Central America is pasture.[46]

The sweeping advance of ranching into forests in Latin America cannot be explained by the profitability of beef production, however. Real estate speculation is the overriding motive. For the land speculator, ranching is the cheapest way to claim property: it takes little investment or labor (ranches employ just one person per 1,500 hectares on typical spreads in the Brazilian Amazon), and states recognize pasture as the kind of "productive" land use to be rewarded with a property title. Land values can skyrocket when roads come through, and with Latin America's high inflation rates, urban investors are especially keen on buying assets that retain their value, such as land.[47]

The problems with animal agriculture mostly fall in the category of "too much

of a good thing." Too much meat consumption leads to illness. Too much meat production leads to dependence on grain imports, a food system skewed against the poor, and environmental loss. All the same, if livestock production is linked to a profusion of problems, the root causes of those problems are found in human institutions. Indeed, the livestock industry's shortcomings are faithful reflections of deeper faults in human societies.

## SACRED COWS

Through the ages, governments have favored livestock producers. Today, subsidies and special arrangements persist in many countries, expanding livestock production and often worsening its environmental consequences. Reformulating these policies can yield both environmental and economic benefits. Nations wanting to correct imbalances between their domestic animals and their ecosystems would thus do well to start by scrutinizing their legal codes.

In western industrial nations, government support for livestock and feed producers runs in the billions of dollars. Meat, dairy, and feed producers benefit from guaranteed minimum prices, government storage of surpluses, feed subsidies, and import levies. According to the Organisation for Economic Co-operation and Development (OECD), government programs in its member states provided subsidies to animal farmers and feed growers worth $120 billion in 1990.[48]

Livestock products receive two thirds of OECD countries' agricultural subsidies overall, and feedgrains and soybeans receive a substantial share of the remainder. The European Community gives the largest benefits to animal farmers, while the United States favors feed growers. Among animal products, dairy and beef are most subsidized, followed by pork and poultry.[49]

Agricultural support programs in industrial nations are designed to promote self-sufficiency in food production, to raise farmers' incomes, and to aid rural communities. Often, however, they boost intensive livestock production. Under American and EC crop programs, for example, farmers often profit by growing feedgrains on land they would otherwise use as pasture. Agriculture programs in western nations also tend to support farmers who raise animals and grow feed more than those who grow fruits and vegetables—despite health guidelines advising citizens to eat fewer animal products and more fruits and vegetables.[50]

Centrally planned states have subsidized animal products just as vigorously. China, vowing to "improve" diets by boosting meat production, has created large-scale, western-style feeding facilities to supply meat to urban areas. The Soviet Union and its former East European allies, relying on state feed plants, slaughterhouses, and intensive pig farms, poured hundreds of millions of dollars into their meat industries. Perhaps 20 percent of the Soviet national budget went to food subsidies in 1990, much of it for animal products.[51]

Some subsidies affect the total scale of livestock production little but greatly magnify its environmental impact. On the expansive ranches of Australia's arid and semiarid zones, for example, overgrazing on public lands is encouraged by government incentives. The government of the Northern Territory fines ranchers for failing to meet minimum stocking numbers; it sets no maximums. And in Western Australia, leases for public land cost just 30¢ a year per head of cattle.[52]

Overgrazing on public land in the western United States continues partly because the BLM and the Forest Service subsidize and mismanage cattle grazing. The government charges ranchers just $2 per head of cattle per month on public land—one fifth the average rate on comparable private range, and scarcely one third the government's cost of managing the land. It was only in 1990 that reform-minded Forest Service rangers in a handful of districts began to uphold higher standards for range management. The BLM, on the other hand, remains unreformed. In late 1991, efforts were afoot in the U.S. Congress to raise grazing fees and mandate change at the BLM.[53]

## Agricultural support programs in industrial nations boost intensive livestock production.

The federal government also takes the blame for some waste of irrigation water through what Congress estimates is a $2.2-billion annual subsidy to the beneficiaries of western water projects. Between $500 million and $1 billion of that amount goes to feed and fodder growers. Water from federal irrigation projects is sold to farmers at a fraction of its market value, allowing them to irrigate pastures profitably and grow cheap fodder crops such as alfalfa.[54]

Among middle-income developing nations, support has been just as lopsided. Governments have supplied credit, tax breaks, and technical support to their livestock industries, both to stimulate foreign exports and to satisfy urban consumers. In Costa Rica, $1.2 billion—nearly one third of all state-financed agricultural credit—went to the cattle sector between 1969 and 1985. Ranching operations in the Brazilian Amazon have received equally generous subsidies. Under one program, the state extended new tax credits for ranching investments based on the amount of taxes ranchers already owed. From 1966 to 1983, Brazil's government bestowed at least $600 million in tax credits and $130 million in low-interest loans on ranching in the Amazon.[55]

Despite the subsidies, returns have been fleeting. Through the mid-eighties in Costa Rica, cattle ranching had generated less revenue than it received in loans, reports Sheldon Annis, professor of geography at Boston University. As of early 1987, nearly two thirds of cattle ranchers who had received government loans were behind in their payments. In Brazil, the average ranch repays only a quarter of its production costs, according to John Browder, professor of urban planning at Virginia Polytechnic Institute and State University. Fortunately, some countries have eliminated the more flagrant support programs since the seventies, though favoritism persists. In 1988, Brazil suspended financial support programs for ranching in the Amazon. Deforestation rates have slowed, but some attribute the drop to a failing economy and bad weather.[56]

In Africa, Botswana continues to coddle its ranchers. A 1975 program to halt land degradation, boost rural incomes, and commercialize the cattle sector has succeeded only in the last objective. The state gave 12 percent of tribal lands to commercial ranchers, without limiting their use of crowded communal range. Five percent of ranchers now own 40 percent of the country's herd. In addition, to comply with EC regulations that imported beef must be free of foot-and-mouth disease, the state has built hundreds of kilometers of fencing to separate cattle from wild buffalo believed to transmit the disease. The newest segment will run along the eastern edge of the Okavango delta, a wildlife-rich inland delta, to open up savannas for cat-

tle. Similar fencing in the south has already taken a devastating toll on migrating wildebeests.[57]

Beyond favors to ranchers are the complex policies that sometimes unwittingly encourage grain-fed livestock production. In Mexico, for example, state-set crop prices intended to keep food staples such as corn and wheat cheap for consumers made sorghum more profitable to grow and accelerated its expansion. A crop readily worked by tractors and harvesters, sorghum further benefited from Mexico's generous subsidies to the agricultural machinery industry. And it has had an assured market in the subsidized animal-feeding industry, whose meat products largely feed the Mexican middle and upper classes.[58]

Egypt's agricultural policies also aim to keep staple food grains cheap by setting prices, but instead encourage farmers to shift land from regulated food crops to unregulated—and therefore more profitable—animal feed. By favoring intensive poultry-feeding operations using imported grain, governments throughout the Middle East and North Africa have flooded the cities with cheap broiler meat, while small farmers and herders who raise sheep and goats on local fodder have languished.[59]

International development agencies have contributed to the number of destructive livestock projects in the Third World. In the sixties and seventies, the World Bank, the U.S. Agency for International Development, and the Inter-American Development Bank underwrote livestock projects extensively. The World Bank lent $340 million a year to livestock projects from 1974 to 1979. In Latin America alone, from 1963 to 1985 it funneled $1.5 billion to livestock, most of it to large cattle operations producing beef.[60]

Lending ventures tried to graft Australian ranching onto Latin American soils and Texas ranching onto the savannas of the Sahel, with little understanding of either the local environment or local people. In the impoverished Sahel, aid supported capital-intensive fence building, water drilling, and the breeding of exotic cattle species. Where pastoralists raised goats, sheep, cattle, and donkeys for milk and security, development assistance channeled support to cattle for beef production.[61]

Perhaps the most damaging misconception guiding livestock development in Africa was the belief that common ownership of rangeland was inhibiting production and causing degradation. Based on this idea, aid agencies recommended dividing the land. Since 1972, the World Bank has funded three separate livestock projects in Botswana to support private ranches, which has accelerated land degradation and exacerbated social inequities. Herders excluded from these projects bear the hidden costs—their herds must survive on less land, with less mobility, yet still compete with ranch cattle.[62]

Frustrations over past failures and the seemingly intractable problems of African rangelands have led development agencies to cut back on aid for livestock development. From 1980 to 1985, World Bank lending for such projects fell to $240 million a year, and now stands at roughly $100 million annually. Funding for rangeland development has fallen more dramatically.[63]

Around the world, flawed policies and failing institutions channel livestock production in environmentally damaging and inequitable ways. Containing those damages will require an ambitious campaign to rewrite policies and reform institutions. One country that has already taken on the challenge is New Zealand, where government support for agriculture was pervasive and generous until the early eighties.[64]

In 1984, a new government faced with budget shortfalls and a prolonged economic decline eliminated most subsidies to agriculture in New Zealand, including some of the world's highest price supports for sheep producers. Unexpected environmental benefits emerged: the use of energy-intensive herbicides and fertilizers on pastures—formerly subsidized—fell precipitously; the sheep herd shrank from 70 million to 58 million animals, curtailing overgrazing and methane emissions. Although farm earnings suffered, in the long term New Zealand's wool and dairy products will conquer larger shares of the world market because of their lower costs.[65]

New Zealand's radical approach to ending special favors for livestock producers will not work everywhere. Some countries will have to go slower, allowing the industry to adjust more gradually. But this nation has demonstrated the feasibility of rewriting laws that lead livestock down an unsustainable path. From Texas to Tunisia, only the lack of political will stalls similar action against such subsidies.

## RESTORING LIVESTOCK'S ROLE

A meat-fed world now appears an unrealizable dream. World grain production has grown more slowly than population since 1984, and farmers lack new methods for repeating the gains of the Green Revolution. Supporting the world's current population of 5.4 billion people on an American-style diet would require two-and-a-half times as much grain as the world now produces for all purposes. Assuming that 8–14 billion people in the future could eat the American ration of 220 grams of grain-fed meat a day can be nothing but a flight of fancy.[66]

Of necessity, a sustainable livestock

system would be significantly smaller than the present one. Rich countries should expect to reduce their meat consumption while developing nations slow the growth of their meat intake. A 1980 study by David Pimentel and colleagues at Cornell University estimated the potential for producing meat, milk, and eggs in the United States without using feedgrain. Such a system would save enormously on natural resources, reducing energy inputs by 60 percent, for example. However, it would produce no more than half as much animal protein as the present grain-based system.[67]

Fostering a sustainable livestock industry will rest on reintegrating livestock with crops where such farming systems have disappeared and nourishing them where they survive. It will also require reorienting rangeland management toward maintaining functional ecosystems rather than maximizing beef production. Yet achieving these goals will ultimately depend on fundamental changes both outside and inside the livestock sector.

---

**The price of meat might double or triple if the full ecological costs were included in the bill.**

---

Many of the environmental problems associated with livestock production—whether excessive resource consumption in the First World or forest loss and land degradation in the Third World—have deeper roots. Below the subsidies and biased policies are the more entrenched forces of land speculation, population growth, and resources priced too low to reflect their environmental costs. Changes in livestock-sector policies cannot alter these factors, but addressing them directly would dramatically transform the livestock economy.

Worldwide, large benefits would come

from adopting systems of environmental taxation. Taxing products based on their ecological costs would make fossil fuels far more expensive, reflecting the impacts of fuel combustion on air quality and climate stability. As a result, feed farmers would pay more for synthetic fertilizers and pesticides, encouraging them to use manure instead. Factory-style animal-feeding operations would pay more for grain, encouraging them to decentralize to tap cheaper fodder supplies. All told, the price of meat might double or triple if the full ecological costs—including fossil fuel use, groundwater depletion, agricultural-chemical pollution, and methane and ammonia emissions—were included in the bill.

Other changes outside the livestock sector are equally critical. Where land-ownership is ambiguous, as in the forests of Latin America, securing property rights for tribal groups and settled peasants would strengthen their hand against speculators. Where human numbers are growing too rapidly for traditional land uses to survive, as in Africa, curbing population growth and providing alternative livelihoods for some pastoralists would alleviate pressures on the land. Where state forests are overburdened by villagers gathering fodder and fuelwood, as in India, returning control of the woodland to local communities would help reestablish effective forest management.

If the ultimate success of livestock-production reform depends on actions outside the livestock sector, internal change is also indispensable. In industrial countries, priority must be given to appropriate government programs and regulations for controlling pollution from factory-style production. In the Third World, innovative approaches are sorely needed for restoring traditional, extensive production methods to environmental balance.

Livestock policies in developing countries need to address land degradation first. In Africa, programs can build on pastoralists' practice of tracking shifting fodder supplies. Access to land is the critical foundation. Though much traditional range has disappeared, governments can preserve existing dry-season areas and establish pastoralist associations to regulate their use. Mauritania, for instance, recently granted pastoralists grazing and water rights on their traditional range. Sadly, however, most states ignore pastoralists' need for land security.[68]

Where pastoralists have lost their reserve of dry-season range, alternatives must be found. One promising approach pioneered by the International Livestock Center for Africa (ILCA) in Ethiopia employs "fodder banks." When seasonal rains begin, herders plant leguminous trees in fenced areas of one to four hectares, and feed their cattle there in the dry season when range grass is sparse. In alternate years, crops can be planted to capitalize on the buildup of manure.[69]

Herds may need to be reduced where loss of range or crumbling management traditions now limit herder mobility. The difficulty is that while the total number of cattle may be damaging, each family often owns fewer animals than it needs to survive. Buying out their herds can further impoverish them. To assure economic security outside of cattle, ILCA is examining strategies to help pastoralists bank some of their cattle-derived income. Though fraught with logistical and cultural constraints—banks are often far away and cattle are herders' traditional "bank"—the concept is noteworthy for its attempt to work with, rather than against, pastoralists' efforts to achieve economic security.[70]

Stall feeding is another technology with promise. By confining their animals in pens and gathering grass and fodder, farmers can save farmland, halt over-grazing, and easily collect manure. In Haryana, India, a stall-feeding program salvaged a severely overgrazed watershed. A decade later, grass production in the watershed has quadrupled and many farmers' incomes have risen. The state forestry department now sells grass-collection leases to farmers, which stimulates interest in managing the watershed.[71]

Domesticated animals can sometimes play positive roles in restoring degraded range. The Center for Holistic Resource Management in Albuquerque, New Mexico, is restoring rangeland by managing cattle to mimic the grazing patterns of vanished wildlife herds. Counter to traditional range management practices, cattle are stocked at high densities but kept moving—their hooves creating pockets in the soil that improve water infiltration and seed germination. Going further, some projects are actually replacing cattle with wildlife. Where wildlife herds still roam, as on many of Africa's savannas, selling wild game meat can often provide pastoralists with alternative livelihoods that are ecologically and economically sustainable.[72]

In the end, restoring livestock production to its historical role as a boon to sustainable agriculture will depend on more than rewriting policies and rethinking development strategies. It will require dietary changes among the world's meat eaters. Soaring consumer demand for meat drove the expansion of the livestock industry, so kitchen-counter reforms may be the ultimate arbiter of success or failure in the effort to transform animal agriculture.

In the United States, personal choices to follow nutritional guidelines would bring wholesale changes to livestock production. In 1982, the Iowa-based Council on Agricultural Science and Technology estimated that reducing American fat intake to the recommended maximum of 30 percent of calories would cut national pork consumption 40 percent, beef consumption 20 percent, and poultry consumption 10 percent. Leaner, grass-fed beef and lamb would be in high demand, while the need for corn and soybeans would drop by one fourth.[73]

Government policies can support dietary changes by giving advice on healthful eating. Most Americans, for example, were brought up hearing about a diet balanced between the "four food groups": meat and fish, dairy products, fruits and vegetables, and grains. These categories are now antiquated. Recently the U.S. Department of Agriculture drafted a new "food pyramid" that placed emphasis on grains, legumes, fruits, and vegetables rather than animal foods. Unfortunately, the agency retracted the draft when livestock producers complained.[74]

Likewise, the U.S. beef-grading system favors grain-fed cattle by awarding higher ratings for higher fat content—which increases when animals eat grain. The government could substitute an actual measure of fat content for the vague terms "select," "choice," and "prime" that currently adorn meat labels. Shoppers might think twice about picking up a portion of beef if instead of "choice" the label read "30 percent fat."[75]

Yet governments usually follow rather than lead, and personal choices can provide a springboard for broader policy changes. U.K. food marketers, for example, estimate that 6 million people in the United Kingdom dine on meatless meals most of the time. Average red-meat consumption per person has fallen 14 percent in the United States since 1976. And beef consumption per capita has declined across Europe, as well as in Australia and New Zealand, during the same period.[76]

In addition to health concerns, many people are troubled by the realization that more than one third of the world's grain goes to feeding animals, while 12 in every 100 people go hungry. Although hunger is not a consequence of meat production—most of the world's estimated 630 million hungry people simply cannot afford to buy food—feedgrain could be needed to fight hunger in the future. World grain production per capita has been declining since 1984. If farmers and family planners are unable to reverse this trend, the feedgrain of the affluent will eventually be needed to nourish the hungry.[77]

The global livestock industry, with its manifold supports and as many environmental repercussions, defies simple reform. Many potential revisions, such as ecological taxes, must come from outside the livestock sector. Yet change is possible. Livestock have been boons to the human enterprise for millennia, and with enough pressure for reform, animal agriculture's current transgressions will end. Personal habits, as well as national policies, can shift dramatically when enough people say "enough."

# 6

# Improving Women's Reproductive Health

*Jodi L. Jacobson*

Sexually transmitted diseases. Abortion. Contraception. Childbirth. These are facets of a widespread and deepening—but largely neglected—crisis in women's reproductive health. Taken together, illnesses and deaths from complications of pregnancy, childbirth, and unsafe abortion, from diseases of the reproductive tract, and from the improper use of contraceptive methods top the list of health threats to women of reproductive age worldwide. At least 1 million women will die of reproductive causes this year, and more than 100 million others will suffer disabling illnesses.[1]

The term "reproductive health" is most often equated with one aspect of women's lives: motherhood. Complications associated with various maternal issues are indeed major contributors to poor reproductive health among millions of women worldwide. But this is just one of three components of

An expanded version of this chapter appeared as Worldwatch Paper 102, *Women's Reproductive Health: The Silent Emergency*.

women's reproductive health. (See Table 6–1.) The second is diseases of the reproductive tract, including sexually transmitted diseases (STDs) such as AIDS and syphilis. Such infections are leading contributors to debilitating, sometimes life-threatening conditions such as infertility and cancer. The third component is contraceptive use, a category that includes birth control methods ranging from barrier devices such as condoms and diaphragms to oral contraceptive pills and intrauterine devices (IUDs).

All three aspects of reproductive health are intimately connected. The health of both a pregnant woman and her fetus, for example, can be severely compromised by reproductive tract infections. On the other hand, women may contract such infections through sexual intercourse or as the result of poor handling of childbirth or abortion procedures.

Half the world's 2.6 billion women are now 15 to 49 years of age. Without proper health care services, this group is

**Table 6-1. Threats to Women's Reproductive Health**

| Factor | Possible Health Effects | Root Causes of Poor Health |
|---|---|---|
| Pregnancy | Complications of pregnancy, childbirth, and unsafe abortion | Low status of women; illiteracy, poverty, malnutrition; lack of access to prenatal and postnatal care, safe abortion services, contraceptives, and trained birth attendants |
| Unsafe Sexual Activities; Poor Obstetric/ Gynecological Practices | Reproductive tract infections leading to infertility, ectopic pregnancy, chronic pain, and cancer of reproductive organs | Low status of women; poor access to contraceptives; lack of access to education and health services |
| Contraceptives | May either prevent or promote reproductive tract infections depending on type of method used; can reduce risks from excess fertility or unwanted pregnancy and unsafe abortion | Government policies that restrict access to full range of family planning and contraceptive methods; economic, social, and cultural barriers to use; low status of women |

SOURCE: Worldwatch Institute.

highly vulnerable to problems relating to sexual intercourse, pregnancy, and contraceptive side effects.[2]

Deaths and illnesses from reproductive causes are highest among poor women everywhere. In societies where women are disproportionately poor, illiterate, and politically powerless, high rates of reproductive illness and death are the norm. Women in developing countries, and economically disadvantaged women in the cities of some industrial nations, suffer the highest rates of complications from pregnancy, sexually transmitted diseases, and reproductive cancers in the world. In many countries—such as Bangladesh, Brazil, Nigeria, and Uganda—reproductive causes now account for more than half the deaths of women in their childbearing years.[3]

Several threats to reproductive health—the rapid spread of STDs, the restricted range of contraceptive choices, and the lack of access to safe abortion services—transcend economic classifications, however. These are of concern to every woman, no matter her income or national origin.

Men also suffer from reproductive health problems, most notably STDs. But the number and scope of risks is far greater for women for a number of reasons. One, women alone are at risk of complications from pregnancy and childbirth. Two, women face higher risks in preventing unwanted pregnancy: they bear the burden of using (and suffering potential side effects from) most contraceptive methods, and they suffer the consequences of unsafe abortion. Three, women are more vulnerable to contracting and suffering complications of many sexually transmitted infections.

Lack of access to comprehensive reproductive health care is the main reason so many women suffer and die. Most illnesses and deaths from reproductive causes could be prevented or treated with strategies and technologies well within reach of even the poorest countries. But few nations, rich or poor, have committed themselves to improving health care for women.

## THE TRAGEDY OF MOTHERHOOD

Complications of pregnancy, childbirth, and unsafe abortion are now the leading killers of women of reproductive age throughout the Third World. Data indicate that 20–45 percent of all deaths among women aged 15–49 are from pregnancy-related causes in most developing countries, as opposed to less than 1 percent in the United States and most of Europe.[4]

In fact, in terms of health indicators, there is no more telling measure of the gap between rich and poor countries than the rates of maternal illness and death. Infant mortality, an oft-cited indicator, is only about nine times higher in the Third World than in the industrial world. But the risk of maternal death is often more than 100 times as great.[5]

Repeated childbearing in unsafe circumstances further increases the lifetime risk of dying during pregnancy in the Third World. In Africa, for example, women face a 1-in-21 chance of dying from pregnancy-related causes in their lifetimes. The comparable figures for South Asia and Latin America are 1 in 38 and 1 in 73, respectively. In contrast, the chance of dying in pregnancy in the

United States is 1 in 6,366, and in Northern Europe, 1 in 9,850.[6]

The reasons for these vastly different outcomes are plain. Women in the Third World have all the major risk factors for poor maternal health, including illiteracy, poverty, and poor nutrition; 20 years or more of childbearing each; and inadequate or nonexistent health care. Each of these conditions multiplies severalfold the health risks women face throughout their lifetimes. Each of them also turns pregnancy and childbirth into a life-threatening endeavor.

The World Health Organization (WHO) defines maternal mortality as a death during or within 42 days of a pregnancy from causes related to or aggravated by the pregnancy or its management. At least a half-million women die annually from pregnancy-related causes, 99 percent of them in developing countries. (See Table 6–2.) Although these figures themselves are sobering, experts privately agree that improved data collection might show the actual toll in some areas to be nearly twice as high.[7]

In absolute terms, South Asia has both the largest number of women of reproductive age and the highest number of maternal deaths annually—about 300,-000. Six countries in the region—Ban-

**Table 6-2. Annual Number of Maternal Deaths, by Region, 1986**

| Region | Deaths |
| --- | --- |
| Developing Countries | |
| Asia | 308,000 |
| Africa | 150,000 |
| Latin America | 34,000 |
| Oceania | 2,000 |
| Industrial Countries | 6,000 |
| World | 500,000 |

SOURCE: World Health Organization, *Maternal Mortality Rates: A Tabulation of Available Information* (Geneva: 1986).

gladesh, Bhutan, India, Nepal, Pakistan, and Sri Lanka—account for fully 43 percent of all maternal deaths.[8]

For every woman who dies, many others are left with illnesses or impairments that rob them of their health and productivity, often for the rest of their lives. Pregnancy-related morbidity, or illness, is not well documented at the global level, but available studies suggest the toll is high. In India, for example, a village survey found 16 pregnancy-related illnesses for every maternal death. Extrapolating from this, World Bank researchers calculate that 3–12 percent of all pregnancies worldwide result in serious illness among women. Other studies—from parts of China, Egypt, and Nigeria—have found pregnancy-related illnesses in from 1 to 37 percent of women.[9]

If she experiences complications from pregnancy but escapes death, a woman may be faced with reproductive disabilities that plague her physically and psychologically. Vesico-vaginal fistulae— tears between the walls of the rectum or bladder and the vagina—are a particularly common outcome of obstructed labor. This condition, which usually occurs among adolescents and other women with narrow pelvises, often leads to the collection or uncontrolled leakage of urine and feces; the resultant foul smell ostracizes untold thousands of women and young girls each year. According to Gary Barker and Susan Rich of the Population Crisis Committee, more than 70 percent of pregnancy-related fistulae in Nigeria occur in adolescents.[10]

Another cause of reproductive illness, the widespread practice of female genital mutilation, contributes both to fistulae and to numerous complications in pregnancy. Often known as female circumcision—the cutting away of all or part of the clitoris and surrounding tissues—this practice is common through-

out much of Africa and parts of the Middle East. An estimated 84 million women and girls have been circumcised worldwide. Other reproductive health problems that arise from circumcision include the development of cysts, scars, and infected abscesses, as well as a condition leading to the retention of menstrual blood.[11]

While a given death can always be traced back to a medical condition, the real "causes" are rooted deeply in the social, cultural, and economic barriers faced by females in the Third World throughout their lives. Indeed, the conditions into which a female infant is born may determine her later fate in pregnancy.

Take the case of an individual female born in Angola, India, Peru, or virtually any other developing country. If she survives infancy, this girl will most likely grow up on a diet that does not meet her nutritional requirements. As a child, she will work for several hours each day— assisting her mother by tending siblings, collecting water and firewood, herding small animals, weeding the fields, or selling wares in the marketplace.

Unlike her brother's tasks, these duties will take precedence over going to school; consequently she will receive little or no formal education. She will almost inevitably receive insufficient nourishment to compensate for the energy expended in daily chores, not to mention for proper growth and development. Her parents will likely plan to have her married early in her teens. Later in life, she is taught, her main role will be to bear and rear as many children "as God brings" or her husband desires.[12]

Girls in developing countries are nutritionally disadvantaged by their very citizenship. Data compiled by UNICEF, for example, indicate that the daily per capita calorie supply for all citizens, measured as a percentage of minimum nutritional needs, exceeds 100 percent in only 79 out of 131 countries. And even where it exceeds the minimum, urban and rural differences—not to mention class-based differences—in the adequacy of daily calorie intake are great.[13]

But malnutrition is far more prevalent among females than males in developing countries for reasons that have more to do with gender than geography. Discrimination in the allocation of food—as well as health care and education—is a widespread and well-documented practice in much of South Asia, for example, where strong preferences for male children diminish the "value" of females. Girls are perceived as risky investments in these cultures for a number of reasons, including the sizable dowry their parents usually must provide to prospective husbands.[14]

Studies from Bangladesh, India, Nepal, and Pakistan indicate that boys consistently receive more and better food than their sisters, although the nutritional needs of prepubescent boys and girls are virtually identical. And a maternal health status report from Lesotho asserts that the major contributor to the poor nutritional status of women is "the tradition of feeding men and boys before women and girls, [where] the nutritious foods are served to male members of the families and females would then have the leftovers."[15]

Moreover, women—having internalized their low status—will feed themselves least in the face of limited food and last in most circumstances, even when pregnant. Nearly half the nursing mothers in South Asia consume less than 70 percent of the recommended daily intake of calories. A study conducted in the early eighties showed that 20–45 percent of women of childbearing age in sub-Saharan Africa daily received inadequate calories. "Little wonder," observes Mary Racelis, Africa Regional Director of UNICEF, "that many African women gain minimal weight even in the last trimester of pregnancy."[16]

Traditional practices and superstitions about food also contribute to women's poor nutritional status. In parts of southern Africa, for example, pregnant women are expected to avoid eggs in the belief they cause convulsions in children; certain vegetables and fruits are off limits for similar reasons. Throughout the Middle East and Africa, pregnant women curtail their intake of food because they believe this will lead to a small fetus and easy labor. Food taboos curbing or forbidding the pregnant woman's intake of eggs, fish, fruit, vegetables, meat, and even milk are common in South Asia as well.[17]

---

**World Bank researchers calculate that 3–12 percent of all pregnancies worldwide result in serious illness among women.**

---

Not surprisingly, anemia is widespread among both pregnant and nonpregnant women in developing countries. Anemia—a deficiency in either the quantity or quality of oxygen-carrying red blood cells that impedes a woman's ability to resist infection or survive hemorrhage—may result from deficiencies of iron, folate, or vitamin $B_{12}$. Iron-deficiency anemia is particularly common in women.[18]

More than half of pregnant women and 47 percent of nonpregnant women in developing countries outside China are estimated to suffer from anemia. The prevalence is highest in South Asia and Africa. Forty-five percent of pregnant women in North Africa, 53 percent in Western Africa, and 51 percent in Eastern Africa are anemic. The figures for South Asia are even worse; 56 percent of pregnant women in that region are affected. Anemia may increase the risk of dying in childbirth by a factor of four, and severe anemia is associated with an eightfold risk of maternal death during pregnancy.[19]

Poor nutrition often worsens later in a woman's life because of an increasingly heavy workload, the loss of iron stores through menstruation, and the combined demands of childbearing. These nutritional deficits contribute to what may become lifelong handicaps, such as an increased predisposition to illness, low weight, and stunted physical and mental development. Physical immaturity due to stunted growth subsequently leads to far higher rates of pregnancy-related problems, including obstructed labor, cervical trauma, toxemia, ruptured uterus, infection, and hemorrhage.[20]

Women are therefore physically ill prepared for childbearing, an activity in which they will almost certainly engage repeatedly. And from one pregnancy to another they may never receive medical care. Lack of access to timely and effective basic maternal health care is a critical problem for Third World women, and contributes mightily to maternal health problems.

The share of women who receive prenatal care is one of several indicators of both the adequacy and accessibility of health services—and hence of maternal health in general. A study from Indonesia found that women who received no prenatal care were more than five times as likely to die from pregnancy-related causes as those who attended a prenatal clinic.[21]

Throughout South Asia and much of Africa, however, only a small share of women—20–35 percent—receive adequate prenatal care. A significantly higher proportion are covered throughout Latin America and the Caribbean: more than half of women there have access to prenatal care in every country but El Salvador, Guatemala, Guyana, and Nicaragua. Cuba leads the region, with 98 percent of women receiving prenatal care.[22]

---

## Lack of access to timely and effective basic maternal health care is a critical problem for Third World women.

---

Even so, the existence of prenatal care facilities does not always translate into effective care. In Zimbabwe, for example, where at least 90 percent of pregnant women receive a minimum of one prenatal checkup, most women are not checked until well into their third trimester. One study there concluded that "motivation to come to prenatal care is high [but] most women book late." Less than 20 percent of the women surveyed presented themselves for care before 20 weeks' gestation, making "interventions for treatment of anemia [and other problems], and administration of . . . immunizations difficult," according to the study.[23]

Women are unable to make use of care that is theoretically "accessible" to them for many reasons. One is lack of access to education on the importance of prenatal care. Lack of freedom is another— and often critical—factor. Other influences are the strength of traditional beliefs and practices regarding pregnancy and delivery, costs, and the real or perceived quality of services.

According to various studies, long distances to health facilities (made worse by poor roads and transportation networks) are another obstacle to prenatal care. For example, 96 percent of mothers in two Nigerian villages who had not used a health facility to give birth cited distance as the reason. Surveys in South Asia, Central America, and among

Navajo Indians in the state of New Mexico found similar results regarding the influence of distance on decisions to seek health care.[24]

Poverty plays a major role in transportation and other costs, even when health services themselves are free. In *Too Far To Walk: Maternal Mortality in Context*, public health researchers Sereen Thaddeus and Deborah Maine cite this case from Indonesia: "Women often had to take their younger children to visit a clinic [entailing] not only additional bus fares, but the provision of snacks for all, so a mother with three or four small children may well spend a day's income on a single visit to the 'free clinic.' "[25]

Quality of care is also a vital determinant of the share of women who seek medical treatment. Poor relationships between health care professionals and their clients, long waits, and administrative red tape are but a few of the problems mentioned by women seeking care. Studies show that well-staffed and well-equipped facilities—more the exception than the rule—attract a higher proportion of people in surrounding communities. And women from many developing countries cite other factors—the lack of emotional support and privacy, differences in language and culture between health professionals and their clients, a rude medical staff, and the often-expected "gift" (or bribe) for medical attention—as reasons why they do not make more use of available facilities.[26]

Lacking prenatal care, the majority of women then face the prospect of giving birth without trained medical assistance. Only about a third of all births are assisted by trained attendants in Africa and South Asia, as opposed to 64 percent in Latin America, 93 percent in East Asia, and virtually 100 percent in North America. In many Third World communities, traditional birth attendants—usually village-based women untrained in modern medicine—are the only source of maternal health care or the only affordable alternative to clinics.[27]

Like the women they serve, traditional birth attendants are usually poor, illiterate, and guided by sometimes harmful traditional practices. These range from the insertion of herbs into the birth canal to "ease labor" to the use of unsterilized razor blades, shards of glass, or knives to sever umbilical cords. A limited knowledge of hygiene among traditional birth attendants in some areas is compounded by the often unhealthy environments in which births take place. Because relatively few countries have put resources into training traditional attendants, their potential for reducing illness and deaths related to pregnancy remains untapped.[28]

## In Sufferance and Silence

For much of the past decade, well-deserved attention has been paid to the global spread of the human immunodeficiency virus (HIV) and its deadly consequence, AIDS. The focus on AIDS, however, has obscured a more widespread, equally devastating epidemic: reproductive tract infections. These currently cause far more deaths among women than AIDS does in men, women, and children combined. The rising incidence of both HIV and reproductive tract infections poses grave and unprecedented threats to the lives of women around the world.

Reproductive tract infections—caused by a variety of bacteria, viruses, and protozoa—originate in the lower reproductive tract, which begins at the external genitals and extends to the cervix. They can result in chronic, often debilitating conditions, including vaginal discharge, pain, itching, ulcers, and bleeding; discomfort during intercourse; painful urination; and cervical infection and ulcers.[29]

Without treatment, infections can spread past the cervix to the upper tract, affecting the uterus, fallopian tubes, and ovaries. Syphilis and herpes are reproductive tract infections that may become systemic. AIDS, caused by a blood-borne or "systemic" virus that can enter the body in a variety ways, is not a reproductive tract infection. But it is related in that it, too, is often sexually transmitted.[30]

In women, such infections can occur as a result of sexual intercourse with an infected partner or from poor or harmful obstetric and gynecological practices (including unsafe traditional methods of contraception, childbirth, and abortion), the use of unclean materials to absorb menstrual flow, female genital mutilation, the improper use of some contraceptives, and the unchecked growth of organisms normally present in the reproductive tract.

Worldwide, about 250 million new infections are sexually transmitted each year. Seven infections outrank AIDS in both the numbers of people infected and the annual increase in new cases. Trichomoniasis, a protozoan infection that causes chronic, frequently painful vaginal infections, is increasing by an estimated 120 million new cases each year. (See Table 6–3.) In contrast, there are an estimated 1 million new HIV infections annually.

The distribution of these infections varies by region. Bacterial diseases—chanchroid (which causes genital ulcers), gonorrhea, and syphilis—have generally declined in importance in industrial countries because of effective prevention and treatment. But they are increasing at epidemic rates among low-income populations in the United States. Transmission rates of three viral infections—genital herpes (which also causes genital ulcers), human papillomavirus (the leading cause of cervical cancer),

**Table 6-3. Annual Number of New Sexually Transmitted Infections Worldwide, 1990**

| Disease | Number of New Cases |
|---|---|
| | (million) |
| Trichomoniasis | 120 |
| Chlamydia | 50 |
| Human Papillomavirus | 30 |
| Gonorrhea | 25 |
| Herpes | 20 |
| Syphilis | 4 |
| Chancroid | 2 |
| Human Immunodeficiency Virus (HIV) | 1 |

SOURCE: World Health Organization, "Sexually Transmitted Infections Increasing by 250 Million New Infections Annually," press release, Geneva, December 20, 1990.

and HIV—and of one bacterial infection (chlamydia) are on the rise throughout the industrial world.[31]

Both bacterial and viral infections remain major health problems in developing countries. Good data are relatively scarce, but reproductive tract infections appear to be common in virtually all the developing countries in which they have been studied. Chancroid, for example, is the most common genital-ulcer disease throughout much of Africa, Southeast Asia, and South America.[32]

Dramatic evidence of this epidemic is provided by a study of rural Indian women in the state of Maharashtra. Fully 92 percent of the 650 women examined were found to have one or more gynecological and sexual diseases related to reproductive tract infections, with an astonishing average of 3.6 such infections per woman. Less than 8 percent of the women had ever undergone a gynecological examination. "Obviously," concluded author R. A. Bang and colleagues, "there is a large gap between the need and the care."[33]

Once infected, women face greater health threats than men do. Typical reproductive tract infections in men cause mild to severe genital or urinary tract problems that are easily treated; in rare cases they can cause sterility and death. Women, in contrast, frequently suffer consequences ranging from chronic genital infection to infertility, persistent pain, and death. Infected pregnant women risk higher rates of maternal and infant illness and death. Research now indicates that the genital lesions produced by some reproductive tract infections increase the risk of transmitting or contracting HIV, the incidence of which is already rising rapidly among women.[34]

Moreover, women face innumerable physical and social obstacles to both preventive care and curative treatment of reproductive tract infections. Indeed, around the world millions of women with serious reproductive tract infections suffer in silence. This is partly because many early-stage infections often lack obvious symptoms and so are not easily recognized. More important, the vast majority of women live in countries where routine screening for such infections is simply unavailable.[35]

To make matters worse, women are rarely educated about the prevention of reproductive tract infections. In many developing countries, these infections—sexually transmitted or otherwise—are rife with stigmas, taboos, and the threat of social ostracism. Fear, reinforced by low self-esteem, illiteracy, and the fear of violence from or rejection by their partners, prevents millions of women from reporting or discussing any symptoms that might lead to prompt identification and treatment. Physical and psychological deterrents to care, including strict mores proscribing even married women from discussing sexual problems, can create virtually insurmountable obstacles to disclosure of gynecological ailments.

Ruth Dixon-Mueller, a consultant on women's reproductive health, and Judith Wasserheit, Chief of the Sexually Transmitted Diseases Branch of the U.S. National Institutes of Health, underscore this point in *The Culture of Silence*: "Women [may] accept vaginal discharge, discomfort during intercourse, or even chronic pelvic pain which accompanies some [reproductive tract infections] as an inevitable part of their womanhood . . . something to be endured, along with other reproductive health problems such as sexual abuse, menstrual difficulties, contraceptive side effects, miscarriages, stillbirths, and potentially life-threatening clandestine abortion or childbirth."[36]

---

## Worldwide, about 250 million new infections are sexually transmitted each year.

---

As with pregnancy-related illness, the chronic results of both lower- and upper-tract infections—such as infertility, pain, and malodorous vaginal discharge—receive little attention and are often discounted by doctors. But they have far-reaching impacts on the lives of millions of women. Abnormal discharge can lead to rejection by a woman's partner. Chronic pelvic pain resulting from upper tract infections may interfere with a woman's ability to carry out her daily tasks. Since families in the Third World depend heavily on the productivity of women, these disabilities have consequences far beyond the considerable individual suffering they cause.

Infertility and chronic infections prevent women from sustaining pregnancies and bearing healthy children, a devastating outcome in cultures where a woman's value often depends on her presumed or demonstrated fertility. In parts of Africa and Asia, for example, those unable to bear children are subject to abandonment, abuse, neglect, and even murder. Infertility resulting from reproductive tract infection is believed to be most common in Africa: it is as high as 50 percent in some areas, and as much as 80 percent of infertility is attributable to reproductive tract infections.[37]

Five infections—bacterial vaginosis (the most common vaginal infection), chlamydia, gonorrhea, syphilis, and the human papillomavirus—can lead to permanent disability and even death. Bacterial vaginosis, chlamydia, and gonorrhea, if left untreated, can spread beyond the cervix to the upper reproductive tract, causing pelvic inflammatory disease—an infection of the uterus, fallopian tubes, and ovaries.[38]

Common outcomes of pelvic inflammatory disease include infertility, ectopic pregnancy, chronic pelvic pain, and recurrent infection. An ectopic pregnancy occurs when, because of scarring and inflammation, a fertilized egg becomes lodged in a fallopian tube, dramatically increasing the chances of internal hemorrhage. In developing countries, reproductive tract infections are assumed to cause an estimated 80 percent of ectopic pregnancies and, by extension, a large share of maternal deaths from hemorrhage.[39]

Although a given infection may by itself move from the lower to the upper tract, the risks of the disease spreading internally increase greatly when women with untreated lower-tract infections undergo unsafe abortions or gynecological examinations, have IUDs inserted, or give birth. In industrial countries, 15–20 percent of women with untreated chlamydial or gonoccocal cervical infections who undergo abortion contract pelvic inflammatory disease. Rates in developing countries—where unsafe abor-

tion and gynecological practices are common—are surely much higher.[40]

Different contraceptive methods can significantly alter the risk of reproductive tract infections. Women with IUDs are three to five times more likely to develop pelvic inflammatory disease, for example, than are women not using a contraceptive. Risks for users of IUDs who have never given birth may be twice this level. A number of explanations—including a possible increase in the risks of developing bacterial vaginosis—have been offered to explain this link. Oral contraceptives and barrier methods tend to reduce the risk of upper tract infections.[41]

Bacterial infections such as gonorrhea and chlamydia appear to be widespread and increasing apace in many countries. Clinic-based data indicate a significant share of women throughout the developing world suffer from lower-tract infections related to gonorrhea, for example. As many as 12 percent of women studied in Asia, 18 percent in Latin America, and 40 percent in Africa exhibited evidence of gonorrhea.[42]

In women, chlamydia infections are difficult to trace. Three out of every four afflicted women will have no symptoms. Indeed, in the absence of routine screening, it is the rising incidence of such disabling or fatal conditions as pelvic inflammatory disease, infertility, and ectopic pregnancy that often provides the best measure of where such infections are spreading and how quickly.[43]

Spot surveys of pelvic inflammatory disease and infertility in a number of developing countries suggest the impact of chlamydia is vast: village studies among women in India, Kenya, and Uganda have found rates of pelvic inflammatory disease as high as 20 percent. Judith Wasserheit asserts, "the fertility prognosis is grim in many developing countries in which treatment is delayed or is totally unavailable." Not surprisingly, scarring and blockage of the fallopian tubes from pelvic inflammatory disease is now believed to be the major preventable cause of female infertility in developing countries.[44]

Each year, 1–3 percent of women of reproductive age in urban areas of sub-Saharan Africa contract pelvic inflammatory disease; currently, about 20–40 percent of acute admissions to gynecology wards in Africa are related to chlamydia. In Brazil, although there is no systematic data collection on chlamydia, pelvic inflammatory disease related to this infection is believed to cause many more deaths among women each year than does AIDS.[45]

Chlamydia is now considered the most common sexually transmitted bacterial disease in the industrial world. Even in the United States, precise data on chlamydia infections are relatively sparse. Still, research links the rising incidence there with a fourfold increase in the number of ectopic pregnancies between 1970 and 1990. Among women studied, a history of chlamydia appeared to more than double the risk of such pregnancies. Chlamydia was also found to increase the risks of premature birth in normal pregnancies. The annual bill for direct and indirect medical care associated with chlamydia infection in the United States came to $1.5 billion in the mid-eighties.[46]

The absence of testing and treatment outlets for the human papillomavirus also condemns hundreds of thousands of women in the developing world to death each year. Several strains of human papillomavirus are now linked with cervical cancer; approximately 450,000 cases of these potentially fatal reproductive tract cancers are diagnosed annually worldwide. Of these, an estimated 354,000 occur in Third World women, virtually all of whom die due to lack of access to relatively simple early-treatment measures.[47]

In developing countries, cervical cancer now outranks all other cancers in women combined. The highest incidence is found in Africa and Latin America. In Western Africa, "cervical cancer is the most common malignancy among women . . . two times as common as the next most frequent cancer [breast cancer]," according to Dr. Nancy Kiviat, Director of Pathology Department at Harborview Medical Center in Seattle, Washington. A review of data by the Brazilian National Tumor Registry in 1980 found cervical cancer to be about one-and-a-half times more common nationwide than breast cancer.[48]

---

## In developing countries, cervical cancer now outranks all other cancers in women combined.

---

The majority of deaths from this condition could be prevented with early testing for cancer-related viruses. Cervical cancer causes some 4,500 unneccessary deaths among American women each year, partly because of economic barriers to obtaining the relatively simple diagnostic test known as the Pap smear. According to David Grimes of the U.S. Centers for Disease Control, "if cervical cancer [in the United States] was viewed as an STD then deaths due to this cause alone would far outnumber deaths due to all other reproductive causes combined."[49]

Add to the threats posed by reproductive tract infections the grim reality of HIV infection, and the prognosis for improving women's reproductive health appears bleak indeed. WHO estimates that more than 8 million adults are currently infected with HIV—including 3 million women, most of whom are in their childbearing years. By the end of 1992, an estimated total of 600,000 cases of AIDS will have occurred among women.[50]

Infection via vaginal intercourse is the most common route of transmission for HIV in Africa. About 2.5 million Africans are now believed to carry the virus, nearly 1 million of them in Uganda alone. Zaire and Zambia have the next highest numbers of cases, with 282,000 and 205,000, respectively. In some cities, one in five pregnant women is HIV-infected. Researchers Mead Over and Peter Piot believe that women's lack of access to education is a contributor to higher rates of HIV infection. They note that in Africa, "the highest [HIV prevalence] rates are observed in those countries with the poorest record on female education."[51]

In many other regions, the rate of increase in HIV infection among women is now rising exponentially. Data from Asia indicate HIV is beginning to spread rapidly there. In some countries, most notably India and Thailand, studies of prostitutes in several urban areas found HIV infection in between 10 and 70 percent of subjects. In 1986, according to the Thai government, 17 males were infected for every female; by 1990, that ratio had fallen to five males for every female. Data from WHO indicate about 200,000 women in Asia are now infected.[52]

As heterosexual transmission of HIV becomes the dominant route of infection in most regions of the world, Over and Piot note that "proportionately more women and more poor people will be among those with HIV infection and AIDS." In other words, HIV is now following the socioeconomic pattern of most reproductive tract infections. This is the case in both North and South America; in many cities of these two regions AIDS is now the leading cause of death among women aged 20–40. Without a concerted campaign to reduce the incidence of reproductive tract infec-

tions and HIV, and to treat existing infections, the number of women dying of reproductive health causes will continue to spiral upward.[53]

## FAMILY PLANNING FOR HEALTH

Vast potential exists for family planning—the use of contraceptives or other pregnancy prevention strategies—to improve women's reproductive health. Relying on family planning methods to space or limit births improves the health of both mothers and children. Used correctly, several methods—such as condoms, diaphragms, and hormonal pills—can assist women and their partners in preventing transmission of reproductive tract infections. Perhaps most important, access to good-quality family planning services enables individuals to exercise a basic human right—to decide freely the number and spacing of their children.

Contraceptive services alone are inadequate for safeguarding women's reproductive health. Unfortunately, these services invariably are offered to the exclusion of, rather than in addition to, assistance with a broader spectrum of reproductive health issues. Such issues include unwanted pregnancy, reproductive tract infections, and infertility—conditions that most women face at least once during their lives.

Moreover, rather than meeting women's varied needs, governments and policymakers have devised programs that are often extremely limited in scope. Too few provide a wide enough array of contraceptive methods to ensure women may both achieve an acceptable balance of personal risks and preferences in contraceptives and switch methods as reproductive needs change. Too few offer adequate counseling services. And too few provide follow-up care to combat the high rates at which women who ask for birth control abandon contraceptive methods they are currently using.

A large number of government-supported family planning programs worldwide deny access to adolescents and unmarried women, although these groups are very likely to resort to abortion, whether or not it is legal, to deal with unwanted pregnancy. Most family planning clinics, even in countries where abortion is legal, do not offer abortion services; most are not well equipped to treat complications of botched abortions where the procedure is illegal. Nor do the majority of clinics test for or treat reproductive tract infections.[54]

A number of international organizations, including the U.S. Agency for International Development, have begun to reflect in their rhetoric the need for reproductive health care that moves beyond conventional family planning programs. Nevertheless, the availability of comprehensive services—and the willingness to tackle controversial issues such as the need for safe abortion services—is still more the exception than the rule. Where they do exist, they are usually provided by nongovernmental organizations that can reach only a small share of women in need. Although this pattern generally holds true in both industrial and developing countries, women in the Third World are particularly underserved by family planning.[55]

To a large degree, family planning programs limit their own potential effectiveness by choosing as yardsticks of success measures that do not reflect the populations in need of service. One such measure is contraceptive prevalence— the share of women of reproductive age using birth control. This is the primary gauge of success in most family planning programs throughout the Third World today.[56]

Contraceptive prevalence rates, invariably measured among married women of reproductive age (including those in consensual unions, such as are common in the Caribbean), suggest the degree to which married women are seeking to space or limit births and what methods they are using. A general increase in these rates in a number of Asian and Latin American countries since the late seventies implies a revolution in attitudes toward smaller families. The share of married women using contraception has risen from 31 to 50 percent in Tunisia, from 30 to 53 percent in Mexico, from 18 to 48 percent in Indonesia, and from 7 to 27 percent in Kenya, for example.[57]

---

## Contraceptive services alone are inadequate for safeguarding women's reproductive health.

---

But contraceptive prevalence rates give little or no information on why women adopt particular methods, whether they are using them safely and effectively, or whether they have access to a full range of choices. Nor do they indicate how far family planning programs go toward improving women's reproductive health. In fact, in some countries with persistent and growing reproductive health problems, family planning programs still get good marks simply because prevalence rates have risen significantly.

According to traditional measures, for example, Brazil is a family planning success story. Approximately 57 percent of married women of reproductive age use contraception. Widespread adoption of birth control has helped reduce birth rates considerably: the average number of children per woman of reproductive age fell from 5.8 in 1970 to 3.3 in 1990. Obviously, Brazilian women have exhibited an intense desire to regulate their fertility. Government policies regulating access to contraceptive methods, however, are structured such that they are forced to put their health at risk to do so.[58]

A recent study by the World Bank concludes that Brazilian women's reproductive health needs are "poorly met," in part because government policies limit access to reversible contraceptives, such as condoms, diaphragms, and IUDs. Forty-one percent of Brazilian contraceptive users are sterilized. According to the World Bank report, "many women resort to sterilization despite its irreversibility because of the lack of alternative methods." Their decisions can also be traced to the virtual absence of consumer information and education programs on contraception, and the lack of family planning services in most public health service posts.[59]

Sterilization is not always a forced choice. It can often be a popular option in countries where many women are in the latter half of their reproductive years and already have as many children as they want. This is the case in the United States, where 28 percent of contraceptive users are sterilized. But in a number of countries, high rates of female sterilization suggest a lack of alternatives. The rates are fairly high in India, Nepal, and the Dominican Republic, for example, where family planning programs are weak and women lack access to information on and supplies of alternatives. Conversely, contraceptive use in Colombia, Costa Rica, Mexico, and Jamaica, where contraceptive options are more varied, is more evenly distributed across a number of methods.[60]

By restricting the range of contraceptive choices, the Brazilian government has actually raised rather than reduced reproductive health risks. There are few assessments of women's reproductive health in other countries as comprehensive as the World Bank's study on Brazil. But evidence indicates the situation among women in many developing countries is just as bad or worse. A rise in the incidence of unsafe abortion and sexually transmitted diseases from a number of countries lauded for the success of their programs in reducing fertility rates suggests the widespread neglect of women's reproductive health.

**Climbing rates of teenage pregnancy and unsafe abortion are clear evidence that most programs are not reaching a large pool of clients.**

Despite considerable reductions in birth rates since the early seventies, for example, a report on Mexico from a conference on women's reproductive health concluded that "women and girls suffer from 'traditional' health problems such as anemia, infection, and malnutrition, maternal mortality, and cancer of the cervix, as well as 'modern' illnesses such as depression, obesity, and STDs. Health services for most, regardless of income, are very poor, failing to provide information, counseling, or appropriate medical care." Adrienne Germaine, Vice President of the International Women's Health Coalition, and Peggy Antrobus, Director of Development Alternatives for Women in a New Era, argue that "policy makers still ask why women's health should occupy a special place despite the evidence of low contraceptive prevalence, rising rates of adolescent pregnancy, septic abortions, and high rates of sexually transmitted diseases and pelvic infection."[61]

Another concept that universally influences but simultaneously limits the scope and content of family planning programs is "unmet need." This is usually measured as the share of married women of reproductive age who express a desire to have no more children but are not currently practicing family planning. It also may include married women who want another child but would like to postpone the next birth. These measures are used to determine the extent of unfulfilled demand for family planning information and supplies.[62]

But these definitions of unmet need exclude large numbers of women: those who are unmarried; adolescents at risk of pregnancy; women who are currently using an effective method ineffectively, sporadically, or in spite of indications of method-related health risks; those who wish to switch methods due to changes in health or life cycle; and those who have recently undergone an abortion and are not practicing family planning.

Nevertheless, the unmet need for family planning among many of these groups is making itself readily apparent in certain troubling trends. Climbing rates of teenage pregnancy and unsafe abortion, and the widespread rejections of contraceptive methods, are clear evidence that most programs are not reaching a large and growing pool of clients. The exclusion of these women from conventional measures gives an indication of what might better be called "ignored needs."

Other types of unmet or "ignored" needs are harder to pinpoint without more complete information. Without data, it is impossible to determine why and how women use different types of contraceptives, for example. The implicit assumption underlying current measures of need is that women who state a desire to limit or space births but are not practicing contraception will be glad to use whatever is available to meet this "need." In effect, unmet need is identified as a simple matter of supply or distribution.

But in countries where choices are limited, women not using contraceptives might just as frequently be expressing an unmet need for a wider range of alternatives, better information on the options available, and more education on how to handle possible side effects. Likewise, women may be expressing an "unmet need" for cheaper or closer supplies or services. In other words, it is not just a matter of how many cycles of pills a government ministry has on hand, but whether or not women want oral contraceptives at all, and what other options might be opened to them.

## MEETING WOMEN'S NEEDS

In the absence of a concerted international campaign to provide comprehensive reproductive health care, the prognosis for the next generation of women is poor. Estimates based on the rising incidence of unsafe abortion, reproductive tract infections, and AIDS, along with the growing unmet need for family planning, indicate that by the end of this decade reproductive causes will kill at least 2 million women a year.[63]

The obstacles to changing this lie not in the need for undiscovered medical techniques or the creation of vast and costly new health establishments. What is required is commitment and leadership on the part of national and international bodies to reorient reproductive health care strategies and expand the populations of women they seek to reach. Rescinding all non-health-related restrictions on the import, sale, and distribution of available contraceptives is of paramount importance to improving reproductive health. The repeal of restrictive abortion policies is no less essential.

Broadening the concept of family planning and reformulating programs to focus primarily on women's health needs are key first steps. Conventional measures alone indicate that unmet need for family planning is enormous: more than 300 million married women now express the desire for access to birth control but cannot obtain methods suitable to their needs. Researchers estimate that filling the unmet need among married women alone would reduce maternal deaths in Africa by 17 percent, in Latin America by 33 percent, and in Asia by 35 percent. Countless deaths and illnesses among teenagers and single women of all ages would also be prevented if their needs were met.[64]

To improve maternal health, networks need to be established connecting individual pregnant women with a variety of services—including prenatal, delivery, and emergency obstetric care. Health care services need to be high-quality, close to home, provided by trusted members of the community, and respectful of women's fears and concerns. The core of this network would be community-based health workers who could screen pregnant women and refer high-risk cases to hospitals. In most cases, these and other trained health workers could also provide prenatal and delivery care, family planning services, and education to the community at large. Traditional birth attendants can be an important part of the health worker corps. Per capita investments of about $1.50 per year should enable most countries to put into action these elements of a "safe motherhood" program.[65]

Experience shows such efforts can dramatically increase women's access to good maternal care. A pilot program to provide traditional birth attendants to 41 villages in Gujurat, India, was established in the early eighties by the Society for Education, Welfare, and Action–Rural. By 1990, this group succeeded in halving the rate of maternal deaths in the region. Similarly successful pilot programs have been established in Brazil, Zimbabwe, and elsewhere.[66]

Exploring and publicizing the social and human costs of poor reproductive health is part of the process of building such commitment. Gathering and analyzing information on the root causes of maternal illness and death, on high rates of reproductive tract infections, and on the cultural constraints to more widespread adoption of contraceptives is essential to devising strategies that work. Women should be involved at every level of the design and management of these efforts.

Screening for and treatment of reproductive tract infections are critical aspects of primary reproductive health care. Many governments and health agencies, particularly in the developing world, have shied away from such initiatives because they are believed to be too costly. But this is not the case. Clinic-based techniques for the diagnosis of vaginal infections cost from 3–6¢ each. And screening Third World women just once during their reproductive years for the presence of human papillomavirus or early signs of cervical cancer would cut deaths from cervical cancer in half. In the words of WHO researcher Andre Meheus, "if the cost . . . in developing countries is assessed in terms of hospitalization, infertility, pelvic inflammatory disease, ectopic pregnancy, and low birth weight for infants . . . screening would be very cost-effective."[67]

Much of the money needed for a comprehensive reproductive health care strategy in developing countries could be raised by reordering priorities and improving the efficiency with which health resources are now used. Health care budgets are inadequate everywhere and need desperately to be increased. But currently available funds are often poorly allocated. Even the least developed countries typically spend 60–80 percent of public health budgets on urban hospitals, although only a small share of their people will ever seek hospital services. Charles C. Griffin, a health economics researcher at the U.S.-based Urban Institute, finds "in some African countries . . . a single national hospital may consume 75 percent of the government health budget."[68]

While redirecting spending will assist in improving women's reproductive health, no amount of money can compensate for the lack of political commitment to improving the status of women. Private organizations can act as catalysts in empowering women in villages and towns throughout the Third World. Indeed, this is already happening: throughout Africa, Asia, and Latin America, community-based groups are bringing women together to share problems and find solutions on issues ranging from sexuality and reproductive tract infections to domestic violence and the availability of credit.

In essence, improving the status of women's reproductive health—and social and economic standing—is the most fundamental of all development challenges. Until women gain access to comprehensive reproductive health care, the cry of "health for all" will remain a bitterly empty promise.

# 7

# Mining the Earth

## *John E. Young*

Human welfare and mineral supplies have been linked for so long that scholars demarcate the ages of human history by reference to minerals: Stone, Bronze, and Iron. Cheap and abundant minerals provided the physical foundation for industrial civilizations. Societies' overall prosperity still correlates closely with per capita use of mineral products.

Industrial nations' abiding preoccupation with minerals is thus not surprising. In the United States, for example, periodic waves of concern over future mineral supplies have led to the appointment of at least a half-dozen blue-ribbon panels on the subject since the twenties. In 1978, a U.S. congressional committee requested a study whose title expressed the central question of virtually all these inquiries: Are we running out?[1]

Recent trends in price and availability of minerals suggest that the answer is "not yet." Regular improvements in exploitive technology have allowed the production of growing amounts at declining prices, despite the exhaustion of many of the world's richest ores. For many minerals, much of the world has yet to be thoroughly explored.

The question of scarcity, however, may never have been the most important one. Far more urgent is, Can the world afford the human and ecological price of

satisfying its voracious appetite for minerals? Today's low mineral prices reflect only the immediate economics of extraction: purchases of equipment and fuel, wages, transportation, financing, and so on. They fail to consider the full costs of devastated landscapes, dammed or polluted rivers, the squalor of mining camps, and the uprooting or decimation of indigenous peoples unlucky enough to live atop mineral deposits.

Although minerals remain essential for human survival, the negative effects of today's unprecedented extraction rates threaten to outweigh the benefits. Where mining is regulated to protect the environment, it still causes substantial damage; where regulated poorly or not at all, it creates environmental disaster areas. Around the world, mining and mineral processing play an important role in such environmental problems as deforestation, soil erosion, and air and water pollution. Globally, the mineral sector is one of the largest users of energy, thus contributing to air pollution and global warming.

The environmental impacts of mineral extraction are particularly severe in developing countries, which produce a large portion of the world's mineral supplies but use a relatively small share. Responsibility for the majority of the damage ultimately lies with those who use the most minerals—the fifth of humanity who live in industrial nations, enjoying material comforts others only dream of.

Reducing the mineral intake of rich nations is thus a top priority. Hope for success lies in the economic maturity of these countries: a certain amount of minerals is required for the infrastructures of prosperous societies, such as housing, office buildings, schools, hospitals, and transportation systems. Beyond these basics, the quantity of materials used need not determine the quality of life. After a certain point, people's welfare may depend more on the caliber of a relatively small number of silicon microchips than on the quantities of copper, steel, or aluminum they use.

The sooner the whole world reaches such a point, the better. At the end of the minerals- and energy-intensive development path taken by today's industrial nations lies ecological ruin. Mining enough to supply a world that has twice as many people, all using minerals at rates that now prevail only in rich countries, would have staggering environmental consequences. To avert such a fate, a new development strategy is needed—one that focuses on the improvement of human welfare while minimizing the need for new supplies of minerals.

## MINERALS IN THE GLOBAL ECONOMY

Large-scale use of minerals began with the Industrial Revolution and grew rapidly from then on. World use of many minerals reached within an order of magnitude of today's levels by late in the nineteenth century. From 1750 to 1900, world minerals use increased tenfold while population doubled. Since 1900, it has jumped at least thirteenfold.[2]

Growth in production and use of individual minerals has been even more extraordinary. Annual production of pig iron—the crude metal that is usually converted into steel—now stands at 552 million tons, 22,000 times what it was in 1700. Outputs of copper and zinc are 560 and 7,300 times greater than in 1800. Although aluminum was not available commercially until 1845 and was far too expensive for large-scale production until the modern electrolytic process was invented in 1886, smelters currently turn out 18 million tons of the metal each year.[3]

The term "minerals" encompasses a wide variety of substances taken from the earth. They are generally divided into four groups: metals, such as aluminum, copper, and iron; industrial minerals—such as lime and soda ash—that are valued for special qualities; construction materials, such as sand and gravel; and energy minerals, such as uranium, coal, oil, and natural gas (which are outside the scope of this chapter).[4]

Of the nonfuel minerals, stone, sand, and gravel are produced most widely and in the largest quantities. (See Table 7–1.) The principal use of the estimated 20 billion tons of such materials taken from the ground in 1990 was in construction, most often as filler in concrete. Ubiquitous in the earth's crust, they are generally used near the site where they are found. Other nonmetals are more valuable and typically travel further from mine to user. These include phosphates and potash (important ingredients in chemical fertilizers), lime (a major component of the cement that binds concrete), soda ash (an alkaline material used in many chemical processes), clays such as kaolin (an important ingredient in ceramics), and salt (most of which is used in the chemical industry, not in food).[5]

As a class, metals are the most important and valuable minerals extracted.

**Table 7-1. Estimated World Production of Selected Minerals, 1990**

| Mineral | Production[1] |
|---|---|
| | (thousand tons) |
| Metals | |
| Pig Iron | 552,000 |
| Aluminum | 18,100 |
| Copper | 8,920 |
| Manganese | 8,600 |
| Zinc | 7,300 |
| Chromium | 3,784 |
| Lead | 3,350 |
| Nickel | 949 |
| Tin | 216 |
| Molybdenum | 114 |
| Titanium | 102 |
| Silver | 15 |
| Mercury | 6 |
| Platinum-Group Metals | 0.3 |
| Gold | 0.2 |
| | |
| Nonmetals | |
| Stone | 11,000,000 |
| Sand and Gravel | 9,000,000 |
| Clays | 500,000 |
| Salt | 191,000 |
| Phosphate Rock | 166,350 |
| Lime | 135,300 |
| Gypsum | 99,000 |
| Soda Ash | 32,000 |
| Potash | 28,125 |

[1]All data exclude recycling.

SOURCES: Manganese from Thomas S. Jones, U.S. Bureau of Mines (USBM), Washington, D.C., private communication, October 15, 1991; chromium from John F. Papp, USBM, Washington, D.C., private communication, October 15, 1991; USBM, *Mineral Commodity Summaries 1991* (Washington, D.C.: 1991); figures for stone, sand and gravel, and clays are Worldwatch Institute estimates based on USBM, *Mineral Commodity Summaries.*

Iron is the world's preeminent metal. Thirty times as much iron is produced as any other metal. Steel—the cheap, strong material into which most iron is converted—costs about one third as much by weight as aluminum, its most common substitute, and dominates

world metal sales. The estimated value of the steel sold each year is about five times the total for all other metals, and four of the nine metals immediately below iron on the production list—manganese, chromium, nickel, and molybdenum—are primarily used in steelmaking.[6]

Aluminum is second to iron both in quantity and value of production. It is extremely important in aircraft construction because of its light weight, and is also made into beverage cans, the most common application in the world's largest user of aluminum, the United States. Copper is primarily used as an electrical conductor; zinc provides corrosion-resistant coatings for other metals; lead is used in electrical batteries and as an octane-boosting gasoline additive; and tin serves as a coating for steel cans.

The use of minerals is heavily concentrated in rich nations, and the disparities in use are most dramatic for metals. In 1988, the top eight industrial-nation users of aluminum, copper, and lead took two thirds of world supplies. Eight or fewer wealthy countries swallowed over half the iron ore and three fifths of zinc, tin, and steel supplies. The concentrations were even greater in the past. Throughout the sixties, the industrial nations absorbed more than 80 percent of world steel production and at least 90 percent of other metals.[7]

Steady demand increases fueled rapid expansion in minerals output until the seventies, when growth rates dropped substantially. From 1950 to 1974, use of eight economically important minerals grew 2–9 percent each year, on average. By 1974–87, average growth rates for the same eight all fell under 2 percent. In the case of tin, use actually shrank.[8]

Five factors appear to underlie the slackening demand for minerals, and for metals in particular. Most involve basic changes in the economies of the chief users. First, industrial economies have grown more slowly since the oil crisis of 1973. Second, these nations are shifting away from heavy industry and toward services and high technology. The pharmaceutical and electronics industries, for example, are among the fastest-growing sectors in industrial economies, and are far less materials- and energy-intensive than traditional extractive and manufacturing industries.[9]

Third, recycling has reduced demand for metals (though not for other minerals, which are not easily recycled). Precious metals such as gold, silver, and the platinum group (platinum, palladium, rhodium, ruthenium, iridium, and osmium, which are important as catalysts in automobile pollution-control devices and many chemical reactions) are recycled the most because of their high value. In the United States, tight regulation of lead—because it is highly toxic—has brought about a 64-percent recycling rate. Fifty-nine percent of U.S. iron and steel production and at least 10 percent of world steel production now derives from scrap rather than fresh ore. Aluminum recycling is particularly widespread because its manufacture from scrap takes less than 10 percent as much energy as its production from ore. Worldwide, nearly a third of the aluminum used in 1987 was recycled.[10]

Fourth, new materials, such as plastics, ceramics, and high-technology composites, are now competing with metals in many applications, from airplanes to construction, and are increasingly substituted for them. Copper, for example, is being supplanted by glass fiber and polyvinyl chloride in communications and plumbing uses. Fifth, and probably most important, industrial nations have in general completed their basic infrastructure of roads and buildings, and now need mineral products primarily to replace worn-out equipment and structures, not for new construction.

For all these reasons, minerals use is now growing faster in developing countries than in wealthier nations. Between 1977 and 1987, for example, the Third World's share of aluminum and copper use grew from 10 to 18 percent, and that of zinc from 16 to 24 percent. The increases are heavily concentrated in Mexico, Brazil, India, and the newly industrializing nations of East Asia.[11]

World minerals production is widely distributed, although production of some individual minerals is limited to a few nations. For instance, known deposits of cobalt, chromium, and the platinum-group metals are concentrated in a few countries, making supplies vulnerable to local political developments.[12]

Many of the world's great minerals users are in decline as producers. West European countries, for instance, have already depleted their high-grade mineral reserves and now rely mostly on imports. Japan imports virtually all the minerals it uses. The United States is still an important producer of many minerals, but gets nearly all its bauxite and alumina (the refined bauxite used by aluminum smelters), three fourths or more of its nickel, chromium, and tin, and about a third of its iron ore and zinc from foreign sources. The Soviet Union still produces large amounts of minerals despite a long history of mining. The list of important producers also includes such developing nations as Brazil, Chile, China, and Zaire. (See Table 7–2.)[13]

Each major industrial region looks to a corresponding part of the Third World for most of its mineral imports: the United States to Latin America, Western Europe to Africa, and Japan to Asia and Oceania. Mineral trade relationships also often reflect old colonial ties. For instance, Zaire supplies Belgium, its former ruler, with 62 percent of its imported copper, and Zambia supplies 30 percent of British imports of that metal.[14]

**Table 7-2. Major Mineral-Producing Countries, 1990**

| Mineral | Country | Share in World Production |
|---------|---------|---------------------------|
|         |         | (percent) |
| Bauxite | Australia | 37 |
|         | Guinea | 16 |
| Chromium | South Africa | 32 |
|          | Soviet Union | 32 |
| Cobalt | Zaire | 58 |
|        | Zambia | 16 |
| Copper | Chile | 17 |
|        | United States | 17 |
| Gold | South Africa | 30 |
|      | United States | 15 |
| Iron Ore | Soviet Union | 26 |
|          | Brazil | 17 |
| Lead | Australia | 16 |
|      | United States | 15 |
| Manganese | Soviet Union | 36 |
|           | South Africa | 16 |
| Molybdenum | United States | 53 |
|            | Chile | 15 |
| Nickel | Soviet Union | 23 |
|        | Canada | 22 |
| Phosphate Rock | United States | 28 |
|                | Soviet Union | 24 |
| Platinum Group | South Africa | 48 |
|                | Soviet Union | 45 |
| Silver | Mexico | 17 |
|        | United States | 14 |
| Tin | Brazil | 24 |
|     | Malaysia | 14 |
| Titanium | Soviet Union | 46 |
|          | Spain | 25 |
| Tungsten | China | 52 |
|          | Soviet Union | 21 |
| Zinc | Canada | 17 |
|      | Australia | 13 |

SOURCE: U.S. Bureau of Mines, *Mineral Commodity Summaries 1991* (Washington, D.C.: 1991).

Mineral "reserves"—an often misunderstood concept—consist of deposits whose existence has been documented by detailed surveying and that are judged to be minable at a cost no higher than current market prices. At current use rates, global reserves of economically important minerals range from about 20 years of supply (lead, tin, and zinc) to 224 years (bauxite). Although 20 years may seem alarmingly short, there is little danger of the world soon running out. Mineral resources—deposits whose presence is indicated by preliminary surveys or other geologic evidence but that are not yet economically viable—are far greater than reserves, and exploration is constantly moving deposits from the resources to the reserves category. In recent decades, mineral reserves have generally grown at least as fast as production.[15]

Much of the best reserves now lie in developing countries, since industrial nations have a much longer history of mining. The Soviet Union and the former members of the Warsaw Pact also possess large reserves of many important minerals, including iron ore, manganese, chromium, and nickel, and their potential resources are enormous. However, economic and political turmoil in the former socialist countries makes them unlikely sites for new mineral projects, which usually require large capital investments and long lead times before production can begin.[16]

Overall, scarcity of mineral deposits does not appear likely to constrain the production of most important minerals in the foreseeable future. Much more probable, however, are reductions in output due to environmental concerns.

## LAYING WASTE

Mining is the quintessential dirty industry. As the German scholar Georgius Agricola put it in his 1550 treatise on mining: "The fields are devastated by mining operations . . . the woods and groves are cut down, for there is need of an endless amount of wood for timbers, machines, and the smelting of metals. And when the woods and groves are felled, then are exterminated the beasts and birds. . . . Further, when the ores are washed, the water which has been used poisons the brooks and streams, and either destroys the fish or drives them away."[17]

Four centuries later, mining's environmental effects remain much the same, but on a vastly greater scale. Modern machinery can do in hours what it took men and draft animals years to do in Agricola's time. Larger equipment reflects the growing scale of the industry. A typical truck used in hard-rock mining in 1960 weighed 20–40 tons, for example; in 1970 it weighed in at 80–200 tons. The size of the shovels used to move ore increased from 2 to 18 cubic meters over the same period. Such technological advances allowed world mineral production to grow rapidly—and proportionately increased the harm to the environment.[18]

Mining and smelting have created large environmental disaster areas in many nations. (See Table 7–3.) In the United States, for example, which has a long history of mining, 48 of the 1,189 sites on the Superfund hazardous-waste cleanup list are former mineral operations. The largest Superfund site stretches across the state of Montana, down a 220-kilometer section of Silver Bow Creek and the Clark Fork River. Water and sediments in the river and a downstream reservoir are contaminated with arsenic, lead, zinc, cadmium, and other metals, which have also spread to nearby drinking-water aquifers. Soils throughout the local valley are contaminated with smelter emissions.[19]

The Clark Fork Basin was the site of more than 100 years of mining and smelting, including what was at one time the largest open pit in the world, the Berkeley Pit copper mine. The pit and a network of underground mine workings contain more than 11 billion gallons of acid mine water that rises a little higher each year, threatening local aquifers and already-tainted streams with contamination. The Clark Fork Coalition, a local environmental group, estimates that cleaning up the pit and other sites in the area could cost over $1 billion. A proposed large new copper mine in the Cabinet Mountains area of northwest Montana now endangers another section of the Clark Fork's drainage.[20]

The environmental damage done in producing a particular mineral is determined by such factors as the ecological character of the mining site, the quantity of material moved, the depth of the deposit, the chemical composition of the ore and the surrounding rocks and soils, and the nature of the processes used to extract purified minerals from ore. Damage varies dramatically with the type of mineral being mined. For example, stone ranks first in production, but its extraction probably causes less overall harm than that of several metals. Since stone and other construction materials are usually taken from shallow or naturally exposed deposits and used with little or no processing, the environmental impacts are mostly limited to land disturbance at the quarry or gravel pit, and relatively few wastes are generated.

At the other end of the damage spectrum, metals are produced through a long chain of processes, each of which involves pollution and the generation of waste. Copper production, for instance, typically involves five stages. First, soil and rock (called overburden) that lie above the ore must be removed. The ore is then mined, after which it is crushed and run through a concentrator, which physically removes impurities. The concentrated ore is reduced to crude metal at high temperatures in a smelter, and

**Table 7-3. Selected Examples of Environmental Impacts of Minerals Extraction and Processing**

| Location/Mineral | Observation |
| --- | --- |
| Ilo-Locumbo Area, Peru copper mining and smelting | The Ilo smelter emits 600,000 tons of sulfur compounds each year; nearly 40 million cubic meters per year of tailings containing copper, zinc, lead, aluminum, and traces of cyanides are dumped into the sea each year, affecting marine life in a 20,000-hectare area; nearly 800,000 tons of slag are also dumped each year. |
| Nauru, South Pacific phosphate mining | When mining is completed—in 5–15 years—four fifths of the 2,100-hectare South Pacific island will be uninhabitable. |
| Pará state, Brazil Carajás iron ore project | The project's wood requirements (for smelting of iron ore) will require the cutting of enough native wood to deforest 50,000 hectares of tropical forest each year during the mine's expected 250-year life. |
| Russia, Soviet Union Severonikel smelters | Two nickel smelters in the extreme northwest corner of the republic, near the Norwegian and Finnish borders, pump 300,000 tons of sulfur dioxide into the atmosphere each year, along with lesser amounts of heavy metals. Over 200,000 hectares of local forests are dying, and the emissions appear to be affecting the health of local residents. |
| Sabah Province, Malaysia Mamut Copper Mine | Local rivers are contaminated with high levels of chromium, copper, iron, lead, manganese, and nickel. Samples of local fish have been found unfit for human consumption, and rice grown in the area is contaminated. |
| Amazon Basin, Brazil gold mining | Hundreds of thousands of miners have flooded the area in search of gold, clogging rivers with sediment and releasing an estimated 100 tons of mercury into the ecosystem each year. Fish in some rivers contain high levels of mercury. |

SOURCE: Worldwatch Institute, based on sources documented in endnote 19.

the metal is later purified, through re-melting, in a refinery.

Most of today's mines are surface excavations rather than underground complexes of tunnels and shafts, so the miner's first task is to remove whatever lies over a mineral deposit—be it a mountain, a forest, a farmer's field, or a town. For any given mineral, surface mining produces more waste than working underground. In 1988, U.S. surface mines produced 11 times as much waste per ton of ore as underground mines did. That same year, overburden accounted for more than a third of the 3.3 billion tons of material handled at non-fuel mines. Such material, while it may be chemically inert, can clog streams and cloud the air over large areas. If the overburden contains sulfur compounds —common in rock containing metal ores—it can react with rainwater to form sulfuric acid, which then may contaminate local soils and watercourses.[21]

Similar but more severe effects often stem from mining and from the disposal of tailings, the residue from ore concentration. Up to 90 percent of metal ore ends up as tailings, which are commonly dumped in large piles or ponds near the mine. The finely ground material makes contaminants that were formerly bound up in solid rock (such as arsenic, cadmium, copper, lead, and zinc) accessible to water. Acid drainage, which exacerbates metal contamination, is often a problem, since sulfur makes up more than a third of the ores of many metals, including copper, gold, lead, mercury, nickel, and zinc. Tailings also usually contain residues of organic chemicals—such as toluene, a solvent damaging to human skin and to the respiratory, circulatory, and nervous systems—that are used in ore concentrators. Ponds full of tailings cover at least 3,500 hectares in the Clark Fork area and 2,100 hectares at the Bingham Canyon copper mine in Utah.[22]

A particularly dramatic example of the impact of tailings disposal is the Panguna copper mine on Bougainville, an island in Papua New Guinea that since mid-1989 has been controlled by secessionist rebels. Before it was closed, the mining operation dumped 600 million tons of metal-contaminated tailings—130,000 tons each day—into the Kawerong River. The wastes cover 1,800 hectares in the Kawerong/Jaba river system, including a 700-hectare delta at its mouth, 30 kilometers from the mine. No aquatic life survives in the river. Local anger at the destruction of the area by mining was a major cause of the civil war.[23]

Smelting, the next stage of the extraction process, can produce enormous quantities of air pollutants. Worldwide, smelting of copper and other nonferrous (noniron) metals releases an estimated 6 million tons of sulfur dioxide into the atmosphere each year—8 percent of total emissions of the sulfur compound that is a primary cause of acid rain. Nonferrous smelters can also pump out large quantities of arsenic, lead, cadmium, and other heavy metals. If they lack pollution control equipment, aluminum smelters emit tons of fluoride, which can concentrate in and kill vegetation and, in severe cases, animals that eat contaminated plants.[24]

**The Panguna copper mine in Papua New Guinea dumped 600 million tons of metal-contaminated tailings into the Kawerong River.**

Uncontrolled smelters have produced some of the world's best-known environmental disaster areas—"dead zones" where little or no vegetation survives. Such an area around the Sudbury, Ontario, nickel smelter in Canada measures 10,400 hectares; in the United States, a dead zone surrounding the Copper Hill smelter in Tennessee covers 7,000 hectares. In Japan, about 6,700 hectares of cropland are too contaminated for rice production; 400,000 hectares of agricultural land have been lost to metal smelting in the United Kingdom since Roman times. Acid fallout destroyed fish populations in lakes 65 kilometers away from the Sudbury smelter. And between 1896 and 1936, a smelter at Trail, British Columbia, killed virtually all conifers within 19 kilometers and retarded tree growth up to 63 kilometers away.[25]

New dead zones, such as the area surrounding the Severonikel nickel smelter in Russia, are still being created. Smelters in industrial countries are now often required by law to have pollution control equipment, but few in developing countries or the formerly socialist nations have any such controls. For each kilogram of copper produced, 12.5 times more sulfur dioxide is released to the air from Chilean smelters than from those in the United States.[26]

The grade of an ore—its metal content in percentage terms—is a critical factor in determining the overall impact of metal mining. The average grade of copper ores, for example, is lower than that for any of the other major metals. Four centuries ago, copper ores typically contained about 8 percent metal; the average grade of ore mined is now under 1 percent. One consequence of the drop in grade is that at least eight times as much ore now must be processed to obtain the same amount of copper. An estimated 990 million tons of ore were mined to produce about 9 million tons of copper in 1990.[27]

---

**Utah's Bingham Canyon copper mine is the largest human excavation in the world.**

---

Even this figure understates the total amount of material moved, since it does not include overburden. The scale of the industry is apparent, however, in the size of the holes it creates. Some 3.3 billion tons of material—seven times the amount moved for the Panama Canal—have been taken from Utah's Bingham Canyon copper mine. Now 774 meters deep, this mine is the largest human excavation in the world. It gained another distinction in 1987 when its operator, Kennecott Copper, inadvertently reported its toxic chemical releases to the Environmental Protection Agency's Toxics Release Inventory (a national toxic-chemicals reporting system from which the mining industry is exempt). Out of the 18,000 industrial facilities reporting, the Bingham Canyon mine came in fourth in total toxic releases and first in metals. The company discon-

tinued reporting the following year, but the scale of its releases spurred legislative efforts in 1991 to include the mining industry in the inventory in the future.[28]

Gold mining also requires the processing of large amounts of material, since the metal occurs in concentrations best measured in parts per million. For example, the operators of the Goldstrike mine in Nevada—the largest in the United States—each day move 325,000 tons of ore and waste to produce under 50 kilograms of gold. In Brazil's Amazon Basin, thousands of small-scale gold miners are using a technique called hydraulic mining to extract as much as 120 tons of gold per year. This involves blasting gold-bearing hillsides with high-pressure streams of water, and then guiding the water and sediment through sluices that separate tiny amounts of gold, which is heavier, from tons of non-valuable material, which then pollutes local rivers.[29]

Since 1979, when the price of gold soared to an all-time high of $850 per ounce, a gold rush has swept the world. Waves of gold seekers have invaded remote areas in Brazil, other Amazonian countries, Indonesia, the Philippines, and Zimbabwe. Dramatic environmental damage has resulted. Hydraulic mining has silted rivers and lakes, and the use of mercury—an extremely toxic metal that accumulates in the food chain and causes neurological problems and birth defects—to capture gold from sediment has contaminated wide areas. Miners release an estimated 100 tons of mercury into the Amazon ecosystem each year.[30]

In North America, heap leaching, a new technology that allows gold extraction from very low-grade ores, is now in wide use. Miners spray cyanide solution, which dissolves gold, on piles of crushed ore or old tailings. After it passes through the ore, the liquid is collected and eventually the gold is extracted from it. Both cyanide-solution collection reservoirs and the contaminated tailings left behind after leaching pose hazards to wildlife and groundwater. In October 1990, for instance, 10 million gallons of cyanide solution spilled from a reservoir at the Brewer Gold Mine, near Jefferson, South Carolina, into a tributary of the Lynches River. The spill, caused by a dam break after a heavy rain, killed as many as 10,000 fish. Thousands of birds also die each year when they mistake cyanide impoundments for lakes.[31]

Fossil-fuel-powered machinery has allowed mining to expand to such a degree that its effects now rival the natural processes of erosion. An estimated 23 billion tons of nonfuel minerals are taken from the earth each year. Taking overburden into account, the total amount of material moved could easily top 30 billion tons—about twice the amount of sediment carried each year by the world's rivers.[32]

An estimated half-million hectares of land—including mines, waste disposal sites, and areas of subsidence over underground mines—are directly disturbed by nonfuel mining each year. Most of this land will bear the scars indefinitely. Historian Elizabeth Dore, describing the effects of 500 years of mining on the Bolivian landscape, writes: "Silver and tin are gone; in their place rise mountains of rock, slag, and tailings. . . . Saturated with mercury, arsenic, and sulfuric acid, the irridescence of these rubbish heaps provides a psychedelic reminder of the past." The damage is not limited to the mine site. As Dore puts it, mining initiates "a chain of soil, water, and air contamination" that can alter the ecosystems of large areas.[33]

Moving billions of tons of material and crushing and melting rock requires large amounts of energy, and supplying it can cause major damage to local ecosystems. Ever since Agricola's time, for example, wood-fired smelters have threatened nearby forests. In southern England, the Sussex iron industry was effectively wiped out when it destroyed the local woods that provided its fuel supply. In the late nineteenth century, more than 2 million cords of wood were used as smelter fuel in Nevada's Comstock Lode—described by one observer as "the tomb of the forests of the Sierras."[34]

Today, demand for energy to extract and process minerals is playing a major role in the deforestation and inundation of large parts of the Amazon Basin. A huge iron ore mining and smelting project at Carajás, in the Brazilian state of Pará, threatens a large area of tropical forest. The project's 20 planned pig-iron smelters will need an estimated 2.4 million tons of charcoal each year, which if produced from native trees will require an estimated 50,000 hectares of forest to be logged annually. According to ecologist Philip Fearnside, high costs make it unlikely that plantations will supply much of the wood, and the state enterprise that owns the project has thus far done little to develop plantation production. The mine is expected to operate for 250 years.[35]

The iron ore facilities are only one piece of Brazil's colossal Grande Carajás Project, a vast state-run development scheme that also includes bauxite, copper, chromium, nickel, tungsten, tin, and gold mines; mineral processing plants; hydroelectric dams; deep-water ports; and other enterprises. Another element of the project, the Albrás aluminum smelter, now takes up to a quarter of the electricity output of the enormous—and enormously destructive—Tucuruí hydroelectric station. The smelter, a major justification for the dam's construction, receives power at one fourth the cost of generation (and one third the average cost of Brazilian electricity).[36]

Aluminum production is particularly energy-intensive. Unlike most other metals, which can be obtained by simply heating the ore, aluminum forms such tight chemical bonds that it can only be economically extracted through a process involving the direct application of electrical current. Modern aluminum smelters require 13–18 kilowatt-hours of electricity to produce a kilogram of metal. Additional energy is used in mining bauxite, and in processing it into the alumina that is smelted. All told, aluminum production requires an estimated 3.8 billion gigajoules (GJ) of energy each year—around 1 percent of world energy use. Much of that energy is purchased at unusually low rates.[37]

Though figures are sparse, the mineral industry is clearly among the world's largest users of energy, and thus a major contributor to the impacts of energy use, including climate change. For instance, copper production takes an estimated 0.8 billion GJ of energy each year. More energy probably goes into steelmaking than any other mineral industry: in the United States, which produces only 11 percent of the world's supply, steelmaking required 2.2 billion GJ in 1988.[38]

The efficiency of energy use in smelting and refining metals has improved over time. Today's U.S. aluminum smelters, for example, use between half and two thirds as much electricity as those built in the late forties. Some new copper smelting technologies use as much as 40 percent less energy than traditional methods. But while smelting has improved, long-term trends in ore grades and accessibility of deposits tend to increase the energy used per unit of metal mined. Declining ore grades increase energy needs, because more ore must be mined, greater quantities of waste material must be handled, and more effort is required to concentrate and smelt the ore. And as more remote, deeper deposits are mined to replace those more easily reached, more energy is required in order to dig bigger holes and transport the ore.[39]

Tight regulation of mining waste disposal, water pollution, and air emissions could help limit mining's environmental impact. This sector is subject to a broad range of environmental rules in industrial countries. In the United States, for example, widely regarded as a leader in such regulation, smelter emissions are regulated under the Clean Air Act and mining-caused water pollution under the Clean Water Act. Unfortunately, federal regulation of mining itself, however, has been and remains quite weak. The Environmental Protection Agency has done little to regulate disposal of mining wastes, despite their status as the single largest category of waste produced. In the Resource Conservation and Recovery Act of 1976, Congress specifically exempted mining wastes from regulation as hazardous waste. In general, the states play a more important role in mining regulation, and the level of attention and enforcement varies dramatically.

Mining and mineral processing are little regulated in developing countries. While many of them have broad environmental protection laws in place, specific regulation of the minerals industries is rare. Where environmental laws do exist, funding and staff for enforcement are usually scarce. Chile, for example, has comprehensive and stringent environmental rules for mining that are virtually unenforced. The Chilean government has been particularly loath to force state-owned mineral operations to comply with the laws. At times, the prospect of major revenue from projects leads government officials to simply ignore environmental rules or studies. At the Ok Tedi copper and gold mine in Papua New Guinea, the government allowed the project's operators—an international consortium of private firms—to dump up to 150,000 tons of tailings a day into the nearby Fly River rather than containing them at the mine site, despite studies showing the potential for major damage to the river system.[40]

## AT WHAT COST?

While mineral prices have fluctuated dramatically, the overriding trend in recent decades has been downward, with most of the plunge occurring during the dozen years following the 1973 oil crisis. After adjusting for inflation, the International Monetary Fund (IMF) index of nonfuel mineral prices declined by half between 1974 and 1986. (See Figure 7-1.) Real prices recovered somewhat in the late eighties, but have never returned to the levels of the fifties, sixties, and early seventies. They were again in decline in 1990 and 1991, and are projected by IMF analysts to go even lower.[41]

Why are mineral prices so low? One reason is that many nations subsidize development of their domestic mineral resources. Since the twenties, for example, the United States has offered mining companies generous tax exemptions called depletion allowances. Miners can deduct from 5 to 22 percent of their gross income, depending on the min-

eral. Unlike conventional depreciation, depletion allowances are not based on capital investments made by the company. In fact, the allowances may be taken for as long as the mine operates—even after the company's investment is fully recovered. In addition, mining companies may also deduct much of the cost of exploring for and developing mineral deposits.[42]

The lost taxes added up to a $5-billion subsidy to the U.S. mining industry over the last decade. The President's budget projects that the 1992 subsidy will be $560 million. According to the Joint Committee on Taxation of the U.S. Congress, the Treasury could gain $2 billion over the next five years if the mineral industry were taxed on the same basis as others.[43]

The U.S. mining industry receives another large but uncalculated subsidy through virtual giveaways of federal land under the General Mining Act of 1872. This legal relic of the frontier era allows those who find hard-rock minerals (such as gold, silver, lead, iron, and copper) in public territory to buy the land for $12 per hectare or less. Since the government retains no rights to the land, the Treasury does not receive royalties on minerals taken from it, in contrast to the situation with oil, gas, and coal found on public land. Even very low royalty levels would yield large sums, since miners took $4 billion worth of hard-rock minerals from former federal lands in 1988.[44]

Japan offers loans, subsidies, and tax incentives for exploration and development of domestic mineral deposits. Similarly, the French government offers financial assistance for minerals exploration, and also makes direct investments in mineral projects through the Bureau de Recherches Geologiques et Minières (BRGM), a state-owned enterprise. Germany is considerably less generous, but does offer direct support for explora-

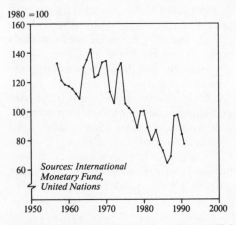

1980 = 100

*Sources: International Monetary Fund, United Nations*

**Figure 7-1. Index of Real Nonfuel Mineral Prices, 1957–91**

tion. Most industrial nations must now look abroad for new mineral supplies, however. Japan's domestic mineral resources are, by the geological luck of the draw, quite limited. Western Europe was once quite rich in minerals, but demand during two centuries of industrial development has depleted most major deposits.[45]

Industrial nations have thus also tried to ensure continued access to cheap minerals supplies through their international trade and aid policies. The Japanese government subsidizes foreign mineral projects of Japanese companies through low-interest loans, loan guarantees, and direct government investments. The state-owned BRGM helps French companies with funding for exploration and development of overseas projects, and Germany offers investment guarantees, minimum rate-of-return guarantees, and favorable loans for foreign mineral investments by its companies. These nations and the United States have also often supported efforts by development institutions, including the World Bank, to finance mineral projects in developing countries—at times with the explicit intention of securing future minerals sources.[46]

**Powerful political and economic interests support continued subsidies for domestic mineral production.**

Historically, nations have justified subsidies for minerals extraction on national security grounds. Minerals are critical to arms production, and supplies have often been equated with military power. Progress in the arms race between the United Kingdom and Germany prior to World War I was measured in steel production. The aluminum industry would not be what it is today were it not for the many forms of special support given by national governments that during World War I came to understand the metal's importance in modern warfare. The role of aluminum in World War II was summed up by a U.S. analyst in 1942 with the following equation: "Electric power→ aluminum→ bombers→ victory."[47]

Today, powerful political and economic interests support continued subsidies for domestic mineral production. While the mining industry and manufacturers who purchase mineral products benefit from this practice, taxpayers end up with the bill and markets are skewed toward use of virgin rather than recycled materials. One analyst estimated in 1977 that U.S. tax subsidies for virgin materials—including wood products as well as minerals—made such items about 10 percent cheaper than they would be otherwise. The actual impact of subsidies on virgin materials prices is probably greater, since other, unquantified subsidies were not taken into account.[48]

Given the growing dependence of rich nations on foreign mineral supplies and their willingness to assist with the development of these resources, developing nations would seem well positioned to benefit from their mineral wealth. But the people of mineral-exporting developing countries have gained little from mining. Indeed, many of these nations seem to have been dragged down economically by their dependence on these exports.

At least a dozen developing countries get a third or more of their export revenues from minerals. (See Table 7–4.) For these nations, the effect of 15 years of falling prices has been less export revenue with which to purchase the manufactured goods—from tractors to televisions to pharmaceuticals—they import. Reduced foreign exchange earnings have also made it difficult or impossible

**Table 7-4. Share of Minerals in Value of Total Exports, Selected Countries,
Late Eighties[1]**

| Country | Mineral(s) | Share |
|---|---|---|
| | | (percent) |
| Botswana | diamonds, copper, nickel | 89 |
| Zambia | copper | 86 |
| Liberia | iron ore, diamonds | 60 |
| Jamaica | bauxite/alumina | 58 |
| Zaire[2] | copper, diamonds | 57 |
| Chile | copper | 50 |
| Togo | phosphates | 50 |
| Peru | copper, zinc, iron ore, lead, silver | 45 |
| Mauritania | iron ore | 41 |
| Papua New Guinea | copper | 40 |
| Bolivia | zinc, tin, silver, antimony, tungsten | 35 |
| Guyana | bauxite | 33 |
| South Africa | gold | 30 |

[1]Minerals are listed in order of total export value.   [2]1985–86.
SOURCES: Zaire from United Nations Conference on Trade and Development, *Handbook of International Trade
and Development Statistics* (New York: United Nations, 1990); all others from International Monetary Fund
(IMF), *International Financial Statistics*, August 1991; IMF, *International Financial Statistics Yearbook* (Washington, D.C.: 1990).

for many mineral producers to repay
their international debts. They are
among the world's most indebted nations. On average, the dozen developing
countries listed in the table bear external
debts 1.5 times greater than their gross
national product (GNP). By comparison,
the average ratio of debt to GNP among
the nations the World Bank classifies as
severely indebted is 0.6.[49]

Zambia provides a dramatic example
of what can happen when a nation gets
trapped between heavy debt and falling
prices for its main export. The country
went into an economic tailspin when the
price of copper, which provides 86 percent of its export revenue, dropped
sharply in the early eighties. The results
were calamitous: twice as many Zambian
children died from malnutrition in 1984
as in 1980. A series of IMF-prescribed
economic recovery plans—which cut domestic spending and devalued the national currency in an attempt to boost
mineral exports and reduce the external

debt—have failed to rescue Zambia from
the grip of export dependence.[50]

The current plight of Third World
minerals exporters is the product of a
collision between economic development strategies and unforeseen trends
in the mining industry and minerals use.
Unfortunately, the projected positive
trends in minerals demand and prices
that were the foundation of the economic plans of many exporters during
the sixties and seventies have vanished
in the last decade.

Throughout the fifties, privately
owned companies essentially controlled—through a loose oligopoly—the
prices of most major minerals, owned
most major projects, and garnered the
bulk of the profits. Although cyclical
swings were not eliminated, prices were
maintained at profitable levels by the
combination of steadily increasing demand and industry control. Companies
cut production during economic slumps
in the major consumer nations, and an-

ticipated economic upturns with investments in new capacity. The power of private firms made it very difficult for Third World governments to impose substantial local taxation or royalty requirements on foreign-owned mineral firms. If they did, the mining companies—which often owned not only mines but also smelting and refining facilities—could keep local tax bills to a minimum by selling their ores to their own processing subsidiaries at low prices.[51]

But in the tide of nationalism of the sixties and seventies, many governments—including newly independent nations and some long-independent ones just learning to flex their muscles—tried to increase their share of the profits from mining through higher taxes, new royalty requirements, and measures against transfer pricing. Some of them, including Bolivia, Chile, Guinea, Guyana, and Zaire, imposed minimum local ownership requirements or nationalized foreign-owned mines. Inspired by the example of the Organization of Petroleum-Exporting Countries, producers of some commodities, including bauxite, copper, and iron ore, banded together in attempts to increase prices.[52]

**Far too often, indigenous people are simply pushed aside in the rush to mine valuable deposits.**

At the same time, the World Bank and other international development institutions promoted an economic strategy that emphasized the use of mining revenue as working capital for industrialization and overall economic growth. Optimistic mineral price projections fueled a rush of investment in mining projects. An increasing number were undertaken by state-owned enterprises rather than private firms, so national governments ended up bearing the debt. Although World Bank investments in mineral projects did not take an exceptionally large share of its lending—under 3 percent of the total from 1966 to 1991—the contributions leveraged considerable funding from other sources. For example, the Bank contributed only $60 million of the $501 million required for the Guelbs iron-ore project in Mauritania, with the balance coming from European, Arab, and Japanese institutions. Private banks, awash in billions of dollars amassed by the newly wealthy oil-exporting countries, also plowed newfound capital into mineral projects.[53]

Minerals projects are expensive. They are also often connected more closely to the outside world than to the host country. For instance, the Guelbs project—which consists of an iron mine and ore concentrator, a port, and a railroad to connect them—has virtually no links with the rest of Mauritania's economy, which it dwarfs. When financing was arranged in 1979, the investment required for the first phase of the project topped the nation's gross domestic product, which then stood at $470 million.[54]

As long as future demand appeared strong, however, and prices remained fairly high, such projects seemed viable. Mineral export revenues grew during the seventies. But in the early eighties, the bubble burst. Softening minerals demand collided with rapid production expansion to create an unprecedented, sustained drop in mineral prices. The decline was exacerbated by the tendency of nationalized mines to continue producing in large quantities despite falling prices. While private producers cut back their output, some nations, such as Zambia, had become too dependent on mineral revenue to reduce production; a few, such as Chile, even expanded production in an attempt to make up for lost revenues, and prices were driven even lower.[55]

The overall result of these developments was a dramatic transformation of the world mineral industry—from a relatively stable, lucrative oligopoly to an unpredictable, intensely competitive business. This change undermined overnight the development strategy followed by many Third World minerals producers. No longer, as the authors of a 1990 study put it, can mineral resources "be regarded as buried treasure." In other words, if mineral projects are hard pressed to pay for themselves, they cannot be expected to provide much help in economic development beyond the mine.[56]

The other, often forgotten side of developing countries' involvement in mining is the effects on local people and their environment. The rush to produce more minerals and gain export revenue has had devastating consequences for those whose homelands are underlain by minerals.

Developers and funders of large mining projects have rarely considered the future of local people during project planning—or when deciding to proceed in the first place. The Panguna copper mine on Bougainville, which led to a civil war, is a particularly dramatic example. Local people received little compensation for the lands they owned or for the destruction of their home territory, while the mine was a huge source of income for the national government. Before the rebels succeeded in closing it in 1989, the mine was yielding 17 percent of Papua New Guinea's operating revenue and 40 percent of its export income.[57]

Far too often, indigenous people are simply pushed aside in the rush to mine valuable deposits. In the Amazon, for example, the Yanomami, an interior tribe who avoided contact with the outside world until recent decades, are dying off rapidly. Thousands of miners have crowded their homeland in the northern Brazilian states of Roraima and Amazonas, polluting local rivers with sediment and mercury and bringing unfamiliar diseases to the indigenous population. It is estimated that at least 15 percent of the Yanomami have died from malaria.[58]

The Brazilian government was for many years unwilling to do anything substantial to save the Yanomami, and local and state officials have long been active supporters of the area's mining operations. As the then-governor of Roraima put it in 1975, "an area as rich as this cannot afford the luxury of conserving half a dozen Indian tribes who are holding back the development of Brazil." But in 1990 and 1991, under heavy pressure from human rights organizations and other governments, President Fernando Collor de Mello sent in federal police to expel miners from Yanomami lands. The police action and the departure of many inexperienced, unsuccessful operators have reduced the number of miners substantially, but the indigenous people are still threatened. Their future now largely hangs on whether President Collor signs an executive decree prepared in July 1991 establishing a 9-million-hectare Yanomami reserve, where mining would be banned. As of early November 1991, Collor had not yet acted.[59]

## Digging Out

Ever since Agricola, the destruction from mineral production has been justified in the name of human progress. The sixteenth century scholar was quite conscious of mining's effects on the environment, yet argued that without metals "men would pass a horrible and wretched existence in the midst of wild beasts." In an absolute sense, Agricola was right: civilizations have always depended heavily on minerals for survival—and still do.[60]

But as Lewis Mumford put it in his classic *Technics and Civilization*, "One must admit the devastation of mining, even if one is prepared to justify the end. . . . What was only an incidental and local damage in [Agricola's] time became a widespread characteristic of Western Civilization just as soon as it started in the eighteenth century to rest directly upon the mine and its products." Mining's effects on the earth are now on the same scale as those of natural forces.[61]

In the short run, the most obvious way to reduce the damage is to regulate the environmental impacts of mining more closely. There is considerable room for improvement of current mining practices—in increased attention to environmental safeguards, more sensitivity to local people and their concerns, and better planning for the indirect impacts of mineral development.

In the United States, several laws now up for revision—including the Resource Conservation and Recovery Act, the Clean Water Act, and the General Mining Act—offer lawmakers a chance to strengthen or add environmental provisions related to mining. In developing countries, several major mineral producers, including Chile, Brazil, and Peru, have recently started looking at mineral production's impacts on the environment and are attempting to improve the regulation of such activities.[62]

In the long run, however, mining regulation offers relatively limited benefits. Even well-managed mines are often enormously destructive. Careful reclamation may reduce erosion and pollution problems at mine sites, but ecological complexity and high costs usually preclude restoring the land to its previous condition. High energy use in mining and smelting makes reuse and recycling of metal-containing products

almost always preferable to virgin production.

The ultimate solution to the problem of mining's environmental destruction rests in profound changes in minerals use and the global economy. No country has yet developed and put into place comprehensive policies on the use of minerals and other raw materials. The assumption that prosperity is synonymous with the quantities of minerals taken from the earth has underlain the industrial development strategies of both capitalist and socialist nations. But that theory is open to question. The environmental damage from nonstop growth in mineral production will eventually outweigh the benefits of increased materials supplies—if it does not already.

The way out of the trap lies in a simple distinction: it is the extraction and processing of minerals, not their use, that poses the greatest threat. The ultimate goal of industrial nations' policies has always been to champion the production of virgin minerals. Although such an approach has effectively promoted mining, it has also helped make minerals artificially cheap. This has led to widespread waste of mineral products, and has diverted funds that might have been spent more productively in other economic sectors.

An alternative goal would be to maximize conservation of mineral stocks already circulating in the global economy. Such a policy could help reduce inflows of new materials and the environmental damage required to produce them. The world's industrial nations, the leading users of minerals, offer the most obvious opportunities for cutting demand. Minerals use there is still rising, but increases have been slower in the last two decades than before. A growing body of evidence suggests that per capita needs for virgin minerals have already peaked in the world's industrial market nations, and that major shifts are under way in the mix of minerals needed.[63]

National governments could accelerate the transition to more materials-efficient economies through basic changes in policies that govern the exploitation and use of raw materials. Tax policy is the obvious place to start. Taxing rather than subsidizing production of virgin minerals would create greater incentives for their more efficient use. It could also provide governments with a significant source of revenue.

---

**It is the extraction and processing of minerals, not their use, that poses the greatest threat.**

---

Many technical possibilities exist for using minerals more efficiently. The most obvious is recycling, as there is ample room to increase recycling rates for many metals. In the United States, for instance, only two base metals, aluminum and iron (usually in the form of steel), are recycled at rates exceeding 24 percent. Beyond that, however, even more opportunity lies in making mineral-containing products more durable and repairable. A 1979 study by the U.S. Office of Technology Assessment concluded that reuse, repair, and remanufacturing of metal-containing products were the most promising methods of conserving metals. Governments could promote such practices by requiring manufacturers to offer longer warranties or to take products back at the end of their useful lives. Deposit/refund systems—for items as diverse as beverage containers and automobiles—can encourage consumers to return products for reuse instead of throwing them away.[64]

A particularly promising initiative is that under way by several European auto manufacturers, including BMW, Mercedes-Benz, Peugeot, Renault, Volkswagen/Audi, and Volvo, to make their vehicles entirely and easily recyclable. Engineers at the various firms are designing cars with an eye toward easy disassembly, reuse, and recycling of various parts, and are attempting to minimize the use of nonrecyclable or hazardous materials. The approach could easily be adopted for other products.[65]

Another option is to substitute more benign materials for those whose production is the most environmentally damaging. Such judgments are inherently difficult, since comparison of the environmental impacts of different materials is an inexact science. But some minerals stand out from the crowd. Production of copper, for example, is exceptionally destructive. The use of optical fibers, made of glass, in place of copper communications wires is an encouraging example of a shift to a less-damaging substitute. Fiber optics also offer a much greater information-carrying capacity than copper wire. The large amounts of energy required for aluminum production make it a logical candidate for replacement with other materials in applications where its light weight does not itself save even greater amounts of energy. The energy taxes now proposed as measures to reduce carbon emissions would speed shifts to less energy-intensive minerals and other materials.

More difficult than shifting industrial nations to a minerals-efficient economy will be the search for a path to a sustainable future for developing countries. For those now heavily dependent on mineral exports, a rapid decline in demand could have dire consequences. Development planners need to recognize that mineral projects have generally failed to deliver long-term economic success, and that current trends in minerals markets and use make mining an unpromising sector for future investment. More attention—

and funding—needs to be devoted to diversifying the economies of mineral-producing nations and regions. Industrial nations should consider devoting a substantial share of any taxes levied on virgin minerals to development assistance for those nations. One prerequisite for successfully rehabilitating those economies is relief from the crushing burden of international debt.

The greatest challenge, however, lies in the search for a Third World development strategy that allows poor countries to improve human welfare dramatically without using and discarding hundreds of kilograms of metals and other minerals per person each year. Roughly four fifths of the world now lives in countries that generally have yet to build the roads, bridges, buildings, and other basic infrastructure that provide the operating framework for rich nations' economies. These nations will inevitably need more minerals as their development proceeds.[66]

But basic choices in development plans—in the location, scale, density, and character of urban development, for example, or in the type of transportation systems—could have dramatic impacts on the amount and mix of materials needed, and on the environmental costs of producing them. Development planners should take minerals needs into account, just as they already consider energy use, food production, water use, and so on. The urgency of this final issue cannot be overstated: if more countries follow the development path of the rich industrial nations, world demand for minerals will continue to rise for many years. Given current geographical trends in production, it is the Third World itself that will suffer most of the environmental damage from meeting the demand.

# 8

# Shaping Cities

## *Marcia D. Lowe*

In his 1,000-page tome, *The History of the City*, historian Leonardo Benevolo concludes that the world's foremost urban model is the ancient Greek city, or *polis*. Describing the *polis* as dynamic but stable, in balance with nature, and growing manageably even after reaching a large size, Benevolo writes, "It is for these qualities . . . that the Greek city has always been, and will remain, a valid model for all other urban developments."[1]

But today's cities, hardly emulating their well-planned Greek predecessors, provide neither equilibrium with nature nor stability for their residents. A sprawling Bangkok has devoured some 3,200 hectares of farmland—an area more than half the size of Manhattan—every year for a decade. Parched Las Vegas may soon build a 1,600-kilometer pipe network to mine water from surrounding, ecologically fragile regions. Tens of thousands of poor people in Cairo live in the above-ground burial vaults and graveside shelters of a vast cemetery. Even heavily polluted Athens has little more than a name in common with its exemplary past.[2]

An expanded version of this chapter appeared as Worldwatch Paper 105, *Shaping Cities: The Environmental and Human Dimensions*.

Only one in 10 people lived in cities when this century began; more than half will by the century's end. Today the vast bulk of urban population growth occurs in developing countries. The populations of Third World cities, now doubling every 10–15 years, overwhelm governments' attempts to provide clean water, sewerage, adequate transport, and other basic services. Cities in industrial countries are gaining people much more slowly, yet even as their growth rates slow or core populations decline, these urban areas continue to spread outward. In industrial and developing countries alike, chaotic, uncontrolled urban growth—whether measured in rising numbers or in the amount of space humans spread out upon—draws on ever more land, water, and energy from surrounding regions to meet people's needs.[3]

As a Nigerian tribesman once remarked to a visiting researcher, land belongs to all people—many of whom are dead, a few living, and countless yet unborn. The way cities physically evolve—and the way their development is planned—has profound impacts on human and planetary well-being. Their further growth can either recognize the limits of the natural environment, or it can destroy the resources on which current and future societies depend; it can meet people's needs equitably, or it can enrich some while impoverishing or endangering others. The world needs an urban planning ethic that is sensitive to these environmental and human dimensions.[4]

## URBAN PLANNING AROUND THE GLOBE

Virtually all cities share some land-related concerns, such as congestion and pollution from motor vehicles, a lack of affordable housing, and the cancerous growth of blighted districts. Of course, prescriptions for better urban planning are not the same for all parts of the world. Many land use issues in industrial countries seem mainly concerned with the quality of urban life, and those in Third World cities are often questions of life and death. But all cities, whether surrounded by affluent suburbs or makeshift shantytowns, now need to plan land use far more carefully than in the past—before the developing world's urban crises turn into catastrophes, and the industrial world's problems become issues of survival.

The extent to which cities control the use of land varies widely. Japan and Western Europe have the world's most comprehensive urban land use controls; their cities are generally compact, laid out for efficiency in transport, water and energy use, and building materials. Japan protects farmland with strict zoning and tax policies. Its suburbs are of moderate, not low, density. Much of Japan's urban activity is concentrated in Tokyo and along the dense Tokaido corridor between that city and Osaka. This compact, linear form has allowed great efficiency in transport, including development of the world's first high-speed train, which has been running since 1964. However, the country's 33 million automobiles—nearly twice as many as in all other Asian countries combined—still plague Japanese cities with extreme traffic congestion, especially in the Tokyo area.[5]

Western Europe has a long tradition of actively controlling land use so that the small amount of available space serves the public's interest more than that of private developers. Paris, a city for nearly 2,000 years, has planned and regulated land use since the Middle Ages. Many of England's urban areas, still fulfilling a farsighted decree by Queen Elizabeth I in 1580, are ringed by green belts intended to protect farmland and prevent sprawl. But in postwar decades the automobile has had a profound effect on Europe's compact character, fueling suburbanization. In the fifties and sixties, some older European cities embraced the U.S. model, demolishing corner shops and cafes to make way for urban freeways. Later, planners tried to contain suburbanization by diverting growth into smaller satellite towns. Since the mid-seventies, they have turned their attention to revitalizing shrinking inner cities.[6]

Control of land use in Eastern Europe and the Soviet Union has not been as effective as might be assumed for centrally planned economies. Urban planning there is not well coordinated with economic decisions, and sometimes reflects rivalries among government ministries. Extreme water, air, and soil contamination from poor placement and regulation of polluting industries is a critical concern. Although urban planners in these countries historically have supported public transport and promoted urban densities high enough to make it viable, in recent years land use has become less efficient. Nearly all new housing has sprung up at the edges of cities, with few accompanying shops, jobs, or schools, resulting in excessively long commutes. Ongoing political reform and the creation of market economies pose the risk that the region's cities will become more automobile-oriented, perpetuating the environmentally destructive patterns of western industrial cities.[7]

Among industrial regions, North America and Australia have the weakest planning traditions. Governments on these continents have done relatively little to guide development beyond separating industrial areas from those zoned for commerce and housing. Many have enforced low-density zoning in an effort to curb urban expansion—a move that, ironically, achieves just the opposite. Zoning codes that restrict residential density, usually by requiring each house to occupy its own large lot, have forced development to consume even greater tracts of open space. And to accommodate new, outlying communities, roads have been extended farther outward, attracting even more spread-out growth.[8]

Even older U.S. cities are becoming more dispersed now than in the pre-automobile era. Growth in the New York metropolitan region has turned to sprawl; while population has grown only 5 percent in the past 25 years, the developed area has increased by 61 percent—consuming nearly a quarter of the region's open space, forests, and farmland. Many people move out to the suburbs and exurbs seeking open space and bonds with nature that come only in a rural setting. Yet most of these residents continue to maintain an urban lifestyle—commuting to jobs in the city and demanding urban amenities from a suburban shopping mall near their home. The result is neither urban nor rural living but a destructive compromise that the environment cannot sustain.[9]

Developing countries have the loosest controls over how cities develop. Local governments in Asia, Africa, and Latin America often have neither the authority to guide land use nor the funds to provide basic services. Municipalities are fiscally dependent on central governments, which are themselves struggling under crushing debt burdens. With few exceptions, urban planning is a relatively recent phenomenon in developing countries, even in the capitals. In India, it reportedly began with Delhi's Master Plan in 1962. In Nigeria, the first systematic effort to plan cities did not begin until 1971; the capital, Lagos, still has no designated metropolitan government and no formally defined urban area. The Lagos State Ministry of Works has a Master Plan Unit, but implementation of its strategies is scattered among various other ministries that have their own priorities.[10]

---

**All cities now need to plan land use far more carefully than in the past.**

---

The Third World is burdened by several enormous, rapidly growing cities—including São Paulo, Shanghai, and Mexico City—whose sheer size and instability create problems on an entirely different scale. As early as 1964, researcher Ronald Wraith used a single word to denote these giant cities racked with pollution and rimmed by shantytowns: "Megalopolis—the city running riot with no one able to control it." Since then, megacities have become increasingly characteristic of the developing world. In 1950, only three of the world's 10 largest cities were in the Third World; by 1980, seven of them were there. (See Table 8–1.)[11]

Although skilled land use planning is badly needed in these megacities, its effectiveness is limited in the absence of

**Table 8-1. Population of World's 10 Largest Metropolitan Areas, 1950 and 1980, With Projections for 2000**

| City | 1950 | City | 1980 | City | 2000 |
|---|---|---|---|---|---|
| | (million) | | (million) | | (million) |
| New York | 12.3 | Tokyo | 16.9 | *Mexico City* | *25.6* |
| London | 8.7 | New York | 15.6 | *São Paulo* | *22.1* |
| Tokyo | 6.7 | *Mexico City* | *14.5* | Tokyo | 19.0 |
| Paris | 5.4 | *São Paulo* | *12.1* | *Shanghai* | *17.0* |
| *Shanghai* | *5.3* | *Shanghai* | *11.7* | New York | 16.8 |
| *Buenos Aires* | *5.0* | *Buenos Aires* | *9.9* | *Calcutta* | *15.7* |
| Chicago | 4.9 | Los Angeles | 9.5 | *Bombay* | *15.4* |
| Moscow | 4.8 | *Calcutta* | *9.0* | *Beijing* | *14.0* |
| *Calcutta* | *4.4* | *Beijing* | *9.0* | Los Angeles | 13.9 |
| Los Angeles | 4.0 | *Rio de Janeiro* | *8.8* | *Jakarta* | *13.7* |

SOURCE: United Nations, *World Urbanization Prospects 1990* (New York: 1991).

other kinds of change. One reason is that most of the physical growth takes place in illegal, unplanned squatter settlements, rendering useless even existing mechanisms for guiding land use. Called *favelas* in Brazil, *bidonvilles* in French-speaking West Africa, *ishish* in the Middle East, and *kampungs* in Indonesia, these illegal communities hold 30–60 percent of the population of many Third World cities. The unhealthy conditions in these settlements can only be addressed fully through extensive economic and social reforms that attack the root causes of poverty—not just in cities but also in the rural areas that urban migrants abandon in search of economic opportunities. The effectiveness of land use planning is also limited in the absence of family planning programs. (Only in Africa does migration account for the bulk of today's urban growth; nearly two thirds of the increase in much of Asia and Latin America results from the fertility of people already in cities.) Finally, planners in the Third World's giant cities face colossal environmental problems, from deadly air pollution in Mexico City, to indiscriminate dumping of toxic wastes in Alexandria, to the ac-

tual sinking of cities such as Bangkok, Jakarta, and Shanghai due to the overdrawing of groundwater.[12]

## TRANSPORT'S MISSING LINK

A city's land use defines its transport system more than any traffic planner or engineer can. The pattern of urban development dictates whether people can walk or cycle to work or whether they need to travel dozens of kilometers; it determines whether a new bus or rail line can attract enough riders. In short, a city's transport system functions better if things are closer to home. By failing to see land use planning as a transport strategy, many of the world's cities have allowed the automobile to shape them. Few could foresee that this orientation would plague cities with traffic jams, deadly accidents, noise, and smog, while marginalizing people who do not own cars.

To achieve efficiency in transport, urban areas around the globe need to adopt new land use controls and revise existing ones. But it is important not to confuse planning future growth with attempting to slow or stop it. People in many metropolitan areas, particularly in the United States, have reacted to worsening congestion and loss of open space by starting slow-growth and no-growth movements. Yet it is impossible to halt further development; by prohibiting growth in their own jurisdictions, communities merely shift it to neighboring areas—where controls are looser and more conducive to further sprawl. More important, future development presents an invaluable opportunity to remedy past errors. If cities do not want to be frozen in their current auto-dependent patterns, they need to turn new growth to their advantage by filling in underused space to make the urban area more compact. In sum, communities would do well to focus their attention on controlling the pattern, not the pace, of growth.[13]

Several improvements in the way cities handle land use can reconcile communities' growth and transportation concerns. Antiquated zoning laws, in particular, need updating. In most industrial countries, planners have continued to segregate homes from jobs, shops, and other centers of activity long after the end of the heavy industrial period, when protecting public health required keeping slaughterhouses and smokestacks out of residential areas. Even though most of today's commercial and industrial sites no longer pose health threats, zoning in much of the industrial world still separates different activities. In the United States, the concept of incompatible land uses is absurdly magnified; vast tracts of housing are largely abandoned in daytime, while monolithic commercial districts stand empty at night. Many neighborhoods are little more than throughways for car drivers en route to somewhere else. In some new communities on the fringes of Los Angeles, a third

of commuters travel more than 80 kilometers daily each way.[14]

Unfortunately, most developing countries have imported these compartmentalized zoning laws. Among the most serious repercussions are excessive distances between homes and jobs; for example, many office workers in São Paulo now spend two to three hours commuting each way. Although poorly regulated and heavily polluting industries still predominate in the Third World—making it necessary to separate factories from homes—zoning codes often segregate other, mutually dependent land uses. Many Asian cities were more dynamic and had greater internal variety before they adopted western-style zoning. Throughout Asia, Latin America, and Africa, zoning that isolates activities unduly burdens public transport by creating distances too long for a walk or bicycle ride. As a result, many vital services are well out of reach for the vast majority.[15]

A more rational approach to zoning in both the developing and industrial worlds would be to integrate homes not only with workplaces but with other amenities, so that they are easily accessible by walking, cycling, or public transport. Such reforms ideally would not hamper developers or impose uniformity, but instead would lift restrictions that inhibit mixed use and create unnaturally one-dimensional districts. Zoning laws need to be specific and carefully conceived, however; the real estate market, if left without controls, may fail to mix different land uses sufficiently. Purely market-led development can also accentuate the existing segregation of activities that results from racial and social discrimination.

The key to making integrated zoning work well as a transport strategy is to encourage urban development that is dense enough to promote alternatives to cars. A general guideline is the concentration of people needed to make a public transport system viable: a U.S. setting, for instance, typically requires at least 17 dwellings per hectare in a given area to support reasonably frequent local bus service, 22 dwellings for light rail, and 37 dwellings for an express bus that many passengers can reach on foot. These moderate densities can be reached by mingling clustered, single-family homes with garden apartments and two- to six-story apartment buildings.[16]

It is not too late for well-established cities to improve their land use patterns; dispersed areas can be made more compact by filling in underused space. Even in cities where most areas are overcrowded, a surprising amount of land in other parts is vacant or underused. For example, only about half of the urbanized land in Bogotá is actually developed, suggesting it could be used much more effectively for homes, commercial developments, and parks. Although much underuse of property results from speculation, local governments also frequently hold large amounts of vacant real estate. Surplus government buildings, tax-foreclosed land, and other public holdings often stay idle while growth mushrooms outward at the city's edge.[17]

**In many cities, the most transport-efficient land use pattern combines a dense, well-mixed downtown with several outlying, compact centers of activity.**

One priority for increasing density in residential areas is to allow homeowners to rent out small apartments within their houses. The size of the average household in industrial countries is shrinking steadily as couples have fewer children and as more people choose living ar-

rangements other than the nuclear family. As a result, many homes can accommodate an extra unit in a converted basement, garage, or attic, or even an added story. According to a 1985 estimate, 12–18 million U.S. homes have surplus space that may be suitable for apartments. Local governments in Canada and Europe encourage this as a way to provide needed housing and make better use of space. Most U.S. communities, in contrast, prohibit apartments in houses in single-family zones. In recent years, however, housing-short communities in California, New Jersey, and Massachusetts have changed regulations to promote this arrangement.[18]

Many large cities are finding that the most transport-efficient land use pattern combines a dense, well-mixed downtown with several outlying, compact centers of activity—all linked by an extensive public transport system. This way, people can walk, cycle, and take short public transport trips within a given area, and can reach other areas via express bus or rapid light rail. In a strategy to ease dependence on the automobile, planners in Canadian cities such as Toronto and Vancouver have achieved such a many-centered layout. Each includes a number of high-density, diverse centers focused around public transport links.[19]

In many cities, popular misconceptions about high-density development inhibit adoption of these practical land use patterns. Planners and the public, particularly in North America, often assume that moderate and high-density land uses are synonymous with crime and unhealthy conditions. Yet there is no scientific evidence of such a link. For example, a recent report on the world's 100 largest cities found that Hong Kong—the most densely populated one, with 403 people per hectare—has fewer murders per capita than all but 11 of the other 99. The infant mortality rate there, at 7 deaths per 1,000 live births, is lower than that of all but five other cities. These data, together with the poor scores on crime and public health of several low-density cities, suggest that where high density and crime coincide, other, more powerful forces are at work; there is no inherent relationship between population density and urban social ills.[20]

Similarly, high and moderate urban densities in themselves do not create a harsh physical environment. Copenhagen and Vienna—two cities widely associated with urban charm and livability—each have a relatively high "activity density" (the number of residents and jobs in the city, including both its central business district and outer areas), at 47 and 72 people per hectare respectively. In contrast, low-density cities such as Phoenix (13 people per hectare) often are dominated by unwelcoming, car-oriented commercial strips and vast expanses of concrete and asphalt. With appropriate planning and design, dense urban areas can lend themselves to greater vitality, more inviting spaces, and even higher use of trees and other plants than sprawled tracts typically have.[21]

Beyond mixing activities and enhancing urban density, using land use planning as a transport strategy involves improving the design of streets. A hierarchical street system is most efficient, combining a finely meshed grid of small streets with slightly larger ones and with a few main arterials. Cul-de-sacs, dead ends, and meandering streets—all of which have been popularized to reduce traffic in residential neighborhoods—have only increased auto dependence overall by creating distances too long for walking and making it too difficult for buses to circulate.

Street designs need to take into account the needs of cyclists and pedestrians. All city and suburban streets need sidewalks for people who are on foot. The effectiveness of bicycle paths and lanes depends on their giving cyclists and drivers equal access to various destinations—not, as often happens, relegating cyclists to out-of-the-way routes so that motor vehicles can have free reign. An outstanding example is in the Dutch city of Delft, where a comprehensive cycle network is based on a hierarchical street pattern combining a subdistrict system of bicycle paths and lanes with larger, district- and city-wide networks designed for longer trips.[22]

Many cities are linking stretches of verdant space along rivers, canals, or old rail lines into continuous paths for cycling, horseback riding, jogging, and walking. For urbanites, these "greenways" bring fresh air and nature closer to home. If designed carefully, they also can create corridors for protecting wildlife. In the United States, where greenways in Washington, D.C., Seattle, and other cities have become major routes for bicycle commuters, an estimated 500 new greenway projects (led largely by citizens' groups) are currently in process. Many Dutch, Danish, and German cities and towns are connected with extensive path networks, and footpaths are common in much of Europe. The city of Leicester, England, is planning to convert an abandoned rail line into the Great Central Way, a car-free route that will bisect the entire city from north to south.[23]

One of the most important factors in a city's physical appeal, and in the quality of urban transport, is the amount of space devoted to automobile parking. Zoning and building codes that require extravagant garages or car parks have unintended, negative effects; massive expanses of parking create an intimidating setting and deter pedestrians by increasing the distances between buildings. Moreover, the lure of convenient parking leads many people to choose driving, even where the finest public transport is available. In the United States, minimum parking requirements are particularly lavish—often making new developments devote more space to cars than to the building's actual floor area. Many cities in developing countries also overemphasize parking. In Delhi, the zoning code demands that commercial and civic buildings provide abundant parking at ground level. In Lima, by the early eighties buildings in up to 10 percent of the city's center had been torn down for parking lots.[24]

Nearly as influential as the amount of available parking in determining the attraction of driving is the price drivers pay. Realizing this, many European cities are now capping the amount of parking provided or even banning free parking downtown. Paris plans to remove some 200,000 parking spaces. Geneva prohibits car parking at workplaces in the city's center (motivating commuters to use the excellent public transport system), and Copenhagen bans all on-street parking in the downtown core. Where car parking is provided, it is best placed underground or behind buildings. This saves space, helps keep cities lively and compact, and makes buildings more accessible to people on foot.[25]

Fortunately for the world's polluted, traffic-clogged cities, there are some outstanding models for adopting land use as a transport strategy. These cities owe their success not only to carefully guided growth but also to systematic, coordinated investments in public transport, cycling, and walking. Portland, Oregon, for example, is a rapidly growing city of roughly 500,000 people within a metropolitan area of 1.3 million. Instead of giving in to ever-greater automobile dependence and sprawl, Portland has encircled itself with an Urban Growth Boundary, an invisible line similar to England's green belts, beyond which new development is not allowed. Reinforced by zoning reforms, the Urban Growth Boundary allows Portland to grow quickly but compactly.[26]

In roughly two decades, Portland has successfully fended off sprawl and claimed valuable city space back from the automobile. The city has increased its housing density by encouraging a blend of multi- and single-family homes in pleasant, compact patterns. Its vibrant downtown boasts such green spaces as Tom McCall Waterfront Park, once an expressway, and Pioneer Courthouse Square, formerly a parking lot. City officials welcome new office construction but restrict the amount of accompanying parking. Since the early seventies, the volume of cars entering the downtown has remained the same even though the number of jobs there has increased by 50 percent.[27]

Investments in public transport have also paid off in Portland. A highly popular transit mall reserves an 11-block stretch of two avenues in the commercial district for buses. Today, 43 percent of all Portland's commuters to downtown ride buses and a light rail system, a higher ridership rate than in most other U.S. cities its size. (Seattle, by comparison, has a rate of 38 percent, Denver 29 percent, and Buffalo 25 percent.) The shift to public transport is believed to be partly responsible for dramatic improvements in the air above Portland; the number of air quality violations has dropped from one every three days in the early seventies to zero in 1989.[28]

Under a statewide law enacted in 1973, Oregon requires all cities and counties to create local land use plans that adhere to mandatory state goals, which include open space protection and the setting of urban growth boundaries. A new state Transportation Planning Rule, adopted in 1991, actually requires Portland to consider different land use scenarios when evaluating transport improvement options. Efficient land use continues to hold great promise; according to a 1989 estimate, vacant and underused land in the central city still amounted to nine times the space needed to accommodate Portland's projected growth rate over the next 20 years.[29]

Another successful model is Curitiba, Brazil, a city of about 1.5 million and the capital of the southeastern state of Paraná. By the end of the sixties, Curitiba was going the way of other auto-dominated cities, with severe traffic congestion, sprawl, and a sorely inadequate bus system. In the seventies, a mayor who formerly had headed the municipal planning commission initiated a series of transport and land use changes that have markedly improved the situation. (See Table 8–2.)[30]

Curitiba's transport system is based on express bus lines that run in reserved lanes, interdistrict buses that connect the express routes, and frequent feeder

**Table 8-2. Curitiba, Brazil: Effects of Transport and Land Use Measures Since Mid-Sixties**

| Measures | Effects |
| --- | --- |
| Public transport: Main corridors have an express bus lane; major bus routes have a station every 400 meters; system is faster and cheaper than those of other Brazilian cities | Curitiba's bus system now serves more than 1.3 million passengers daily, 50 times as many as 20 years ago |
| Provisions for pedestrians and cyclists: City has an extensive cycleway network; pedestrians have priority in the downtown; public squares have been improved | Once-declining shopping districts are now robust, lively; the city has more meeting spots in which people can gather |
| Traffic calming: Some streets are closed to autos; in others, speed limits and trees slow car traffic | Curitiba's rate of accidents per vehicle is the lowest in Brazil |
| Land use policies: New development is concentrated in existing urban space instead of sprawling outward; emphasis is on making the best use of developed area | A former gunpowder/munitions storage was turned into a theatre; an old glue factory is now a community center; green area per inhabitant has expanded from 0.5 square meters to today's 50 |
| Careful integration of transport and land use policies: Planners encourage higher densities around major transport corridors, and try to ensure that each area includes a mix of homes, jobs, and services | Gasoline use per vehicle in Curitiba is 30 percent less than in other Brazilian cities its size; people in Curitiba spend about 10 percent of their income on transport, one of the lowest rates in Brazil |

SOURCES: Jaime Lerner, *The Curitiba Mass Transit System* (Washington, D.C.: International Institute for Energy Conservation (IIEC), 1989); Michael Philips, *Energy Conservation Activities in Latin America and the Caribbean* (Washington, D.C.: IIEC, 1990); Charles L. Wright, "A Characteristics Analysis of Non-Motorized Transport," *UMTRI Research Review*, March/April 1990; Christina Lamb, "Brazil City in Vanguard of Fight Against Pollution," *Financial Times*, August 30, 1991.

routes linking neighborhoods to the main system. As an integrated public transport network, this system has received worldwide attention. By closely coordinating land use with the bus system, Curitiba has established strong transport corridors that can be augmented relatively easily to accommodate future growth. For example, the city plans to upgrade some of its more heavily used express bus routes to light rail. As the population and public transport ridership both expand even further, these existing rights-of-way could host a high-capacity rapid rail system if necessary.[31]

One out of five people in Curitiba owns a car—for Brazil, an ownership rate second only to Brasilia's—yet gasoline use per vehicle is 30 percent lower than the average for eight comparable Brazilian cities. Although cities in the poorest developing countries may not be able to replicate Curitiba's high-quality transport system, these guiding concepts provide a sound basis for their future growth. Worldwide, cities at all levels of economic development could draw heavily on Curitiba's experience.[32]

## ROOM ENOUGH FOR ALL

Nearly every urban area has two faces— one well-housed and connected to a variety of services and amenities, and the other, ill-housed and excluded from many such opportunities. Often the disadvantaged are physically isolated. Millions of poor people live in the developing world's squatter settlements, where governments ignore their existence; others are shut out of the industrial world's communities by a lack of affordable housing or appropriate jobs. Concentrated in segregated pockets, poor city dwellers everywhere are burdened with a disproportionate share of urban hazards—ranging from toxic waste dumps to high-speed traffic—because they lack the political power to keep such threats out of their neighborhoods.

Although the most profound of these metropolitan problems are rooted in fundamental social forces such as ethnic and class discrimination, land use in cities and suburbs is also a potent factor. Geographic isolation reinforces deprivation by excluding the poor from services through which they could improve their lives; it separates entire groups from economic and educational opportunities to help themselves out of poverty.

Many localities' land use controls shut out affordable housing. In addition to no-growth measures that push housing prices up as supply cannot fully respond to demand, several other regulations make it uneconomical to build anything other than expensive homes. As noted earlier, some communities limit residential development to single-family homes, requiring each to be built on a spacious lot. And to make developers help pay for accompanying infrastructure, many local governments levy a flat fee on all new housing, regardless of its value. Although builders' fees are useful for discouraging urban sprawl when they are combined with smaller lot sizes and urban growth boundaries, flat charges disproportionately inflate the cost of small homes. Combined with large-lot zoning, such fees can both promote sprawl and discriminate against affordable housing.[33]

Exclusionary land use controls are ostensibly based on concern about exceeding current infrastructure capacity or damaging the environment. But many such regulatory barriers actually stem from communities' efforts to keep out certain groups of people. Local zoning and other land use regulations in the United States, for example, frequently reflect communities' elitism or racial and ethnic prejudice. In 1991, a blue-ribbon commission reported to President Bush that in some areas excessive regulations, often based on this type of exclusionary motivation, add 20–35 percent to the price of a new house—putting most of them far beyond the reach of low- and moderate-income households.[34]

Municipalities can enhance the supply of affordable housing by replacing exclusionary regulations with controls that promote a variety of housing types. In Oregon, Portland has used this strategy successfully. Because of changes in local zoning plans, 54 percent of all recent residential development in the region consists of apartments, duplexes, and other affordable housing, compared with the 30-percent maximum allowed by previous zoning. This policy has helped keep Portland housing prices reasonable, unlike those in other fast-growing cities. Measured in relation to households' income, housing there is two to three times as affordable as in other West Coast cities, such as Seattle, San Jose, San Francisco, and Los Angeles.[35]

Removing exclusionary regulations also improves low-income people's access to other important opportunities. Mixed communities' stronger tax base makes them more able than monolithic low-income and minority ones to offer good schools, libraries, hospitals, and other public services. Their greater economic vitality attracts essential businesses, including grocery stores and banks. The more stable conditions in diverse neighborhoods, by creating a safer environment for investment, reduce the likelihood that minorities and the poor will be denied loans and other financial assistance because they live in areas that lenders consider a financial risk. Well-integrated communities would thus remove a geographic barrier to much-needed financial services.

Greater diversity would also help communities address the increasingly common problem of mismatched housing and job locations. In many urban areas in industrial countries, employment in retail and fast-food businesses is increasingly moving out to the suburbs, leaving disadvantaged inner-city residents with little access to blue-collar jobs that match their skills. The imbalance is particularly manifest in the United States, where workers are unable to follow the flight of jobs to the suburbs because of exclusionary land use controls. Made worse by a lack of adequate public transport for commuting to outlying areas, the mismatch results in unemployment among inner-city residents while suburban employers face a labor shortage. Fully addressing this situation requires not only reforms in land use controls but also the removal of other economic and social barriers, such as discriminatory hiring.[36]

## Local zoning and other land use regulations in the United States frequently reflect communities' racial and ethnic prejudice.

In much of the developing world, where far greater numbers of people lack even rudimentary shelter, a different approach is required to ensure that land use accommodates the urban poor. Faced with high real estate prices and concentrated landownership, people with little or no income have virtually no hope of obtaining land or housing legally. In many cases, even the process of acquiring and using land—quite aside from its price—is unaffordable. A study in Peru, for example, found that it would take a group of low-income families nearly seven years of petitioning and bureaucratic interchanges with government offices to obtain a vacant lot on which to build homes. For each person, the process would cost more than 50 times the minimum monthly wage.[37]

Because the poor can neither afford formal housing nor meet these official requirements, they find informal, creative ways to get shelter. Thus an estimated 70–95 percent of new housing in most Third World cities is unauthorized. The informal route is highly effective; according to the Peru study, the value of illegal housing built in Lima between 1960 and 1984 exceeded $8.3 billion, or 47 times the amount spent by the state on low-income housing.[38]

Most governments in the developing world ignore or harass the settlements they consider illegal, although some tolerate them. A few progressive authorities extend legal tenure to settlements on publicly owned land. Squatter invasions of private land pose obvious tenure conflicts, however. Such disputes can sometimes be resolved through land sharing arrangements between illegal occupants and landowners, in which the inhabitants agree to leave one portion of the disputed area in exchange for the right to buy or lease a smaller portion at an affordable price. Clearly preferable to eviction, landsharing schemes are well established in several countries, including the Philippines and Indonesia.[39]

---

**An estimated 70–95 percent of new housing in most Third World cities is unauthorized.**

---

In industrial as well as developing countries, it is important to increase the supply of land for affordable housing. One way is to release undeveloped and underused public land. Cities can also create land banks of tax-delinquent land. Typically, local governments foreclose on derelict property and sell it—often to speculators who let the land become tax-delinquent again. In land banking, the city can hold such properties and resell them only for socially productive uses. This strategy is especially useful for sparking redevelopment of vacant property in declining inner-city neighborhoods. Applied successfully in several North American cities—including St. Louis, Missouri; Saskatoon, Saskatchewan; and Edmonton, Alberta—land banking not only has increased the supply of affordable residential land, it has also made existing urban space more compact.[40]

Streamlining regulatory requirements can further help cities make the most of underused and vacant land. There is ample room for reform in such procedures in some countries; a recent international survey found, for instance, that getting permits to build a medium-sized factory—a procedure that takes about eight months in Britain, six weeks in Belgium, five weeks in the United States, and four weeks in Canada—may take several years in India. This longer process idles productive land, hinders entrepreneurs, and postpones expansion of the city's tax base.[41]

Among the strategies with the greatest potential for encouraging the productive use of idle land are measures to prevent speculation, whereby landowners in nearly all free-market societies hold property as an investment for future windfall gains rather than putting it to current use. Speculation puts upward pressure on real estate prices and wastes great amounts of urban land.[42]

Several taxation strategies can discourage speculation by making urban land less attractive as an investment vehicle. The Netherlands, Singapore, Sweden, and Taiwan are among the countries in which regulatory and tax discouragements have deterred speculation. One method is to tax vacant or blighted land according to its true worth in the market. Local governments typically assess such properties at far less than the market value, effectively rewarding property owners for keeping land idle. More accurate property assessment, by contrast, encourages redevelopment. For example, after Southfield, Michigan, began in 1963 to assess vacant land at its true market value, new housing and building construction exceeded that in all of Detroit, an adjacent city 30 times its size. Cities can go a step further by taxing vacant land more heavily than developed parcels. It is critically important, however, to combine these tax strategies with clearly defined growth frontiers—such as England's green belts and Portland's Urban Growth Boundary—that contain development within the existing urban area.[43]

Another strategy is to use a differential property tax, levying a higher charge on land than on buildings. This dual approach is now in effect in 15 U.S. cities—mostly in Pennsylvania, which, unlike most other states, has specific "enabling" legislation that allows localities to make such a change. When Pittsburgh introduced a sharply graded dual tax system in 1978, the number of vacant lot sales, new building permits, and new dwellings quickly increased. At the same time, demolitions declined. Cities in Denmark levy land taxes and a separate, lower tax on buildings. The majority of localities in New Zealand have adopted—on the vote of local property holders themselves—land tax systems from which buildings are entirely exempt. And in Australia, most local governments also exclude buildings from property tax. Such strategies would be particularly valuable in East European cities, to ensure that future private development is compact.[44]

For any city to reconcile its two faces requires far more than reforms in land use policy. Racial and class discrimination and income disparities are formidable factors in the exclusion of groups and the decline of central cities. Yet enlightened land use planning can be a powerful check on these forces. As urban planning professor Alan Altshuler of Harvard University has noted, "Even the most 'neutral' planning [is] inescapably political in failing to question, and tending to reinforce, the existing distribution of power and wealth in society."[45]

## HUMANE CITIES

For a strictly human invention, a city can be a harsh place for people. To walk along many urban streets is to brave a gauntlet of noise, smog, and the danger of being struck by a motor vehicle. If poorly planned, city landscapes may offer few glimpses of nature and little relief from relentless concrete and asphalt. Although nearly every city has its own lively districts filled with character and local color, large expanses are devoid of such urban charms. Neighborhoods often have no inviting places for friends to meet or children to play. Veering far from the model of the Greek *polis*, many cities fail to create vibrant public spaces or to include people in the decisions that will shape their own communities.

Making urban areas more humane includes planning the use of street space. In cities all over the world, automobile traffic needs to be held in check. The London Planning Advisory Council concluded in a recent study that traffic restraint is "the only way of improving the environment of central and inner London." Many European cities have redesigned roads in order to "calm" traffic. Typically this entails reduced speed limits and strategically placed trees, bushes, flowerbeds, or play areas along or in the roadway—gentle inducements that make drivers proceed slowly and yield the right-of-way to pedestrians, cyclists, and children at play. Traffic calming is most common in Germany and the Netherlands, and is being applied increasingly to residential streets and main roads throughout northern Europe. It is beginning to catch on in Australian communities and in Japan, in "compromise streets."[46]

Greenery further softens a city's rough edges. Devoting more urban space to trees and other plants can provide habitat for a surprising diversity of birds and other wildlife, giving city dwellers a needed bond with nature. Growing numbers of cities are conserving their remaining wild spaces and creating nature reserves in built-up areas. For example, the Nature Conservancy Council, a central U.K. government agency, now supports city reserve projects in more than 60 urban areas. A share of the funding is specifically aimed at greening inner cities and public housing projects, which typically lack natural amenities.[47]

Communities in many cities use food-growing plots to restore greenery to barren neighborhoods and to supplement the diets and incomes of inner-city residents. Copenhagen's residents cultivate "allotment" gardens at the city's edge, and schoolchildren in the Hague learn to grow vegetables in communal tracts. Urban gardens are common in many East European and Soviet cities. New York has 700–800 community gardens. More than 2 million gardeners in U.S. cities, including many elderly, young, and disabled workers, tend neighborhood plots and solar greenhouses. In a particularly successful gardening project initiated by a regional food giveaway program in Peoria, Illinois, people who used to receive free food are now cultivating vegetables for the same program.[48]

A major obstacle to growing food crops safely in many urban areas is the health threat from air, soil, or water contamination. Areas exposed to industrial emissions or air pollution from heavy traffic are generally inappropriate for growing food. Thoroughly washing grains, fruits, and vegetables may remove airborne pollutants, but not soil- or waterborne lead and other heavy metals that have moved through the plant and concentrated in edible fruit, roots, or leaves. Where agricultural extension is available, people can request a soil test to determine if the plots are safe. In mildly polluted areas, low levels of airborne dust and particulates can be screened by planting trees and other nonfood plants around food crops.[49]

Better planning and design can create city spaces that are friendly and safe enough for people to gather and enjoy themselves. Yet in their attempts to attract people to a given area, planners and designers often repeat familiar mistakes. Urban social critic William Whyte has noted how cities can avoid these pitfalls. To accommodate more people in a congested street, for instance, it is more effective to expand the pedestrian space, not the room given large vehicles carrying one person each. Relegating street vendors to a single area makes less sense than allowing them to space themselves in small, frequent clusters. A park or courtyard is much safer if it is not walled off but rather made visible from the street. Spikes placed on ledges to ward off "undesirables" provide less public security than do comfortable surfaces that invite plenty of people to linger in the same space.[50]

In her 1961 classic, *The Death and Life of Great American Cities*, Jane Jacobs advanced the notion that by providing "eyes on the street," people-filled areas become less vulnerable to crime. She reasoned, "The safety of the street works best, most casually, and with least frequent taint of hostility or suspicion precisely where people are using and enjoying the city streets voluntarily." Compact developments welcome pedestrians and foster conviviality, Jacobs noted. Also important are short city blocks, a diversity of building types and activities, and people of different ages.[51]

Similarly, economic strategies to save central cities can succeed only if new physical developments are attractive and welcoming. Whyte warns against the approach that many of the world's large cities are now taking: building giant, fortress-like complexes that not only do not blend with the city's downtown but that repel the people outside with a solid blank wall facing the street. He notes, for example, that visitors to a new convention center in Houston drive from the freeway to the center's parking garage, walk through enclosed skyways to various offices, shops, hotels, and restaurants, and then drive away, "without ever having to set foot in Houston at all."[52]

One of the most important planning tools for a humane city is a planning process that involves the public. Experience has made abundantly clear the repercussions of imposing land use decisions without community influence or consent. In the worst extreme, insensitive planning can obliterate whole neighborhoods, as happens in slum clearance projects thinly veiled as urban renewal. But even in milder cases, planners can easily err in trying to "clean up" what they view as problems, thus sterilizing a community's natural charm or failing to respect its history and character. A more participatory planning process helps avert such losses, and is likelier to address the specific needs of the elderly, handicapped, children, and other groups.

Neighborhood organizations can provide an effective liaison with the city administration and planning council. In several U.S. cities, including Atlanta, Cincinnati, and Washington, D.C., such groups play a legal role in zoning and other land use decisions. Baltimore gives funding and technical assistance to its neighborhood groups to facilitate their participation in the urban planning process.[53]

Finally, urban land use planning needs to keep up with evolving societies. In many developing countries, particularly in Africa and Latin America, roughly half the low- and moderate-income households seeking shelter in cities in the near future will be headed by single mothers. For these families it will be important to facilitate small-scale commercial work in the home.[54]

In the industrial world, the nuclear family consisting of a commuting father and a mother who stays at home with children is no longer the dominant model. Only 40 percent of households in the United Kingdom are traditional families. In the United States, two-earner families predominate, and single-parent families are the fastest-growing family type. As the makeup of households changes, the need for a different urban environment will be increasingly felt in residential neighborhoods. Land use controls can help cities and suburbs respond to that need by accommodating not only more mingling of homes and jobs but also the encouragement of shared living arrangements for smaller households, the generation of small businesses in homes, and the availability of day care for children and the elderly.[55]

## A Groundwork for Urban Land Use Policy

By all accounts, the growth of cities is an undeniable fact of the future. At current rates of expansion, the world's population will double in 40 years, the urban population will double in 22, and the Third World urban population in 15—with momentous consequences for both human life and the environment. Family planning programs are crucial for slowing urban population increase, particularly in developing countries. Yet the industrial countries' experience demonstrates that even cities with declining populations often commit the transgressions of growth: lacking prudent land use planning, they continue to expand into surrounding regions, squandering natural resources on which future generations depend. In rich and poor countries alike, there is an urgent need to ensure that cities do not further destroy the natural environment and so undermine the human prospect.[56]

**Unlike attempts to slow or stop growth, carefully guided development can make cities better able to meet people's needs.**

That cities will grow does not mean they must inevitably expand into surrounding forests or farmlands. Many have so much underused space that they could develop for decades to come without bulldozing another square meter of undisturbed land. Industrial countries have tremendous scope for making urban growth more compact by establishing green belts and growth boundaries, and by requiring further development to occur only within those lines. In the developing world, great potential for filling in underused space lies in the redistribution of urban landownership, which—particularly in Latin America and Asia—is often extremely skewed. In Greater Bombay, for example, 2,000 hectares of vacant land now owned by a

single family could house most of the city's squatters, slum residents, and sidewalk dwellers.[57]

With land use planning that confines development within existing boundaries, cities can protect both their own future and that of rural areas far beyond their visible reach. Compact growth can conserve energy and protect water resources while arresting destructive sprawl. And unlike attempts to slow or stop growth, carefully guided development can make cities better able to meet people's needs. Prohibiting further development can shut out many groups of people—and by restricting the supply of housing, it tends to inflate the price of homes. More compact growth, in contrast, can help create diverse communities and promote smaller, more affordable housing.

To achieve these goals for cities everywhere, three conditions must be met. First, the general public and decision makers need better access to information about the characteristics of a community's population and the probable consequences of various planning decisions. Second, cities and surrounding areas need a greater degree of regional cooperation to prevent individual localities' land use from producing problems in other jurisdictions. Third, urban areas in virtually all countries need stronger support from their national governments, giving them greater budgetary power to plan their own long-term development strategies.

The first of these imperatives, adequate information, is critical yet often lacking even in the most rudimentary form. Nigeria, the most populous country in sub-Saharan Africa, has not had an official census since 1963. Developing countries seldom have enough information on the age, sex, education, or employment of their populations. Their governments are particularly short of data on fertility, mortality, and migration. Often they also lack clear records concerning who owns what; many cities' land registering systems are so inadequate that when the government itself wants to buy a parcel, it may take several years to find out who owns it. Such information gaps inhibit the efficiency of real estate markets, and form a barrier to the full use of available land.[58]

Information is only effective, however, if planners are trained in how to use it. For instance, responding appropriately to societal changes such as an aging population or a shift to smaller households requires education in the use of demographic data. Similarly, estimating the likely effects of new zoning or other land use controls on property values is difficult without a background in economics and real estate. And foreseeing the probable consequences of various land use changes—from the coastal impacts of beachfront development to the global warming implications of car-dependent suburbs—demands a thorough knowledge of environmental issues.

It is also important that urban planners and elected officials stay up to date on public opinion. Many local authorities resist bold planning decisions because of unfounded fears about public reaction. In a recent survey of German cities, people overwhelmingly favored greater emphasis on public transport even if that meant less support for automobiles. Varying by city size, the extent of popular support for public transport ranged from 95 percent in Berlin to 93 percent in Munich, 88 percent in Hamburg and Düsseldorf, and a low of 58 percent in Troisdorf. Yet a separate poll of local politicians in the Munich area found that most were certain their constituents would favor the car over public transport.[59]

Planners, as well as the general public, could benefit from a fuller grasp of how land use controls work. Although the issues of urban growth and land use controls are widely debated, they are seldom adequately understood. Public campaigns are important for dispelling misconceptions such as the belief that low-density zoning protects open space or that high-density land use is linked to crime and unhealthy conditions. With such information, decision makers and citizens alike are better equipped to calculate the full consequences of their choices. If communities learn to focus on controlling the pattern of growth rather than its amount or pace, they can avoid adopting restrictions that inadvertently worsen problems such as traffic congestion and the lack of affordable housing.

The second precondition of effective urban planning—regional cooperation—can help resolve conflicts between the interests of a particular locality and those of the broader region. For example, many localities, in competing for high tax-yielding development, misuse zoning powers to shut out land uses that yield little tax revenue or require public spending for social services. Such "fiscal" zoning leads communities to exclude low-income housing, leaving neighboring jurisdictions with the burden of providing affordable homes. Fiscal zoning can also accelerate the economic drain from central cities, as suburbs seek to replenish public coffers by establishing massive commercial zones to attract taxpaying businesses.

Cooperation among competing localities is difficult to achieve without specific laws at the state or provincial level. In the United States, such legislation has successfully countered fiscal zoning in Minnesota since 1971. All the localities in the Minneapolis-St. Paul region are required to pool a portion of their commercial and industrial tax base—thus reducing the competition among various communities for commercial and industrial development. The localities put 40 percent of any increases in their business tax proceeds into a pool, which is then distributed throughout the metropolitan region according to each community's population and overall tax base. This system has not only reduced the usual incentives to court the most lucrative land uses throughout the region, it has narrowed the gap between the per-capita tax base of the richest and poorest communities from a ratio of roughly 13 to 1 to a more equitable 4 to 1.[60]

Ideally, state or provincial laws can require each locality's land use to be compatible with specified regional interests but leave the actual planning process up to the local community. In the United States, such legislation has given new force to urban planning in eight states, including Oregon, Florida, and New Jersey. All cities and counties in these states are required to plan their own development according to stipulated goals, such as energy conservation, protection of open space, and provision of affordable housing. These statewide requirements both enhance regional cooperation and give cities the backing they need to apply a comprehensive, long-term vision to their land use planning. In fact, it is largely because of Oregon's land use law—together with the state's efforts to reduce the pressure on small farmers to sell to developers—that the Portland region has been able to increase the density of development and keep urban growth from invading surrounding rural areas.[61]

Finally, effective urban planning cannot be carried out without strong support from national governments. To make wise land use decisions, cities need more generous national funding for infrastructure, education, and social services. Experience in industrial countries has demonstrated that placing the burden of all these costs on property taxes can lead local governments to act irresponsibly—by allowing ecologically de-

structive development of valuable open space, for instance, or excluding low tax-paying land uses such as affordable housing. Deteriorating municipal services, along with failing roads, bridges, and sewerage systems in major urban areas worldwide, testify to the need for giving more money to cities.

At the same time, it is important that such investments not be made at the expense of rural areas or secondary cities. Particularly in the Third World, strong rural development strategies—to create off-farm employment, for example—offer people a vital alternative to migrating to already-overburdened cities. In many developing countries, where the consolidation of population, power, and wealth in capitals and other megacities is extreme, national funding support is crucial for helping secondary urban areas attract some of the urban development now concentrating in the big cities.[62]

To ensure that cities' use of national resources is compatible with sound land use principles, governments can withhold funds from projects that fail to conform to designated standards. Under the U.S. Clean Air Act amendments of 1990, for example, regional transportation plans have to meet specific air quality targets in order to receive federal highway funds. Many metropolitan areas will be able to achieve the needed reductions in emissions only through lower dependence on automobiles. In 1991 the U.S. Congress began considering legislation that would reward states for encouraging urban land use planning as a way to solve transport problems. Under the proposed legislation, states in which the number of vehicle miles travelled per person increased by more than 10 percent would receive a 10-percent cut in their federal highway funds—money that would then go to states where the per capita figure had declined by more than 10 percent.[63]

The world's urban problems help shape people's existence within and outside cities, and can deeply alter the lives of future generations. Land use planning is not sufficient to address these problems, but it is undeniably necessary. There is much to learn from the enduring model of the ancient *polis*, and from the resolve of Athenians who more than two millennia ago undertook this oath: "We will strive for the ideals and sacred things of the city, both alone and with many . . . we will transmit this city not only not less, but greater, better and more beautiful than it was transmitted to us."[64]

# 9

# Creating Sustainable Jobs in Industrial Countries

*Michael Renner*

"Save a Logger. Kill an Owl." exhorts a bumper sticker popular in the U.S. Pacific Northwest, where timber companies have suggested that measures to protect an endangered species from extinction will cost the jobs of tens of thousands of loggers. As the provocative slogan suggests, the northern spotted owl has become a symbol of the seemingly intractable conflict between jobs and environmental protection—and of the larger tensions between the health of the economy and that of the natural world on which it ultimately depends.

For centuries, economy has ruled at the expense of ecology. Global production has depended on the ability to deplete one nonrenewable source after another, to draw down the earth's regenerative capacity, and to treat the world's waterways and atmosphere as mere waste receptacles. Some people assume that the only way to stop this spree of

An expanded version of this chapter appeared as Worldwatch Paper 104, *Jobs in a Sustainable Economy*.

borrowing from the earth is to turn this situation upside down—to sacrifice human well-being on the altar of ecological purity.

But environmental and economic health are interdependent, and one can be pursued without imperiling the other. Contrary to the "jobs versus owls" rhetoric, less damaging ways of producing, consuming, and disposing of goods are completely consistent with the goal of full employment because they tend to be far more labor-intensive. Although there are undoubtedly situations in which new environmental laws throw individual workers out of their jobs, such cases are in fact rare, and often balanced by jobs created in pollution control or in entirely new fields.

The challenge is to create millions of new jobs in areas already plagued by massive unemployment. In industrial countries that have led the assault on the environment and are now faced with leading the rescue, official unemployment figures have grown from 3 percent in the early sixties to 7.5 percent in the late eighties. In a world in which a billion people will be added to the population in the next 12 years, in which industries are in constant flux, and in which international shifts in the jobs market occur quickly and unpredictably, the difficulty of gainfully employing everyone who wants to work can only get worse.[1]

Conventional approaches to economic development—which produce enormous amounts of pollution and consume huge quantities of energy and materials in the pursuit of ever higher rates of economic growth—often fail to deliver one of the most important products of any economy: enough jobs. The dilemma is that achieving anything near full employment would, under such circumstances, require even higher—and utterly unsustainable—levels of growth. This predicament is particularly severe for developing countries, since the resource-intensive or extractive industries on which they depend are likely to decline.[2]

---

**Conventional approaches to economic development often fail to deliver enough jobs.**

---

The most difficult challenge is political. Corporate threats to close down factories often succeed in mobilizing workers and communities to oppose environmental regulations—even though these communities would be among the first to benefit from their implementation. This "job blackmail" makes it harder to forge coalitions between the labor and environmental movements. But the rise of endemic unemployment and the erosion of real wages since the seventies have compelled labor leaders to take a new look at their interests.[3]

Many of them now understand that ecological health and economic well-being are inseparable. On the one hand, the economy cannot depend forever on depleting natural resources, degrading ecosystems, and rendering large areas unfit for habitation. On the other hand, it is hard to see how ecological sustainability can be achieved in the absence of economic well-being. As a report by the United Steelworkers of America put it: "In the long run, the real choice is not jobs or environment. It's both or neither. What kind of jobs will be possible in a world of depleted resources, poisoned water and foul air, a world where ozone depletion and greenhouse warming make it difficult even to survive?"[4]

## RESTRUCTURING THE ECONOMY

If environmental degradation is not to become irreversible, fundamental changes in the way goods are produced, used, and disposed of are unavoidable. A sustainable society will have to give greater emphasis to conservation and efficiency, rely more on renewable energy, and extract nominally renewable resources only to the degree that they can regenerate themselves. It will need to minimize waste, maximize reuse and recycling, avoid the use of hazardous materials, and preserve biodiversity. And it will need to develop more environmentally benign production technologies, and to design products to be more durable and repairable.

As progress is made toward these goals, the worst environmental offenders, including the oil, coal, chemical, and motor vehicle industries, will shrink; some may eventually disappear altogether. In their place, new industries will emerge. Just as automobiles, synthetic chemistry, and throw-away products characterized life during much of the twentieth century, so will the features of an environmentally sustainable economy—energy-efficient appliances and homes, short commutes, bike paths, solar power plants, and recycling centers—reshape life in the twenty-first.

Although such dramatic changes may be hard to imagine, they have ample historical precedent; modern economies are anything but static. From the Industrial Revolution onward, economic activity and employment have continually shifted—from agriculture to manufacturing to services. Among the members of the Organisation for Economic Cooperation and Development (OECD), industrial employment gradually declined from 35 to 30 percent of total employment between 1960 and 1988, agricultural jobs fell from 22 to 8 percent, and service jobs climbed from 43 to 62 percent. The composition of industry itself is continuing to change: in OECD countries, traditional industries such as textiles, iron and steel, and metals processing are declining, while electronics, telecommunications, and biotechnology are gaining. The question is not whether economies will change as a result of environmental concerns, but in what directions they will evolve, what the job prospects will be, and how governments can guide and smooth the process.[5]

Conventional economic theory holds that a dynamic economy sheds jobs in mature industries but creates sufficient new employment in emerging ones. Increasing labor productivity—the ability to make a product with fewer employees—is generally seen as a desirable outcome. Overall, the ranks of the work force have grown because the total volume of goods and services produced has expanded dramatically, offsetting the labor-saving effects of automation. Yet while the microelectronics revolution has spawned whole new industries, it has also reduced the need for labor through-

out the economy. Since the seventies, virtually every country has been struggling with pervasive structural unemployment—and with the unsettling discovery that economic growth is no longer always accompanied by a commensurate increase in the number of jobs. (See Figure 9–1.)[6]

High unemployment stems from the same economic choices that cause industries to destroy the environment. In his 1976 book *The Poverty of Power*, Barry Commoner summarized: "The amount of energy and capital needed to accomplish the same task has increased; the amount of labor used to produce the same output has decreased; the impact on the environment has worsened." The efficiency of industrial energy use has risen 30 percent since 1973, but capital and energy are still being substituted for human labor, which is in chronic surplus.[7]

The U.S. economy epitomizes these trends. Between 1950 and 1986, the output of the U.S. manufacturing sector, adjusted for inflation, more than tripled. But while the amount of energy used also nearly tripled and the quantity of capital (measured by the value of machinery and buildings) increased fourfold, the input of labor (measured by the

Figure 9-1. Rise in GNP and Civilian Employment in the United States, 1950–88

total number of hours worked) rose by only about a third. As a result, the productivities of these inputs—the relative amounts required to produce a particular product—diverged dramatically. While capital productivity remained almost unchanged until 1974 and then fell by almost 20 percent over the next decade, labor productivity increased 2.5-fold.[8]

Five manufacturing industries—primary metals; paper; oil refining; chemicals; and stone, clay, and glass—are notable for their high use of energy and capital and their low labor needs. They are also by far the biggest polluters. Among them, they account for 80–85 percent of both energy use and toxics releases within the U.S. manufacturing sector—but for only 17 percent of its employment. (See Table 9–1.) They use 21 percent of the energy consumed in the U.S. economy as a whole, but provide only 3 percent of the jobs. Similarly, high levels of energy consumption and pollution in the transportation, electric utility, and mining industries are accompanied by low levels of employment.[9]

Polluting industries are thus at best a marginal—and now shrinking—source of jobs. In most countries, the energy and chemical industries each account for less than 3 percent of total employment. Even in the absence of environmental policies, many of these jobs are disappearing due to increased automation.

**Table 9-1. United States: Employment, Pollution, and Energy Use, by Economic Activity, 1987/88**

| Industry | GDP | Employment | Toxics Release | Energy Use |
|---|---|---|---|---|
| | (percent of all manufacturing) | | | |
| Refining and Coal Products | 3.9 | 0.8 | 3.7 | 31.2 |
| Chemicals | 9.0 | 5.5 | 58.4 | 21.2 |
| Primary Metal | 4.3 | 4.0 | 12.5 | 14.0 |
| Paper | 4.6 | 3.6 | 13.6 | 11.5 |
| Food Products | 8.7 | 8.4 | 1.4 | 4.8 |
| Stone, Clay, and Glass | 3.2 | 3.1 | 0.5 | 4.7 |
| Lumber and Wood Products | 3.2 | 3.9 | 0.2 | 2.0 |
| Transportation Equipment | 5.8 | 10.6 | 1.6 | 1.7 |
| Fabricated Metal | 7.1 | 7.4 | 1.5 | 1.7 |
| Nonelectrical Machinery | 9.5 | 10.7 | 0.4 | 1.4 |
| Electrical Machinery | 10.0 | 10.7 | 1.4 | 1.1 |
| Printing and Publishing | 6.8 | 8.0 | 0.3 | 0.6 |
| Other Manufacturing[1] | 23.8 | 23.3 | 4.2 | 4.1 |
| All Manufacturing[2] | 100.0 | 100.0 | 100.0 | 100.0 |

[1]Tobacco, textiles, apparel, furniture and fixtures, rubber and miscellaneous plastics, instruments, leather, and miscellaneous manufacturing.   [2]Columns may not add to 100 due to rounding.
SOURCES: Worldwatch Institute, based on U.S. Department of Commerce, Bureau of the Census, *1987 Census of Manufactures* (Washington, D.C.: U.S. Government Printing Office, 1990); U.S. Department of Energy, Energy Information Administration, *Manufacturing Energy Consumption Survey: Consumption of Energy 1988* (Washington, D.C.: U.S. Government Printing Office, 1991); Environmental Protection Agency, *The Toxics Release Inventory* (Washington, D.C.: U.S. Government Printing Office, 1989).

For example, a quarter of all U.S. refining jobs were eliminated between 1982 and 1990. And despite rising production, U.S. coal mining jobs fell sharply during the eighties, from 250,000 to 150,000. With further gains in labor productivity, additional losses are expected in the nineties. Similar patterns are found in Europe.[10]

Throughout the world, industrial economies and employment are continuing to shift from manufacturing to the service sectors, which consume little energy and are still relatively labor-intensive. Where the bulk of breadwinners were once farmers and factory workers, they are now computer operators, administrators, accountants, and clerks. But services can never entirely replace manufacturing, and the exodus of workers from this sector will not reduce the need for manufactured products. Demand for them will endure, but until manufacturers change their fundamental methods of production, industrial pollution will continue to cripple both people and the environment.

**Many of the industries needed in an environmentally sustainable economy are far more labor-intensive than today's resource-based industries.**

The initial response of government regulators and industry executives to environmental problems was to add pollution control devices to existing plants, and to build waste treatment facilities. Some 75–80 percent of total pollution abatement expenditures in OECD countries—worth at least $200 billion annually—are devoted to such "tailpipe" devices, with the remainder going to preventive measures. Few jobs have been lost as a result of pollution control

regulations. Instead, these outlays created at least 5 million jobs directly and indirectly in the United States and Western Europe.[11]

Yet even sophisticated control equipment can only reduce—never eliminate—industrial pollutants. Confronted with this inherent shortcoming, the world is now being pushed toward more fundamental changes that can prevent pollution rather than just contain it. Improving energy efficiency is one of the most cost-effective strategies. Since the seventies, considerable headway has been made, but the technical opportunities are far from exhausted. And efficiency can be improved not only in specific kinds of machinery, but in consumption patterns. In transportation, for example, switching from cars and trucks to trains will yield large savings, because trains are much more efficient.[12]

Pollution avoidance, as distinguished from control, is catching on in many countries. Governments in Denmark, Finland, France, Germany, the Netherlands, and Norway have begun to encourage the development of "clean" technologies. In the United States, the Environmental Protection Agency (EPA) established an Office of Pollution Prevention in 1987, and 10 states passed laws aimed at reducing toxics use. A growing number of companies are beginning to explore pollution prevention and waste avoidance.[13]

Manufacturing technologies can be modified to reduce waste and eliminate hazardous substances. The resulting savings often make this approach less expensive than installing pollution control equipment. In the electronics industry, for instance, where chlorofluorocarbons have been used extensively to clean soldering debris from circuit boards, more benign water-based alternatives are increasingly used, and manufacturing methods are being revamped so that circuit boards do not need cleaning at all.[14]

Many products are already being replaced by more environmentally benign alternatives. For example, phosphate-free detergents and chlorine-free paper are being introduced in many countries. And biodegradable products are being substituted for synthetic chemical ones. But much greater change lies ahead. Since large amounts of energy and raw materials go into goods production—manufacturing an American car takes about as much energy as the car itself uses in two years of driving—a move away from "planned obsolescence" is essential. And at the end of a product's useful life, recycling and reuse are preferable to the environmentally unsound practices of landfilling and incineration.[15]

Some products are indispensable in a modern society, even though current methods of their production, consumption, or disposal pose environmental problems. But there are other products whose environmental costs are out of all proportion to their utility. For them, the challenge is less to find suitable replacements than to curtail or even ban their use altogether. Much of today's packaging fits that description. In the United States, for example, as much as half of all paper production and nearly a quarter of all plastics sold go into packaging.[16]

As the economy is restructured, employment will be affected in three ways. In some cases, additional jobs will be created—as in the manufacturing of pollution control devices added to existing production equipment. In others, employment will be substituted—as in shifting from fossil fuels to renewables, or from auto manufacturing to rail car manufacturing. In yet other circumstances, jobs may be eliminated without replacement—as, again, when packaging materials are discouraged or banned.

The employment effects will be most noticeable in extractive and basic materials industries and in the regions, like Louisiana, Oregon, or Germany's Ruhr Valley, that depend most on them. Fortunately, many of the industries needed in an environmentally sustainable economy are far more labor-intensive—employing more people per dollar of output—than today's resource-based industries.

The jobs impact of a more sustainable economy will inevitably extend beyond national boundaries. To the extent that countries pursue policies that let them reduce the use of imported energy and materials, exporting nations will suffer adverse economic consequences, particularly if they depend heavily on a single commodity such as oil or bauxite. Even without the adoption of comprehensive environmental policies, developing countries are already confronted with this issue; some of the raw materials they export have been replaced by synthetic substitutes. Ecological and economic sustainability can only be addressed adequately, therefore, if the world community works cooperatively to create new industries that will both enhance the environment and provide millions of rewarding new jobs.

## ENERGY EFFICIENCY AND RENEWABLES

Reduced consumption of fossil fuels is one of the clearest prerequisites of a sustainable energy economy. The combustion of oil and coal on a massive scale makes breathing hazardous in many cities, generates acid rain that decimates crops and forests, and is a principal contributor to global warming. Using energy more efficiently and switching to renewable energy are practical ways of tackling these problems.[17]

Avoiding energy use via improved efficiency is cheaper and creates more jobs than supplying energy from either conventional or renewable energy sources. On the supply side, renewables create more jobs than conventional energy industries because their capital requirements, with the exception of photovoltaic cells, are much more modest and their labor needs greater. Generating 1,000 gigawatt-hours of electricity per year, for example, requires 100 workers in a nuclear power plant and 116 in a coal-fired plant, but 248 workers in a solar thermal facility and 542 on a wind farm.[18]

If the amount of energy required for heating, cooling, transportation, or industrial processes can be reduced by relying more on conservation, the resulting savings can be respent elsewhere in the economy. The same is true if renewable energy systems can be built with lower capital costs than conventional ones. To the extent that such diverted spending goes to areas that are more labor-intensive than conventional energy industries, there will be a further net gain in employment.[19]

**A study in Alaska found that state spending on weatherization creates more jobs per dollar of outlays than any other type of capital project.**

The costs and the energy and labor requirements of alternative energy technologies relative to conventional ones are bound to change. The difference in labor-intensity between fossil and solar technologies may become less pronounced, as equipment for the latter is manufactured in larger batches and the new facilities become more automated. Another important factor is the cost of supplying energy. Wind and solar tech-

nologies are well on the road to becoming cost-competitive. Oil prices are now much lower than in the late seventies and early eighties. But if the growing recognition that the market price for oil does not reflect the enormous environmental damage inflicted by its use leads to the adoption of "green" taxes, oil's cost to consumers will be pushed upward, boosting the outlook for renewables. The European Community proposed in September 1991 that its members put a surcharge of $10 on each barrel of oil by the year 2000, and a $14 tax on an equivalent amount of coal.[20]

Residential weatherization is a particularly labor-intensive process. A study by Steve Colt of the University of Alaska at Anchorage found that state spending on weatherization creates more jobs per dollar of outlays than any other type of capital project—almost three times as many direct jobs as highway construction, for example.[21]

In the United States, New York has spent the most on low-income weatherization. The Center for the Biology of Natural Systems (CBNS) at Queens College, New York City, analyzed the economic impact of the state's Weatherization Assistance Program from 1976 to 1989. As of 1989, a total of 254,000 housing units, or 14 percent of those eligible, had been weatherized. The study estimated that roughly 23,000–30,000 job-years of net employment were generated during that period, or 60–80 jobs per $1 million of expenditure.[22]

Across the United States, 4.2 million low-income households, 19 percent of those eligible, have so far been weatherized. Although New York state is not entirely representative of conditions nationwide, the CBNS findings permit a rough approximation of the number of jobs that could be created if all low-income housing units were weatherized. Keeping in mind that average U.S. weatherization costs per unit are 30 percent lower than in New York, a total of 1.4 million to 1.8 million job-years might be generated. Assuming that similar conditions hold for weatherizing all U.S. households, the total weatherization job potential is 6 million to 7 million job-years.[23]

One of the most comprehensive U.S. studies of the economic impact of a substantial commitment to solar and conservation was prepared in 1979 by Leonard Rodberg for the Joint Economic Committee of the U.S. Congress. Assuming an annual investment of $115 billion (in 1989 dollars), Rodberg found that more than 2 million jobs might have been created in 10 years—a quarter of them in conservation and the rest in solar energy. The decrease in consumption of non-renewable fuels—45 quadrillion Btus less by 1990 than was projected at the time under a business-as-usual approach—would have led to the loss of about 1 million jobs in primary-energy and electricity-generating industries. But respending the associated savings in energy outlays elsewhere in the economy would have brought additional employment gains, for a net increase of almost 3 million jobs as a whole.[24]

More recently, a study was prepared for the Great Lakes Governors to determine the economic effects of increasing the use of biomass energy. In 1985, more than 32,000 people in the Great Lakes states were working directly or indirectly with this energy source. Increasing the use of biomass by 50 percent between 1985 and 1995 would have generated 50,900 new jobs in operations and maintenance, 17,500 in manufacturing and construction of new plants and equipment, and 7,900 through the respending of savings. Taking into account the jobs lost by displacement of fossil fuels, the net gain would still be 42,100 jobs by 1995. The bulk of the increase would be in agriculture, fab-

ricated metal products, and the wholesale and retail trade.[25]

A study prepared in 1985 for the Commission of the European Community (EC) analyzed the employment potential of six energy conservation and renewable energy technologies in Denmark, France, the United Kingdom, and West Germany. It found that some 34 million tons of oil equivalent could be saved and an average of 142,000 job-years gained by the year 2000. Since only six technologies and four out of 12 member countries were included in the study, the authors suggest that a full-fledged conservation and renewables program could yield a minimum of 530,000 job-years for the EC as a whole, or an average of about 3,800 jobs per million tons of oil equivalent of primary energy saved.[26]

Although a shift from fossil fuels to solar energy entails job losses in the former industry, there are overlaps among the kinds of suppliers and skills required. For example, materials needed for the production of solar collectors for space and water heating include glass or plastic for the collector cover; copper, aluminum, and steel for frames and absorber plates; and fiberglass or a rigid foam for insulation. The prospective suppliers are all established industries.[27]

Many of the skills needed for manufacturing solar systems are "similar to those required for conventional construction projects and heating system installation," according to Rodberg. Thus, work opportunities exist for a variety of occupations, including sheet metal workers, carpenters, plumbers, pipefitters, and construction workers.[28]

The economies that would gain the most by boosting efficiency and substituting locally available renewables are those that now depend on imported energy. The losers would be those regions and countries whose economies depend on the export of fossil fuels—mainly in the Middle East. Such countries will need support to broaden their economic base as the world checks its thirst for fossil fuels.[29]

To date, the solar and conservation potential remains largely unfulfilled, though millions of people in developing countries are now employed processing charcoal and other biomass fuels. Unfortunately, low oil prices and a lack of tax incentives and government research and development support have held back the commercial takeoff of many of the renewable industries. U.S. employment in the solar industry, for example, was estimated at only about 20,000 in the mideighties. Nonetheless, many of the renewable energy sources are now poised for rapid growth, propelled by new government policies that take account of their environmental advantages compared with fossil fuels.[30]

## RAILROADS VERSUS HIGHWAYS

Transportation—centered on the use of cars and trucks—is a major user of fossil fuels, and therefore an important source of urban air pollution, acid rain, and global warming. Many nations are awakening to their unhealthy addiction to a mode of transportation that is excessively energy-intensive and polluting. Although recent attempts to mitigate these problems have focused on limited measures such as catalytic converters, alternative fuels, and, to a lesser extent, improved fuel economy, the magnitude of the challenge suggests that a wholesale restructuring of the transportation industry is required to make it sustainable.

The motor vehicle industry is a cornerstone of the modern industrial economy. It contributes almost 7 percent of global economic output and employs more than 4 million people. Automobiles account for about 4 percent of all industrial employment in the United States and Spain, 6 percent in Britain and Canada, 7 percent in Japan, and 8–9 percent in France, Italy, Sweden, and the former West Germany. Vehicle sales continue to grow but, due to automation, employment has expanded much less. For example, sales revenues for West German auto companies more than doubled from 1977 to 1987, but the number of jobs grew by less than one quarter.[31]

Rail systems virtually everywhere have been systematically disadvantaged. Deutsche Bundesbahn, the German federal railway system, has steadily lost ground in both passenger and freight transport. Between 1967 and the late eighties, its share fell from 9 to 6 percent of passenger transportation and from 31 to 22 percent of freight transport. Moreover, the railway's investment in a few high-speed passenger train connections comes increasingly at the expense of maintaining service on lesser routes. In freight transport, this railway system seems destined to become a mere adjunct to trucking. All told, employment has been halved in the postwar period, to the point where schedules often cannot be met and the remaining employees are forced to work overtime. In the former East Germany, similar problems loom as cars and trucks take center stage in the wake of unification. A quarter of the 250,000 rail workers are to be laid off over the next five years.[32]

While the railroads languish, the trucking industry is booming. In western Germany, it has grown nearly fivefold between 1960 and 1988, capturing 56 percent of the country's freight transport. Employment grew almost 50 percent between 1978 and 1989. The trucking boom in Europe is likely to continue for some years, fueled by lowered tariff barriers in the European Community, the opening of commerce with Eastern Europe, and growing adoption of the "just-in-time" system of production, whereby factories rely on frequent, precisely timed deliveries of materials and parts.[33]

Considering the priority accorded cars and trucks, it is not surprising that these industries provide more jobs than public transportation does. Indeed, highway vehicle–related jobs in the former West Germany outnumber rail-related jobs by five to one. (See Table 9–2.) Since the data omit jobs both at supplier firms for rail-vehicle manufacturing and in track construction and maintenance, however, the ratio may actually be closer to three to one. This imbalance is much more severe in the United States, where car reliance is higher, intercity rail transport is mostly limited to freight, and the manufacture of trolleys and subway cars has virtually ceased. And due to rising automation, U.S. freight railroad employment has

been cut almost in half during the past decade.[34]

An environmentally sustainable economy will require a reversal of this still-rising dependence on cars and trucks. For this to happen, rail-based transport will need to be given priority. In some respects, the transportation system of the future will resemble that of 80–100 years ago, before the automotive revolution. It will not be a true return to the past, however, since there are now great opportunities for technological and other improvements.

Although the car and trucking industries employ millions of people, their contribution to the overall job market is not commensurate with their dollar output. German figures show that highway construction generates the fewest jobs of any public infrastructure investment. Spending 1 billion deutsche marks ($580 million) on highways yields only 14,000–19,000 jobs, compared with about 22,000 jobs in railway tracks, or 23,000 in light rail track construction.

**Table 9-2. West Germany: Land Transportation Employment, 1987–89**

| Activity | Jobs | Share[1] |
|---|---|---|
| | (thousand) | (percent) |
| Motor Vehicles | 2,507 | 83 |
|   Manufacturing and Repair of Motor Vehicles[2] | 1,680 | 55 |
|   Automotive Dealers | 300 | 10 |
|   Gasoline Stations and Other Services | 100 | 3 |
|   Truck Freight Transport | 427 | 14 |
| Rail Systems | 523 | 17 |
|   Railway and Light Rail Manufacturing | 100 | 3 |
|   Railways | 277 | 9 |
|   Urban Mass Transit Systems | 146 | 5 |
| Total | 3,030 | 100 |

[1]Totals may not add due to rounding.   [2]Including supplier firms.
SOURCES: Compiled from Markus Hesse and Rainer Lucas, *Verkehrswende. Ökologische und Soziale Orientierungen für die Verkehrswirtschaft,* Schriftenreihe des IÖW 39/90 (Berlin and Wuppertal: Institut für Ökologische Wirtschaftsforschung (IÖW), 1990); Markus Hesse and Rainer Lucas, *Die Beschäftigungspolitische Bedeutung der Verkehrswirtschaft in Nordrhein-Westfalen,* Forschungsprojekt im Auftrag des Instituts für Landes- und Stadtentwicklungsforschung (Berlin and Wuppertal: IÖW, 1990).

Similarly, a 1988 assessment found that the number of jobs created in building urban bike paths compares favorably with that in highway construction.[35]

One of the most important employment questions is the extent to which the skills now used in the automotive industries are adaptable to the operation of rail systems. Markus Hesse and Rainer Lucas of the Institute for Ecological Economics Research in Wuppertal, Germany, conclude that given some overlaps and similarities in skill patterns, the shifts should not be too difficult. Both motor vehicle manufacturing and railroads require a broad distribution of occupations. The skills needed to construct highways, railway tracks, and bike paths—such as engineering, concrete pouring, and trucking—are relatively similar, although workers will need to adapt from one to the other.[36]

At present, a shift from cars and trucks toward railroads, subways, light rail lines, and buses offers alternative job opportunities for at least part of the work force that now manufactures, assembles, operates, or services cars and trucks. In the decades to come, however, a more radical reorientation aimed at reducing overall transportation needs—by redesigning cities, for example, to bring jobs and commercial centers closer to residential centers—and at increasing the share of nonmotorized modes may ultimately mean fewer jobs in transportation. But the latter goal will take longer to achieve, allowing for a relatively smooth transition.[37]

# RECYCLING MATERIALS, RETAINING JOBS

From extraction to processing and disposal, the use of raw materials—wood, metals, and minerals—requires large amounts of water and energy and inflicts immense damage on the environment. But most products can incorporate fewer materials while providing the same services. And instead of designing goods for quick disposal, making them more sturdy allows for their repair and reuse. In short, avoidance is the best strategy for reducing the volume of trash that releases heavy metals, dioxins, furans, and other pollutants into the environment. At the end of a product's useful life, recycling offers the best means of reducing the waste stream and energy needed to manufacture products from virgin materials.[38]

Recycling is already an important source of jobs; it is a more important employer than metal mining in the United States. But no government statistics on recycling jobs are compiled and comparatively little research has been done on the subject. Jim Quigley of the Center for the Biology of Natural Systems has surveyed various recycling operations to determine how much material it takes, per year, to create one job. Assessing programs in several states, he found that recycling programs vary widely in their labor intensity, but generate on average one job for every 465 tons of materials handled annually. Put differently, for each million tons of waste, approximately 2,000 jobs are created. Thus under current conditions—with 13 percent of the 180 million tons of U.S. municipal solid waste recycled in 1988—more than 50,000 people may be employed.[39]

Other studies suggest that the number is even higher. The ALCOA company estimates that at least 30,000 people in the United States are involved in the recycling of aluminum alone—equal to twice the employment in the primary aluminum production industry. And boosting the recycling rate would open up a far larger number of jobs. According to Quigley, increasing the rate to 75 percent could yield some 375,000 jobs in the United States.[40]

Compared with incineration and landfilling, recycling offers more employment and is cheaper, due to its much lower capital requirements. Building waste-burning plants and manufacturing the machinery they use creates more temporary jobs than the more modestly equipped recycling centers do. But recycling offers a large number of permanent jobs in operations and maintenance activities. For each 1 million tons of materials processed, recycling facilities in Vermont, for example, generate 550–2,000 jobs, depending on the kind and size of facility. But for incinerators, the range is 150–1,100 and for landfills, 50–360 jobs. Facilities in New York City are much larger, and the resulting economies of scale mean that more waste is handled per employee than in Vermont. The key results, however, are the same: recycling creates far more jobs than do either landfills or incinerators.[41]

According to Barry Commoner, director of CBNS, an improved materials recovery program could boost the recycling rate in New York City from 18 percent to 75 percent. Pursuing that route instead of burning waste would both save money and create new jobs. At about $500 million, the cost of building an incinerator is three times that of recycling facilities that can handle the same amount of trash. Even a more modest goal—recycling one quarter of the city's waste by April 1994 as mandated by law—would create about 1,400 jobs, or more than four times the number generated if the same volume of waste were incinerated.[42]

While recycling offers large economic benefits, the gain is not without pain. It implies, after all, that fewer raw materials are mined, smelted, and made into products. Recycling aluminum beverage cans, for example, means that less bauxite is needed, with inevitable repercussions in producer countries such as Australia, Jamaica, and Guinea. And there will be fewer jobs in the energy industry, since aluminum recycling saves energy compared with aluminum produced from virgin materials. The same is true for glass recycling, and even more so for reusing a bottle instead of melting it to make new glass. Recycling paper inevitably means less demand for wood pulp, and fewer jobs in logging and paper mills.

---

**At least 30,000 people in the United States are involved in the recycling of aluminum alone.**

---

Still, these losses may not be large, since the energy and wood pulp industries are not big employers. Jim Quigley of CBNS, for example, has calculated that the 3 million tons of waste newspaper recycled in the United States in 1987 (one quarter of the total annual newsprint consumption) may have displaced up to 7,400 jobs. The overall job gains are still likely to outweigh the losses, however. A 1986 West German study, for instance, showed that although increasing the share of throwaway beverage containers from 15 percent to 90 percent would create an additional 15,000–20,000 jobs, the implied abandonment of reusable and recyclable bottles would at the same time cause the loss of 90,000 jobs. Thus the fledgling recycling industry has already become an important employer—and offers the potential for many more jobs in the future.[43]

## FROM LOGGING TO STEWARDSHIP OF FORESTS

In our urban society, the misconstrued conflict between environmental and economic well-being is often fought most bitterly over some of the resources least seen or understood: old-growth forests. Considered major sanctuaries of biodiversity, they have become battlegrounds in a struggle over basic human priorities, as focused in the "owls versus jobs" debate. The passion of environmentalists is fully matched by the ire of loggers who—often rightly—see their livelihoods as threatened.

The spotted owl issue epitomizes some of the distortions that have characterized the "jobs versus environment" debate. The focus on a single endangered species, intrinsically important as it is, has drawn much of the public's attention away from the larger challenge of protecting complex ecosystems that play vital roles in maintaining the health of thousands of other species as well—including our own. Likewise, it overlooks the other benefits of old-growth forests, such as their roles in the purification of water, cleansing of air, prevention of soil erosion, and stabilization of climate—not to mention as recreation sites. At the same time, the focus on lost logging jobs has neglected the larger impacts on employment.

Timber industry officials assert that as many as 150,000 jobs could be lost through implementation of the Thomas Report—the April 1990 recommendation by a task force of government scientists that more than 1.2 million hectares of federal forest land be set aside as protected habitat for the spotted owl. The task force itself, however, estimated the number at 12,000–20,000 jobs. The Forest Service and the Bureau of Land Management (BLM), meanwhile, claim that saving the spotted owl would cost up to

28,000 jobs by the year 2000, including indirect and induced employment. These studies all ignore future job losses that due to mechanization will occur even in the absence of any environmental measures—losses that argue for a broader rethinking of employment in the region. In addition, they fail to account for positive employment effects of old-growth forest protection.[44]

The Pacific Northwest timber industry was shedding jobs well before the spotted owl controversy erupted. And future employment prospects are clouded not so much because of environmental restrictions but because the industry is literally running out of its own resource, because it continues to mechanize its operations, and because it exports large quantities of unprocessed logs.

No more than 10–15 percent of an estimated 6–8 million hectares of original old-growth forest in the Pacific Northwest remains today. Darius Adams of the University of Washington expects timber harvests on public land in the western United States to drop by at least 40 percent by the end of this decade, even without environment-inspired limits. The strong emphasis on short-term profit maximization during the eighties has accelerated the cutting process in some cases. So-called leveraged buyouts that liquidate a company's assets to finance its own takeover have led timber companies to engage in massive clearcutting operations that rapidly exhaust the forest resource base and imperil long-term employment. In the Pacific Northwest, conservationists estimate that at current cutting rates, all old-growth logging will disappear within 20 years.[45]

From 1977 to 1987, logging in Oregon's national forests increased by 16 percent, but timber employment dropped—due to automation—by more than 12,000 jobs, or 15 percent. It took 10 workers to process 1 million board feet of wood in 1977, compared with eight workers 10 years later. Workers who retained their jobs were forced to take pay cuts of up to 25 percent in order to compete with nonunion loggers in the southeastern United States. And future job losses from automation are likely to far exceed any cuts that might result from environmental protection measures. Jeff DeBonis, founder of the Association of Forest Service Employees for Environmental Ethics, argues that "even' if the current, unsustainable level of cut continued for the next 45 years, the Pacific Northwest wood products industry would still lose at least 35,000 jobs" due to mechanization.[46]

Timber companies often find it profitable to export unprocessed logs. In 1988, one quarter of the cut in Oregon and Washington was shipped out in the form of raw logs. Jeff Olson, an economist with the Wilderness Society in Portland, has calculated that the United States loses 4–5 jobs for every 1 million board feet of unprocessed logs exported. A recent Forest Service/BLM report whose publication the Bush administration sought to suppress suggests that a ban on shipping raw logs abroad would generate some 15,000 domestic jobs. Other proponents of such a policy have presented even higher estimates.[47]

If current trends continue, the job outlook for the timber industry will be bleak with or without environmental policies. Yet there is a silver lining: the economy of the Pacific Northwest region is becoming more broadly based and less dependent on timber extraction. Between 1975 and 1987, all other sectors of the economy in that region grew rapidly. As a result, the logging and wood products industries' share of the gross product of Washington and Oregon dropped by half, to 3.5 percent.[48]

Unless displaced loggers and mill workers receive assistance to make the transition to new careers, the availability of jobs in other industries will be of little comfort. While the Pacific Northwest economy as a whole is becoming more diversified, individual communities may have few immediate alternatives. The U.S. Forest Service could alleviate the problem by providing temporary income support for loggers instead of subsidizing logging on federal lands, but the Bush administration opposes any special aid program.[49]

## The economy of the Pacific Northwest region is becoming more broadly based and less dependent on timber extraction.

The Redwood Employee Protection program, set up for workers displaced by the expansion of the Redwood National Park in the late seventies, provided salaries, fringe benefits, pensions, and training and relocation benefits. Its record is mixed, since it failed to bring new jobs to the lumber towns or to initiate any innovative training programs. Richard Kazis and Richard Grossman have commented in *Fear at Work* that "a large number of former lumber-jacks and millworkers have been left to grow hopeless on the government dole." And even though the timber companies had reaped sizable profits, they were not required to contribute anything to the program.[50]

Despite the animosity between loggers and environmentalists, efforts are under way to bridge the gulf of misunderstanding and develop a joint approach. Headwaters, an environmental group based in southern Oregon, hopes to help communities overcome their dependence on extractive resources and adapt to the demands of a sustainable economy. Together with other organizations, it has been working with local union woodworkers to set up two worker-owned companies to seek forest management contracts and to process, ship, and market forest products. They plan to use natural selection methods that allow the harvest of other products besides timber. Similarly, the Labor-Environmental Assessment and Planning Project in Oregon, still in its formative stage, intends to study the implications and feasibility of extensive environmental reclamation and restoration activities.[51]

Reforestation and rehabilitation activities and small-scale logging operations tend to be highly labor-intensive. Additional employment gains might be reaped by reducing the emphasis on cutting trees in favor of other activities such as harvesting fruits, fodder, and medicinal plants.[52]

Making the transition from a purely extractive industry to stewardship requires considerable training and education—and will open up professional opportunities in such areas as silviculture, botany, marketing, planning, and communication. Just what level of cutting is truly sustainable and how many jobs could be secured in the long run remains to be determined. While these tasks may not necessarily present profit-making opportunities for timber companies, they are essential for the survival not just of endangered species like the northern spotted owl, but for the earth as a whole.

## MAKING THE TRANSITION

As the world moves toward an economy that emphasizes reduction in the absolute amounts of materials processed, as well as substitutions in the kinds of materials consumed, profound changes in the job market are inevitable. Any major industrial shift is likely to be painful, and as this one proceeds there is much for policymakers to be concerned about.

The extractive and basic materials industries, in particular, are bound to be hit hard. Whole classes and age groups of workers may find their jobs threatened. Some regions may see their industrial base disappear. And lack of education or training may leave many workers ill equipped to find jobs in a sustainable economy.

A well-planned, forward-looking government policy is thus essential if societies are to ensure that people have rewarding jobs in the future. No longer can they afford to simply leave the jobs question to the "free market," or to maintain the disincentives to job creation that are embodied in many existing policies. New policies are needed to discourage the exploitation of virgin materials, the consumption of nonrenewable sources of energy, and reliance on highly polluting modes of transportation; to encourage the development of nonpolluting manufacturing and processing technologies; and to stimulate the production of more benign and durable goods. Regionally targeted incentives can attract new investment to those areas most affected by the decline or disappearance of heavily polluting industries. Where market forces alone are insufficient, government procurement programs can stir demand for environmentally sound products.

The development of more sustainable industrial policies can also be facilitated by improved public access to information about the environmental impacts of specific corporate activities. Employers faced with environmental regulations may be tempted to use the threat of job layoffs as a cudgel to thwart needed legislation. In the United States, some public "right-to-know" legislation exists, but its scope is limited. The Clean Air and Clean Water acts include provisions that give workers laid off because of employers' compliance with the laws the right to request an EPA investigation—

but only after a factory has been closed. The establishment of corporate eco-audits (detailing environmental impacts of products, production processes, and materials handled) would allow workers and communities to confront environmental job blackmail, and would make it clear to employees and the public alike that economic and environmental health are interdependent.[53]

Although a sustainable economy promises to create a host of new jobs, the transition is likely to be difficult for some industries, regions, and communities. That difficulty will be compounded by the high levels of unemployment that already exist. Automation continues to make many positions obsolete even as millions of young people search for work each year. A variety of measures—restructuring corporate taxes, providing retraining assistance and income support to displaced workers, and sharing work more equitably—could help to smooth the transition.

A restructuring of the tax system could make it more appealing to companies to hire more people rather than install more machines. One proposal envisions a levy on corporate energy use as a financing mechanism for social security funds. The charge would permit a reduction in the social security tax rate, perhaps by as much as one third. For employers, gross wage costs would decline even though net wages remain unaffected. Labor would become relatively less costly, and therefore more attractive to employers. Although labor-saving machinery already installed would not be abandoned, the proposal would help put a brake on future job displacements. A West German proposal estimated that, depending on the size of an energy tax and the degree to which employers rely on overtime, the demand for labor could grow by 750,000 to 1.5 million jobs, or 3–6 percent of the country's total employment in 1988.[54]

Another financial instrument in need of recalibration is the capital depreciation allowance. Setting depreciation schedules is a difficult task because of the varying rates at which different kinds of production equipment wear out. But to the extent that companies are permitted to write off taxes on machinery at a rate faster than it actually wears out, the cost of capital is effectively lowered and the replacement of workers by machines is encouraged.[55]

No matter how many jobs will eventually be created in a sustainable society, there is still a need to help workers who lose their jobs due to the decline of polluting industries. Existing laws provide some training, income support, counseling and placement services, and relocation assistance, but are clearly not equal to the task. U.S. federal outlays for worker retraining have been slashed in half since 1980. In 1987, public spending on employment and training programs, measured as a share of gross domestic product, came to only 0.3 percent in the United States, compared with 0.7 percent in France, Spain, and the United Kingdom, with 1 percent in West Germany, and with 1.7 percent in Sweden.[56]

---

**Although a sustainable economy promises to create new jobs, the transition is likely to be difficult for some industries, regions, and communities.**

---

In the United States, the Oil, Chemical and Atomic Workers Union has proposed the creation of a comprehensive "Superfund for Workers" to provide people displaced from environmentally destructive industries with up to four years of financial support so they could pursue vocational retraining or a career shift through an extended program of study. Possible variations include seed money and other assistance to help start a small business, or partial income supplements for those who seek less well paid work. The annual cost for 1 million workers might come to $40 billion.[57]

Not all of this would be a net addition to public expenditures, however, because funds currently devoted to unemployment compensation and other assistance programs could be marshaled for this purpose—and because a program that enables laid-off workers to rejoin the economy as active participants also adds to tax revenues. A variety of benefits have been proposed in the U.S. Congress for displaced coal miners and loggers, but none of the relief measures have been linked to the tax, investment, and research and development policies needed to bring about the shift toward sustainability.[58]

Considering that large numbers of people are already out of work and more are seeking work for the first time every year, the challenge is not only to create as many rewarding jobs as possible but to share available work more equitably. European trade unions have long championed worktime reductions as a means of providing employment for more people. This could be accomplished by shortening hours, cutting the number of workdays per week, extending vacation time, lowering the retirement age, offering parental leave and sabbaticals for continued education, or experimenting with job-sharing arrangements. Individual countries vary widely in the length of average annual worktime and therefore their potential for reductions.[59]

Although many people prefer to spend less time in the factory or at the office, working fewer hours is often not a practical option for them, because in a commodity-intensive economy they are compelled to seek full-time employment. Yet a key component of sustainability—the production of more-durable goods—provides a crucial underpinning for such a move. When goods do not wear out rapidly, they need not be replaced as frequently. More-durable goods are likely to have higher purchase prices than throwaways, but over time people will spend less on furniture, appliances, and clothing. Hence there is less need for paid work to achieve a given material standard of living.[60]

A more sustainable economy promises great environmental and economic benefits, though the transition will not be without pain. It will produce many losers, particularly among extractive and heavy industries. But the evidence is strong that the winners will outnumber them: more jobs will be created in energy efficiency, recycling, and public transportation than will be lost in the oil and coal industries, car manufacturing, and waste disposal. In fact, automation is a much more important cause of job loss than environmental protection is. And while extractive industries tend to be geographically concentrated, jobs arising out of energy conservation, renewables, and recycling are likely to be more evenly spread.

The overall changes—for industry and for the world—will be profound. Shifting to an environmentally sustainable society is a task equal in its scope, complexity, and ultimate importance to the profound transformations wrought by the Industrial Revolution. What is different now is that humanity already has at its disposal many of the tools and much of the knowledge required to make the transition. It still needs to gather the vision and political will to embrace the policies that can save the planet.

# 10

# Strengthening Global Environmental Governance

## *Hilary F. French*

The past year has been marked by unparalleled activity in environmental diplomacy. Unlike the headline-grabbing proclamations of ecological concern heard from world leaders a few years back, recent efforts have been accompanied by little fanfare. But in negotiations around the globe—from Geneva to Nairobi to Washington—diplomats have started the hard work of forging a global consensus on the pressing environmental issues of our time.

Negotiations are now under way on two major treaties—one to address the accelerating loss of the earth's biological diversity and the other to combat global warming. Discussions have also begun on a statement of principles covering forest management that may lay the groundwork for an actual treaty. Meanwhile, diplomats are busily preparing for the United Nations Conference on Environment and Development (UNCED), dubbed the Earth Summit, to be held in Brazil in June 1992. This meeting, which commemorates the twentieth anniversary of the Stockholm U.N. Conference on the Human Environment, will review all the major environmental and development challenges facing the world community and adopt an action plan on sustainable development.[1]

International cooperation on environmental protection is of course not new: as far back as 1872 Switzerland made an effort to establish a European organization to protect the nesting sites of migratory birds. But the scale of international negotiations is growing rapidly. More than 150 environmental treaties have been adopted, the majority since 1970. They include accords on diverse subjects—including acid rain, ocean pollution, endangered species protection, hazardous wastes export, and the preservation of Antarctica. As the current flurry of diplomatic activity indicates, environmental issues have in the space of a few years become a central feature of international relations. (See Table 10–1.)[2]

At the institutional level, the United Nations Environment Programme (UNEP), created at the 1972 conference

**Table 10-1. Selected Environmental Agreements**

| Agreement | Description |
| --- | --- |
| Convention on Long-Range Transboundary Air Pollution | Adopted in Geneva in 1979, after negotiations under the auspices of the U.N. Economic Commission for Europe. Strengthened joint research and monitoring programs. A July 1985 sulfur dioxide protocol calls for a 30-percent reduction in emissions or their transboundary flows from 1980 levels by 1993. A nitrogen oxides protocol in November 1988 calls for a freeze on emissions at 1987 levels in 1994, as well as further discussions beginning in 1996 aimed at reductions. A volatile organic compounds protocol may have been ready for signing by the end of 1991. |
| London Dumping Convention | Adopted in 1972. Negotiations convened by the U.N. International Maritime Organization; 66 countries are now party to it. Originally outlawed dumping radioactive and other wastes deemed "highly dangerous" into the ocean. A recent amendment outlaws dumping of all forms of industrial waste by 1995; a ban on ocean incineration of wastes is to take effect by the end of 1994. |
| Convention on International Trade in Endangered Species of Wild Flora and Fauna | Adopted in 1973; 108 parties. Aims to protect endangered species by restricting their import and export and trade in products made from them. It prohibits entirely trade in species threatened with extinction, as in the ban on the ivory trade imposed in 1990. |
| Commercial Whaling Ban | A 1982 amendment to the 1946 International Convention for the Regulation of Whaling negotiated by the International Whaling Commission. Bans all commercial whaling. |
| Basel Convention | Adopted in March 1989. Treaty calls for international adherence to "prior informed consent" for hazardous waste export. It has been signed by 53 countries, but ratified by only 13; 20 ratifications are needed before it will be legally binding. |
| Antarctica Treaty | Signed in 1959 by 12 nations. Signatories agreed to put aside conflicting national claims to the continent and jointly manage it "in the interests of all mankind." A 1991 agreement prohibits all mining exploration and development for 50 years and protects wildlife, regulates waste disposal and marine pollution, and provides for increased scientific monitoring of the continent. |

SOURCE: Worldwatch Institute, based on sources documented in endnote 2.

in Stockholm, has worked to catalyze and coordinate environmental action within the United Nations. Many other U.N. agencies and international institutions, including the United Nations Development Programme (UNDP), the In-ternational Fund for Agricultural Development, and the U.N. Population Fund are also involved to some degree in programs promoting sustainable development.[3]

But despite limited advances, the

overall state of the global environment continues to deteriorate at an alarming rate. (See Chapter 1.) Existing treaties are often not adequate to the tasks they are charged with. For some critical environmental threats, no treaty exists at all. UNEP, though it has done a laudable job of fulfilling its limited mandate, does not in its current form have the institutional stature to marshall the needed quantum leap in cooperation.

If the world is to effectively address the pressing environmental problems on the global agenda, stronger international governance will be needed. Countries find themselves simply unable to take effective national action on problems that transcend boundaries. No matter how much nations try to protest, there is no avoiding the fact that national sovereignty—the ability of states to control events within their territory—is undermined in a world where borders are routinely breached by pollution, financial flows, refugees, and other forces. Environmental decisions made in one country also influence others through international trade.[4]

Stronger international governance will evolve both from better utilization of existing mechanisms and, over time, through the development of new ones. But strengthening international institutions does not necessarily imply the creation of one global super agency. Rather, innovations are likely to arise from disparate sources. For instance, the small offices charged with implementing a given treaty often forge valuable new governing techniques. Nongovernmental organizations (NGOs) are also at the forefront of international mobilizing: several, most prominently Friends of the Earth, Greenpeace, and the World Wide Fund for Nature, are far-flung organizations responsive to global constituencies rather than to parochial national interests.

The tasks delegated to international institutions by governments are best limited to those that absolutely require cooperation for resolution. Explained Maurice Strong, Secretary-General of UNCED, in a 1987 speech: "The prime organizing principle for any system of governance should be that responsibility for every activity should be vested in the level closest to the people affected at which it can be managed most effectively." He suggests that by this criteria the number of issues dealt with at the global level would be far more limited than those on the currently overcrowded United Nations agenda.[5]

Though economic and environmental interdependence continue to accelerate, international institutional development is not keeping pace. Existing treaties and institutions represent an embryonic attempt to create the international mechanisms that are required. Governments must use them as a springboard for the more fundamental governance changes that are needed to set the world on a sustainable course.

## GUARDING THE COMMONS

In his seminal 1968 essay "The Tragedy of the Commons," ecologist Garrett Hardin compared the international environmental predicament with the degradation of medieval common grazing lands—individual herders pursued short-term economic gains to the detriment of everyone's long-term future, knowing that one individual's efforts to conserve the resource base would be overwhelmed by the actions of others. Concluded Hardin: "Ruin is the destination toward which all men rush, each pursuing his interest in a society which believes in the freedom of the commons. Freedom in a commons brings ruin to us all."[6]

The world is now facing for the first time the challenge of devising international rules to govern the global commons. One of the most difficult tasks is defining what parts of the planet fall into this category: countries are understandably reluctant to cede sovereignty on what they have long considered national resources. Among the hundreds of treaties that regulate portions of the global commons, two ambitious efforts stand out—the Law of the Sea adopted in 1982 and the Montreal Protocol on ozone depletion, completed in 1987 and revised in 1990. Both offer important lessons for future negotiations.

The Law of the Sea treaty was the product of more than a decade of often contentious negotiations. Coastal nations had been laying ever growing claims to their territorial waters in order to exploit energy reserves, mineral resources, and fisheries. This competed with other interests vital to some countries, including the traditional freedom of the seas for navigation and the need to cooperate in controlling pollution and overfishing.[7]

---

**The Law of the Sea treaty was the product of more than a decade of often contentious negotiations.**

---

The final bargain preserved freedom of navigation subject to some limited controls even within nation's territorial waters—defined as those within 12 miles of their shores. Coastal nations were granted the right to manage all economic activities such as fishing and oil and mineral development within a 200-mile "exclusive economic zone." As a result, coastal and island countries in theory now control access to the resources contained in 40 percent of the ocean,

with just six countries (Australia, Indonesia, Japan, New Zealand, the Soviet Union, and the United States) holding claim to a third of the total. The Law of the Sea has for this reason been called the "greatest territorial grab in history" by some critics. Seen in a more positive light, however, the 200-mile zone was considered essential to conserving and managing fisheries that would otherwise be subject to uncontrolled foreign and domestic harvesting.[8]

In return for recognizing their territorial and economic rights, the treaty obligated coastal nations to protect the marine environments in areas under their control. Those ratifying the convention are expected to participate in treaties aimed at controlling diverse sources of ocean pollution including discharges and runoff from cities and agriculture, ocean dumping of wastes, releases from boats, oil exploration and drilling, mining, and air pollution deposited in the ocean.[9]

The Law of the Sea treaty provided a foundation for eventually negotiating separate agreements under the auspices of the International Maritime Organization and UNEP. To date, international treaties cover ocean dumping, vessel discharges, transportation of oil and hazardous materials, and emergency response to accidents. Four regional agreements cover land-based sources of pollution such as sewage and agricultural runoff. In addition, UNEP has developed an extensive regional seas program that encourages the negotiation of legally binding conventions for these shared resources.[10]

Another major element of the Law of the Sea bargain was an agreement to regard the high seas—outside the 200-mile territorial limit—as the "common heritage of mankind." The only similarly recognized piece of the earth is the continent of Antarctica, which 12 countries agreed to safeguard for the benefit of all humanity under the Antarctica Treaty of 1959.[11]

The Law of the Sea convention also called for the creation of an International Seabed Authority that would cooperatively mine the deep seabed for minerals if it became economically attractive to do so. As part of the bargain, industrial countries agreed to facilitate the transfer of some of the needed mining technology. The treaty provided for a licensing system for private mining activities, with a share of the revenues to go to developing countries in recognition of their stake in the global resource.[12]

At the time, the seabed provisions were hailed by many observers as a historic jump in international cooperation. They were seen by developing countries as a means to move toward a "New International Economic Order" that would lift them out of poverty through mandatory technological and financial transfers. But the seabed provisions proved a major roadblock to worldwide acceptance of the treaty. Several industrial countries refused to sign or ratify the convention unless changes were made in these sections. The position of the U.S. government was the biggest obstacle. Rather than trying to negotiate changes that would make the treaty acceptable, the Reagan administration came to office with an inflexible stance that antagonized many other countries and eliminated any possibility of consensus.[13]

Nearly 10 years after its completion, the treaty has still not entered into force because only 50 of the needed 60 countries have ratified it. Ironically, the seabed mining provisions have proved to be something of a period piece. No deep seabed mining is likely to take place for several decades, at least, and the ocean floor is deemed unlikely to ever become the pot of gold once envisioned. Efforts at the moment are focused on reaching a compromise that would be acceptable

to the holdouts so that the convention can be ratified.[14]

Despite the treaty not being officially implemented, the seemingly endless Law of the Sea negotiations were not in vain. Many treaty provisions are being observed as customary international law around the world, with positive effects on fish stocks, ocean pollution, and freedom of the seas. And the treaty established some useful precedents for future environmental diplomacy. The principle that the ocean is the "common heritage of mankind" may be relevant to other efforts to manage shared resources and territories, and the provision of U.N. financial and technical assistance to help developing countries protect coastal areas established the need to link obligations with the means to meet them, though the amounts provided are far from adequate.[15]

One aspect of the Law of the Sea that will only be put in practice if the treaty enters into force is its pathbreaking dispute settlement provisions. Countries are offered a range of options for settling conflicts. In some instances, national courts have jurisdiction but are required to be open to foreign claims. In other cases, international procedures apply, ranging from informal consultation through binding judicial proceedings. A Tribunal of the Law of the Sea to be set up in Hamburg would be the option of last resort. In a special Seabed Chamber, corporations and individuals would have standing. The distinctive feature of the system is that it is mandatory: parties would be required to accept the judgment of this international court, rather than just having the option of referring disputes to it.[16]

Unlike the somewhat tarnished image of the Law of the Sea, the treaty to protect the ozone layer is widely hailed as a landmark in environmental diplomacy. Evidence mounted in the early eighties that the ozone layer—which protects the earth from harmful ultraviolet radiation that can cause skin cancer, damage marine life, and lower agricultural yields— was being depleted by reactions high in the atmosphere involving chlorine- and bromine-containing industrial chemicals such as chlorofluorocarbons (CFCs) and halons. As a first international step in responding to the threat, 20 nations, including most of the primary CFC-producing countries, signed a convention in Vienna in March 1985. It created a mechanism for cooperation on research and data gathering and included a political commitment to take action at a later date.[17]

In September 1987, after more alarming scientific evidence had been gathered, the Montreal Protocol on Substances that Deplete the Ozone Layer was signed. It called for emissions of CFCs in industrial countries to be cut in half by 1998, and for halon emissions to be frozen at 1986 levels by 1992. Developing countries were granted deferrals to compensate for their low levels of production. The treaty also restricted the purchase of CFCs from nonsignatories to prevent shifts of production in order to escape regulation. The U.S. Environmental Protection Agency (EPA) estimated that the emissions reductions called for by the protocol would prevent 1.2 million cataract cases around the world, 137 million cases of skin cancer, and 27 million skin cancer deaths—a significant achievement by any measure.[18]

In the world of international diplomacy, which moves at a notoriously glacial pace, the ozone negotiations were extraordinarily speedy. In little more than two years the world community had moved from the commitment-free Vienna Convention to a treaty binding countries to a system of international regulation that would affect powerful commercial interests and products widely used in everyday life. Just over a

year after the Montreal Protocol was adopted—on January 1, 1989—it had received enough ratifications to enter into force.[19]

One strength of the protocol was its provision for further updating as new scientific information became available. The ink was barely dry on the treaty when worrisome new evidence did indeed emerge, confirming that ozone depletion was already taking place over the heavily populated northern hemisphere. Furthermore, the new data suggested that the atmospheric models underlying the Montreal Protocol had actually underestimated the pace of depletion— dangerous amounts of ozone loss would occur even if it were fully implemented by all nations.[20]

---

**The single most important ingredient in the ozone treaty's success was the creation of the fund to help developing countries.**

---

Faced with this disturbing information, the parties to the protocol decided to return to the negotiating table. After a series of meetings, 93 nations agreed in June 1990 to stop using CFCs altogether by 2000 and to extend the treaty's provisions to several previously unregulated ozone-depleting chemicals. Developing countries, led by India and China, argued forcefully that it was unfair of industrial countries to expect the Third World to incur the costs of switching to CFC substitutes to solve a problem they had little role in creating. After intensive bargaining and a last-minute policy reversal by the United States, participants agreed to establish a fund of up to $240 million to help developing countries purchase CFC substitutes. China and several other developing countries subsequently ratified the convention, although as of November 1991 India had not.[21]

In *Ozone Diplomacy*, U.S. Chief Negotiator Richard Eliot Benedick distills several "elements of success" from the unusually swift ozone saga. He underscores the important role played by the international scientific community, UNEP, and international NGOs such as Friends of the Earth. They were able to form a consensus for action that transcended parochial national interests. Early U.S. leadership was another important factor. According to Benedick, the United States consistently urged the reluctant Europeans, Japanese, and Soviets to act. He attributes this to an informed and vocal public, which had already succeeded in forcing the passage of the strictest national ozone protection legislation in the world. American industry, in turn, came to favor international regulation over national laws in order to level the global playing field.[22]

Perhaps the single most important ingredient in the treaty's success was the creation of the fund to help developing countries make the transition to CFC substitutes—a lesson that can be applied to treaties on biodiversity and climate and to the Earth Summit. Key developing countries would not have supported the treaty had its call for technical and financial assistance not been backed up in this way. Growing CFC use in nonsignatory nations could then have overwhelmed reductions by treaty signers. Unfortunately, the fund is off to a slow start, with only $22 million of the $53 million pledged for 1991 having been raised as of late September 1991, and no projects under way yet.[23]

Though the ozone agreement is a pinnacle in international environmental diplomacy, the world community cannot afford to become complacent. Indeed, new scientific information released in 1991 showing depletion proceeding twice as fast as expected over parts of the northern hemisphere has spurred a call to revise the treaty once more. Possible steps include accelerating the phaseout of CFCs and more tightly controlling some of the proposed CFC substitutes that, though less damaging, have themselves been identified as ozone depleters. Parties to the treaty are still considering how to ensure that countries honor their commitments, though they have decided that assistance from the ozone fund depends on good-faith efforts to comply with the treaty's terms.[24]

## FORGING STRONGER TREATIES

Weighed against the magnitude of the environmental problems facing the world, the experience to date with global environmental governance is not encouraging. Treaties often take a long time to negotiate, ratify, and enter into force. The need to accommodate the diverse opinions and conditions of more than 100 nations can lead to a least common denominator effect, in which the treaty reflects the desires of the most reluctant party to the negotiations. And even the relatively weak treaties now in force rarely include effective means of ensuring that countries meet their obligations.

The treatymaking process can be improved in a variety of ways. One is to rely on "soft law"—declarations and action plans that do not need to be formally ratified and are not legally binding but that help create an international consensus and lay the groundwork for the negotiation of binding treaties later. This approach has been used successfully in many areas, such as UNEP's regional seas program. The action plan that is to emerge from the Earth Summit, known as Agenda 21, falls into this category.[25]

If a binding treaty is deemed the best route, a variety of models exist. Among international relations specialists, the convention-protocol approach followed in the ozone talks and the comprehensive strategy of the Law of the Sea negotiations are often viewed as competing archetypes. The traditional view cites the relative success of the ozone treaty as a vindication of the step-by-step negotiating method. Although early international discussions on climate change focused on negotiation of a "Law of the Atmosphere" analogous to the Law of the Sea, the proponents of the ozone model triumphed and the discussions are now following the convention-protocol model. To those frustrated with this incremental approach, Richard Benedick points out that "premature insistence on optimal solutions could have the unintended effect of bogging down the negotiations and prolonging the entire process."[26]

**It is important that treaties include provisions to facilitate updating should new scientific information become available.**

But there is also a danger that letting countries sign a framework treaty without requiring them to make any firm promises provides an easy political out that can delay progress toward actual reductions. Notes Jim MacNeill, the former Secretary General of the World Commission on Environment and Development: "An empty framework convention enables our leaders to cop out of these discussions and gain credit for doing so. . . . It is much like an author going to a publisher with a table of contents, asking for an advance and getting it on the promise that his children or grandchildren will write the narrative."[27]

In addition, segmenting a problem into manageable chunks—as protocols do—can reduce the opportunities for imaginative bargaining between countries that might improve the ultimate outcome. James Sebenius of Harvard University's Kennedy School of Government points out that in the climate negotiations a forested country like Brazil might readily agree to an energy efficiency protocol but refuse to sign one on forestry. Similarly, the United States—one of the world's biggest energy consumers—might be willing to commit to a forestry protocol but not an energy one. In this case, little progress would have been made toward actually solving the problem. However, if the two protocols were part of one process, deals could be struck that make it advantageous for each party to take some action in areas it would normally resist. Sebenius argues for a compromise that allows for imaginative bargaining without being so complex as to bring the process to a standstill.[28]

The success of the ozone negotiations can be linked more to factors such as the development of profitable substitutes for CFCs and mounting scientific information about the threat than to its convention-protocol approach. Similarly, the last-minute accession to power of the Reagan administration and the revolutionary nature of some of the provisions of the Law of the Sea probably account more for its failure to enter into force than the treaty's comprehensive nature, so it would be unwise to dismiss it as an altogether faulty model for future negotiations. Both experiences are relevant to the challenges ahead.

Whatever the model, it is important that treaties include provisions to facilitate updating should new scientific information become available or political conditions change in a way that would make a stronger agreement possible. Annexes, for example, can be revised without having to ratify a whole new treaty. Instead, they are automatically binding unless one party to the treaty expressly objects. The decision in 1990 to phase CFCs out entirely required only an adjustment to the Montreal Protocol's annex, which meant that it took effect immediately with no need for a time-consuming ratification process. Another way to speed the process along is to require that any country signing a treaty be bound to accept at least one future protocol. This makes it possible to agree to a treaty expeditiously while still holding the signatory to a concrete obligation. Use of such tools is being considered in the talks on global warming.[29]

An additional approach is to gradually delegate to an international agency the power to set environmental standards. These can then be adapted in response to changing conditions. Already, some technical agencies such as the International Telegraph Union have this power, as does the International Labour Organisation (ILO). The governing bodies charged with implementing some environmental treaties, such as marine pollution accords and the Antarctica Treaty, also have regulatory responsibilities. In some cases, these bodies, which were set up to implement treaties and which are composed of representatives of member states, can agree to set standards by two-thirds majority rather than unanimous vote. This helps overcome the least common denominator problem.[30]

However, the key to the success or failure of most treaties lies not in the negotiation process but in the internal political dynamics of participating nations and in public opinion. Countries or groups of countries often set the ball rolling by making voluntary pledges. An informal "30-percent club" of European countries that committed to a 30-percent reduction in sulfur dioxide emissions

helped create the political will for an acid rain agreement. In the global warming talks, Germany spurred progress by vowing to cut its carbon emissions 25 percent by 2005. This enabled the European Community (EC) to commit to stabilizing carbon emissions by the year 2000, and it put pressure on the United States to follow suit.[31]

On a more negative note, political scientists give the term "blocking coalition" to groups of nations that can prevent the creation of strong treaties because they together account for the preponderance of the problem. Sometimes, only one country—a "veto state"—can scuttle an agreement. Reversals of position by this government can then become critical. With the acid rain issue, for example, Germany was a veto state until a sudden change of heart in response to new scientific information pumped life into long-stalled negotiations. In the bargaining over a ban on commercial whaling, Japan long played this role. In the global warming talks, the United States wears the veto-state mantle. The priority then becomes influencing the veto state or the members of the blocking coalition, through international political persuasion and domestic public pressure.[32]

## IMPROVING COMPLIANCE

Reaching an agreement is only half the battle. The next major challenge is seeing that countries stand by their signatures once a treaty is in effect. Unlike national governments, international agencies do not have police powers. Most treaties do not even stipulate any sanctions. There is a paucity of data on compliance with existing environmental agreements, so nobody really knows to what extent signatories are keeping their word. Although there is no reason to think that countries routinely flout treaty commitments, compliance is clearly less than perfect.[33]

One of the most powerful tools to encourage compliance today is to require collection of data and to give all interested parties free access to the information. Nations are sometimes required to submit detailed annual reports both on data directly relevant to the treaty, such as sulfur dioxide emissions in the case of the acid rain accords, and on actions they have taken to comply. Treaty secretariats, if they have the resources, can keep tabs on compliance and bring breaches to the attention of other governments. If the information is made public, NGOs and others can shine a spotlight on those countries that have not followed through on commitments. But making freedom of environmental information a reality is often a difficult struggle. During the ozone talks, Greenpeace waged a long and only partially successful battle for data to be made publicly available. Under the Antarctic treaties, documents were restricted for a long time and meetings were closed. Only under outside pressure has the veil of secrecy recently begun to lift.[34]

With most environmental treaties, the requirements for data reporting and monitoring are perfunctory at best. But there are several international institutions outside the environmental realm that take this job more seriously. The U.N. and European Commissions on Human Rights have powers to monitor compliance and to demand explanations from signatories for reported lapses. The International Labour Organisation also keeps tabs on whether members are following through on their obligations. Under a two-stage process, initial pressure is often enough to bring a state into line. Both management and labor actually form part of the governing body of the ILO through a unique tripartite sys-

tem in which these groups share equal standing with governments. The Human Rights Commissions and the ILO rely in no small measure on input from NGOs for identifying violators.[35]

In some cases, on-the-ground monitoring and inspections may be necessary to ensure that governments are keeping their word. This is particularly the case for agreements that cover economically important activities: countries will not want to take on international commitments that might affect their economic position unless they are certain that everyone is playing by the same rules.

In one example of an innovative approach, satellite monitoring is being used to enforce compliance with bilateral agreements covering the use of driftnets in the Pacific Ocean between the United States and Japan, South Korea, and Taiwan. Once the United States detects a possible violator, coast guard officials are allowed to board the suspicious vessel and detain it if necessary until the appropriate national authority arrives on the scene. The International Atomic Energy Agency also conducts inspections under the Nuclear Non-Proliferation Treaty to ensure that material from civilian nuclear power plants is not being diverted toward military ends. But the 1991 discovery that Iraq, a treaty signatory, was well on its way to developing a bomb despite the inspections demonstrates the need to strengthen the system—possibly by providing for unannounced visits. Recent arms control treaties' provisions for on-site inspections have also broken new ground in this area that may one day prove helpful to international environmental agreements.[36]

Once a violator is identified, there must be some means of taking that government to task. The International Court of Justice (the World Court) at the Hague could be an important instrument if nations used it as originally intended. Most treaties provide for voluntary rather than mandatory use of the World Court to resolve disputes involving international obligations, and most nations have not agreed to have disputes against them heard at the World Court without their consent. Granting the Court more automatic jurisdiction and giving NGOs and international organizations the right to initiate suits would markedly improve its usefulness. Under these circumstances, enough cases might even be brought to merit the creation of a special environmental chamber. The European Community has demonstrated the utility of an international judiciary. Countries suspected of violating EC laws—environmental and otherwise—are brought before the European Court. Though it does not yet have the power to impose sanctions, the public shaming resulting from a negative ruling is often sufficient to get the offending government to change its ways.[37]

Occasionally, sanctions are needed to spur compliance with an environmental treaty. Short of military force, one of the most practical options is trade sanctions, which are being turned to with growing frequency. An international ban on the purchase of wildlife products from Thailand was recently imposed by countries party to the Convention on Internatonal Trade in Endangered Species of Wild Flora and Fauna, for example, on the grounds that illegal traders were shipping their goods through that country. An early 1991 report from the U.S. International Trade Commission identifies 19 international environmental agreements that use some form of trade sanction to improve compliance.[38]

Environmentalists are concerned that using sanctions for this purpose will be restricted by trade bodies such as the General Agreement on Tariffs and Trade (GATT). A September 1991 ruling of a GATT dispute resolution panel

heightened their fears. The group upheld a Mexican charge that a U.S. embargo on Mexican tuna caught in ways that kill more dolphins than U.S. fishers are allowed to violated GATT rules. Consideration of the ruling by the full GATT General Council has been deferred by joint agreement of the United States and Mexico, so the final outcome is not clear. Yet the ruling itself was a clear signal that GATT must be reformed to recognize explicitly the legitimate and important role of sanctions in enforcing environmental treaties.[39]

Effective environmental agreements need to include carrots as well as sticks. Indeed, in many instances sanctions are inappropriate, as the problem is not so much a lack of desire to comply as an inability to, given the shortages of investment capital and access to environmentally beneficial technologies in poorer nations.

---

**Effective environmental agreements need to include carrots as well as sticks.**

---

Although everyone recognizes the need for technology transfer, actually accomplishing it can be difficult. A primary problem is that patents in industrial countries are often held in private hands, making it difficult for governments to transfer them on noncommercial terms. In most negotiations, such as those over ozone and climate change, developing countries have argued that industrial countries must find ways around this problem. Yet industrial countries maintain that patent protection (a form of intellectual property rights) is needed to give the private sector incentive to develop new technologies. Given this conundrum, industrial countries are emphasizing that many useful technologies are publicly held. What is needed in these cases is facilitating information exchange and cooperation between those in control of technologies and those in need of them.[40]

In the biodiversity negotiations, the intellectual property rights and technology transfer issues are being raised with an added twist. In this case, developing countries are seeking legal recognition of their rights to indigenous knowledge of the attributes of local plant and animal varieties. The Third World argues that if they permit genetic materials to be sent North, then biotechnologies should be transferred South in exchange. At the very least, they are pushing for some form of compensation for the profits that northern pharmaceutical and seed companies make using the South's biological riches. (See Chapter 2.)[41]

Whatever the treaty, one of the most practical means of accomplishing technology transfers and helping developing countries to cover other costs incurred by treaty obligations is to create an international fund. Developing countries can then purchase either the needed products directly or the licenses to manufacture them domestically. The ozone fund has paved the way. Though there is wide recognition that similar arrangements will be needed for future treaties, industrial-country reluctance to commit to adequate sums is proving a major sticking point in the negotiations on biodiversity, global warming, and the Earth Summit's Agenda 21. It was also one of the reasons that plans for a forest treaty have been put on a back burner.[42]

One promising development is the creation of the $1.5-billion Global Environment Facility (GEF) to help finance environmental projects in developing countries. The fund is under the joint management of the World Bank, UNEP, and UNDP. It will concentrate on projects to slow global warming, preserve biodiversity, protect international waters, and combat ozone depletion. Industrial countries look to it as the logical institution to manage future trust funds created under any new treaties, an arrangement now being considered for the ozone fund.[43]

But developing countries would prefer any "Green Funds" to be independent of the World Bank, which they perceive to be in the pocket of the industrial world. Even some northern countries are beginning to acknowledge the need to develop more democratic decision making procedures for the fund that would give southern countries more control. If it is to be effective, the GEF will also need to overcome the World Bank's reputation for secrecy and its penchant for large development projects that do not involve local people in their design or implementation.[44]

Beyond specific environmental funds, paving the way for developing-country participation in international environmental treaties will require deeper economic reforms such as debt relief, the reduction of trade barriers, and poverty alleviation so that the countries are able to pay attention to longer-term environmental concerns. Without these measures, developing countries may find themselves simply unable to meet their international commitments.[45]

## REGULATING THE INTERNATIONAL MARKETPLACE

Air and water are not the only channels for pollution to cross national boundaries: the global economy has a similar effect. Rapidly growing world trade and the location of factories owned by multinational corporations also diminish national control over environmental quality. The globalization of the economy has meant that a growing amount of environmental governance is now taking place through the back door, via international trade organizations.

One way in which the global economy transmits environmental problems around the world is through the export of hazardous waste and products. A series of highly publicized waste export incidents in 1988 brought attention to the waste trade. For example, the saga of the *Khian Sea*'s round-the-world tour in search of a dumping ground for ash from Philadelphia's waste incinerator grabbed headlines for several months. Greenpeace estimates that at least 10 million tons of waste have been exported to Eastern Europe or developing countries since 1986. The pesticide trade is also a concern. According to the U.S. General Accounting Office, about 25 percent of the 180,000–270,000 tons of pesticides that the United States exports each year are either banned or restricted for use at home.[46]

The international community has moved to regulate this toxic trade by requiring "prior informed consent," meaning that a country planning such exports has to obtain the permission of the receiving country before a shipment can proceed. Some countries and regional agreements ban this trade outright rather than regulate it. Although exporting countries have argued that bans violate the "sovereign" right of the receiving country to decide for itself if it wishes to accept a shipment, it is the developing countries most often at the receiving end that generally prefer bans. This is apparently one right that the Third World feels it can do without.[47]

In the most extreme form of dangerous exports, whole industries sometimes move to parts of the world where environmental regulations are relatively lenient. Products can be shipped back to the head office's home country, meaning that consumers get the benefit of the product while shifting the environmental costs onto others. In some cases, manufacturers who stay put and comply with domestic environmental laws can find themselves at a competitive disadvantage.[48]

---

**A growing amount of environmental governance is now taking place through the back door, via international trade organizations.**

---

H. Jeffrey Leonard, President of the private Global Environment Fund, found in a detailed examination of location decisions that there has been no wholesale exodus of industry to developing countries in response to stricter environmental legislation at home. Flight has occurred, however, in the case of some very hazardous industries, including asbestos, benzidine dyes, a few pesticides, and some mineral-processing companies. Leonard also found that some countries—including Ireland, Mexico, Romania, and Spain—deliberately kept environmental standards lenient to try to attract foreign investment. Even when firms relocate in search of cheap labor, they can take advantage of lax environmental regulations to cut costs even further.[49]

Patterns of timber harvesting have also shifted in response to new environmental laws. When Thailand announced a much lauded policy to ban commercial logging in 1989, it took an important step toward preserving its own forests. But the domestic logging industry simply turned to neighboring Laos and Myanmar, where deforestation is also occurring at a rapid rate. Similarly, Japan has limited the logging of its own forests, but imports large quantities of tropical timber from neighboring Southeast Asia.[50]

The question of how to control environmentally damaging trade is a difficult one. To discourage hazardous exports, industrial countries could act unilaterally and require firms operating overseas to meet domestic standards. Although some companies are doing this on a voluntary basis, no country requires it as a matter of government policy. However, Japan's Ministry of International Trade and Industry is considering instituting such a policy.[51]

A second option is to impose an import duty on products made in factories with lax environmental standards. By one interpretation, this would simply be a means of internalizing pollution costs into the market price of the product. This would prevent an exporting country from profiting from a hidden subsidy in avoided pollution control costs, in effect "ecological dumping." But developing countries—bitter from long experience with trade barriers to their products erected by industrial countries—perceive these levies as thinly disguised protectionism. GATT agrees with the developing countries on this point and forbids such levies.[52]

A fairer way to prevent pollution export while still ensuring free trade would be to develop international standards that would both create a level playing field and guarantee a high level of environmental protection. This idea has been raised several times over the years, but faces many political hurdles: nations are reluctant to relinquish this kind of regulatory power to an international agency, developing countries do not want to be saddled with large pollution control costs, and environmentalists fear that any agreed legislation would reflect the least common denominator.[53]

Still, free trade bodies are playing a growing role in the negotiation of international environmental standards. The trend is most pronounced in the European Community, which has promulgated hundreds of common environmental laws since the early seventies. To prevent a least common denominator effect, countries are allowed under the EC's constitution to go beyond the common standard and enact stricter domestic measures if they wish. Some ambiguities in the Community's founding Treaty of Rome, however, left environmentalists concerned that countries wanting to impose domestic product standards that impede free trade would be charged with violating EC rules.[54]

## GATT is in need of an overhaul in order to inject some environmental sensibilities into it.

A 1988 ruling of the European Court of Justice helped allay these fears. The United Kingdom and a coalition of beer manufacturers had brought suit against Denmark, claiming that a law outlawing the use of cans for beer and soft drinks and requiring that Danish bottles be returnable was a disguised attempt to protect Denmark's beer industry. The Court ruled that the returnable bottle law did indeed constitute a barrier to trade, but it upheld the main provision anyway, finding that the law's environmental benefits in saved energy and reduced waste justified a minor constraint on trade. The ruling established that EC members may enact environmental regulations that impede free trade, so long as protecting the environment rather than domestic industries is the goal of the legislation. An important precedent for future disputes has been set, though there is still considerable room for disagreement over which motivation weighs heaviest in a policymaker's mind.[55]

Similar issues are being raised in the negotiations now under way for a U.S.-Mexico free trade agreement. Fearing that free trade considerations could require lowering U.S. standards to Mexican levels, U.S. environmental groups and Congress forced the Bush administration in May 1991 to ensure that no U.S. environmental laws will be loosened. In addition, the administration agreed to develop with Mexico an environmental plan that will in theory strengthen standards and enforcement at Mexican plants just across the border in order to preclude an investment boom in hazardous industries there. But a draft plan issued in August is weak on funding commitments and enforcement provisions, and the administration is under pressure to revise it substantially.[56]

There is growing recognition that GATT itself is in need of an overhaul in order to inject some environmental sensibilities into it. Created to guarantee free trade after World War II, the treaty clearly does not reflect adequately the growing importance of environmental matters on the international agenda. There have been calls from several quarters for the negotiation of a GATT environmental code that would stipulate when environmental concerns might take precedence over the treaty's free trade mission. A moribund GATT working group on the relationship between trade and the environment is being reactivated to discuss these matters. Over the course of time, GATT may be a forum from which common, or at least comparable, environmental standards will emerge. But reaching a global consensus on such standards will be much more difficult than in bilateral and regional agreements, since it will involve some 100 countries at different stages of economic development and with varying levels of commitment to environmental protection.[57]

# TOWARD EFFECTIVE GLOBAL ENVIRONMENTAL GOVERNANCE

Central to the task of strengthening global environmental governance is reform of the vast United Nations system. Created after World War II, the organization reflects the priorities and power structures of that era. If it is to respond effectively to global environmental threats, far-reaching changes will be required.

In the spring of 1989, 17 Heads of State signed a revolutionary though little-noticed document entitled the Declaration of the Hague that provided some indication of the magnitude of the needed institutional innovations. These leaders of countries as varied as Brazil, France, India, Japan, and West Germany agreed that the problems of ozone depletion and global warming required the creation of a new or newly strengthened institution within the U.N. system that would be empowered to take decisions "even if, on occasion, unanimous agreement has not been achieved." This body would be able to impose penalties for violations of its decisions. Disputes would be referred to the World Court for a binding settlement. Said Prime Minister Gro Harlem Brundtland of Norway about the declaration: "The principles we endorsed were radical, but any approach which is less ambitious would not serve us."[58]

The Hague Declaration is revolutionary because it goes beyond existing concepts of international law, which are based on the notion of a compact between sovereign states that cannot be bound to an international agreement without their express consent. But in a world with porous borders, countries are increasingly unable to influence events within their own boundaries. And the treaty system now in place is unable to solve the problems, given its slow pace and the ability of a country that causes a large share of the problem either to not participate or to drag others down to the lowest common denominator. The Hague signatories decided that when it comes to the global environment, sovereignty must be "pooled" if it is to be exercised.[59]

Nearly three years later, the Hague Declaration has slipped from sight. Its primary promoters, the Heads of State of France, the Netherlands, and Norway, may simply have given up on the idea in the face of inevitable resistance from the United States and the Soviet Union, which were not invited to the conference out of fear they would scuttle the deal. Overcoming the old rule of unanimous consent of states would, after all, require the very unanimity the Declaration itself was designed to overcome—an international relations chicken-and-egg syndrome. Still, more than 30 nations eventually signed the Declaration. It thus represents the achievement of a remarkable degree of consensus on what must ultimately be done to save the planet.[60]

Though the Hague Declaration is no longer a live proposal, it is widely recognized that some reform of international environmental institutions is needed. A number of proposals have been put forth by both governments and private groups, many of them in preparation for the Earth Summit. They range from relatively limited proposals, such as strengthening UNEP, to far more ambitious ideas such as creating an environmental security council. (See Table 10–2). The goal of many of the proposals is to merge the U.N.'s environment and development capacities so that the linkages between them are recognized, and sustainable development is promoted. Although it is difficult at the time of this writing, in November 1991, to know what will happen at the Earth Summit in Brazil, the prevailing view is that

any reforms agreed to there will be primarily limited to existing institutions.[61]

UNEP is a prime candidate for reform. Though it is widely acknowledged to have done a good job with the minimal resources the international community has put at its disposal, its limited budget—until recently smaller than that of some U.S. nongovernmental environmental groups—is pitiful given the size of the task. An additional problem is UNEP's somewhat marginal position within the United Nations. Though it is charged with coordinating the system's response to environmental issues, it has little ability to influence the programs of other agencies with much larger budgets. Not being a specialized agency, it has no regulatory powers and limited programmatic activities.[62]

There is wide agreement that UNEP should be strengthened, but no consensus exists on how to do it. Some countries favor narrowing its priorities and focusing its efforts on those things they perceive it does best, such as data gathering and facilitating treaty negotiation. Others favor upgrading it to a specialized agency. At the very least, UNEP's budget is increasing. The organization's governing council (composed of contributing countries) recently approved a $150-million budget for 1992, up from $59 million in 1989. The council agreed to work toward further increases in the future.[63]

It is also likely that some effort to better coordinate U.N. agency sustainable development programs will emerge from the conference in Brazil. The United States has proposed reviving a moribund environmental coordination board composed of high-level representatives of relevant specialized agencies, particulary UNEP and UNDP. A proposal to create a sustainable development commission consisting of senior government officials to review environment and development activities of the

**Table 10-2. Selected Proposals for Reforming the U.N. System to Incorporate Environmental Issues**

| Proposal | Description |
| --- | --- |
| Expand Role of Security Council | Would give Security Council chief jurisdiction over environmental problems that have security implications. |
| Create Environmental Security Council | Would provide a new body to deal specifically with environmental emergencies and their long-term consequences. |
| Create New U.N. General Assembly Committee | Would deal specifically with environmental and sustainable development issues. |
| Transform the Trusteeship Council | Would designate certain global resources (such as the Amazon forest) as "biosphere trusts." In return for meeting standards proposed by the Council, administering country would receive debt relief or some other payment through the U.N. system. |
| Strengthen Economic and Social Council | Would transform ECOSOC into central U.N. organ for in-depth environmental policy discussions and promotion of sustainable development. |
| Create Sustainable Development Commission | Based on model of Human Rights Commission, would meet annually to review implementation of decisions of UNCED. Goal would be to provide more accountability on part of U.N. agencies and governments before other governments and nongovernmental groups. |
| Create New High-Level Coordinating Mechanism | Would review programs of all U.N. agencies and recommend how they could best contribute to sustainable development goals. |
| Strengthen UNEP | Would either focus efforts on its existing strengths, such as information collection and dissemination programs, and correspondingly expand cooperative activities with UNDP (such as the Global Environment Facility), or broaden UNEP's mandate and elevate it to a specialized agency. |
| Create Green Peacekeeping Force | Would establish U.N. force that would be available to assist on site of an environmental disaster. |

SOURCE: Adapted from Patricia A. Bliss-Guest, U.S. Council on Environmental Quality, "Proposals for Institutional Reform of the UN System to Promote Sustainable Development Policies," presented at Twentieth Annual Amercian Bar Association Conference on the Environment, Warrenton, Va., May 18, 1991.

international system and monitor implementation of Agenda 21 throughout the U.N. system is also being seriously considered.[64]

Events in Brazil will lay the groundwork for a more ambitious look at United Nations reform proposed for 1995. An independent group of current and past world leaders including Willy Brandt, Jimmy Carter, Václav Havel, Julius Nyerere, and Eduard Shevardnadze has called for a World Summit on Global Governance to be held that year—the fiftieth anniversary of the founding of the United Nations. In their statement, called the Stockholm Initiative, they called for the summit to reexamine the organization's structure and operating procedures in light of altered world priorities and conditions since 1945. Decisions taken in 1995 would undoubtedly affect the way the United Nations handles environmental matters.[65]

For instance, the composition of the Security Council would likely be reviewed. Its current permanent membership of the five post–World War II powers is hardly representative of today's world community. Only when the Council has broader representation can it seriously be considered as a forum where international environmental conflicts might be addressed. Logical candidates for permanent Security Council seats include the European Community, India, and Japan. The 1995 summit would also likely reconsider the requirement that decisions be made by unanimous vote in the Security Council, giving each permanent member a veto. Changing this would represent a fundamental transformation of international law on a par with that envisioned by the Hague Declaration.[66]

The role of the Economic and Social Council (ECOSOC) would also probably be reconsidered at the 1995 Summit, if not before then by the General Assembly. ECOSOC was originally intended to coordinate the far-flung U.N. system's activities in all areas not pertaining to military security. It would in theory be a logical place to handle sustainable development issues. But a continually expanding membership and a lack of any real authority over the U.N. specialized agencies has hamstrung the council. To resuscitate it, the United Nations Association–USA proposes creating a small board composed of high-level government representatives who would oversee the work of the unwieldy body. It would include the major states of each region and a representative group of smaller countries, and have some measure of real authority over U.N. specialized agencies.[67]

**Events in Brazil will lay the groundwork for a more ambitious look at United Nations reform proposed for 1995.**

Most of the more ambitious reform proposals face a considerable hurdle—the need to revise the U.N. Charter if they are to be implemented. The permanent members of the Security Council are likely to strongly resist considering proposals that would require this for fear of opening a "Pandora's box." However, the reform process could receive a boost from the appointment of the new Secretary General in late 1991. Many called for the designation of someone capable of steering the organization toward a more prominent role in promoting sustainable development.[68]

Global governance reforms will need to go beyond changing institutional machinery. Effective governance will require opening the process to far more extensive public participation than is now allowed. Today's international laws and institutions are compacts between governments, not people. Provisions for public review and comment and the possibility of bringing citizen suits do not exist at the international level, nor is there the equivalent of an elected parliament. NGOs are not routinely granted the right to intervene in international negotiations, though they have been allowed to do so to a limited degree in the preparations for UNCED and in the climate talks.[69]

Cooperative efforts between environmentalists from all corners of the planet to build a global movement to press for strong treaties will also be important. Already, the seeds of such cooperation have been laid through groups like the International Climate Action Network, the World Rainforest Network, and the unprecedented international NGO effort to organize for the Earth Summit.[70]

Countries will not actively participate in international governance unless they feel they have something to gain from it. There is the obvious potential benefit of staving off problems such as climate change and the loss of biodiversity. But for developing countries, this will not be ample incentive. Any calls for strengthened global governance will continue to be viewed warily so long as industrial countries do not offer the things developing countries most need—financial and technological assistance to combat environmental problems, and help with structural economic problems such as debt and deteriorating terms of trade that exacerbate Third World poverty and environmental degradation.

Creating an effective system of international environmental governance is a formidable challenge on the path to a sustainable future. It will require wide departures from business as usual. But there is little choice. Unless governments move quickly, the world faces a future of climbing global temperatures, depleted fisheries, reduced agricultural yields, diminished biological diversity, and growing human suffering.

# 11

# Launching the Environmental Revolution

*Lester R. Brown*

In June 1992, the United Nations is holding its Conference on Environment and Development in Rio de Janeiro. Coming 20 years after the U.N. meeting in Stockholm that officially launched the international environmental movement, this so-called Earth Summit will dwarf its predecessor. With some 10,000 official delegates from 150 countries and up to 20,000 concerned citizens and activists scheduled to participate in a parallel Global Forum, it will be the largest U.N. conference ever held.[1]

As part of their preparation for the meeting, governments prepared reports on the state of their environments. Most focus on national achievements—a reduction in air pollution here or a successful reforestation program there. But overall, global environmental trends are not reassuring. The health of the planet has deteriorated dangerously during the 20 years since Stockholm.

As a result, our world faces potentially convulsive change. The question is, In what direction will it take us? Will the change come from strong worldwide initiatives that reverse the degradation of the planet and restore hope for the future, or will it come from continuing environmental deterioration that leads to economic decline and social instability?

Muddling through will not work. Either we turn things around quickly or the self-reinforcing internal dynamic of the deterioration-and-decline scenario will take over. The policy decisions we make in the years immediately ahead will determine whether our children live in a world of development or decline.

There is no precedent for the change in prospect. Building an environmentally sustainable future depends on restructuring the global economy, major shifts in human reproductive behavior, and dramatic changes in values and lifestyles. Doing all this quickly adds up to a revolution, one defined by the need to restore and preserve the earth's environmental systems. If this Environmental Revolution succeeds, it will rank with the Agricultural and Industrial Revolutions as one of the great economic and social transformations in human history.

Like the Agricultural Revolution, it will dramatically alter population trends. While the former set the stage for enormous increases in human numbers, this revolution will succeed only if it stabilizes population size, reestablishing a balance between people and the natural systems on which they depend. In contrast to the Industrial Revolution, which was based on a shift to fossil fuels, this new transformation will be based on a shift away from fossil fuels.

The two earlier revolutions were driven by technological advances—the first by the discovery of farming and the second by the invention of the steam engine, which converted the energy in coal into mechanical power. The Environmental Revolution, while it will obviously use new technologies, will be driven primarily by the restructuring of the global economy so that it does not destroy its natural support systems.

The pace of the Environmental Revolution will be far faster than that of its predecessors. The Agricultural Revolution began some 10,000 years ago and the Industrial Revolution has been under way for two centuries. But if the Environmental Revolution is to succeed, it must be compressed into a few decades.

Progress in the Agricultural Revolution was measured almost exclusively in the growth in food output that eventually enabled farmers to produce a surplus that could feed city dwellers. Similarly, industrial progress was gauged by success in expanding the output of raw materials and manufactured goods. The Environmental Revolution will be judged by whether it can shift the world economy onto an environmentally sustainable development path, one that leads to greater economic security, healthier life-styles, and a worldwide improvement in the human condition.

Many still do not see the need for such an economic and social transformation. They see the earth's deteriorating physical condition as a peripheral matter that can be dealt with by minor policy adjustments. But 20 years of effort have failed to stem the tide of environmental degradation. There is now too much evidence on too many fronts to take these issues lightly.

Already the planet's degradation is damaging human health, slowing the growth in world food production, and reversing economic progress in dozens of countries. By the age of 10, thousands of children living in southern California's Los Angeles basin have respiratory systems that are permanently impaired by polluted air. Some 300,000 Soviet citizens are being treated for radiation sickness. The accelerated depletion of the stratospheric ozone layer in the northern hemisphere will lead to an estimated additional 200,000 skin cancer fatalities over the next half-century in the United States alone. Worldwide, millions of lives are at stake. These examples, and countless others, show that our health is closely linked to that of the planet.[2]

A scarcity of new cropland and fresh water plus the negative effects of soil erosion, air pollution, and hotter summers on crop yields is slowing growth of the world grain harvest. Combined with continuing rapid population growth, this has reversed the steady rise in grain output per person that the world had become accustomed to. Between 1950 and 1984, the historical peak year, world grain production per person climbed by nearly 40 percent. Since then, it has fallen roughly 1 percent a year, with the drop concentrated in poor countries. With food imports in these nations restricted by rising external debt, there are far more hungry people today than ever before.[3]

On the economic front, the signs are equally ominous: soil erosion, deforestation, and overgrazing are adversely affecting productivity in the farming, forestry, and livestock sectors, slowing overall economic growth in agriculturally based economies. The World Bank reports that after three decades of broad-based economic gains, incomes fell during the eighties in more than 40 developing countries. Collectively, these nations contain more than 800 million people—almost three times the population of North America and nearly one sixth that of the world. In Nigeria, the most populous country in the ill-fated group, the incomes of its 123 million people fell a painful 29 percent, exceeding the fall in U.S. incomes during the depression decade of the thirties.[4]

---

**The decline in living conditions once predicted by some ecologists has become a reality for one sixth of humanity.**

---

Anyone who thinks these environmental, agricultural, and economic trends can easily be reversed need only look at population projections. Those of us born before the middle of this century have seen world population double to 5 billion. We have witnessed the environmental effects of adding 2.5 billion people, especially in the Third World. We can see the loss of tree cover, the devastation of grasslands, the soil erosion, the crowding and poverty, the land hunger, and the water pollution associated with this addition. But what if 4.7 billion more people are added by 2050, over 90 percent of them in the Third World, as now projected by U.N. demographers?[5]

The decline in living conditions that was once predicted by some ecologists from the combination of continuing rapid population growth, spreading environmental degradation, and rising external debt has become a reality for one sixth of humanity. Moreover, if a more comprehensive system of national economic accounting were used—one that incorporated losses of natural capital, such as topsoil and forests, the destruction of productive grasslands, the extinction of plant and animal species, or the health costs of air and water pollution, nuclear radiation, and increased ultraviolet radiation—it might well show that most of humanity suffered a decline in living conditions during the eighties.

Today we study the archaeological sites of civilizations that were undermined by environmental deterioration. The wheatlands that made North Africa the granary of the Roman Empire are now largely desert. The early civilizations of the Tigris-Euphrates Basin declined as the waterlogging and salting of irrigation systems slowly shrank their food supply. And the collapse of the Mayan civilization that flourished in the Guatemalan lowlands from the third century B.C. to the ninth century A.D. may have been triggered by deforestation and soil erosion.

No one knows for certain why the centers of Mayan culture and art fell into neglect, nor whether the population of 1 million to 3 million moved or died off, but recent progress in deciphering hieroglyphs in the area adds credence to an environmental decline hypothesis. One of those involved with the project, Linda Schele of the University of Texas, observes: "They were worried about war at the end. Ecological disasters, too. Deforestation. Starvation. I think the population rose to the limits the technology could bear. They were so close to the edge, if anything went wrong, it was all over."[6]

Whether the Mayan economy had become environmentally unsustainable before it actually began to decline, we do not know. We do know that ours is.

## MECHANISMS OF CHANGE

Converting to an environmentally sustainable economy in the time available depends on accelerating the process of change. But what are the mechanisms of change?

Social change occurs in response either to new information or to new experience. Atmospheric chemists, for instance, reported in the mid-eighties that the chlorofluorocarbons (CFCs) used in air conditioning, refrigerators, and plastic foams were evaporating into the upper atmosphere and damaging the stratospheric ozone layer that protects us from dangerous ultraviolet radiation. As a result, the use of CFCs is now being phased out. None of us has ever seen the ozone layer, much less observed its depletion. Nonetheless, the world responded—a classic case of new information leading to policy changes.[7]

Five years ago, CFC manufacturers were opposed to the suggested phaseout, regularly challenging the scientific evidence, much as coal producers are now questioning the science underlying the greenhouse effect. But when a few leading producers considered what would be in the long-term interest of their companies, they moved rapidly to gain the lead in developing alternatives. In a similar fashion, once a leading oil or coal company starts to invest heavily in the solar-hydrogen economy, the heir apparent to fossil fuels, others are likely to follow.[8]

Sometimes new information alone will not bring about change. A smoker bombarded with data every few weeks from yet another study on the adverse health effects of this addiction may continue to smoke cigarettes, rationalizing away their life-threatening quality. But the day that person experiences difficulty breathing and is diagnosed with lung cancer, he or she will almost certainly stop smoking. In this instance, new experience did what new information could not do.

To what extent will new information alone sustain the Environmental Revolution and to what extent, as with the smoker, will it take some painful new experience? With nuclear power, some governments elected not to invest in this energy source based on the studies that warned of the risk of potentially catastrophic accidents. Others rejected nuclear power only after the May 1986 explosion at Chernobyl, when the risk became a reality. This experience will forever color how the world looks at the various options for meeting energy needs.[9]

Our choice now is either to rally behind the Environmental Revolution or to continue on the current path, moving toward a world where famine expands beyond the capacity of international relief agencies, where cancer reaches epidemic proportions, and where the decline in living conditions now under way in some 40 countries continues to spread, dropping more and more of the world's poor below the survival level.

We know what we have to do and we have the technologies needed for the Environmental Revolution to succeed. The basic reference points are the same for government policymakers, corporate planners, and individuals making lifestyle decisions: Does this policy or action lower carbon emissions? Does it reduce the generation of toxic wastes? Does it slow population growth? Does it increase the earth's tree cover? Does it cut CFC emissions? Does it reduce air pollution and acid rain? Does it reduce radioactive waste generation? Does it lessen soil erosion? Does it protect the planet's biodiversity?

Social and economic change always starts with individuals, even when it occurs within large organizations. Some of the conditions of sustainability can be satisfied by individual life-style decisions or by local community action. Couples can help stabilize population by having only two children. Individuals can use energy more efficiently. But phasing out CFCs, replacing fossil fuels with solar energy, or protecting the planet's biodiversity depends on national governments and international agreements. Without clear policy guidance from governments, corporations, which control a large share of the world's investment capital, are not likely to make the required changes in investment patterns.

Neither government policy formulation nor corporate investment decisions are made in a vacuum. Strong visionary leaders can accelerate the Environmental Revolution, but in democracies, government policies and priorities broadly reflect the concerns and priorities of the people. Whether policy changes come quickly enough depends on whether public understanding of environmental threats and their social consequences is strong enough to support these changes and whether the public holds politicians accountable at the ballot box for environmental decisions.

Although the Environmental Revolution has been described here largely in environmental and economic terms, it is in the most fundamental sense a social revolution: the product of changing values, of seeing ourselves again as a part of nature rather than apart from nature, of recognizing our dependence on the earth's natural systems and resources and on the goods and services they provide.

## THE PIVOTAL ROLE OF GOVERNMENTS

Today there is a vast gap between what governments are doing and what they need to do for the Environmental Revolution to succeed. Most are taking some steps in the right direction, but even the most progressive countries are still in the early stages of the transformation.

Some governments are evaluating the policy instruments they can use to restructure the economy—tax policies, subsidies, regulations, R&D funding, procurement policies. Of all the instruments available, the partial replacement of income and other taxes with environmental taxes is by far the most effective tool to move the economy onto an environmentally sustainable path.

---

**The Environmental Revolution is the product of seeing ourselves again as a part of nature rather than apart from nature.**

---

Taxing environmentally destructive activities, such as carbon emissions, the generation of hazardous waste, and the use of virgin materials, permits the market to operate unimpaired, taking advantage of its inherent efficiencies while steering it in an environmentally sustainable direction. For example, taxing carbon emissions discourages the use of fossil fuels, while encouraging investments in energy efficiency and renewable sources of energy.

Environmental taxes address a principal weakness of market economies, namely that the costs of environmentally destructive economic activities are often not borne by those responsible for the damage. The costs of the respiratory illnesses of children in Mexico City are not borne by the motorists who generate the pollution. The costs of dealing with rising sea level in low-lying developing countries will not be borne by the industrial nations largely responsible for the carbon emissions that are driving climate change. As German environmental analyst Ernst von Weizsacher observes, "Prices do not tell the ecological truth." Environmental taxes provide a means of incorporating these indirect costs into the economy, correcting the shortcomings of the market.[10]

At present, Europe is leading the world in the use of tax policy for environmental purposes. In September 1991, the European Community (EC) proposed that its member governments replace some existing taxes with an energy tax equal to $10 per barrel of oil, a sum that would raise the 1991 market price of $20 per barrel by half as it was phased in during the nineties. Applied to all fossil fuels and nuclear power, the tax is designed to reduce carbon emissions and nuclear waste while fostering investments in energy efficiency and renewable sources. Even before the tax was announced, industry groups, fearing this unilateral initiative would damage their competitive position, had come out in opposition. Nonetheless, if this measure is passed by the Council of Ministers representing the member governments, as expected, it will be a major new step in forging a strong Community environmental policy. EC environment commissioner Carlo Ripa di Meana says that "with this initiative the Commission is looking to give the Community the role of catalyst at the international level."[11]

Further evidence of Europe's leadership comes from Germany. When the government decided in early 1991 to rebuild the transportation and telephone systems of what was formerly East Germany, it elected to boost the tax on gasoline by 50¢ per gallon to help finance the program. This raised the tax per gallon to $1.85 (compared with a U.S. tax of roughly 30¢) and pushed the price, including tax, to nearly $4 per gallon, sending a clear signal to motorists. By discouraging gasoline use, this tax will help reduce the acid rain that is destroy-ing German forests, improve air quality in the notoriously polluted eastern German cities, lower the carbon emissions destabilizing the earth's climate, and reduce the oil imports that could weaken the country's economy.[12]

Getting rid of subsidies that are ill-conceived or outdated can also speed the transformation. In the Soviet Union, where energy is supplied at prices far below those of the world market, there is little incentive to use energy efficiently. As a result, more than twice as much is used to produce a dollar's worth of goods and services as in Japan, the most energy-efficient industrial economy. Subsidies of pesticide use in developing countries have led to the excessive, sometimes reckless use of farm chemicals. In the United States, subsidies such as those embodied in the federal policy of selling timber rights to logging companies at a fraction of cost encourage tree cutting at the expense of paper recycling.[13]

Carefully used, however, subsidies can accelerate the Environmental Revolution. For example, in the late seventies California adopted a tax write-off to supplement the federal subsidy of investments in renewable energy resources. This, coupled with key regulatory changes that opened up the electricity market to generators other than electric utilities, set the stage for the state's emergence as a world leader in this field. With 30 million people and an economy larger than Canada's, California today generates more electricity from both wind farms and solar thermal power plants than does the rest of the world combined. This forward-looking state also leads in development of geothermal energy, accounting for roughly a third of the global total. Along with biomass-fired power plants, these renewable sources provide Californians with enough electricity to meet the residential needs of 4 million households. Because of a bold governmental initiative taken over a decade ago, the world now has a window on the future, an early view of what an environmentally sustainable energy economy might look like.[14]

Procurement policies are also an effective means of shifting priorities. For example, in government bureaucracies where the principal raw material is paper, a decision to buy only recycled products helps create a market, encouraging the industry to invest in mills that use recycled stock rather than freshly cut trees. Similarly, replacing inefficient incandescent light bulbs in government offices with the new compact fluorescent ones that use only one fourth as much electricity would help create a viable market for the large-scale manufacture of mini-fluorescents while familiarizing both employees and the public with this energy-saving technology.[15]

Although no government has an environmentally sustainable development strategy, some are starting to put the components of one into place. As governments focus on steps to slow global warming, Germany, a long-time coal producer, has emerged as the leader, committing itself to a 25-percent reduction in carbon emissions by 2005. Close behind are Australia, Austria, Denmark, and New Zealand, each of which has pledged to cut emissions 20 percent during the same period.[16]

While some industrial countries are starting to phase out fossil fuels to stabilize climate, some developing countries are committing themselves to eventually stabilizing population size. Prominent among these is China, where over one fifth of humanity lives. Bangladesh, with a more intermediate goal, hopes to reduce the average number of children per woman from 4.9 in 1990 to 2.3 percent in 2000. Nigeria's goal is to bring this number down from 6.2 in 1990 to 4 in 2000. And Mexico plans to cut its 1990

population growth in half by the year 2000.[17]

On the waste management front, Denmark has emerged as a model by banning throwaway beverage containers, thus sharply reducing garbage generation. By forcing a shift to refillable containers, it has cut the energy invested in beverage containers by two thirds or more and lowered air and water pollution accordingly. Employment, meanwhile, may have increased, since reusing beverage containers is more labor-intensive than manufacturing new ones.[18]

Among industrial countries, the Netherlands has pioneered the use of bicycles for personal transportation. With a bicycle fleet of 12 million for a population of 15 million, this compact country has more than twice as many bicycles as cars. In Groningen, the largest city in northern Netherlands, bicycles already account for half of all trips.[19]

Some national governments, including Australia, the Netherlands, Norway, and Sweden, have begun to formulate broader environmental plans, including setting national goals. The motivation for Australia's plan came largely from the extensive land degradation that is undermining grain and livestock production, two cornerstones of its economy. Tree planting, which will ameliorate these threats, is a centerpiece of the plan. By the end of this decade, if Australia achieves its goal of planting 1 billion trees, forest cover will be restored on nearly half the land stripped of trees since European settlement began some two centuries ago.[20]

The Netherlands, densely populated and faced with heavy pollution from industry, transportation, and agriculture, has adopted the most detailed and comprehensive plan of any government. The Dutch National Environmental Policy Plan calls for only a 3- to 5-percent cut in carbon emissions by 2000, but it includes an ambitious halving of the nitrogen and phosphorus flowing into rivers from fertilizer runoff, sewage, and industrial discharge. It also aims for a sharp reduction in emissions of both sulfur dioxide and nitrous oxides from power plants. Using a combination of grants and taxes, the goal is to get more people out of their cars and onto bicycles for shorter trips and into trains for longer ones.[21]

These examples are drawn mostly from industrial countries, largely because Third World governments are too preoccupied with poverty, and particularly its spread over the past decade, to respond to global environmental threats. The challenge to national governments and the international community is to deal simultaneously with poverty and environmental degradation. As the Iron Curtain goes down, the Poverty Curtain has become ever more visible. The ideological fault line that divided the world for nearly a half-century has disappeared, only to be replaced by an economic fault line dividing the world between North and South.

While he was president of the World Bank, Barber Conable noted that "as the 1990s unfold, success in reducing poverty should be 'the' measurement of global economic progress." It is difficult to imagine an effective international environmental effort if a strong net flow of capital from rich countries to poor ones is not restored. As others have noted, when we reach the point where half the world watches the other half starve to death on television, civilization will have come to an end.[22]

If deepening poverty continues to threaten the survival of part of humanity in the short run, the Environmental Revolution will fail. People facing starvation today are not likely to worry about the effects of climate change tomorrow. We can no longer separate the future habitability of the planet from the current distribution of wealth.

This new reality distinguishes this decade from those that have gone before. It is not possible for part of the world to follow one path and the rest to follow another. No country can stabilize its climate in isolation. No country, acting unilaterally, can preserve the earth's biological diversity. If even one country continues to discharge large quantities of CFCs into the atmosphere, then people everywhere are doomed ultimately to rising levels of skin cancer, more frequent cataracts, the suppression of immune systems, and the associated vulnerability to infectious diseases.

The poor have something the rich desperately need, namely their cooperation in preserving the global economy's environmental support systems. If affluent societies are unwilling to help the poor deal with lifethreatening poverty, the developing world may be reluctant to devote much time or resources to these threats. Although governments of rich nations such as the United States may resist it, a meaningful sustainable development strategy anywhere must now embrace the satisfaction of basic human needs everywhere.

---

**We can no longer separate the future habitability of the planet from the current distribution of wealth.**

---

Fortunately, the end of the cold war offers an opportunity for restructuring national priorities, for investing in the Environmental Revolution—in health care and family planning, tree planting, soil conservation, energy efficiency, renewable energy resources, CFC substitutes, clean water, pollution reduction, and reuse and recycling.

In effect, the Environmental Revolution depends on redefining security. Robert McNamara—uniquely suited to comment on this as both former U.S. Secretary of Defense and former President of the World Bank—argues that the time has come for a massive global reduction in military expenditures. Observing that Third World military expenditures totaled roughly $170 billion in 1988, nearly as much as was spent for health care and education combined, he urges that they be roughly cut in half over the remainder of this decade. To facilitate this he recommends that the superpowers continue to reduce both conventional and nuclear arms, that the U.N. Security Council guarantee the territorial integrity of nations, and that financial aid to developing countries be tied to reductions in military expenditures. At the October 1991 World Bank annual meeting in Bangkok, both new Bank president Lewis Preston and Michel Camdessus, head of the International Monetary Fund, announced that they would henceforth work with borrowing countries to curb military spending.[23]

---

**Accustomed to passing on the expense of environmental destruction and disruption to society at large, corporations are not eager for wholesale reform.**

---

At this point, given the resources needed for the Environmental Revolution, national governments may want to examine the experience of Costa Rica, which abolished its army in 1949, leaving the maintenance of law and order to the police. As a result of this bold move, Costa Rica was able to spend more on education, health, and family planning, and is now among Third World leaders in such basic social indicators as infant and maternal mortality, literacy, and life expectancy. Indeed, life expectancy

there is 77 years, two years more than in the United States.[24]

Given the deteriorating state of the planet and all that portends, there is now a need for other similarly bold initiatives by national governments. Such actions are not a substitute for international cooperation, but they can provide a strong psychological boost for all of humanity.

## CORPORATIONS FACING CHANGE

Of all the sources of resistance to the Environmental Revolution, none is greater than that coming from corporate boardrooms. Accustomed to internalizing profits while externalizing costs, by passing on the expense of environmental destruction and disruption to society at large, corporations are not eager for wholesale reform. Although some companies are actively supporting the transformation, they are often younger firms, not those in the old-line industries. Unfortunately, too many companies assume that exploitation of the environment for dumping waste or acquiring raw materials is essential to their success, much as factory owners early in the Industrial Revolution thought their survival depended on the exploitation of child labor.

Corporations are facing an enormous amount of change in the years ahead, some far more than others. Much of the change will originate with governments as public environmental concerns translate into environmental taxes, regulations, and procurement policies. Some will come from environmentally sensitive consumers. And some will come from environmentally sensitive corporate leaders within the business community. Corporations will change in response to environmental threats, but will they do it with foresight, anticipating the adjustments needed? Or will they delay, possibly pushing society to the brink of catastrophe?

Since mid-century, corporate investment patterns have been shaped by the enormous worldwide growth in consumer purchasing power interacting with advancing technology and new products. Research and development on new products, combined with market research on what consumers needed or could be persuaded to buy, provided the grist for long-term corporate production planning. The fourfold expansion of the global economy over the last 40 years, coupled with the internationalization of markets, created a unique growth opportunity for enterprising firms. During the latter part of this four-decade span, pollution control regulations and the banning of environmentally destructive products, such as CFCs or dangerous pesticides, began to affect business investments—but only in a minor way.[25]

In the years ahead, environmental influences can be expected to increasingly dominate the evolution of the global economy. Phasing out fossil fuels, shifting to a reuse-recycle economy, protecting the stratospheric ozone layer, reducing air pollution and acid rain, minimizing hazardous waste generation, and adapting to water scarcity are among the environmental influences shaping the economic future of corporations.

The economic restructuring in prospect is not trivial. The shift from fossil fuels to a solar-hydrogen energy system will affect every sector of the economy, from transportation to food. At present, transport systems are largely fueled by oil, either gasoline, diesel fuel, or jet fuel. As the shift away from fossil fuels progresses, the use of electricity for transportation, now confined largely to rail systems, will likely become common for automobiles and trucks. And in locales distant from cheap electricity-generating sites, hydrogen is likely to become the fuel of choice for cars, trucks, and buses, as well as for airplanes everywhere. Efforts to reduce air pollution in California are leading to regulations on manufacturers that will require 2 percent of all cars sold in the state after 1998 to have zero emissions—that is, to be electric. The city of Los Angeles signed a $7-million contract to help a Swedish firm, Clean Air Transport Svenska, start to manufacture electric cars. The company hopes to begin selling them in Los Angeles in early 1993. And General Motors plans to market its new electric car there by the mid-nineties.[26]

Efforts to put agriculture on a more sustainable footing will lead to more comprehensive nutrient recycling and integrated pest management strategies, affecting the market for fertilizers and pesticides. The food processing industry in industrial countries, now using more energy in processing, packaging, and distributing food than farmers use in producing it, may face even greater changes.[27]

Local limits on the earth's waste-absorptive capacity are forcing industries to redesign their manufacturing processes to generate less waste. Already doing this in response to government regulations, firms will find an even greater incentive to cut waste as environmental taxes are levied, such as those recently adopted on plastic bags in Italy and nonreturnable beer and soft drink containers in Finland.[28]

The oft-repeated notion that the business of business is business recognizes the obligation that corporations have to their stockholders, and implicitly the difficulties in unilaterally responding to environmental concerns that would put them at a competitive disadvantage. This short-term concern with profits contrasts sharply with the long-term nature of environmental concerns, setting up an inherent conflict in corporate management. Given the highly competitive setting in which firms operate, some corporate leaders welcome government regulation or environmental taxes as it permits them to reduce environmental damage without being put at a short-term competitive disadvantage.

Using their well-developed commercial instincts, corporations attempt to exploit consumer environmental concerns in marketing their products, often confusing buyers with their advertising claims. The principal antidote to this practice is the emergence of so-called eco-labels, an approach pioneered in West Germany more than 10 years ago. The Blue Angel labeling program there has evaluated over 3,500 products in some 50 categories. In Canada, products bearing the Environmental Choice label first appeared on the shelves in 1989. Other European countries are modeling their labeling systems after that of Germany. Japan is launching an eco-mark program and the United States has two relatively new product evaluation groups, Green Cross and Green Seal, with the latter directed by a board consisting largely of leaders of environmental and consumer groups.[29]

The premise underlying these programs is that environmentally sensitive consumers will alter their buying habits if given relevant information about products they routinely purchase. Decisions made by millions of consumers each day add up to major shifts in consumer demand. This, in turn, affects product design, method of manufacture, and even whether some products appear at all. In Canada, where surveys indicate that 80 percent of the public is willing to pay 10 percent more for environmentally benign products, companies are obviously eager to exploit this concern by getting the seal on as many products as possible. Among other things, these programs evaluate such things as the energy efficiency of household appliances and the recycled material content of products. In the case of Canada, for ex-

ample, reusable diapers were given the seal of approval while throwaway diapers were not.[30]

When public concern over environmental deterioration first surfaced, corporations often fought new regulations, arguing that industries and jobs would flee overseas. They typically reacted superficially, spending more on environmental advertising than on environmental action. These issues were, they believed, something to be dealt with by the public relations office, not by corporate planners or plant managers.

A number of firms have now moved beyond this and are beginning to assess their own operations in environmental terms, including such things as energy efficiency, paper recycling, and hazardous waste generation. This is an important step, given the share of the global economy accounted for by the corporate sector. For example, in mid-1991 AT&T released an environmental strategy paper outlining near-term goals. This far-flung corporation, which employs some 275,000 workers worldwide, plans by the end of 1994 to phase out CFC use, to reduce waste from manufacturing processes by 25 percent and paper use by 15 percent, and to achieve a 35-percent paper recycling rate; by the end of 1995, it expects to cut toxic air emissions by 95 percent. Impressive though these goals are, the list is instructive as much for what it omits—goals for the reduction of carbon emissions and some hazardous wastes—as for what it includes.[31]

At the next level, the challenge for companies is to ask whether there is a place for their products in an environmentally sustainable economy. For some, the changes in prospect are rather modest. Manufacturers of electrical household appliances, for instance, can concentrate mostly on making them more energy-efficient and designing them so they can more easily be repaired or recycled. Companies now building gasoline-powered automobiles can shift to electric or hydrogen-powered cars without vast investments. Firms that produce incandescent light bulbs can make the switch to compact fluorescents simply by modifying their manufacturing facilities.

Many products manufactured on a relatively limited scale today have an enormous market potential in an environmentally sustainable world. Prominent among these are refillable beverage containers, compact fluorescent light bulbs, bicycles, photovoltaic cells, thermally efficient building materials, heat pumps, wind electric generators, high-speed rail cars, contraceptives, rooftop solar water heaters, and water-efficient plumbing appliances. Within the construction industry, the rapid growth areas will include building solar power plants, electrolysis plants to produce hydrogen fuel, and commuter rail systems, and refurbishing and retrofitting older buildings to boost their energy efficiency.

Another group of companies will have to take a more fundamental look at their products simply because there will be no place for them in an environmentally sustainable economy. For example, if climate stabilization is the goal, then coal and oil companies can either try to maintain the status quo and face a difficult, potentially bleak future or they can help develop renewable energy sources. Given the heavy damage from coal burning, some governments might one day even ban the use of coal, much as they have CFCs or nuclear power.

Some companies by their very nature contribute to carbon reductions. In California, several firms have raised over $2.5 billion in private capital markets for investment in wind-turbine manufacture and wind farms, thus helping demonstrate that wind power is a viable energy source, one with a potential comparable to that of hydropower, which now supplies one fifth of the world's electricity. Companies producing goods that directly or indirectly reduce carbon emissions, such as photovoltaic cells, bicycles, and fax machines (which reduce the need for postal and private delivery services) are well positioned to help build an environmentally sustainable economy and to profit from it.[32]

---

**The challenge for companies is to ask whether there is a place for their products in an environmentally sustainable economy.**

---

Like everyone else, corporations have a stake in a sustainable future. It is hard to sustain profits in a declining economy. Those within a given industry that see the need for change and move to the forefront will fare better than those who attempt to maintain the status quo. Current circumstances raise an intriguing question: are corporate interests and the survival of civilization now so intertwined that companies assuming a major environmental responsibility are likely to benefit economically simply because they are responding to a deeply felt public concern about the future? Two corporate successes come to mind: The Body Shop and Ben & Jerry's.

The Body Shop, a U.K.-based international chain of outlets specializing in hair and skin care products launched by Anita Roddick, is a model of a corporation where economic and environmental interests are tightly intertwined. The firm buys raw materials from indigenous people such as Indians in the Amazonian rain forest, packages its shampoos and lotions in refillable containers, and does not use animals to test its products. It is committed to environmentally sustainable development and human rights. Shop salespeople solicit signatures on petitions to save the rain forest and distribute membership forms for Amnesty International.[33]

Starting with one shop 15 years ago, the company now has over 600 outlets in some 18 countries, with sales in 1990 of nearly $400 million. With such growth in sales and profits, The Body Shop has little trouble attracting investors. Perhaps even more important, this success appears to be affecting the long-standing leaders in the field, such as Estée Lauder, who are now adopting some of The Body Shop's environmental practices. According to *Business Week*, "Roddick has rewritten the rules for the $16 billion global cosmetics business."[34]

It is now possible to visualize companies supporting the Environmental Revolution even more vigorously, becoming politically active on behalf of environmental issues. Ben Cohen of Ben & Jerry's, a $90-million-a-year Vermont-based ice cream firm, notes that political action on behalf of a corporation's economic interests is standard operating procedure. Cohen, whose company devotes 7.5 percent of its profits to funding social and environmental projects, believes it altogether appropriate, even in a sense obligatory, for his publicly owned firm to lobby on behalf of broader issues. For example, Ben & Jerry's used a bit of humor and a billboard on the Southeast Expressway outside of Boston to oppose nuclear power with a sign that said, "STOP SEA-BROOK, keep our customers alive and licking."[35]

Roddick and Cohen each have a clearly articulated and strongly held vision of the kind of world they want. This permeates the entire structure of their firms, and translates into an enviable bottom line. Unfortunately, only a handful of corporations have such visionaries at their helms. Whether the success of this new genre of socially and environmentally active firms will lead to the

adoption of their goals by more and more of the corporate community remains to be seen.

The political activities of these two firms raise an interesting question about corporate responsibilities and interest in an environmentally sustainable economy. Since corporations have a stake in such a future, perhaps they should be actively working for it in ways that go beyond the traditional boundaries of corporate activity. If large companies routinely post lobbyists in the capitals of countries where they operate to look after narrow corporate interests, why shouldn't they have environmental lobbyists there as well working hand in hand with those from environmental groups to ensure a sustainable future?

## MOBILIZING FOR CHANGE

Unless more of us become environmentally active, both as individuals and in organized groups, the Environmental Revolution will not succeed. Success depends on overcoming human inertia, vested economic interests in the status quo, and some of the structural impediments of society. The behavior of corporate leaders is shaped by the pressures of short-term profit-making. Politicians are influenced by short-term reelection concerns and by special interest groups. But environmental groups can take the long view, speaking for future generations. Without a much stronger public interest community mobilizing for rapid change, there is a risk of sacrificing the future on the altar of short-term profits and reelection worries.

Individuals can do many things acting independently, including voting for environmentally sensitive candidates, but the Environmental Revolution depends on systemic change, and that requires a means of concentrating and sustaining pressure for change. Individuals can sort beverage containers for recycling, but they cannot replace throwaway containers with refillable ones. That requires an organized effort to change public policy: either an outright ban on their use, as in Denmark, or a stiff tax on throwaways, as in Finland.[36]

The energy fueling the process of change comes from millions of individuals and thousands of environmental groups, ranging from large international organizations with millions of supporters, such as Greenpeace—with its 5 million supporters and offices in 24 countries—to local, single-issue groups. Local groups include rubber tappers trying to save the Amazon rain forest, a group in India protesting a large dam, a women's group in Kenya planting trees, communities in the Soviet Union opposing construction of nuclear power plants, and ones in the United States urging cleanup of toxic waste sites. These groups research issues, educate the public, litigate when necessary, and organize citizens to press local and national governments to abandon environmentally destructive policies. In many societies, they are the only effective counterweight to special interest groups.[37]

While public interest groups help generate the information that drives social change, it is the communications media that disseminates it. The difficulties for the media of covering such a complex set of issues are evident. There is a tendency, for example, to treat the environment like drugs, inflation, or other staples of daily journalism. But there are differences: With inflation, prices that go up today may come down tomorrow. But a species that disappears today will not reappear tomorrow.

Like society at large, newspaper editors sometimes have difficulty immediately grasping the importance of environmental issues, covering events and trends that are of limited consequence while ignoring some that matter. Within the media, there is a preoccupation with economic trends, partly because data are readily available to measure them, but it is environmental trends that are shaping our future.

American newspapers regularly report the dollar's changed value versus the yen over the past 24 hours. In effect this measures the shift in the relative strength of the U.S. and Japanese economies. But it doesn't have much to do with the health of the global economy and the human prospect. What about the 100 or more plant and animal species that were condemned to extinction yesterday, reducing the diversity of life on earth and with consequences that few can fully comprehend?[38]

We know from this morning's paper that the price of a barrel of oil went up 19¢ on the futures market yesterday. But what about the 56 million tons of carbon dioxide that were spewed into the planet's atmosphere by burning fossil fuels during the same period? And what about the 66 million tons of topsoil lost from the world's croplands yesterday— soil that will take centuries to replace?[39]

Newspapers and magazines closely follow minor shifts in the political composition of electorates, but pay comparatively little attention to the changing chemical composition of the atmosphere. Political shifts may be dramatic, but they are transient. Alterations of the atmosphere, on the other hand, affect the habitability of the planet not only for ourselves, but for generations to come.

Forty years ago environmental issues only occasionally made it into the news simply because there was not much happening. But as the world economy has expanded fourfold since then, pushing demands on the earth's natural systems beyond their carrying capacity, the incidence of damage has increased disproportionately. Likewise, if adding 2.5 billion people to the world over 40 years has wreaked such havoc with the earth, what will be the effect of adding nearly 5 billion over the next six decades?[40]

This may be an appropriate time for media organizations to systematically reassess the resources devoted to coverage of major fields such as politics, the economy, and the environment. If environmental trends are indeed shaping our future, perhaps newspapers should have a daily environment section, just as they have a daily business section. Perhaps there should be at least as many environmental columnists on the editorial page as there are political ones. And perhaps television news programs should have a daily environment report as well as a business one. Within the environmental section of the paper, a reporter could be assigned to cover species extinctions and their consequences in the same way that an economic reporter often specializes in corporate bankruptcy proceedings.

**Unless more of society mobilizes in support of the Environmental Revolution, it will not succeed.**

At issue for the media, and society at large, is how to accelerate change on a scale not previously seen except when mobilizing for war. The Environmental Revolution by definition depends on an extraordinary amount of social change, a compression of history—squeezing centuries of change into decades.

Social change is not usually a smooth process. In the Soviet Union, democratization accelerated sharply under the leadership of Mikhail Gorbachev in 1985 in the form of glasnost. When the Committee of Eight attempted its ill-fated coup d'état in 1991, it became the precipitating event that unleashed the forces of democracy and set the stage for dismantling the Soviet Empire.

Thus far, social change in response to environmental threats has also been a gradual process, slowly gaining momentum. Like democratization in the Soviet Union, it faces enormous obstacles in the form of people wedded to the status quo. Just as many Communist Party officials and bureaucrats resisted, there are many powerful vested interests in the existing world economic system, interests that are resisting the Environmental Revolution.

No one knows what the environmental equivalent of the Soviet coup d'état will be, the event that puts the Environmental Revolution on the fast track. It could be a crop-damaging rise in summer temperatures in the U.S. grain belt that creates chaos in world grain markets, or a nuclear accident in France that exposes millions of Europeans to excessive radiation, forcing massive population relocations.

The issue is not our survival as a species, but rather the survival of civilization as we know it. Individually and collectively we have to decide whether we are prepared to make the efforts needed to reverse the trends that are undermining the future of civilization. Unless more of society mobilizes in support of the Environmental Revolution, it will not succeed.

Can societies mobilize quickly enough to bring about the changes needed? Can multinational corporations, for example, go beyond the obvious steps mentioned earlier to assume major responsibility for the earth's environmental future? What if a major corporation, recognizing its stake in a sustainable future, announced that it would devote 2 percent of its profits to helping close the family planning gap in the Third World? What if IBM or Du Pont or Phillips or Mitsubishi announced a major commitment to stabilizing the earth's climatic systems through public education and investment?

What if national governments were to take unilateral initiatives to help restore the planet's health? What if Japan were to launch a program to reverse the deforestation of the planet and committed itself to doing so by the end of this decade?

If we are individually wealthy, counting ourselves among the 202 billionaires and the 3 million or so millionaires in the world, should we continue with business as usual? Or should we be using our wealth to support the Environmental Revolution, since the possession of great wealth will mean little in a world descending into chaos?[41]

Some of the world's wealthy, such as Sir James Goldsmith, who made much of his fortune in the food industry, are beginning to respond to the planet's plight. In October 1990, the *Sunday Times* of London reported: "In a financial world that has recently become inured to shocks, last Wednesday brought an announcement that was greeted with disbelief. Sir James Goldsmith—corporate predator extraordinaire, scourge of board rooms, one of the most feared men on Wall Street— was retiring from business. From now on, he said, he would devote his energies and much of his fortune of more than $1 billion to ecological and environmental causes." The article went on to say that Goldsmith would not be a figurehead but an active environmental campaigner, lobbying, speaking, publishing, and funding projects. Great wealth, the 57-year-old billionaire argued, was of no value in a crumbling world.[42]

An even more recent experience in California also raises hope that the well-off will join the fray. Hal Arbit, a wealthy investor distressed by the destruction of the state's forests, pitted his resources against those of the Louisiana Pacific,

Pacific Lumber, and Simpson Timber companies, bankrolling a campaign for a new forest policy. As a result of his support of a lobbying effort orchestrated by the Sierra Club, the California legislature passed a landmark timber bill in September 1991 that banned clear-cutting in old-growth forests, reduced clear-cuts on less mature timber land from 120-acre parcels to 20-acre ones, and expanded the buffer zones between clear-cuts, thus putting forestry in the state on an environmentally sustainable footing. The governor vetoed this particular bill because he claimed it would have imposed "unnecessary economic hardship on companies," but a slightly modified version is being negotiated and is expected to pass and be signed into law.[43]

The emergence of individuals who are committed to change is not always predictable. Dr. Vladimir Chernousenko, the nuclear physicist who was appointed scientific supervisor of the emergency cleanup at Chernobyl, produced a detailed report estimating that the process has claimed between 5,000 and 7,000 lives to date. But the government has declined to release his findings. Chernousenko believes not only that nuclear power is not a viable energy source, but that it is the most dangerous environmental threat in the world today. Dismissed from the Institute for Theoretical Physics in Kiev for speaking out on these issues, he is dedicating the rest of his life—now estimated at no more than two years, since he himself is a victim of radiation sickness—to publishing a detailed account of Chernobyl. After hearing him speak at a conference in Mexico, author Peter Matthiessen wrote that he was stirred by the "exhilarating spectacle of a brave man set free by his own passionate commitment to the truth even while penniless and dying."[44]

Far away in the Andean highlands of Ecuador, an Italian priest, Father Antonio Polo, has dedicated himself to environmentally sustainable development. He helped the farmers in the village of Salinas build a cheese factory, one that has now been replicated in seven other villages in the province. Profits from the factories are reinvested in grassland improvement, veterinary medicines, and community health programs. He has also launched a successful reforestation effort that has created hundreds of hectares of forests. When the villagers discovered they could grow mushrooms in the shade of the trees, this spurred yet another local industry. Father Polo's work demonstrates how projects can simultaneously protect the environment while raising the standard of living.[45]

These are but four examples of how individuals can make a difference. Indeed, social change, by definition, depends on broad-based participation in the process. We can all contribute, but what are we as individuals prepared to do? Are we willing to commit ourselves to a particular goal such as a national ban on the use of throwaway beverage containers, the creation of a bicycle-friendly local transportation system, or the adoption of a national population stabilization policy? Given the stakes, how much of our spare time can we spend organizing, lobbying, and writing letters to our elected political leaders? Is it worth an hour a week of volunteer time? Ten, or perhaps even 20, hours a week?

If the Environmental Revolution is to succeed, it will need the support of far more people than it now has. In addition to overcoming vested interests, it must also overcome human inertia. Up until now the Environmental Revolution has been viewed by society much like a sporting event—one where thousands of people sit in the stands watching, while only a handful are on the playing field actively attempting to influence the outcome of the contest. Success in this case depends on erasing the imaginary sidelines that separate spectators from participants so we can all get involved. Saving the planet is not a spectator sport.

# Notes

## Chapter 1. Denial in the Decisive Decade

1. William K. Reilly, Administrator, U.S. Environmental Protection Agency (EPA), "Statement on Ozone Depletion," Washington, D.C., April 4, 1991; species estimate from Edward O. Wilson, *The Diversity of Life* (Cambridge, Mass: Harvard University Press, forthcoming); atmospheric levels of carbon dioxide from Daniel A. Lashof and Dennis A. Tirpak, eds., "Policy Options for Stabilizing Global Climate," EPA report to Congress, December 1990, and Tim Worf, Scripps Institution of Oceanography, La Jolla, CA., private communication, September 26, 1991; warmest years from P.D. Jones, Climatic Research Unit, University of East Anglia, Norwich, U.K., "Testimony to the U.S. Senate on Global Temperatures," Commerce Committee, U.S. Senate, October 11, 1990, and from William K. Stevens, "Separate Studies Rank '90 As World's Warmest Year," *New York Times*, January 10, 1991; deforestation rate from "New Deforestation Rate Figures Announced," *Tropical Forest Programme* (IUCN Newsletter), August 1990; population growth figures from Population Reference Bureau (PRB), *1991 World Population Data Sheet* (Washington, D.C.: 1991).

2. Remarks of José Lutzenberger, Secretary of State for Environment, Brazil, at the launching of The Nature Conservancy's Parks in Peril Program, Washington, D.C., November 15, 1990.

3. Frank L. Picard, *Intervention: Ending the Cycle of Addiction and Codependence* (New York: Prentice Hall Press, 1989).

4. Income distribution from U.N. Development Programme (UNDP), *Human Development Report 1991* (New York: Oxford University Press, 1991); $1 per day figure from World Bank, *World Development Report 1991* (New York: Oxford University Press, 1991).

5. Lack of safe water from *The International Drinking Water Supply and Sanitation Decade: Review of Decade Progress* (Geneva, Switzerland: World Health Organization, 1990); reproductive health problems from Jodi L. Jacobson, *Women's Reproductive Health: The Silent Emergency*, Worldwatch Paper 102 (Washington, D.C.: Worldwatch Institute, June 1991); all other data from UNDP, *Human Development Report 1991*.

6. Net transfers to developing countries averaged $4.7 billion per year during 1981–90, according to World Bank, *World Debt Tables 1990–91: External Debt of Developing Countries, Vol. I* (Washington, D.C.: 1990), and to the Debt and International Finance Division, World Bank, Washington, D.C., private communication, September 30, 1991.

7. For a further discussion of these issues, see Gareth Porter and Janet Welsh Brown, *Global Environmental Politics* (Boulder, Colo.: Westview Press, 1991).

8. Global military spending figure from Ruth Leger Sivard, *World Military and Social Expenditures 1991* (Washington, D.C.: World Priorities, 1991); world population from PRB, *1991 World Population Data Sheet*; family planning figure from Nafis Sadik, *The State of the World Population 1991* (New York: U.N. Population Fund, 1991).

9. UNDP, *Human Development Report 1991*; Keith Schneider, "Military Has New Strategic Goal In Cleanup of Vast Toxic Waste," *New York Times*, August 5, 1991.

10. Sivard, *World Military and Social Expenditures 1991* (based on latest available figures from 1987).

11. Mahbub ul Haq, "A Peace Agenda for the Third World," *Development* (Journal of the Society for International Development), No. 1, 1991; see also Robert S. McNamara, "The Post-Cold War World and Its Implications for Military Expenditures in the Developing Countries," address to the World Bank Annual Conference on Development Economics, Washington, D.C., April 25, 1991.

12. U.S. energy savings is Worldwatch estimate based on Department of Energy (DOE), Energy Information Agency (EIA), *State Energy Price and Expenditure Report 1988* (Washington, D.C.: September 1990), and on DOE, EIA, *Monthly Energy Review September 1991* (Washington, D.C.: 1991); California Energy Commission, *Energy Efficiency Report* (Sacramento, Calif.: 1990).

13. Energy savings from low-flow showerheads from Michael Shepard, "How to Improve Energy Efficiency," *Issues in Science and Technology*, Summer 1991.

14. "Beijing Ministerial Declaration on Environment and Development," Ministerial Conference of Developing Countries on Environment and Development, Beijing, June 18–19, 1991; see also "Minister Vows to Vigorously Support Plan for a Third World 'Green' Fund," *International Environment Reporter*, July 17, 1991.

15. *World Bank News*, May 9, 1991; see also David Reed, *The Global Environment Facility: Sharing Responsibility for the Biosphere* (Washington, D.C.: Multilateral Development Bank Program, World Wide Fund for Nature, 1991).

16. David Gardner, "EC Nears Deal on Energy Tax to Combat Global Warming,"

*Financial Times*, October 14, 1991; tax on leading industrial nations refers to members of the Organisation for Economic Co-operation and Development; James Poterba, "Tax Policy to Combat Global Warming: On Designing a Carbon Tax," in Rudiger Dornbusch and James M. Poterba, eds., *Global Warming: Economic Policy Responses* (Cambridge, Mass.: MIT Press, 1991).

17. Organisation for Economic Co-operation and Development, *Development Co-operation: Efforts and Policies of the Members of the Development Assistance Committee* (Paris: in press).

18. Sandra Postel, "Toward a New 'Eco'-nomics," *World Watch*, September/October 1990; David Pearce et al., *Blueprint for a Green Economy* (London: Earthscan Publications Ltd., 1989); see also Robert Goodland et al., eds., *Environmentally Sustainable Economic Development: Building on Brundtland* (Paris: UNESCO, 1991).

19. Mahabub Hossain, *Credit for Alleviation of Rural Poverty: The Grameen Bank in Bangladesh*, Research Report 65 (Washington, D.C.: International Food Policy Research Institute, 1988); Alexander M. Counts, "Bangladesh: Help the Poor, Not the Rich," *Washington Post*, May 14, 1991; John C. Ryan, "Goods from the Woods," *World Watch*, July/August 1991.

20. Michael Weisskopf, "2 California Utilities Vow Emissions Cuts," *Washington Post*, May 21, 1991; International Fund for Agricultural Development, *IFAD Annual Report 1989* (Rome: 1990).

21. Sara Parkin, "Power & Green Politics," *Resurgence*, May/June 1991.

## Chapter 2. Conserving Biological Diversity

1. Species numbers from Nigel E. Stork, "Insect Diversity: Facts, Fiction and Speculation," *Biological Journal of the Linnean Society*, Vol. 35, 1988, and from E.O. Wilson, "The

Current State of Biological Diversity," in E.O. Wilson and Frances M. Peter, eds., *Biodiversity* (Washington, D.C.: National Academy Press, 1988); soil from John Lancaster, "Protecting a Wealth of Species," *Washington Post*, May 24, 1991.

2. Edward O. Wilson, *The Diversity of Life* (Cambridge, Mass: Harvard University Press, forthcoming), based on assumed total of 10 million tropical rain forest species; World Resources Institute (WRI) et al., *Global Biodiversity Strategy: Guidelines for Action to Save, Study, and Use Earth's Biotic Wealth Sustainably and Equitably* (Washington, D.C.: 1992). For other recent scientific estimates, see Walter V. Reid, "How Many Species Will There Be?" in J. Sayer and T. Whitmore, eds., *Tropical Deforestation and the Extinction of Species* (Gland, Switzerland: International Union for Conservation of Nature and Natural Resources (IUCN), forthcoming), which predicts that deforestation will commit 0.1–0.5 percent of tropical forest species (or 10,000–50,000 species out of 10 million) to extinction per year, and Jared Diamond, "Playing Dice with Megadeath," *Discover*, April 1990, which assumes that current trends will result in the loss of 90 percent of tropical forests and half their 30 million species over the next century, or 150,000 species per year.

3. WRI et al., *Global Biodiversity Strategy*; Larry Harris, Department of Wildlife and Range Sciences, University of Florida, Gainesville, Fla., private communication, July 7, 1991.

4. Aldo Leopold, *A Sand County Almanac, With Essays From Round River* (New York: Sierra Club/Ballantine Books, 1966).

5. Species from Walter V. Reid and Kenton R. Miller, *Keeping Options Alive: The Scientific Basis for Conserving Biodiversity* (Washington, D.C.: WRI, 1989); loss of nearly half of tropical forests from Norman Myers, *Deforestation Rates in Tropical Forests and Their Climatic Implications* (London: Friends of the Earth, 1989); 17 million hectares from William

Booth, "Tropical Forests Disappearing at Faster Rate," *Washington Post*, September 9, 1991; Ismail Serageldin, *Saving Africa's Rainforests* (Washington, D.C.: World Bank, 1991).

6. James Brooke, "Amazon Forest Loss is Sharply Cut in Brazil," *New York Times*, March 26, 1991; Atlantic forests from Mark Collins, ed., *The Last Rain Forests* (London: Mitchell Beazley, 1990); John R. McNeill, "Deforestation in the Araucaria Zone of Southern Brazil, 1900–1983," in John F. Richards and Richard P. Tucker, eds., *World Deforestation in the Twentieth Century* (Durham, N.C.: Duke University, 1988).

7. Prairies from *Final Consensus Report of the Keystone Policy Dialogue on Biological Diversity on Federal Lands* (Keystone, Colo.: Keystone Center, 1991); cedars from Reid and Miller, *Keeping Options Alive*; Sandra Postel and John C. Ryan, "Reforming Forestry," in Lester R. Brown et al., *State of the World 1991* (New York: W.W. Norton & Co., 1991); Spencer B. Beebe, "Conservation in Temperate and Tropical Rain Forests: The Search for an Ecosystem Approach to Sustainability," paper presented at the 56th North American Wildlife and Natural Resources Conference, Edmonton, Alta., Canada, March 25–29, 1991; Keith Moore, *Coastal Watersheds: An Inventory of Watersheds in the Coastal Temperate Forests of British Columbia* (Vancouver: Earthlife Canada Foundation and Ecotrust/Conservation International, 1991).

8. U.N. Environment Programme (UNEP), *Environmental Data Report*, 3rd ed. (Oxford: Basil Blackwell, 1991); Thomas E. Dahl, *Wetlands Losses in the United States 1780's to 1980's* (Washington, D.C.: U.S. Department of the Interior, Fish and Wildlife Service, 1990); "Sustaining Wetlands: International Challenge for the 90s," final report of the Sustaining Wetlands Forum, Ottawa, Ont., Canada, April 1990; prairie wetlands from Peter Lee, "Viewpoint," Environment Alberta, *Environment Views*, September 1990.

9. World Conservation Monitoring Center (WCMC), *Global Biodiversity 1992* (draft) (Cambridge: forthcoming); Ecuador from Don Hinrichsen, *Our Common Seas: Coasts in Crisis* (London: Earthscan, 1990), and from Monica Herzig Zürcher and Alejandro Toledo Ocampo, "The Nineties: Another 'Lost Decade' for Latin American Wetlands?" *IWRB News* (International Waterfowl and Wetlands Research Bureau), January 1991; *Biodiversity Action Plan for Indonesia* (draft) (Ciloto, W. Java, Indonesia: National Planning Agency et al., 1991).

10. Boyce Thorne-Miller and John Catena, *The Living Ocean: Understanding and Protecting Marine Biodiversity* (Washington, D.C.: Island Press, 1991); Pamela Hallock-Muller, "Coastal Pollution and Coral Communities," *Underwater Naturalist*, Vol. 19, No. 1, 1990.

11. Susan M. Wells, ed., *Coral Reefs of the World* (Gland, Switzerland: IUCN and UNEP, 1988); Jon Miller, "Troubled Waters," *Far Eastern Economic Review*, March 15, 1990; Philippines diversity from Les Kaufman, "Marine Biodiversity: The Sleeping Dragon," *Conservation Biology*, December 1988.

12. Bleaching dates from Ernest H. Williams Jr. and Lucy Bunkley-Williams, "Coral Reef Bleaching Alert," *Nature*, July 19, 1990; Raymond L. Hayes and Thomas J. Goreau, "The Tropical Coral Reef Ecosystem as a Harbinger of Global Warming," paper presented at the 2nd International Conference on Global Warming, Chicago, April 8–11, 1991.

13. "No Money for Hawaiian Snails," *Oryx*, January 1991. The sources for Table 2–2 are: amphibians from David B. Wake, "Declining Amphibian Populations," *Science*, August 23, 1991, from David Towns and Ian Atkinson, "New Zealand's Restoration Ecology," *New Scientist*, April 20, 1991, and from Radhakrishna Rao, "India: Bullfrog Extinction," *Third World Week*, November 23, 1990;

birds from N. J. Collar and P. Andrew, *Birds to Watch: The ICBP Checklist of Threatened Birds* (Cambridge: International Council for Bird Preservation, 1988), and from Barry R. Noon and Kimberly Young, "Evidence of Continuing Worldwide Declines in Bird Populations: Insights from an International Conference in New Zealand," *Conservation Biology*, June 1991; fish from Jack E. Williams et al., "Fishes of North America Endangered, Threatened, or of Special Concern: 1989," *Fisheries*, November/December 1989, from "Fishing and Pollution Imperil Coastal Fish, Several Studies Find," *New York Times*, July 16, 1991, and from Leslie S. Kaufman et al., "A Decade of Ecological Change in Lake Victoria," New England Aquarium, Boston, Mass., unpublished; invertebrates from Wilson, *The Diversity of Life*, from Organisation for Economic Co-operation and Development (OECD), *State of the Environment 1991* (Paris: 1991), and from WRI et al., *Global Biodiversity Strategy*; mammals from W. L. Hare, ed., *Ecologically Sustainable Development* (Fitzroy, Australia: Australian Conservation Foundation et al., 1990), and from OECD, *State of the Environment 1991*; carnivores from "Saving the Wild Cats: A Manifesto on Cat Conservation," *Tiger Paper*, January/March 1990, and from Jane E. Brody, "Boom in Poaching Threatens Bears Worldwide," *New York Times*, May 1, 1990; primates from IUCN, *1990 IUCN Red List of Threatened Animals* (Gland, Switzerland, and Cambridge: 1990); reptiles from Species Survival Commission, Tortoise and Freshwater Turtle Specialist Group, *Tortoises and Freshwater Turtles: An Action Plan for their Conservation*, 2nd ed. (Gland, Switzerland: IUCN, 1991), and, for sea turtles, from IUCN, *1990 IUCN Red List of Threatened Animals*.

14. G. Carleton Ray, "Coastal-Zone Biodiversity Patterns," *Bioscience*, July/August 1991.

15. Soviet Union from Carl Safina and Ken Hinman, "Stemming the Tide: Conservation of Coastal Fish Habitat in the United

States," Summary of a National Symposium on Coastal Fish Habitat Conservation, Baltimore, Md., March 7–9, 1991; Malaysia from Jared M. Diamond, "The Present, Past and Future of Human-Caused Extinctions," *Philosophical Transactions of the Royal Society of London*, Vol. B 325, 1989.

16. UNEP, *Environmental Data Report*; Chris McIvor, "Namibia Fights to Save its Fish," *New African*, May 1991.

17. Wake, "Declining Amphibian Populations"; Marcia Barinaga, "Where Have All the Froggies Gone?" *Science*, March 2, 1990; Rao, "India: Bullfrog Extinction."

18. Reid and Miller, *Keeping Options Alive*; Peter H. Raven, "Biology in an Age of Extinction: What Is Our Responsibility?" Plenary Address, Fourth International Congress of Systematic and Evolutionary Biology, College Park, Md., July 1–4, 1990.

19. Southern Africa (which includes Botswana, Lesotho, Namibia, South Africa, and Swaziland) from Jeffrey A. McNeely et al., *Conserving the World's Biological Diversity* (Gland, Switzerland, and Washington, D.C.: IUCN et al., 1990); Philip Shabecoff, "Plant Lovers' Ambitious Goal Is No More Extinctions," *New York Times*, November 13, 1990.

20. Reid and Miller, *Keeping Options Alive*.

21. Cary Fowler and Pat Mooney, *Shattering: Food, Politics, and the Loss of Genetic Diversity* (Tucson: University of Arizona Press, 1990); Indonesian rice from *Biodiversity Action Plan for Indonesia*, and from WRI et al., *Global Biodiversity Strategy*.

22. Reid and Miller, *Keeping Options Alive*; Victoria Griffith, "Diseases Put Brazil's Oranges at Risk," *Financial Times*, June 14, 1991; Stephen B. Brush, "Farmer Conservation of New World Crops: The Case of Andean Potatoes," *Diversity*, Vol. 7, Nos. 1 and 2, 1991.

23. Willa Nehlsen et al., "Pacific Salmon at the Crossroads: Stocks at Risk from Califor-

nia, Oregon, Idaho, and Washington," *Fisheries*, March/April 1991.

24. IUCN, *1990 United Nations List of National Parks and Protected Areas* (Gland, Switzerland, and Cambridge: 1990); Chile from George Ledec, "A Proposed Strategy for the World Bank to Promote Increased Conservation of Biological Diversity in Latin America and the Caribbean," unpublished paper, April 1989; M.I. Dyer and M.M. Holland, "The Biosphere-Reserve Concept: Needs for A Network Design," *Bioscience*, May 1991; John C. Ryan, "Belize's Reefs on the Rocks," *World Watch*, November/December 1991.

25. Parks from WCMC, *Global Biodiversity 1992*; Janis Alcorn and Augusta Molnar, "Deforestation and Forest-Human Relationships: What Can We Learn from India?" paper presented at meeting of the American Anthropological Association, New Orleans, La., November 1990; James Rush, *The Last Tree: Reclaiming the Environment in Tropical Asia* (New York: The Asia Society, 1991); Kuna from Mac Chapin, "Losing the Way of the Great Father," *New Scientist*, August 10, 1991; William Harp, "Ecology and Cosmology, Rain Forest Exploitation Among the Emberá-Chocó," paper presented at Humid Tropical Lowlands Conference: Development Strategies and Natural Resource Management, Panama City, Panama, June 17–21, 1991; Tukano from Jason W. Clay, *Indigenous People and Tropical Forests: Models of Land Use and Management from Latin America* (Cambridge, Mass.: Cultural Survival, 1988).

26. J. Michael McCloskey and Heather Spalding, "A Reconnaissance-Level Inventory of the Amount of Wilderness Remaining in the World," *Ambio*, Vol. 18, No. 4, 1989; Janis B. Alcorn, "Ethics, Economies, and Conservation," in Margery L. Oldfield and Janis B. Alcorn, eds., *Biodiversity: Culture, Conservation and Ecodevelopment* (Boulder, Colo.: Westview Press, forthcoming); Arturo Gómez-Pompa and Andrea Kaus, "Conservation by Traditional Cultures in the Trop-

ics," in Vance Martin, ed., *For the Conservation of Earth* (Golden, Colo.: Fulcrum, 1988).

27. Richard Evans Schultes, "Ethnobotanical Conservation and Plant Diversity in the Northwest Amazon," *Diversity*, Vol. 7, Nos. 1 and 2, 1991; tribes from Eugene Linden, "Lost Tribes, Lost Knowledge," *Time*, September 23, 1991; Charles R. Clement, "Amazonian Fruits: Neglected, Threatened and Potentially Rich Resources Require Urgent Attention," *Diversity*, Vol. 7, Nos. 1 and 2, 1991.

28. Christopher A. Myers and Aniruddh D. Patel, "Saving Asia's Wildlife," *World Monitor*, January 1991.

29. Organization of American States (OAS) and National Park Service (NPS), U.S. Department of Interior, *Inventory of Caribbean Marine and Coastal Protected Areas* (Washington, D.C.: 1988); Mark Brazil, "Where Eastern Eagles Dare," *New Scientist*, May 4, 1991.

30. Jim Fulton, Member of Canadian Parliament, letter to Lucien Bouchard, Minister of Environment, February 6, 1990; Czechoslovakia from Jim Thorsell, "The IUCN Register of Threatened Protected Areas of the World," paper presented to the 34th Working Session of IUCN Commission on National Parks and Protected Areas, Perth, Australia, November 26–27, 1990; *Biodiversity Action Plan for Indonesia*; Europe from Patrick C. West and Steven R. Brechin, eds., *Resident Peoples and National Parks: Social Dilemmas and Strategies in International Conservation* (Tucson: University of Arizona Press, 1991); marine areas from OAS and NPS, *Inventory of Caribbean Marine and Coastal Protected Areas*, and from "Focus on: Marine Protected Areas," in WRI, *World Resources 1988–89* (New York: Basic Books, 1988).

31. Poland from Thorsell, "The IUCN Register of Threatened Protected Areas"; Yasmin D. Arquiza, "Toll on the Atoll," *Far Eastern Economic Review*, March 15, 1990.

32. John A. Dixon and Paul B. Sherman, *Economics of Protected Areas: A New Look at Benefits and Costs* (Washington, D.C.: Island Press, 1990); Alcorn, "Ethics, Economies, and Conservation."

33. Michael Wells et al., *People and Parks: Linking Protected Area Management with Local Communities* (Washington, D.C.: World Bank et al., 1991).

34. Ibid.; "Villagers Rally for Dam Project in National Park," *Bangkok Post*, November 21, 1990.

35. Mike De Mott, "Peru: Wildlife Area Focus of Ecological Debate," *Latinamerica Press*, June 20, 1991.

36. Wells et al., *People and Parks*.

37. Daniel B. Botkin, *Discordant Harmonies: A New Ecology for the Twenty-First Century* (New York: Oxford University Press, 1990); on ancient clearance of seemingly pristine Amazonian jungle, see Anna Roosevelt, "The Historical Perspective on Resource Use in Tropical Latin America," in Center for Latin American Studies, University of Florida, *Economic Catalysts to Ecological Change* (Gainesville, Fla.: 1990); toxic wastes have been found in fish of the deep ocean, see Thorne-Miller and Catena, *The Living Ocean*.

38. Monte Hummel, *A Conservation Strategy for Large Carnivores in Canada* (Toronto: World Wildlife Fund Canada, 1990); J. M. Thiollay, "Area Requirements for the Conservation of Rain Forest Raptors and Game Birds in French Guiana," *Conservation Biology*, June 1989; C.M. Pannell, "The Role of Animals in Natural Regeneration and the Management of Equatorial Rain Forests for Conservation and Timber Production," *Commonwealth Forestry Review*, Vol. 68, No. 4, 1989; Elliott A. Norse, *Ancient Forests of the Pacific Northwest* (Washington, D.C.: Island Press, 1990); Carlos A. Peres, "Humboldt's Woolly Monkeys Decimated by Hunting in Amazonia," *Oryx*, April 1991; Reed F. Noss, "Sustainability and Wilderness," *Conservation Biology*, March 1991.

39. Reed F. Noss, "What Can Wilderness Do For Biodiversity?" in P. Reed, ed., *Preparing to Manage Wilderness in the 21st Century* (Asheville, N.C.: U.S. Department of Agriculture, Forest Service, 1990); Craig L. Shafer, *Nature Reserves: Island Theory and Conservation Practice* (Washington, D.C.: Smithsonian Institution, 1990).

40. Adrian Barnett and Aléxia Celeste da Cunha, "The Golden-Backed Uacari on the Upper Rio Negro, Brazil," *Oryx*, April 1991.

41. Alan B. Durning, *Poverty and the Environment: Reversing the Downward Spiral*, Worldwatch Paper 92 (Washington, D.C.: Worldwatch Institute, November 1989).

42. Paul R. Ehrlich and Edward O. Wilson, "Biodiversity Studies: Science and Policy," *Science*, August 16, 1991; Reed Noss, "A Native Ecosystems Act (Concept Paper)," *Wild Earth*, Spring 1991; Z. Naveh, "Some Remarks on Recent Developments in Landscape Ecology as a Transdisciplinary Ecological and Geographical Science," *Landscape Ecology*, Vol. 5, No. 2, 1991.

43. Andrew Gray, "Indigenous Peoples and the Marketing of the Rainforest," *The Ecologist*, November/December 1990; James Brooke, "Venezuela Befriends Tribe, but What's Venezuela?" *New York Times*, September 11, 1991.

44. Sue Armstrong, "The People Who Want Their Parks Back," *New Scientist*, July 6, 1991; Alcorn, "Ethics, Economies, and Conservation."

45. Gregor Hodgson, "Drugs from the Sea," *Far Eastern Economic Review*, April 11, 1991; Philippe Rasoanaivo, "Rain Forests of Madagascar: Sources of Industrial and Medicinal Plants," *Ambio*, December 1990.

46. Medicines from Elaine Elisabetsky, "Sociopolitical, Economical and Ethical Issues in Medicinal Plant Research," *Journal of Ethnopharmacology*, No. 32, 1991; rattan from Jenne H. De Beer and Melanie J. McDermott,

*The Economic Value of Non-timber Forest Products in Southeast Asia* (Amsterdam: Netherlands Committee for IUCN, 1989).

47. Fikret Berkes, ed., *Common Property Resources: Ecology and Community-Based Sustainable Development* (London: Belhaven Press, 1989); De Beer and McDermott, *The Economic Value of Non-timber Forest Products*; John Kurien, *Ruining the Commons and Responses of the Commoners: Coastal Overfishing and Fishermen's Actions in Kerala State, India* (Geneva: UN Research Institute for Social Development, 1991).

48. De Beer and McDermott, *The Economic Value of Non-timber Forest Products*; fish from Oliver T. Coomes, "Rain Forest Extraction, Agroforestry, and Biodiversity Loss: An Environmental History from the Northeastern Peruvian Amazon," paper presented to the 16th International Congress of the Latin American Studies Association (hereinafter, LASA Congress), Washington, D.C., April 6, 1991; Rodolfo Vasquez and Alwyn H. Gentry, "Use and Misuse of Forest-harvested Fruits in the Iquitos Area," *Conservation Biology*, December 1989; 2–3 percent figure from Cultural Survival, "Cultural Survival Enterprises Direct Assistance Projects FY1989–1990," Cambridge, Mass., no date; market control from Stephan Schwartzman, "Marketing of Extractive Products in the Brazilian Amazon," Environmental Defense Fund, Washington, D.C., October 29, 1990.

49. John O. Browder, "Social and Economic Constraints on the Development of Market-Oriented Extractive Reserves in Amazon Rain Forests," *Annals of Economic Botany*, forthcoming; Americas Watch, *Rural Violence in Brazil* (Washington, D.C.: Human Rights Watch, 1991); goal of one fourth of Brazilian Amazon from Luis Fernando Allegretti, Institute for Amazon Studies, Curitiba, Brazil, speech to LASA Congress, April 4, 1991; Guatemala from Conrad Reining, "Non-Timber Forest Products and the Peten, Guatemala: Why Extractive Reserves Are Critical for Both Conservation and Development,"

Conservation International, Washington, D.C., unpublished paper, March 1991; Peru from Coomes, "Rain Forest Extraction."

50. Import tax from Environmental Defense Fund, "Rubber Tappers Demonstrate in Brasilia," press release, Washington, D.C., April 2, 1991; plantations from Nigel J.H. Smith and Richard Evans Schultes, "Deforestation and Shrinking Crop Gene-Pools in Amazonia," *Environmental Conservation*, Autumn 1990.

51. Douglas Daly, "Extractive Reserves: A Great New Hope," *Garden*, November/December 1990; Charles M. Peters, "Plenty of Fruit But No Free Lunch," *Garden*, November/December 1990.

52. Peters, "Plenty of Fruit"; Henrik Borgtoft Pedersen and Henrik Balslev, "Economic Botany of Ecuadorean Palms," paper presented at conference arranged by Conservation International and Asociación Nacional para la Conservación de la Naturaleza on "The Sustainable Harvest and Marketing of Rain Forest Products," Panama City, Panama, June 20–21, 1991.

53. Charles M. Peters et al., "Oligarchic Forests of Economic Plants in Amazonia: Utilization and Conservation of an Important Tropical Resource," *Conservation Biology*, December 1989; Christine Padoch, Institute of Economic Botany, New York Botanical Garden, speech to American Association for the Advancement of Science (AAAS) Annual Meeting, Washington, D.C., February 18, 1991.

54. Agnes Kiss, ed., *Living With Wildlife: Wildlife Resource Management with Local Participation in Africa* (Washington, D.C.: The World Bank, 1990).

55. Ibid.; Oliver Kanene, "Poacher's Pay-Off," *Panoscope*, January 1991; Zimbabwe figure from Mary-Lu Cole, "A Farm on the Wild Side," *New Scientist*, September 8, 1990.

56. Forest ownership figure from Robert Repetto, "Deforestation in the Tropics," *Scientific American*, April 1990; Mark Poffenberger, "Facilitating Change in Forestry Bureaucracies," in Mark Poffenberger, ed., *Keepers of the Forest: Land Management Alternatives in Southeast Asia* (West Hartford, Conn.: Kumarian Press, 1990); Conner Bailey and Charles Zerner, "Role of Traditional Fisheries Resource Management Systems for Sustainable Resource Utilization," presented at Forum Perikanan Dalam Pembangunan Jangka Panjang Tahap II: Tantangan dan Peluang, Sukabumi, West Java, Indonesia, June 18–21, 1991; Dale Lewis et al., "Wildlife Conservation Outside Protected Areas—Lessons from an Experiment in Zambia," *Conservation Biology*, June 1990.

57. Figure of 97 percent from Arthur Mitchell et al., "Community Participation for Conservation Area Management in the Cyclops Mountains, Irian Jaya, Indonesia," in Poffenberger, ed., *Keepers of the Forest*; George Marshall, "The Political Economy of Logging: The Barnett Inquiry into Corruption in the Papua New Guinea Timber Industry," *The Ecologist*, September/October 1990; "Putting Teeth in Logging Laws," *Asiaweek*, August 30, 1991.

58. Postel and Ryan, "Reforming Forestry"; A.J. Hansen et al., "Conserving Biodiversity in Managed Forests: Lessons from Natural Forests," *Bioscience*, June 1991.

59. Pannell, "The Role of Animals in Natural Regeneration"; Postel and Ryan, "Reforming Forestry"; Marguerite Holloway, "Hol Chan: Marine Parks Benefit Commercial Fisheries," *Scientific American*, May 1991; A.T. White, "The Effect of Community-Managed Marine Reserves in the Philippines on Their Associated Coral Reef Fish Populations," *Asian Fisheries Science*, Vol. 2, 1988; Wendell Berry, "Preserving Wildness," *Wilderness*, Spring 1987.

60. Genetic vulnerability from Gary Paul Nabhan, *Enduring Seeds: Native American Agri-*

*culture and Wild Plant Conservation* (San Francisco, Calif.: North Point Press, 1989), and from Fowler and Mooney, *Shattering.*

61. Earl Young, Belize Fisheries Department, Coastal Zone Management Unit, private communication, July 2, 1991; Ann Y. Robinson, "Conservation Compliance and Wildlife," *Journal of Soil and Water Conservation*, January/February 1989; David Baldock, *Agriculture and Habitat Loss in Europe* (Gland, Switzerland: World Wide Fund for Nature International, 1990); Robert M. May, "Avian Analyses," *Nature*, October 25, 1990.

62. David F. Bezdicek and David Granatstein, "Crop Rotation Efficiencies and Biological Diversity in Farming Systems," *American Journal of Alternative Agriculture*, Vol. 4, Nos. 3 and 4, 1989; Peter G. Kevan et al., "Insect Pollinators and Sustainable Agriculture," *American Journal of Alternative Agriculture*, Vol. 5, No. 1, 1990.

63. Baldock, *Agriculture and Habitat Loss in Europe*; Robinson, "Conservation Compliance and Wildlife"; Defenders of Wildlife, *In Defense of Wildlife: Preserving Communities and Corridors* (Washington, D.C.: 1989).

64. Subsidies from WRI et al., *Global Biodiversity Strategy*; Holly B. Brough, "A New Lay of the Land," *World Watch*, January/February 1991.

65. Keystone Center, *Oslo Plenary Session Final Consensus Report: Global Initiative for the Security and Sustainable Use of Plant Genetic Resources* (Oslo: 1991); Damien Lewis, "The Gene Hunters," *Geographical Magazine*, January 1991.

66. Nabhan, *Enduring Seeds*; Miguel A. Altieri, "Traditional Farming in Latin America," *The Ecologist*, March/April 1991; Oldfield and Alcorn, *Biodiversity.*

67. Altieri, "Traditional Farming"; Robert Chambers et al., eds., *Farmer First: Farmer Innovation and Agricultural Research* (London: Intermediate Technology, 1989); Patricia

Allen and Debra Van Dusen, eds., *Global Perspectives on Agroecology and Sustainable Agricultural Systems*, Proceedings of the 6th International Scientific Conference of the International Federation of Organic Agriculture Movements (Santa Cruz: University of California, 1989).

68. Reed F. Noss, "Wildlife Corridors," in D. Smith, ed., *Ecology of Greenways* (Minneapolis: Univ. of Minnesota, forthcoming); Lowell W. Adams and Louise E. Dove, *Wildlife Reserves and Corridors in the Urban Environment: A Guide to Ecological Landscape Planning and Resource Conservation* (Columbia, Md.: National Institute for Urban Wildlife, 1989).

69. Kathleen Landauer and Mark Brazil, eds., *Tropical Home Gardens* (Tokyo: United Nations University, 1990); Kenneth A. Dahlberg, "Fields, Fisheries, Grasslands, Forests: Towards More Regenerative Systems," draft paper presented at AAAS annual meeting, Washington, D.C., February 17, 1991.

70. Nabhan, *Enduring Seeds.*

## Chapter 3. Building a Bridge to Sustainable Energy

1. The $5-per-barrel figure is in 1991 dollars per barrel, based on 1971 figure of 30¢ per kilowatt-hour, provided by James Schlesinger, former U.S. Secretary of Energy, private communication, July 11, 1991; nuclear cost figures reflect a change in real prices, from Christopher Flavin, *Reassessing Nuclear Power: The Fallout from Chernobyl*, Worldwatch Paper 75 (Washington, D.C.: Washington, D.C., March 1987); "World List of Nuclear Power Plants," *Nuclear News*, August 1991.

2. See Table 3–2 for references for these figures. This chapter's focus on the potential to use natural gas as a transition fuel is intended to complement the detailed analyses of energy efficiency and renewables in earlier editions of *State of the World.*

3. U.S. Department of Energy (DOE), *National Energy Strategy, First Edition 1991/1992*

(Washington, D.C.: U.S. Government Printing Office, 1991); Karen Schmidt, "Industrial Countries' Responses to Global Climate Change," *Environmental and Energy Study Institute Special Report*, Washington, D.C., July 1, 1991.

4. DOE, *National Energy Strategy*; Daniel Yergin, *The Prize: The Epic Quest for Oil, Money & Power* (New York: Simon & Schuster, 1990).

5. World oil consumption from British Petroleum (BP), *BP Statistical Review of World Energy* (London: various years); industrial-country data for 1990 from BP, *BP Statistical Review of World Energy* (London: 1991), and from Organisation for Economic Co-operation and Development (OECD), *In Figures* (Paris: 1991); developing-country data for 1989 from United Nations, *Yearbook of Energy Statistics* (New York: 1991), and from Central Intelligence Agency (CIA), *Handbook of Economic Statistics* (Washington, D.C.: 1990).

6. Motor Vehicle Manufacturers Association, *Facts and Figures '91* (Detroit, Mich.: 1991).

7. "World List of Nuclear Power Plants"; BP, *BP Statistical Review* (various years).

8. Carbon emissions based on Gregg Marland et al., *Estimates of CO$_2$ Emissions from Fossil Fuel Burning and Cement Manufacturing, Based on the United Nations Energy Statistics U.S. Bureau of Mines Cement Manufacturing Data* (Oak Ridge, Tenn.: Oak Ridge National Laboratory, 1989), and on Thomas A. Boden et al., *Trends '91* (Oak Ridge, Tenn.: Oak Ridge National Laboratory, in press); BP, *BP Statistical Review* (1991).

9. Worldwatch Institute estimates based on Marland et al., *Estimates of CO$_2$ Emissions*, on Boden et al., *Trends '91*, and on BP, *BP Statistical Review* (1991).

10. Third World share of fossil energy use from BP, *BP Statistical Review* (various years); long-term carbon outlook is a Worldwatch Institute estimate based on projected leveling off of industrial-country emissions and a 3.8-percent annual increase in developing-country emissions as projected in The Intergovernmental Panel on Climate Change (IPCC), *Climate Change: The IPCC Response Strategies* (Washington, D.C.: Island Press, 1991).

11. People's Republic of China, Ministry of Energy, *Energy in China* (Beijing: 1990); BP, *BP Statistical Review* (1991); Marland et al., *Estimates of CO$_2$ Emissions*; Boden et al., *Trends '91*.

12. BP, *BP Statistical Review* (various years); Boden et al., *Trends '91*; Richard H. Hilt and Marie L. Lihn, "The Clean Air Act's Impact on Natural Gas Markets," *Public Utilities Fortnightly*, October 15, 1991; Edwin Moore and Enrique Crousillat, "Prospects for Gas-Fueled Combined-Cycle Power Generation in the Developing Countries," Energy Series Paper No. 35, World Bank, Washington, D.C., 1991.

13. Editorial, *Financial Times*, January 18, 1991; BP, *BP Statistical Review* (1991).

14. BP, *BP Statistical Review* (1991); industry analysts' projections from "IPAA: U.S. Oil Flow Headed for Further Decline," *Oil & Gas Journal*, May 13, 1991; DOE, Energy Information Administration (EIA), *Monthly Energy Review September 1991* (Washington, D.C.: 1991); Ray Moseley, "Soviet Oil Industry Suffers Deepest Crisis in its History," *Journal of Commerce*, September 17, 1991.

15. DOE, EIA, *Monthly Energy Review September 1991*; William Dawkins, "Middle East to Increase Share of Oil Output," *Financial Times*, June 4, 1991; Overseas Development Council, "The Gulf Crisis: Impact on Developing Countries," *Policy Focus*, No. 3, 1991; Ed Morse, "The Coming Oil Revolution," *Foreign Affairs*, Winter 1990–91.

16. Vahan Zanoyan, "The Middle East and OPEC Dynamics," presented at the Aspen Institute Energy Policy Forum, Aspen,

Colo., July 11, 1991; Caryle Murphy, "Gap Widens Between Arab Rich, Poor; Disparity May Add to Mideast Instability When Crisis is Over," *Washington Post*, November 13, 1990.

17. Philip K. Verleger, Jr., "The Oil Vortex: A Way Out?" *Economic Insights*, September/October 1990; Morse, "The Coming Oil Revolution"; Meena Menon, Staff Reporter, *The Times of India*, Bombay, India, private communication, October 17, 1991; "Europe, Developing Nations Face Serious Oil Shortages," *Journal of Commerce*, October 16, 1990.

18. U.S. Office of Technology Assessment, *Catching Our Breath: Next Steps for Reducing Urban Ozone* (Washington, D.C.: U.S. Government Printing Office, 1989); Laurent Belsie, "Ozone Pollution Reaches 10-Year Highs Across US," *Christian Science Monitor*, August 23, 1988; Prague from Josef Vavroušek et al., *The Environment in Czechoslovakia* (Prague: Department of the Environment, State Commission for Science, Technology, and Investments, 1990); "Vehicular Pollution Makes Breathing Dangerous," *Indian Post* (Bombay), February 11, 1989; Mark A. Uhlig, "Mexico City: the World's Foulest Air Grows Worse," *New York Times*, May 12, 1991; Mary Kay Magistad, "Bangkok's Progress Marked by Health Hazards," *Washington Post*, May 7, 1991.

19. "Sugar Maples Sicken Under Acid Rain's Pall," *New York Times*, May 15, 1991; BP, *BP Statistical Review* (1991); James N. Galloway et al., "Acid Rain: China, United States, and a Remote Area," *Science*, June 19, 1987.

20. U.S. Environmental Protection Agency (EPA), *Clean Air Act Amendments of 1990 Detailed Summary of Titles*, November 1990; John H. Wile, "The Impacts of the 1990 Clean Air Act on Utility Planning," *Energy Outlook* (National Economic Research Associates, Inc., White Plains, N.Y.), February 1991; Hilary F. French, *Green Revolutions: Environmental Reconstruction in Eastern Europe and the Soviet Union*, Worldwatch Paper 99 (Washington, D.C.: Worldwatch Institute, November 1990).

21. Christopher Flavin, *Slowing Global Warming*, Worldwatch Paper 91 (Washington, D.C.: Worldwatch Institute, October 1989); Tim Worf, Scripps Institution of Oceanography, La Jolla, Calif., private communication, September 26, 1991; Schmidt, "Industrial Countries' Responses"; "The Carbon Club," *Atmosphere*, June 1991.

22. Schmidt, "Industrial Countries' Responses"; Matthew L. Wald, "Two Big California Utilities Plan to Cut $CO_2$ Emissions," *New York Times*, May 21, 1991.

23. Daniel A. Lashoff and Dennis A. Tirpak, eds., *Policy Options for Stabilizing Global Climate* (Washington, D.C.: EPA, 1990); Gregg Marland, "Carbon Dioxide Emission Rates for Conventional and Synthetic Fuels," *Energy*, Vol. 8, No. 12, 1983.

24. OECD, *Greenhouse Gas Emissions: The Energy Dimension* (Paris: 1991).

25. Robert L. Bradley, Jr., "Reconsidering the Natural Gas Act," Southern Regulatory Policy Institute Issue Paper No. 5, Roswell, Ga., August 1991; "The Use of Natural Gas in Power Stations," *Energy in Europe* (Commission of the European Communities, Brussels, Belgium), December 1990; Elizabeth A. Bretz, "Gas-turbine-based Combined-cycle Powerplants," *Electrical World*, August 1991; "UDI: Gas is Favorite Fuel of Utilities, IPPs," *Energy Daily*, March 18, 1991; American Gas Association (AGA) Planning & Analysis Group, "Trends in Electric Generation Capacity and the Impacts on Natural Gas Demand," Washington, D.C., January 23, 1988.

26. Moore and Crousillat, "Prospects for Gas-Fueled Combined-Cycle Power Generation"; Robert H. Williams and Eric D. Larson, "Expanding Roles for Gas Turbines in Power Generation," in Thomas B. Johansson et al., eds., *Electricity: Efficient End-Use and New Generation Technologies, and Their Planning Im-*

*plications* (Lund, Sweden: Lund University Press, 1990).

27. Williams and Larson, "Expanding Roles for Gas Turbines in Power Generation"; Alistair Lloyd, "Thermodynamics of Chemically Recuperated Gas Turbines," Princeton University Center for Energy and Environmental Studies, Princeton, N.J., January 1991; Moore and Crousillat, "Prospects for Gas-Fueled Combined-Cycle Power Generation."

28. Williams and Larson, "Expanding Roles for Gas Turbines in Power Generation"; Lloyd, "Thermodynamics of Chemically Recuperated Gas Turbines."

29. Christopher Flavin and Nicholas Lenssen, *Beyond the Petroleum Age: Designing a Solar Economy*, Worldwatch Paper 100 (Washington, D.C.: Worldwatch Institute, December 1990); Idaho National Engineering Laboratory et al., *The Potential of Renewable Energy: An Interlaboratory White Paper*, prepared for the Office of Policy, Planning and Analysis, U.S. Department of Energy, in support of the National Energy Strategy (Golden, Colo.: Solar Energy Research Institute, 1990); U.S. calculation is a Worldwatch Institute estimate based on the fact that coal-fired power plants account for 32 percent of U.S. $CO_2$ emissions; 30 percent gas figure based on the amount of natural gas required to provide 778 billion kilowatt-hours of electricity, assuming a heat rate of 7,000 Btus per kilowatt-hour in a combined cycle plant or 7 cubic feet of natural gas per kilowatt-hour, which means that 5.5 trillion cubic feet of gas would be required. U.S. natural gas use in 1990 was 18.8 trillion cubic feet.

30. Daniel Sperling, ed., *Alternative Transportation Fuels: An Environmental and Energy Solution* (New York: Quorum Books, 1989).

31. Thomas W. Lippman, "More Use of Natural Gas as Motor Fuel Explored," *Washington Post*, February 14, 1990; Allen R. Wastler, "Calif. Natural Gas Supplier Expands Fuel Station Network," *Journal of Commerce*, March 12, 1991; DOE, EIA, *Monthly Energy Review September 1991*; AGA Planning and Analysis Group, "Projected Natural Gas Demand from Vehicles under the Mobile Source Provisions of the Clean Air Act Amendments," Washington, D.C., January 30, 1991.

32. EPA, "Analysis of the Economic and Environmental Effects of Compressed Natural Gas as a Vehicle Fuel," Washington, D.C., April 1990; Jeffrey A. Alson et al., "Motor Vehicle Emission Characteristics and Air Quality Impacts of Methanol and Compressed Natural Gas," in Sperling, *Alternative Transportation Fuels*; AGA Planning and Analysis Group, "An Analysis of the Economic and Environmental Effects of Natural Gas as an Alternative Fuel," Washington, D.C., December 15, 1991.

33. Michael Walsh, automotive emissions consultant, Washington, D.C., private communication, September 13, 1991; Bryan D. Willson, Colorado State University, Fort Collins, Colo., private communication, September 17, 1991.

34. Walsh, private communication; Willson, private communication; Alan Caminiti, United Parcel Service, Greenwich, Conn., private communication, September 27, 1991.

35. Neil Geary, spokesperson, Amoco Company, Chicago, Ill., private communication, October 21, 1991; Wastler, "Calif. Natural Gas Supplier Expands Fuel Station Network"; Jessie Ochoa, public affairs officer, Shell Oil Company, Houston, Tex., private communication, October 21, 1991; AGA, "The Economic and Environmental Effects of Natural Gas as an Alternative Fuel."

36. Brian M. Barnett and W. Peter Teagan, "The Role of Fuel Cells in our Energy Future," Keynote Address, The Second Grove Fuel Cell Symposium, The Royal Institution, London, September 24–27, 1991; "Fuel Cells for Urban Power," *EPRI Journal*, September 1991.

37. EPA, *Methane Emissions and Opportunities for Control: Workshop Results of Intergovernmental Panel on Climate Change* (Washington, D.C.: 1990).

38. Ibid.; Daniel Lashof, "Draft Statement on Methane," Natural Resources Defense Council, Washington, D.C., September 3, 1991.

39. Willson, private communication; John Mueller, Standards, Development, and Support Division, EPA, Ann Arbor, Mich., private communication, October 23, 1991.

40. Robert A. Hefner, "Onshore Natural Gas in China," presented at the World Bank Energy Roundtable Discussion on Gas Development in Less Developed Countries, Paris, March 25–26, 1985.

41. Walter Vergara et al., *Natural Gas: Its Role and Potential in Economic Development* (Boulder, Colo.: Westview Press, 1990).

42. DOE, EIA, *Monthly Energy Review September 1991*; BP, *BP Statistical Review* (1991); Bradley, "Reconsidering the Natural Gas Act."

43. DOE, EIA, *Monthly Energy Review September 1991*.

44. U.S. National Research Council, *Undiscovered Oil and Gas Resources* (Washington, D.C.: National Academy Press, 1991).

45. Robert A. Hefner, "Natural Gas Resource Base and Production Capability Policy Issues," presented at the Aspen Institute Energy Policy Forum, Aspen, Colo., July 13, 1991; AGA Planning and Analysis Group, "Coalbed Methane Resource, Reservoir and Production Characteristics," Issue Brief, Washington, D.C., November 16, 1990.

46. W.L. Fisher, "Factors in Realizing Future Supply Potential of Domestic Oil and Natural Gas," presented at the Aspen Institute Energy Policy Forum, Aspen, Colo., July 13, 1991; Paul D. Holtberg, Gas Research Institute, "Is There Enough Gas?" presented at Americans for Energy Independence seminar on the natural gas outlook, Washington, D.C., October 9, 1991. It is important to distinguish between proven reserve figures—oil and gas that has been clearly identified through exploratory drilling—and the far greater estimates of ultimately recoverable resources.

47. BP, *BP Statistical Review* (1991); Moore and Crousillat, "Prospects for Gas-Fueled Combined-Cycle Power Generation"; Shell International Petroleum Company, *Natural Gas* (London: 1988).

48. C.D. Masters et al., "Resource Constraints in Petroleum Production Potential," *Science*, July 12, 1991; Moore and Crousillat, "Prospects for Gas-Fueled Combined-Cycle Power Generation"; World Bank, *Annual Report 1991* (Washington, D.C.: 1991).

49. Hefner, "Onshore Gas in China."

50. Hoyt Purcell, "Coalbed Methane Still a Threat," *Wilderness Alberta*, Spring 1991.

51. Flavin and Lenssen, *Beyond the Petroleum Age*.

52. Worldwatch Institute estimates based on gas resource estimates cited in this section and on the expectation that the recent growth rate in world gas production of 3.5 percent per year will continue.

53. This scenario is a Worldwatch Institute projection, using Oak Ridge and British Petroleum figures; it is not a prediction but simply an indication of what the effect of a major shift in the fossil fuel mix might be.

54. Flavin and Lenssen, *Beyond the Petroleum Age*; David Stipp, "Wind Farms May Energize the Midwest," *Wall Street Journal*, September 6, 1991; Cynthia Pollock Shea, "Germany Expanding Support Program for Wind Energy, Will Aid 250 MWe," *International Solar Energy Intelligence Report*, March 22, 1991; Leonard S. Greenberger et al., "Domestic Energy Alternatives," *Public Utilities Fortnightly*, January 15, 1991.

55. "Rechargeable Battery Markets Analyzed in New BCC Report," *International Solar Energy Intelligence Report*, February 8, 1991; Fredrick Rose, "Utilities React to Electromagnetic Fields," *Wall Street Journal*, April 11, 1991; Joan M. Ogden and Robert H. Williams, *Solar Hydrogen: Moving Beyond Fossil Fuels* (Washington, D.C.: World Resources Institute, 1989).

56. Carl-Jochen Winter and Joachim Nitsch, eds., *Hydrogen as as Energy Carrier: Technologies, Systems, Economy* (Berlin: Springer-Verlag, 1988); Ogden and Williams, *Solar Hydrogen: Moving Beyond Fossil Fuels.*

57. W. Grasse and F. Oster, eds., *Hysolar Solar Hydrogen Energy Results and Achievements 1985–1989* (Stuttgart: University of Stuttgart, 1990); Winter and Nitsch, *Hydrogen as an Energy Carrier*; Carl-Jochen Winter, "Solar Hydrogen Energy Trade," *Energy Policy*, June 1991.

58. Cost of solar hydrogen as transportation fuel from Ogden and Williams, *Solar Hydrogen: Moving Beyond Fossil Fuels*.

59. Mark A. DeLuchi, "Hydrogen Vehicles," in Sperling, *Alternative Transportation Fuels*; F.E. Lynch and G.J. Egan, "An Introduction Strategy for Hythane, an Alternative Fuel Blend of Hydrogen and Natural Gas," presented to the Committee on Transportation and Air Quality, Transportation Research Board, Denver, Colo., July 16–17, 1990.

60. Lynch and Egan, "An Introduction Strategy for Hythane."

61. Dennis Anderson, World Bank, Washington, D.C., private communication, October 16, 1991; the photovoltaic panels would actually cover just 15 percent of the land area, per John Schaefer and Edgar DeMeo, Electric Power Research Institute, "An Update on U.S. Experiences with Photovoltaic Power Generation," Proceedings of the American Power Conference, April 23, 1990;

U.S. land area used by the military from Michael Renner, "Assessing the Military's War on the Environment," in Lester R. Brown et al., *State of the World 1991* (New York: W.W. Norton Co., 1991).

62. OECD, *Energy Policies and Programmes of IEA Countries 1989 Review* (Paris: 1990).

63. Hilt and Lihn, "The Clear Air Act's Impact on Natural Gas Markets"; Kevin Commins, "Clean Air Act Could Devastate Ill. Coal, Producer Says," *Journal of Commerce*, April 10, 1991; Meridian Corporation, "Energy System Emissions and Materiel Requirements," prepared for Deputy Assistant Secretary for Renewable Energy, Department of Energy, Alexandria, Va., February 1989; Pace University Center for Environmental Legal Studies, *Environmental Costs of Electricity* (New York: Oceana Publications, 1990); Tom McNiff Jr., "Coal-Fired Plant Plans Stoke Conflict in Mass.," *Journal of Commerce*, August 8, 1991; "Carbon Taxes," *Global Environmental Change Report*, June 24, 1991; Andrew Hill, "EC Energy Tax Would Put $10 on Barrel of Oil," *Financial Times*, August 23, 1991.

64. Grasse and Olster, *Hysolar Results and Achievements 1985–1989*; "Germany Spends $58 Million on H, Plus PV Outlays," *The Hydrogen Letter*, October 1991.

65. Peter Keat, "Selling Efficient Kilowatt-hours," *Public Power*, September/October 1991; Ralph Cavanagh, Senior Attorney, Natural Resources Defense Council, San Francisco, Calif., private communication, October 21, 1991.

## Chapter 4. Confronting Nuclear Waste

1. Quote is by Lewis Strauss, commissioner of the U.S. Atomic Energy Commission, before the National Association of Science Writers, New York, September 16, 1954, as cited by Daniel Ford, *The Cult of the Atom* (New York: Simon and Schuster, 1982).

2. Total irradiated fuel figure of 80,000 tons is Worldwatch Institute estimate based on I.W. Leigh and S.J. Mitchell, Pacific Northwest Laboratory, *International Nuclear Fuel Cycle Fact Book* (Springfield, Va.: National Technical Information Service (NTIS), 1990), on Organisation for Economic Co-operation and Development (OECD), Nuclear Energy Agency (NEA), *Nuclear Spent Fuel Management: Experience and Options* (Paris: 1986), on Andrew Blowers et al., *The International Politics of Nuclear Waste* (New York: St. Martin's Press, 1991), on Soviet figures from G.A. Kaurov, Director of the Center of Public Information for Atomic Energy, Moscow, in letter to Lydia Popova, Socio-Ecological Union, Moscow, August 5, 1991, and on East European production based on United Nations, *Energy Statistics Yearbook* (New York: various years), on British Petroleum (BP), *BP Statistical Review of World Energy* (London: 1991), and on above sources.

3. U.S. Department of Energy (DOE), Office of Civilian Radioactive Waste Management (OCRWM), *Integrated Data Base for 1990: U.S. Spent Fuel and Radioactive Waste Inventories, Projections, and Characteristics* (Washington, D.C.: 1990); United Nations, *Energy Statistics Yearbook*; BP, *BP Statistical Review*; Ronald L. Fuchs and Kimberly Culbertson-Arendts, *1989 State-by-State Assessment of Low-Level Radioactive Wastes Received at Commercial Disposal Sites* (Idaho Falls, Idaho: DOE, 1990).

4. Wilson cited in Fred C. Shapiro, *Radwaste* (New York: Random House, 1981).

5. James D. Watkins, Secretary of Energy, Testimony before the Committee on Energy and Natural Resources, U.S. Senate, Washington, D.C., March 21, 1991; William S. Lee, chairman and president, Duke Power Company, Statement before the Secretary of Energy, National Energy Strategy Hearing, Washington, D.C., August 1, 1989.

6. Catherine Caufield, *Multiple Exposures: Chronicles of the Radiation Age* (Chicago: University of Chicago Press, 1989).

7. Ibid.; National Research Council (NRC), *Health Effects of Exposure to Low Levels of Ionizing Radiation: BEIR V* (Washington, D.C.: National Academy Press, 1989); Lowell E. Sever, "Low-Level Ionizing Radiation: Paternal Exposure & Children's Health," *Health & Environment Digest* (Freshwater Foundation, Navarre, Minn.,) February 1991; Alice Stewart, "Low-Level Radiation: The Cancer Controversy," *Bulletin of the Atomic Scientists*, September 1990; Harriet S. Page and Ardyce J. Asire, *Cancer Rates and Risks*, 3rd ed. (Bethesda, Md.: National Institutes of Health (NIH), 1985).

8. NRC, *BEIR V*; "Biological Effects of Radiation," *The New Encyclopedia Britannica*, Macropaedia, Vol. 15 (Chicago: Encyclopedia Britannica, Inc., 1976); Dan Benison, chairman, International Commission on Radiological Protection (ICRP), press conference, Washington, D.C., June 22, 1990. One centisievert is equivalent to one rem, another unit used to measure the biological effect of radiation on the body.

9. R.H. Clarke and T.R.E. Southwood, "Risks from Ionizing Radiation," *Nature*, March 16, 1989; Stewart, "Low-Level Radiation"; G.W. Kneale and A.M. Stewart, "Childhood Cancers in the U.K. and Their Relation to Background Radiation," Proceedings of the International Conference on Biological Effects of Ionizing Radiation, Hammersmith Hospital, London, November 24–25, 1986.

10. Clarke and Southwood, "Risks from Ionizing Radiation."

11. NRC, *BEIR V*.

12. Hylton Smith, Scientific Secretary, ICRP, Didcot, U.K., private communication, March 25, 1991; Caufield, *Multiple Exposures*; John W. Gofman, *Radiation-Induced Cancer from Low-Dose Exposure: An Independent Analysis* (San Francisco: Committee for Nuclear Responsibility, Inc., 1990).

13. Steve Wing et al., "Mortality Among Workers at Oak Ridge National Laboratory: Evidence of Radiation Effects in Follow-Up Through 1984," *Journal of the American Medical Association*, March 20, 1991; Thomas W. Lippman, "Risk Found in Low Levels of Radiation," *Washington Post*, March 20, 1991; Peter Aldhous, "Leukemia Cases Linked to Fathers' Radiation Dose," *Nature*, February 22, 1990.

14. Maureen C. Hatch et al., "Cancer Rates After the Three Mile Island Nuclear Accident and Proximity of Residence to the Plant," *American Journal of Public Health*, June 1991; Wing et al., "Mortality Among Workers"; Seymour Jablon et al., *Cancer in Populations Living Near Nuclear Facilities* (Bethesda, Md.: NIH, 1990).

15. Simon Rippon, "After Five Years, Uncertainties Remain at Chernobyl," *Nuclear News*, June 1991; Robert Peter Gale, "Long-Term Impacts from Chernobyl in U.S.S.R.," *Forum for Applied Research and Public Policy*, Fall 1990; Felicity Barringer, "Chernobyl: The Danger Persists," *New York Times Magazine*, April 14, 1991; Gofman, *Radiation-Induced Cancer*.

16. "Report on Nuclear Program Views Environmental Effects," *O Globo* (Rio de Janeiro), September 30, 1990, translated in Foreign Broadcast Information Service (FBIS) Daily Report/Latin America, Rosslyn, Va., November 2, 1990; Gail Daneker and Jennifer Scarlott, "Nuclear Tragedy Strikes Brazil," *RWC Waste Paper* (Radioactive Waste Campaign, New York), Winter 1987/1988; K.T. Thomas et al., "Radioactive Waste Management in Developing Countries," *IAEA Bulletin*, Vol. 31, No. 4, 1989.

17. Matthew L. Wald, "Nature Helps Spread Taint of Nuclear Waste Into the Environment," *New York Times*, December 10, 1988; Frank P. Falci, "Foreign Trip Report: Travel to USSR for Fact Finding Discussions on Environmental Restoration and Waste Management, June 15–28, 1990," Office of Technology Development (OTD), DOE, July 27, 1990; estimate for cancer deaths is found in International Physicians for the Prevention of Nuclear War and Institute for Energy and Environmental Research, *Radioactive Heaven and Earth: The Health and Environmental Effects of Nuclear Weapons Testing In, On, and Above the Earth* (New York: The Apex Press, 1991), and is based on risk estimates in NRC, *BEIR V*.

18. G. de Marsily et al., "Nuclear Waste Disposal: Can the Geologist Guarantee Isolation?" *Science*, August 5, 1977; Ronnie D. Lipschutz, *Radioactive Waste: Politics, Technology and Risk* (Cambridge, Mass.: Ballinger, 1980).

19. DOE, OCRWM, *Integrated Data Base for 1990*; typical 1,000 megawatt light-water reactor from NRC, Board on Radioactive Waste Management (BRWM), "Rethinking High-Level Radioactive Waste Disposal," National Academy Press, Washington, D.C., July 1990; Lipschutz, *Radioactive Waste*; J.O. Blomeke et al., Oak Ridge National Laboratory, "Projections of Radioactive Wastes to be Generated by the U.S. Nuclear Power Industry," NTIS, Springfield, Va., February 1974.

20. "World List of Nuclear Power Plants," *Nuclear News*, August 1991; Leigh and Mitchell, *International Nuclear Fuel Cycle Fact Book*; BP, *BP Statistical Review*; DOE, OCRWM, *Integrated Data Base for 1990*; International Atomic Energy Agency (IAEA), *Nuclear Power, Nuclear Fuel Cycle and Waste Management: Status and Trends 1990*, Part C of the *IAEA Yearbook 1990* (Vienna: 1990); Table 4–2 is based on Leigh and Mitchell, *International Nuclear Fuel Cycle Fact Book*; on OECD, NEA, *Nuclear Spent Fuel Management*, on Blowers et al., *The International Politics of Nuclear Waste*, on Soviet figures from Kaurov, in letter to Popova, and on East European production based on United Nations, *Energy Statistics Yearbook*, on BP, *BP Statistical Review*, and on above sources.

21. IAEA, *Nuclear Power, Nuclear Fuel Cycle and Waste Management*; OECD, NEA, *Nuclear Spent Fuel Management*; State of Nevada, Agency for Nuclear Projects/Nuclear Waste Project Office, "Storage of Spent Fuel from the Nation's Nuclear Reactors: Status, Technology, and Policy Options," Carson City, Nev., October 1989.

22. Cumbrians Opposed to a Radioactive Environment (CORE), "A Brief Background to Reprocessing and the Thermal Oxide Reprocessing Plant (THORP)," *Thermal Oxide Reprocessing Plant: An Indepth Investigation* (Cumbria, U.K.: undated); Lipschutz, *Radioactive Waste*.

23. OECD, NEA, *Nuclear Energy in Perspective* (Paris: 1989); Fuchs and Culbertson-Arendts, *1989 State-by-State Assessment of Low-Level Radioactive Wastes*.

24. Fuchs and Culbertson-Arendts, *1989 State-by-State Assessment of Low-Level Radioactive Wastes*; Arjun Makhijani and Scott Saleska, *High-Level Dollars, Low-Level Sense: A Critique of Present Policy for the Management of Long-Lived Radioactive Wastes and Discussion of an Alternative Approach* (New York: The Apex Press, in press); nuclear power's share of low-level waste excludes waste from uranium enrichment for reactor fuel.

25. Edward Landa, *Isolation of Uranium Mill Tailings and Their Component Radionuclides from the Biosphere—Some Earth Science Perspectives*, Geological Survey Circular 814 (Arlington, Va.: United States Geological Service, 1980); Peter Diehl, Herrischried, Germany, private communication and printout, June 28, 1991; "Urals Town Contaminated by Radioactive Waste, to be Evacuated," *Izvestiya*, January 11, 1991, translated in FBIS Daily Report/ Soviet Union, Rosslyn, Va., February 5, 1991; DOE, OCRWM, *Integrated Data Base for 1990*; OECD, NEA and IAEA, *Uranium: Resources, Production and Demand* (Paris: 1990).

26. "World List of Nuclear Power Plants"; IAEA, *Nuclear Power, Nuclear Fuel Cycle and Waste Management*; typical 1,000 megawatt pressurized water reactor is from DOE, OCRWM, *Integrated Data Base for 1990*.

27. U.S. Congress, Office of Technology Assessment (OTA), *Complex Cleanup: The Environmental Legacy of Nuclear Weapons Production* (Washington, D.C.: U.S. Government Printing Office, 1991); "'Hot Frogs' Loose at Nuclear Laboratory," *Washington Post*, August 4, 1991.

28. Karen Dorn Steele, "Hanford: America's Nuclear Graveyard," *Bulletin of the Atomic Scientists*, October 1989; Luther J. Carter, *Nuclear Imperatives and Public Trust: Dealing with Radioactive Waste* (Washington, D.C.: Resources for the Future, 1987); DOE, OCRWM, *Integrated Data Base for 1990*; OTA, *Complex Cleanup*; Karen Dorn Steele, "Hanford in Hot Water," *Bulletin of the Atomic Scientists*, May 1991; Scott Saleska and Arjun Makhijani, "Hanford Cleanup: Explosive Solution," *Bulletin of the Atomic Scientists*, October 1990; U.S. General Accounting Office (GAO), "Hanford Single-Shell Tank Leaks Greater Than Estimated," Report to the Chairman, Committee on Governmental Affairs, U.S. Senate, August 1991.

29. Thomas B. Cochran and Robert S. Norris, "A First Look at the Soviet Bomb Complex," *Bulletin of the Atomic Scientists*, May 1991; Thomas B. Cochran and Robert Standish Norris, *Nuclear Weapons Databook: Working Papers—Soviet Nuclear Warhead Production*, NWD 90–3, 3rd rev. (Washington, D.C.: Natural Resources Defense Council, 1991); Cochran quote in Matthew L. Wald, "High Radiation Doses Seen for Soviet Arms Workers," *New York Times*, August 16, 1990; Falci, "Foreign Trip Report: Travel to USSR for Fact Finding Discussions."

30. Cochran and Norris, *Nuclear Weapons Databook: Working Papers—Soviet Nuclear Warhead Production*.

31. Keith Schneider, "Military Has New Strategic Goal in Cleanup of Vast Toxic Waste," *New York Times*, August 5, 1991; OTA, *Complex Cleanup*.

32. NRC, BRWM, "Rethinking High-Level Radioactive Waste Disposal"; Table 4–3 is based on Lipschutz, *Radioactive Waste*, on Frank L. Parker et al., *The Disposal of High-level Radioactive Waste 1984*, Vol. II (Stockholm: Beijer Institute, 1984), on CORE, *Thermal Oxide Reprocessing Plant*, on OECD, NEA, *Feasibility of Disposal of High-Level Radioactive Waste into the Seabed*, Vol. 1 (Paris: 1988), on Frank L. Parker et al., *Technical and Sociopolitical Issues in Radioactive Waste Disposal, 1986*, Vols. IA and II (Stockholm: Beijer Institute, 1987), on IAEA, *Nuclear Power, Nuclear Fuel Cycle and Waste Management*, and on Daniel Gibson, "Can Alchemy Solve the Nuclear Waste Problem?" *Bulletin of the Atomic Scientists*, July/August 1991.

33. Table 4–4 is based on Lipschutz, *Radioactive Waste*; on Report to the Congress by the Secretary of Energy, "Reassessment of the Civilian Radioactive Waste Management Program," Washington, D.C., November 29, 1989; on "World Status of Radioactive Waste Management," *IAEA Bulletin*, Spring 1986; on "World Overview: Radioactive Waste Management," *IAEA News Feature*, May 20, 1988; on Jacques de la Ferté, "What Future for Nuclear Power?" *The OECD Observer*, April/May 1990; on Leigh and Mitchell, *International Nuclear Fuel Cycle Fact Book*; on IAEA, *Nuclear Power, Nuclear Fuel Cycle and Waste Management*; and on OECD, NEA, *Nuclear Spent Fuel Management*.

34. Ferté, "What Future for Nuclear Power?"; see also Donald E. Saire, "World Status of Radioactive Waste Management," *IAEA Bulletin*, Spring 1986.

35. Konrad B. Krauskopf, "Disposal of High-Level Nuclear Waste: Is It Possible?" *Science*, September 14, 1990.

36. Frank L. Parker et al., *The Disposal of High-Level Radioactive Waste 1984*, Vol. I (Stockholm: Beijer Institute, 1984); Carole Douglis, "Stones that Speak to the Future," *OMNI*, November 1985.

37. Cost estimates are from Makhijani and Saleska, *High-Level Dollars, Low-Level Sense*, converted to 1990 dollars.

38. Scott Saleska, Institute for Energy and Environmental Research (IEER), Takoma Park, Md., private communication, July 25, 1991.

39. NRC, BRWM, "Rethinking High-Level Radioactive Waste Disposal."

40. Thomas W. Lippman, "Energy Dept. Set to Ship A-Waste to New Mexico," *Washington Post*, October 4, 1991.

41. Bernd Franke and Arjun Makhijani, "Avoidable Death: A Review of the Selection and Characterization of a Radioactive Waste Repository in West Germany," IEER, Takoma Park, Md., November 1987; Helmut Hirsch, Gruppe Ökologie, Hannover, Germany, private communication, September 25, 1991; Lipschutz, *Radioactive Waste*; Don Hancock, "Getting Rid of the Nuclear Waste Problem: The WIPP Stalemate," *The Workbook*, October/December 1989.

42. Hancock, "Getting Rid of the Nuclear Waste Problem"; Victor S. Rezendes, director, energy issues, GAO, "Nuclear Waste: Delays in Addressing Environmental Requirements and New Safety Concerns Affect DOE's Waste Isolation Pilot Plant," Testimony before the Environment, Energy, and Natural Resources Subcommittee, Committee on Government Operation, U.S. House of Representatives, Washington, D.C., June 13, 1991.

43. Eliot Marshall, "The Geopolitics of Nuclear Waste," *Science*, February 22, 1991; Janet Raloff, "Fallout Over Nevada's Nuclear Destiny," *Science News*, January 6, 1990; Archambeau quote in William J. Broad, "A Mountain of Trouble," *New York Times Magazine*, November 18, 1990.

44. Raloff, "Fallout Over Nevada's Nuclear Destiny"; Lipschutz, *Radioactive Waste*.

45. R. Monastersky, "'Young' Volcano Near Nuclear Waste Site," *Science News*, June

30, 1990; de Marsily et al., "Nuclear Waste Disposal"; clairvoyant reference is found in Diane M. Cameron and Barry D. Solomon, "Nuclear Waste Landscapes," in J. Barry Cullingworth, ed., *Energy, Land, and Public Policy* (New Brunswick, N.J.: Transaction Books, 1990).

46. Carter, *Nuclear Imperatives*; National Academy of Sciences report cited in Shapiro, *Radwaste*; National Academy committee cited in Carter, *Nuclear Imperatives*.

47. Cameron and Solomon, "Nuclear Waste Landscapes."

48. DOE, *Commercial Nuclear Power 1990* (Washington, D.C.: 1990); Lipschutz, *Radioactive Waste*; Carter, *Nuclear Imperatives*.

49. California law quoted in Shapiro, *Radwaste*; Carter, *Nuclear Imperatives*.

50. See Blowers et al., *The International Politics of Nuclear Waste*, or Gerald Jacob, *Site Unseen: The Politics of Siting a Nuclear Waste Repository* (Pittsburgh: University of Pittsburgh Press, 1990) for a complete review of the 1982 Act.

51. Victor Gilinsky, "Nuclear Power: What Must Be Done?" *Public Utilities Fortnightly*, June 1, 1991; Bob Miller, Governor of Nevada, Testimony before the Committee on Energy and Natural Resources, U.S. Senate, Washington, D.C., March 21, 1991; Paul Slovic et al., "Lessons from Yucca Mountain," *Environment*, April 1991.

52. Watkins, Testimony before the Committee on Energy and Natural Resources; Judy England-Joseph, associate director, Energy Issues, Resources, Community, and Economic Development Division, GAO, "Nuclear Waste: DOE Expenditures on the Yucca Mountain Project," Testimony before the Subcommittee on Nuclear Regulation, Committee on Environment and Public Works, U.S. Senate, Washington, D.C., April 18, 1991; Gibson cite in Sandra Sugawara, "Nuclear-Dump Contract Fight Goes to Court,"

*Washington Post*, March 30, 1989; Paul Rodarte, "Military Maneuvers over Native Lands," *Nuclear Times*, Winter 1990/1991.

53. "Chained to Reactors," *The Economist*, February 2, 1991; "World List of Nuclear Power Plants"; Sylvia Hughes, "Secret Report Attacks French Nuclear Programme," *New Scientist*, March 17, 1990; "Two Reports Call for Reorganisation of French Nuclear Power Industry," *European Energy Report*, January 11, 1991; "French Conservatives Join Greens in Nuclear Waste Disposal Protests," *International Environment Reporter*, November 1989; "Rethink on Waste Storage," *Power in Europe*, February 15, 1990; Ann MacLachlan, "French Government Stops Test Drilling at Waste Sites for 'At Least' a Year," *Nuclear Fuel*, February 19, 1990.

54. Fauroux quote in "Council of Ministers Adopts Draft Law on Disposal of Long-Term Radioactive Waste," *International Environment Reporter*, May 22, 1991; "France Passes New Law on Disposal of Nuclear Waste Underground," *European Energy Report*, July 12, 1991; William Dawkins, "French to Make Cleaner Job of Nuclear Waste," *Financial Times*, May 15, 1991; Leigh and Mitchell, *International Nuclear Fuel Cycle Fact Book*.

55. H.P. Berg and P. Brennecke, "Planning in-Depth for German Waste Disposal," *Nuclear Engineering International*, March 1991; "Dispute over Nuclear Waste Raging in German State of Lower Saxony," *International Environment Reporter*, July 3, 1991; "East German Nuclear Plant Hopes Fade as Minister Changes Tack," *European Energy Report*, April 19, 1991; Blowers et al., *The International Politics of Nuclear Waste*.

56. Berg and Brennecke, "Planning in-Depth for German Waste Disposal"; Hirsch, private communication; "Court Gives Federal Government Go-Ahead on Nuclear Waste Disposal Site," *International Environment Reporter*, April 24, 1991; Parker et al., *The Disposal of Radioactive Waste 1984*; Leigh

and Mitchell, *International Nuclear Cycle Fact Book*; "Germany Suspends Storage at East's Morsleben Repository," *Nuclear Europe Worldscan*, March/April 1991.

57. Carter, *Nuclear Imperatives*; Blowers et al., *The International Politics of Nuclear Waste*; Franke and Makhijani, "Avoidable Death"; Parker et al., *Technical and Sociopolitical Issues*, Vols. IA and II; Leigh and Mitchell, *International Nuclear Fuel Cycle Fact Book*.

58. Carter, *Nuclear Imperatives*; Parker et al., *Technical and Sociopolitical Issues*, Vols. IA and II.

59. NRC, "Review of the Swedish KBS-3 Plan for Final Storage of Spent Nuclear Fuel," NTIS, Springfield, Va., March 1, 1984; National Board for Spent Nuclear Fuel, *Evaluation of SKB R&D Programme 89* (Stockholm: 1990); Blowers et al., *The International Politics of Nuclear Waste*; Parker et al., *Technical and Sociopolitical Issues*, Vols. IA and II.

60. Parker et al., *Technical and Sociopolitical Issues*, Vols. IA and II; Karl-Inge Ahall et al., *Nuclear Waste in Sweden: The Problem is Not Solved!* (Uppsala: The Peoples' Movement Against Nuclear Power and Weapons, 1988); "Swedes Accept Waste, Poll Says," *European Energy Report*, December 14, 1990.

61. "World List of Nuclear Power Plants"; Tatsujiro Suzuki, "Japan's Nuclear Dilemma," *Technology Review*, October 1991; "Utility Says More Nuclear Plants Are Almost Impossible in Japan," *Journal of Commerce*, November 7, 1990; Jacob M. Schlesinger, "Japan Energy Plan Spurs Public Fission," *Wall Street Journal*, January 30, 1991.

62. David Swinbanks, "Yen Melts Down Opposition," *Nature*, May 24, 1990; Schlesinger, "Japan Energy Plan Spurs Public Fission."

63. Swinbanks, "Yen Melts Down Opposition"; Schlesinger, "Japan Energy Plan Spurs Public Fission"; Yoji Takemoto, Wisetokyo,

Tokyo, private communication, February 14, 1991.

64. "HLW Disposal Plans Come to Light," *Nuke Info Tokyo*, November/December 1989; "Hokkaido Government Opposes HLW Plan in Horonobe," *Nuke Info Tokyo*, September/October 1990.

65. "German Spent Fuel May Go to China," *Nuclear News*, October 1985; "Joint Research Agreement Reached with China on HLW Disposal," *Nuke Info Tokyo*, November/December 1990.

66. "World List of Nuclear Power Plants"; Charles Mitchell, "Fallout From Chernobyl Accident Still Clouds Soviet Nuclear Plans," *Journal of Commerce*, April 19, 1991; Gabriel Schonfeld, "Rad Storm Rising," *Atlantic*, December 1990; "Urals Town Contaminated by Radioactive Waste, to be Evacuated," *Izvestiya*, January 11, 1991, translated in FBIS Daily Report/Soviet Union, Rosslyn, Va., February 5, 1991.

67. Cochran and Norris, *Nuclear Weapons Databook: Working Papers—Soviet Nuclear Warhead Production*; "Resolution on Nuclear Waste State Program Viewed," *Sovestskaya Rossiya*, June 28, 1990, translated in FBIS Daily Report/Regional Affairs, Rosslyn, Va., July 3, 1990; "Soviet Plans to Construct Waste Facility in Siberia Protested," *Multinational Environmental Outlook*, July 11, 1989; "Oslo Concern on USSR Waste Storage," *European Energy Report*, Eastern Europe Supplement, December 14, 1990; "Nuclear Plans Divide Baltic Neighbors," *New Scientist*, December 1, 1990.

68. Michael Wise, "Nuclear Waste Piles Up in Eastern Europe," *Washington Post*, July 17, 1991; "Resolution on Nuclear Waste State Program Viewed"; "Radioactive Waste Found in Cesky Kras," *Zemedelske Noviny*, Prague, December 4, 1990, translated in FBIS Daily Report/East Europe, Rosslyn, Va., February 13, 1991; "Pollution Found at Bulgarian N-Plant," *Financial Times*, July 25, 1991.

69. Mark Clifford, "A Nuclear Falling Out," *Far Eastern Economic Review*, May 18, 1989; "Nuclear Waste Policy Examined in Light of Protest," *The Korea Times*, November 10, 1990, in FBIS Daily Report/East Asia, Rosslyn, Va., November 21, 1990; Huh Sook, "Overview of Korea Nuclear Program," *Nuclear Europe Worldscan*, March/April 1991; "Nuclear Dumps to be Built on Uninhabited Islands," *Korea Herald*, November 30, 1990, in FBIS Daily Report/East Asia, Rosslyn, Va., January 4, 1991; "Argentine Activist Receives Death Threats," *WISE News Communiqué*, December 21, 1990; C.S. Lee, "Taipower's Backend Management," *Nuclear Europe Worldscan*, March/April 1991; Carl Goldstein, "Nuclear Qualms," *Far Eastern Economic Review*, July 4, 1991; Chris Brown, "Deadly Anti-Nuclear Protest Further Stalls Taiwan Plant," *Journal of Commerce*, October 4, 1991.

70. "World List of Nuclear Power Plants"; Prakash Chandra, "India: Going Nuclear," *Third World Week*, December 23, 1990; Barbara Crossette, "300 Factories Add Up to India's Very Sick Town," *New York Times*, February 6, 1991; Barry D. Solomon and Fred M. Shelley, "Siting Patterns of Nuclear Waste Repositories," *Journal of Geography*, March/April 1988; Department of Atomic Energy, *Annual Report: 1989–1990* (New Delhi: 1990).

71. Chenevier quoted in William Dawkins, "Loud Rumblings from Beneath the Surface," *Financial Times*, December 5, 1990.

72. Lipschutz, *Radioactive Waste*.

73. Makhijani and Saleska, *High-Level Dollars, Low-Level Sense*; Greenpeace and Friends of the Earth, "Radioactive Waste Management: The Environmental Approach," London, November 1987.

74. Estimate of $200 million from U.S. Council for Energy Awareness, "Completing the Task," Washington, D.C., October 1988; $1 billion estimate from Gordon MacKerron, "Decommissioning Costs and British Nuclear Policy," *The Energy Journal*, Vol. 12, Special Issue, 1991; "NE Wants Decommissioning to be Slower, Cheaper," *Nuclear News*, August 1991; Andrew Holmes, "Take It Away, Kids!" *Energy Economist*, July 1991.

75. Makhijani and Saleska, *High-Level Dollars, Low-Level Sense*; Marvin Resnikoff, Radioactive Waste Management Associates, "Memorandum: CANDU Decommissioning," New York, April 22, 1991.

76. Blowers et al., *The International Politics of Nuclear Waste*; "French Ministry of Industry to Prepare National Nuclear Report," *European Energy Report*, November 16, 1990; "Two Reports Call for Reorganisation of French Nuclear Power Industry"; David E. Sanger, "A Crack in Japan's Nuclear Sangfroid," *New York Times*, February 17, 1991; Robert Thomson, "Nuclear Mishap Shakes Confidence in Japan's Programme," *Financial Times Weekend*, February 16–17, 1991; "Travel to the USSR for the First Fact Finding Meeting of the US-USSR Joint Coordinating Committee on Environmental Restoration and Waste Management, November 8–17, 1990," OTD, DOE, December 17, 1990; Zhores Medvedev, *The Legacy of Chernobyl* (New York: W.W. Norton & Co., 1990); Radioactive Waste Campaign, *Deadly Defense: Military Radioactive Landfills* (New York: 1988).

77. See, for instance, NRC, BRWM, "Rethinking High-Level Waste," OTA, *Managing the Nation's Commercial High-Level Radioactive Waste* (Washington, D.C.: U.S. Government Printing Office, 1985), OTA, *Complex Cleanup*, Arjun Makhijani, "Reducing the Risks: Policies for the Management of Highly Radioactive Nuclear Waste," IEER, Takoma Park, Md., May 1989, Carter, *Nuclear Imperatives*, and Jacob, *Site Unseen*, which includes reference to OTA testimony before the U.S. Congress in 1981.

78. Blowers et al., *The International Politics of Nuclear Waste*; Mitchell, "Fallout From Chernobyl Accident Still Clouds Soviet Nu-

clear Plans"; "Ukraine Halts Nuclear Programme as Energy Sovereignty Grows,"
*European Energy Report*, September 21, 1990;
Christopher Flavin, "Italian Voters Reject
Nuclear Power," *World Watch*, January/Feb-
ruary 1988; David Lowry, environmental
consultant, Milton Keyes, U.K., private communication, Washington, D.C., April 29,
1991.

79. Jacob, *Site Unseen*; Wolf Häfele, "Energy from Nuclear Power," *Scientific American*,
September 1990; DOE, *National Energy Strategy, First Edition 1991/1992* (Washington,
D.C.: U.S. Government Printing Office,
1991).

## Chapter 5. Reforming the Livestock Economy

1. Livestock population from U.N. Food
and Agriculture Organization (FAO), *Production Yearbook 1989* (Rome: 1990); Population
Reference Bureau (PRB), *1991 World Population Data Sheet* (Washington, D.C.: 1991).

2. History of domesticated animals from
D.B. Grigg, *The Agricultural Systems of the
World: An Evolutionary Approach* (New York:
Cambridge University Press, 1974); human
population from United Nations, *1985/86
Statistical Yearbook* (New York: 1988), and
from PRB, *1991 World Population Data Sheet*;
livestock population trends from FAO, *World
Crop and Livestock Statistics, 1948–1985*
(Rome: 1987), *Production Yearbook 1988*
(Rome: 1989), and *Production Yearbook 1989*.

3. FAO, *Production Yearbook 1989*.

4. Draft power from James Yazman, pro-
gram officer, Winrock International, Morril-
ton, Ark., private communication, May 30,
1991; Roger Jeffery et al., "Taking Dung-
Work Seriously: Women's Work and Rural
Development in North India," *Economic and
Political Weekly*, April 29, 1989; Frank H.
Baker et al., "The Relationships and Roles of
Animals in Sustainable Agriculture and on

Sustainable Farms," *Professional Animal Scientist*, December 1990.

5. Pastoralist population from Edward C.
Wolf, "Managing Rangelands," in Lester R.
Brown et al., *State of the World 1986* (New
York: W.W. Norton & Co., 1986); H. Breman
and C.T. de Wit, "Rangeland Productivity
and Exploitation in the Sahel," *Science*, September 30, 1983.

6. Gandhi quoted in "Goat: The Poor
Man's Savior," *Green Files* (Centre for Science
and Environment, New Delhi), December
1989; share of meat and milk in Africa from
International Livestock Center for Africa
(ILCA), *ILCA Annual Report 1989* (Addis
Ababa: 1990).

7. By convention, international meat statistics are kept in "carcass weight," which includes bones and other parts that people
generally do not eat. About two thirds of carcass weight is edible, though the exact share
varies depending on the type of meat. The 1
billion meat-eaters and U.S. consumption
figures are Worldwatch Institute estimates,
based on data from U.S. Department of Agriculture (USDA), Foreign Agricultural Service
(FAS), "World Livestock Situation," Washington, D.C., April 1991, and from Linda Bailey, agricultural economist, Economic Research Service (ERS), USDA, Washington,
D.C., private communication, September 11,
1990.

8. Global meat production is Worldwatch
Institute estimate based on FAO, *Production
Yearbook 1989*; pork production trends from
Shayle D. Shagam, *The World Pork Market—
Government Intervention and Multilateral Policy
Reform* (Washington, D.C.: USDA, ERS,
1990), updated from USDA, FAS, "World
Livestock Situation"; beef production from
William F. Hahn et al., *The World Beef Mar-
ket—Government Intervention and Multilateral
Policy Reform* (Washington, D.C.: USDA,
ERS, 1990).

9. Poultry trends from Robert V. Bishop et
al., *The World Poultry Market—Government Inter-*

*vention and Multilateral Policy Reform* (Washington, D.C.: USDA, ERS, 1990); share of world poultry meat from chickens from USDA, FAS, "World Agricultural Production," Washington, D.C., August 1990; development of intensive chicken industry from Gary Vocke, "The Changing Nature of World Agriculture," *National Food Review*, April/June 1990; U.S. share of poultry market from USDA, FAS, "World Agricultural Production."

10. Bishop et al., *World Poultry Market*; Shagam, *World Pork Market*; Hahn et al., *World Beef Market*.

11. Soybeans are grown primarily to produce meal; soybean oil is a by-product. Soybean area from USDA, ERS, Washington, D.C., various private communications, and from FAO, *Production Yearbook 1989*.

12. David Hamilton Wright, "Human Impacts on Energy Flows through Natural Ecosystems, and Implications for Species Endangerment," *Ambio*, July 1990; grazing area from Board on Science and Technology for International Development (BOSTID), National Research Council (NRC), *The Improvement of Tropical and Subtropical Rangeland* (Washington, D.C.: National Academy Press, 1990); cropland is Worldwatch Institute estimate based on share of grain for feed from USDA, FAS, "World Cereals Used for Feed," and on cropland for grain and soybeans from FAO, *Production Yearbook 1989*, excluding cropland growing hay and other fodder crops.

13. Baker et al., "Roles of Animals in Sustainable Agriculture."

14. Grain use is Worldwatch Institute estimate based on H.A. Fitzhugh et al., *The Role of Ruminants in Support of Man* (Morrilton, Ark.: Winrock International, 1978), updated according to meat production trends from FAO, *World Crop and Livestock Statistics, 1948–1985*, *Production Yearbook 1988*, and *Production Yearbook 1989*.

15. Meat figures are expressed in boneless, trimmed, edible weight rather than carcass weight; Soviet chicken from Bishop et al., *World Poultry Market*.

16. David Pimentel, professor, Cornell University, Ithaca, N.Y., private communication, February 22, 1991, and David Pimentel et al., "The Potential for Grass-Fed Livestock: Resource Constraints," *Science*, February 22, 1980; half of agricultural energy is Worldwatch Institute estimate based on David Pimentel and Marcia Pimentel, *Food, Energy and Society* (Baltimore, Md.: Arnold Edward, 1979), and on Richard C. Fluck and C. Direlle Baird, *Agricultural Energetics* (Westport, Conn.: AVI Publishing Co., 1980); gasoline equivalent is Worldwatch Institute estimate based on data in Table 5–3 and on per capita consumption data from Larry Duewer, ERS, USDA, Washington, D.C., private communication, January 15, 1991.

17. Share of irrigation water for livestock from Mark Reisner and Sarah Bates, *Overtapped Oasis: Reform or Revolution for Western Water* (Washington, D.C.: Island Press, 1990), from John M. Sweeten, "Water Use, Animal Waste, and Water Pollution," in H. Russell Cross and Floyd M. Byers, eds., *Current Issues in Food Production: A Perspective on Beef as a Component in Diets for Americans* (Englewood, Colo.: National Cattlemen's Association, 1990), and from private communications with various water experts in western states; Ogallala from John B. Weeks et al., *Summary of the High Plains Regional Aquifer-System Analysis in Parts of Colorado, Kansas, Nebraska, New Mexico, Oklahoma, South Dakota, Texas, and Wyoming* (Washington, D.C.: U.S. Government Printing Office, 1988); irrigated share of hay and feed from Jim Oltjen, professor, Department of Animal Science, University of California, Davis, private communication, February 12, 1991, and from Gerald M. Ward, "Water Use for U.S. Beef Production," Department of Animal Sciences, Colorado State University, Fort Collins, Colo., undated; 3,000-liter figure counts only con-

sumptive use, excludes rainwater on crops, and refers to boneless, trimmed, edible weight, from Oltjen, private communication; comparison to home water use is Worldwatch Institute estimate based on per capita animal product consumption from Duewer, private communication, and on estimate of typical home use.

18. International comparisons from Pimentel and Pimentel, *Food, Energy, and Society*, and from Fluck and Baird, *Agricultural Energetics*; fertilizers from Organisation for Economic Co-operation and Development (OECD), *Water Pollution by Fertilizers and Pesticides* (Paris: 1986); Japan from Hahn et al., *World Beef Market*; New Zealand from B.A. Stout, *Handbook of Energy for World Agriculture* (London: Elsevier Science Publishers, 1990).

19. Manure overview from OECD, *Water Pollution by Fertilizers and Pesticides*; nutrient value of wasted manure is Worldwatch Institute estimate, assuming 80 percent of manure in confined feeding operations is not used to its full potential, based on USDA, ERS, "Economies of Size in Hog Production," Washington, D.C., 1986, and on Pimentel, private communication, May 21, 1991, and following data and methods in Sweeten, "Water Use, Animal Waste," and comparisons with chemical fertilizer from Fertilizer Institute, "Fertilizer Facts and Figures," Washington, D.C., 1990.

20. Netherlands from Ir.F. Langeweg, ed., *Concern for Tomorrow* (Bilthoven, Netherlands: National Institute for Public Health and Environmental Protection, 1989); manure surplus from Commission of the European Communities (EC), *State of the Environment in the European Community 1986* (Brussels: EC, 1987); ammonia from G.J. Heij and T. Schneider, eds., *Dutch Priority Programme on Acidification*, final report second phase Dutch Priority Programme on Acidification (Bilthoven, Netherlands: National Institute of Public Health and Environmental Protection, undated).

21. Health effects of nitrate from World Health Organization (WHO), *Guidelines for Drinking-Water Quality, Vol. 1, Recommendations* (Geneva: 1984), and from Eric P. Jorgensen, ed., *The Poisoned Well* (Washington, D.C.: Island Press, 1989); Commission of the EC, *State of the Environment in the European Community 1986*; Ministerio de Obras Públicas y Urbanización, *Medio Ambiente en España '89* (Madrid: 1989); Department of the Environment, *The Environment in Czechoslovakia* (Prague: State Commission for Science, Technology and Investments, 1990).

22. Rangelands account for 93 percent of all drylands suffering at least moderate desertification, according to Till Darnhofer, deputy director, Desertification Control Program Activity Center, U.N. Environment Programme (UNEP), Nairobi, Kenya, private communication, May 23, 1991; role of cattle in desertification and wildlife loss from BOSTID, *The Improvement of Tropical and Subtropical Rangelands*.

23. Extent of degradation is based on informed opinion of experts, with accuracy limits of plus or minus 10 percent from Darnhofer, private communication; caution from James E. Ellis and David M. Swift, "Stability of African Pastoral Ecosystems: Alternate Paradigms and Implications for Development," *Journal of Range Management*, November 1988, from Ruth Mace, "Overgrazing Overstated," *Nature*, January 24, 1990, and from Gerrit B. Bartels et al., "The Applicability of the Carrying Capacity Concept in Africa: A Comment on the Thesis of De Leeuw and Tothill," in Richard P. Cincotta et al., eds., *New Concepts in International Rangeland Development: Theories and Applications*, proceedings of the 1991 International Rangeland Development Symposium, Washington, D.C., January 14, 1991 (Logan, Utah: Utah State University, Department of Range Science, 1991); higher rainfall areas from D. Layne Coppock, "The Southern Ethiopian Rangelands: Review of Vegetation and Pastoral Dynamics and Implications for Theory

and Management," paper presented at Technical Meeting on Savanna Development and Pasture Production, Woburn, U.K., November 19–21, 1990, Commonwealth Secretariat, London, October 1991.

24. Maryam Niamir, *Community Forestry: Herders' Decision-making in Natural Resources Management in Arid and Semi-arid Africa* (Rome: FAO, 1990).

25. Sahelian countries included in population growth and crop expansion estimates are Burkina Faso, Chad, Gambia, Mali, Mauritania, Niger, and Senegal; population from FAO, *1988 Country Tables* (Rome: 1988), and from PRB, *1991 World Population Data Sheet*; cropland expansion from FAO, *1988 Country Tables* and *Production Yearbook 1989*; Charles Lane, *Barabaig Natural Resource Management: Sustainable Land Use Under Threat of Destruction*, Discussion Paper 12 (Geneva: United Nations Research Institute for Social Development, June 1990); ranches from Olivia Graham, "Enclosure of the East African Rangelands: Recent Trends and Their Impact," Pastoral Development Network (PDN) Paper 25A, Overseas Development Institute (ODI), London, March 1988; increased degradation from Jon Moris, "Interventions for African Pastoral Development Under Adverse Production Trends," African Livestock Policy Analysis Network (ALPAN) Paper 16, ILCA, Addis Ababa, October 1988.

26. Jiri Skoupy, "Developing Rangeland Resources in African Drylands," *Desertification Control Bulletin* (UNEP), No. 17, 1988; Alf Morten Jerve, *Cattle and Inequality. A Study of Rural Economic Differentiation from Southern Kgalagadi in Botswana* (Bergen, Norway: Chr. Michelsen Institute, September 1982).

27. Savanna ecology from R.R. Vera et al., "Development of Improved Grazing Systems in the Savannas of Tropical America," in *Rangelands: A Resource Under Siege*, proceedings of the 2nd International Rangeland Congress, Adelaide, Australia, 1984 (New York: Cambridge University Press, 1986);

overstocking and soil salinization from World Resources Institute, *World Resources 1990–91* (New York: Oxford University Press, 1990).

28. Spain and Portugal from confidential preliminary assessments for U.N. Conference on Environment and Development, Rio de Janeiro, Brazil, June 1992; U.S. from Ed Chaney et al., *Livestock Grazing on Western Riparian Areas* (Eagle, Idaho: Northwest Resource Information Center, 1990), and from Johanna Wald and David Alberswerth, "Our Ailing Public Rangelands: Still Ailing! Condition Report 1989," National Wildlife Federation, Washington, D.C., and Natural Resources Defense Council (NRDC), San Francisco, October 1989.

29. U.S. Department of the Interior, Bureau of Land Management, "State of the Public Rangelands 1990: The Range of Our Vision," Washington, D.C., 1990; share of range severely degraded from confidential preliminary assessments for U.N. Conference on Environment and Development, Rio de Janeiro, Brazil, June 1992; streambanks from Chaney et al., *Livestock Grazing on Western Riparian Areas*.

30. Bill Hare, Australian Conservation Foundation, Fitzroy, Victoria, unpublished memorandum, April 15, 1991; Brian Huntley et al., *South African Environments into the 21st Century* (Cape Town, South Africa: Human & Rousseau Tafelberg, 1989).

31. India and Uruguay populations and pastures from FAO, *Production Yearbook 1989*; decrease in common property from N.S. Jodha, "Rural Common Property Resources: Contributions and Crisis," Foundation Day Lecture, May 16, 1990, Society for Promotion of Wastelands Development, New Delhi; other fodder resources from Centre for Science and Environment, *State of India's Environment 1984–1985* (New Delhi: 1985); increased pressure on forests from Mark Poffenberger, "Joint Management for Forest Lands: Experiences from South Asia," Ford

Foundation, New Delhi, January 1990, and from "Land Degradation Rapidly Spreading," (New Delhi) *Financial Express*, November 16, 1990.

32. H.A. Pearson et al., eds., *Development or Destruction? The Conversion of Forest to Pasture in Latin America* (Boulder, Colo.: Westview Press, in press).

33. Pasture area is conservative because only land used as pasture for more than four years is counted. Pasture and forest area from FAO, *Production Yearbook 1976* (Rome: 1977), and *Production Yearbook 1989*; Panama and Costa Rica from George Ledec, "New Directions for Livestock Policy in Latin America," paper presented at the First Technical Workshop on the Transformation of Tropical Forests to Pastures in Latin America, October 4–7, 1988, Oaxaca, Mexico; Darién province and "fence creeping" from Jeffrey R. Jones, *Colonization and Environment: Land Settlement Projects in Central America* (Tokyo: U.N. University Press, 1990).

34. Susanna Hecht, "Cattle Ranching Development in the Eastern Amazon: Evaluation of a Development Policy," doctoral dissertation, University of California, Berkeley, 1982.

35. Japan Environment Agency and U.S. Environmental Protection Agency, "Methane Emissions and Opportunities for Control: Workshop Results of Intergovernmental Panel on Climate Change, Response Strategies Working Group," Washington, D.C., September 1990; livestock's share of greenhouse warming effect is Worldwatch Institute estimate from ibid.

36. "Protein fiasco" from Michael Lipton, *Poverty, Undernutrition and Hunger*, Staff Working Paper 597 (Washington, D.C.: World Bank, 1983), and from WHO, *Diet, Nutrition and the Prevention of Chronic Diseases*, Technical Report Series 797 (Geneva: 1990); recommended protein consumption from WHO in Pimentel et al., "Potential for Grass-Fed Livestock"; industrial-country protein con-

sumption from FAO, *Production Yearbook 1989*; Committee on Diet and Health, Food and Nutrition Board, NRC, *Diet and Health: Implications for Reducing Chronic Disease Risk* (Washington, D.C.: National Academy Press, 1989).

37. NRC, *Diet and Health*; Surgeon General and American Heart Association from Gregory Byrne, "Surgeon General Takes Aim at Saturated Fats," *Science*, August 3, 1988; WHO, *Diet, Nutrition and the Prevention of Chronic Diseases*.

38. Chen Junshi et al., *Diet, Life-style, and Mortality in China: A Study of the Characteristics of 65 Chinese Counties* (New York: Oxford University Press, 1990); see also Gail Vines, "China's Long March to Longevity," *New Scientist*, December 8, 1990.

39. Junshi et al., *Diet, Life-style, and Mortality in China*; Campbell quoted in Jane E. Brody, "Huge Study of Diet Indicts Fat and Meat," *New York Times*, May 8, 1990.

40. Food self-sufficiency from Vocke, "Changing Nature of World Agriculture"; Taiwan from J.S. Sarma, *Cereal Feed Use in the Third World: Past Trends and Projections to 2000*, Research Report 57 (Washington, D.C.: International Food Policy Research Institute, December 1986); per capita meat and egg consumption updated to 1990 from Bailey, private communication; grain per capita and feed's share of grain updated to 1990 from USDA, FAS, "World Cereals Used for Feed"; imports updated to 1990 from USDA, ERS, *World Grain Database* (unpublished printout) (Washington, D.C.: 1990) and various USDA circulars.

41. Meat and feed consumption from USDA, ERS, "USSR Agriculture and Trade Report," Washington, D.C., May 1989 and May 1990; growth of grain imports—expressed on a net basis—from USDA, FAS, "World Grain Situation and Outlook," March 1990 and May 1991; second largest grain importer from USDA, FAS, "World Grain Situation and Outlook," February 1991.

42. Third World net grain trade from Sarma, *Cereal Feed Use in the Third World*, updated from USDA, ERS, *World Grain Database*, and from USDA, ERS, *World Agriculture, 1970–1989: Trends and Indicators* (Washington, D.C.: 1990); share of coarse grain imports for feed from FAO, *Livestock Development in Developing Countries and Implications for Consumption and Trade of Feeds* (Rome: 1983), updated from USDA, FAS, "World Cereals Used for Feed."

43. Crop competition from David Barkin et al., *Food Crops vs. Feed Crops: Global Substitution of Grains in Production* (Boulder, Colo.: Lynne Reinner Publishers, 1990); feed's share of grain in Egypt from USDA, FAS, "World Cereals Used for Feed."

44. Mexico from Barkin et al., *Food Crops vs. Feed Crops*, and from David Barkin and Billie R. DeWalt, "Sorghum and the Mexican Food Crisis," *Latin American Research Review*, Vol. 23, No. 3, 1988; feed's share of grain from USDA, FAS, "World Cereals Used for Feed"; malnutrition from David Barkin, professor, Autonomous Metropolitan University, Mexico City, Mexico, private communication, May 3, 1991.

45. Barkin et al., *Food Crops vs. Feed Crops*.

46. Sheldon Annis, "Debt and Wrong-Way Resource Flows in Costa Rica," *Ethics and International Affairs*, Vol. 4, 1990; coastal land in pasture from H. Jeffrey Leonard, *Natural Resources and Economic Development in Central America* (New Brunswick, N.J.: Transaction Books, 1987).

47. Susanna B. Hecht, "The Logic of Livestock in the Amazon," *BioScience* (forthcoming); Philip M. Fearnside, "Deforestation in Brazilian Amazonia: The Rates and Causes of Forest Destruction," *The Ecologist*, November/December 1989.

48. Farm programs influence both prices and quantities produced, see Hahn et al., *World Beef Market*, Shagam, *World Pork Market*, Bishop et al., *World Poultry Market*, and Bengt Hyberg et al., *The World Coarse Grain Market— Government Intervention and Multilateral Policy Reform* (Washington, D.C.: USDA, ERS, 1990); OECD, *Agricultural Policies, Markets and Trade: Monitoring and Outlook 1991* (Paris: 1991).

49. OECD, *Agricultural Policies, Markets and Trade*.

50. Hahn et al., *World Beef Market*; U.S. International Trade Commission, *Estimated Tariff Equivalents of U.S. Quotas on Agricultural Imports and Analysis of Competitive Conditions in U.S. and Foreign Markets for Sugar, Meat, Peanuts, Cotton and Dairy Products* (Washington, D.C.: 1990); Baker et al., "Roles of Animals in Sustainable Agriculture."

51. Centrally planned economies from Shagam, *World Pork Market*; Soviet food budget from OECD, *Agricultural Policies, Markets and Trade*.

52. Northern Territory from Hare, unpublished memorandum; D.G. Wilcox and J.F. Thomas, "The Fitzroy Valley Regeneration Project in Western Australia," in Joan A. Dixon et al., eds., *Drylands Management: Economic Case Studies* (London: Earthscan Publications, 1990).

53. "Grazing, BLM Bills: A Volatile Mix?" *Environmental and Energy Study Institute (EESI) Weekly Bulletin* (Washington, D.C.), March 11, 1991; comparison to private fees and government expenses from "Raising the Grazing Fee," *Wilderness*, Winter 1990, and from "Last Roundup on the Range," *U.S. News & World Report*, November 26, 1990; lack of enforcement and emerging reforms from "Bucking Tradition: Moving Toward Sustainable Ranching," *High Country News* (special issue), March 12, 1990, from "The Public Range Begins to Green Up," *High Country News* (special issue), May 7, 1990, and from Lisa Jones, "Overgrazing: Feds Move to End It," *High Country News*, April 8, 1991; congressional action from "Grazing, BLM Bills," and from "Vento BLM Bill to Full Committee," *EESI Weekly Bulletin*, May 20, 1991, up-

dated from Stanley Sloss, Subcommittee on National Parks and Public Lands, U.S. Congress, Washington, D.C., private communication, October 4, 1991.

54. U.S. Congress, House of Representatives, Committee on Interior and Insular Affairs, *Department of the Interior's Efforts to Estimate the Cost of Federal Irrigation Subsidies: A Record of Deceit* (Washington, D.C.: U.S. Government Printing Office, 1989); share accruing to feed and fodder growers is Worldwatch Institute estimate based on share of western irrigation water for livestock discussed above; undercost water sales from Reisner and Bates, *Overtapped Oasis*.

55. Costa Rica from Annis, "Wrong-Way Resource Flows"; John O. Browder, "Public Policy and Deforestation in the Brazilian Amazon," in Robert Repetto and Malcolm Gillis, eds., *Public Policies and the Misuse of Forest Resources* (New York: Cambridge University Press, 1988).

56. Annis, "Wrong-Way Resource Flows"; Browder, "Public Policy and Deforestation"; Amazon subsidies and deforestation from Julia Preston, "Destruction of Amazon Rain Forest Slowing," *Washington Post*, March 17, 1991.

57. Grazing program from Louis A. Picard, *The Politics of Development in Botswana: A Model for Success?* (Boulder, Colo.: Lynne Reinner Publishers, 1987); cattle distribution from Edwin N. Wilmsen, professor, Africa Studies Center, Boston University, Mass., letter to David A. Wirth, NRDC, Washington, D.C., June 5, 1986; Eddie Koch, "Beef Barons Threaten the Okavango," (Johannesburg) *Weekly Mail*, January 11–17, 1991.

58. Barkin and DeWalt, "Sorghum and the Mexican Food Crisis."

59. Egypt's crop prices' effects from Barkin et al., *Food Crops vs. Feed Crops*; regional overview from John C. Glenn, *Livestock Production in North Africa and the Middle East: Prob-

lems and Perspectives*, Discussion Paper 39 (Washington, D.C.: World Bank, 1988).

60. C. de Haan, "Changing Trends in the World Bank's Lending Program for Rangeland Development," in *Low Input Sustainable Yield Systems: Implications for the World's Rangelands*, proceedings of the 1990 International Rangeland Development Symposium, Reno, Nev., February 15, 1990 (Logan: Utah State University, Department of Range Science, 1990); funding in Latin America, expressed in constant 1980 dollars, from Annis, "Wrong-Way Resource Flows."

61. Moris, "Interventions for African Pastoral Development"; de Haan, "World Bank's Lending Program for Rangeland Development."

62. Misconception critique from Ian Livingstone, "Livestock Management and 'Overgrazing' Among Pastoralists," *Ambio*, April 1991; Botswana from David A. Wirth, senior project attorney, NRDC, Washington, D.C., et al., letter to A.W. Clausen, president, World Bank, Washington, D.C., June 24, 1986; hidden costs from Olivia Graham, "A Land Divided: The Impact of Ranching on Pastoral Society," *The Ecologist*, September/October 1989.

63. De Haan, "World Bank's Lending Program for Rangeland Development."

64. Nancy Morgan, "Policy Reform in New Zealand and Australia," in USDA, ERS, "Pacific Rim Agriculture and Trade Report," Washington, D.C., July 1990.

65. Ibid.; David Richardson, "Lambs to the Slaughter in New Zealand," *Financial Times*, February 19, 1991; "New Zealand Farmers Sell Them Sunny Meadows," *Economist*, February 23, 1991.

66. Grain for American-style diet worldwide is Worldwatch Institute estimate based on U.S. per capita grain consumption from USDA, FAS, "World Cereals Used for Feed," on PRB, *1991 World Population Data Sheet*, and

on world grain harvest from USDA, ERS, *World Grain Database*; American meat consumption from Duewer, private communication.

67. Pimentel et al., "Potential for Grass-Fed Livestock."

68. Dry-season range preservation from Ian Scoones, "Economic and Ecological Carrying Capacity Implications for Livestock Development in the Dryland Communal Areas of Zimbabwe," PDN Paper 27B, ODI, London, March 1989; rights to range from Niamir, *Herders' Decision-making in Natural Resources Management*; Mauritania from Cornelius de Haan, livestock advisor, World Bank, Washington, D.C., private communication, May 14, 1991.

69. Moris, "Interventions for African Pastoral Development"; ILCA, *ILCA Annual Report 1989*.

70. Alternative economic security from D. Layne Coppock, "The Borana Plateau of Southern Ethiopia: Synthesis of Pastoral Research, Development, and Change 1980–90," in ILCA, *ILCA Annual Report 1990* (Addis Ababa: forthcoming).

71. Stall-feeding overview from James De Vries, "Zero Grazing: Successfully Using Livestock in Regenerative Farming System," *VITA News* (Volunteers in Technical Assistance, Arlington, Va.), April 1990; Haryana from Poffenberger, "Joint Management for Forest Lands."

72. J. M. Hall, "New Approaches to Rangeland Management using the Holistic Resources Management (HRM) Model in Africa," in *New Concepts in International Rangeland Development*; Shannon Horst, director of public awareness, Center for Holistic Resource Management, Albuquerque, N.M., private communication, May 30, 1991; Agnes Kiss, ed., *Living with Wildlife: Wildlife Resource Management with Local Participation in Africa* (Washington, D.C.: World Bank, 1990).

73. Council on Agricultural Science and Technology from Baker et al., "Roles of Animals in Sustainable Agriculture."

74. Carole Sugarman and Malcolm Gladwell, "U.S. Drops New Food Chart," *Washington Post*, May 27, 1991.

75. Fattier meat from intensive grain-feeding from Thomas R. McKinney and Alison Gold, "United States Feedlots," Rocky Mountain Institute, Old Snowmass, Colo., November 5, 1987; "Cattle Feeding Concentrates in Fewer, Larger Lots," *Farmline*, June 1990.

76. U.K. from Clay Harris, "Carnivores Lose Ground," *Financial Times*, May 10, 1991; U.S. red-meat consumption from Duewer, private communication; per capita beef consumption trends worldwide from Bailey, private communication.

77. Hunger figure from World Bank, *World Development Report 1990* (New York: Oxford University Press, 1990); grain trends from Lester R. Brown, "The New World Order," in Lester R. Brown et al., *State of the World 1991* (New York: W.W. Norton & Co., 1991).

## Chapter 6. Improving Women's Reproductive Health

1. Number of deaths from reproductive causes is Worldwatch Institute estimate based on the cumulative number of deaths of women worldwide from pregnancy-related causes (500,000), cervical cancer related to human papillomavirus (354,000), and AIDS (at least 100,000). This is a conservative estimate in that it excludes deaths from pelvic inflammatory disease, adverse health effects of contraceptive methods used improperly, and deaths from a wide variety of sexually transmitted diseases for which mortality figures do not now exist, especially in developing countries. Moreover, maternal mortality figures are widely believed to be underestimated. Maternal mortality figure from World

Health Organization (WHO), *Maternal Mortality Rates: A Tabulation of Available Information* (Geneva: 1986); deaths due to cervical cancers from K. Stanley et al., "Women and Cancer," *World Health Statistics Quarterly*, Vol. 140, No. 3, 1987; deaths due to AIDS from Dr. James Chin, chief, Surveillance Forecasting and Impact Assessment, Global Programme on AIDS, WHO, "Sexually Transmitted Infections Increasing by 250 Million New Infections Annually," press release, Geneva, December 20, 1990. Illness figure based on calculations from data just cited as well as on estimate of 5 million pregnancy-related illnesses based on calculations from Ann Starrs, *Preventing the Tragedy of Maternal Deaths: A Report on the International Safe Motherhood Conference* (Nairobi: WHO, 1987), and on estimate of 13 million to 15 million new cases of pelvic inflammatory disease annually from calculations made by Judith Wasserheit, chief, Sexually Transmitted Diseases Branch, National Institutes of Health, private communication, May 10, 1991.

2. United Nations (UN), Department of Economic and Social Affairs (DIESA), *World Population Prospects* (New York: 1991); UN, DIESA, *Sex and Age Distributions of Populations* (New York: 1991).

3. Share of deaths from all reproductive causes in four countries is based on George T. Acsadi and Gwendolyn Johnson-Acsadi, "Safe Motherhood in South Asia: Sociocultural and Demographic Aspects of Maternal Health," background paper prepared for the Safe Motherhood-South Asia Conference, Lahore, Pakistan, March 1990, on J. Ties Boerma, "Levels of Maternal Mortality in Developing Countries," *Studies in Family Planning*, July/August 1987, on Chinyelu Okafor and A.A. Olukoya, eds., *Safe Motherhood Nigeria 1990: Women's Perspectives on Maternal Mortality and Morbidity* (New York: Family Care International, 1990), on Mead Over and Peter Piot, "HIV and Other Sexually Transmitted Diseases" (draft), in Dean T. Jamison and W. Henry Mosley, eds., *Disease Control Priorities in Developing Countries* (Wash-

ington, D.C.: World Bank, forthcoming), and on "Pregnancy and Death in Bangladesh," *International Family Planning Perspectives*, September 1990.

4. Starrs, *Preventing the Tragedy*.

5. WHO, *Maternal Mortality Rates*.

6. Starrs, *Preventing the Tragedy*.

7. WHO, *International Classification of Diseases: Manual of the International Statistical Classification of Diseases, Injuries, and Causes of Death*, 9th revision (Geneva, 1987); number of annual maternal deaths from Julia A. Walsh et al., "Maternal and Perinatal Health" (draft), in Jamison and Mosley, *Disease Control Priorities in Developing Countries*.

8. Distribution of maternal deaths by region from Starrs, *Preventing the Tragedy*; share of maternal deaths in six countries from Acsadi and Johnson-Acsadi, "Safe Motherhood in South Asia."

9. Walsh et al., "Maternal and Perinatal Health."

10. Gary Barker and Susan Rich, "Adolescent Fertility in Kenya and Nigeria," Population Crisis Committee, Washington, D.C., 1990; see also Acsadi and Johnson-Acsadi, "Safe Motherhood in South Asia."

11. Hamid Rushwan, "Female Circumcision," *World Health*, April/May 1990.

12. Francine van de Walle and Nassour Ouaidou, "Status and Fertility among Urban Women in Burkina Faso," *International Family Planning Perspectives*, Vol. 11, No. 2, June 1985; Acsadi and Johnson-Acsadi, "Safe Motherhood in South Asia."

13. United Nations Children's Fund, *State of the World's Children 1989* (New York: Oxford University Press, 1989).

14. Acsadi and Johnson-Acsadi, "Safe Motherhood in South Asia."

15. Government of Lesotho Health Ministry, "Lesotho Country Paper," paper pre-

sented at the Conference on Safe Motherhood for the Southern African Development Coordinating Council (SADCC) countries, Harare, Zimbabwe, October 29-November 1, 1990.

16. Acsadi and Johnson-Acsadi, "Safe Motherhood in South Asia"; Mary Racelis, "Sociocultural Factors in Safe Motherhood," paper presented at the Conference on Safe Motherhood for the SADCC countries, Harare, Zimbabwe, October 29-November 1, 1990.

17. Information on food taboos in southern Africa from Marvelous Mhloyi, "Maternal Mortality in the SADCC Region," paper presented at the Conference on Safe Motherhood for the SADCC countries, Harare, Zimbabwe, October 29-November 1, 1990; in Middle East and North Africa from Nahid M. Kamel, "Determinants and Patterns of Female Mortality Associated with Women's Reproductive Role," in Alan D. Lopez and Lado T. Ruzicka, eds., *Sex Differentials in Mortality* (Canberra, Australia: Australian National University, 1983); and in South Asia from Acsadi and Johnson-Acsadi, "Safe Motherhood in South Asia."

18. For a discussion on anemia and strategies to prevent and treat it, see Beverly Winikoff et al., "Women's Health: An Alternative Perspective for Choosing Interventions," *Studies in Family Planning*, July/August 1988.

19. E. DeMaeyer and M. Adiels-Tegman, "The Prevalence of Anaemia in the World," *World Health Statistics Quarterly*, Vol. 38, 1985.

20. Acsadi and Johnson-Acsadi, "Safe Motherhood in South Asia"; Starrs, *Preventing the Tragedy*.

21. Walsh et al., "Maternal and Perinatal Care."

22. Share of women with access to prenatal care in South Asia and sub-Saharan Africa from Starrs, *Preventing the Tragedy*; data on

Latin America from Pan American Health Organization, "Regional Plan of Action for the Reduction of Maternal Mortality in the Americas," paper presented at the Pan American Sanitary Conference, Washington, D.C., September 1990.

23. Government of Zimbabwe, "Zimbabwe Country Paper," presented at the conference on Safe Motherhood for the SADCC countries, Harare, Zimbabwe, October 29-November 1, 1990.

24. Sereen Thaddeus and Deborah Maine, *Too Far To Walk: Maternal Mortality In Context* (New York: Columbia University, Center for Population and Family Health, 1990).

25. Ibid.

26. Ibid.; Anrudh K. Jain, "Fertility Reduction and the Quality of Family Planning Services," *Studies in Family Planning*, January/February 1989; Starrs, *Preventing the Tragedy*.

27. Starrs, *Preventing the Tragedy*.

28. WHO and the International Federation of Gynaecology and Obstetrics (FIGO), "Traditional Birth Attendants: A Resource for the Health of Women," *International Journal of Gynaecolgy and Obstetrics*, Vol. 23, 1985; A. Mangay Maglacas and John Simons, eds., *The Potential of the Traditional Birth Attendant* (Geneva: WHO, 1986).

29. Descriptions of various infections and their consequences derived from WHO, *Sexually Transmitted Diseases Research Needs: Report of a WHO Consultative Group* (Copenhagen: 1989).

30. For a complete discussion of reproductive tract infections, see Ruth Dixon Mueller and Judith Wasserheit, *The Culture of Silence* (New York: International Women's Health Coalition, 1991).

31. L.A. Mtimavalye and M.A. Belsey, *Infertility and Sexually Transmitted Disease: Major Problems in Maternal and Child Health and Family*

*Planning* (New York: The Population Council, 1987).

32. Ibid.

33. R.A. Bang et al., "High Prevalence of Gynecological Diseases in Rural Indian Women," *The Lancet*, January 14, 1989.

34. Mtimavalye and Belsey, *Infertility and Sexually Transmitted Disease*.

35. Dixon-Mueller and Wasserheit, *Culture of Silence*; Mtimavalye and Belsey, *Infertility and Sexually Transmitted Disease*.

36. Dixon-Mueller and Wasserheit, *The Culture of Silence*.

37. Ibid.; Acsadi and Johnson-Acsadi, "Safe Motherhood in South Asia"; Over and Piot, "HIV Infection and Other Sexually Transmitted Diseases"; Michael J. Rosenbert et al., "Sexually Transmitted Diseases in sub-Saharan Africa," *The Lancet*, July 19, 1986; see also WHO, "Prevention and Management of Infertility," *Progress*, No. 15, 1990.

38. Judith Wasserheit, "Reproductive Tract Infections," in *Special Challenges in Third World Women's Health* (New York: International Women's Health Coalition, 1990); Judith Wasserheit, "The Significance and Scope of Reproductive Tract Infections among Third World Women," *International Journal of Gynecology and Obstetrics*, Supplement 3, 1989; Dixon-Mueller and Wasserheit, *Culture of Silence*.

39. Share of ectopic pregnancies related to reproductive tract infections from Dr. C.J. Van Dam, Medical Officer, Sexually Transmitted Disease Programme, WHO, Geneva, private communication, May 1, 1991.

40. Wasserheit, "Reproductive Tract Infection."

41. Wasserheit, "The Significance and Scope of Reproductive Tract Infections."

42. Dixon-Mueller and Wasserheit, *Culture of Silence*.

43. Mtimavalye and Belsey, *Infertility and Sexually Transmitted Disease*; WHO, *Sexually Transmitted Diseases Research Needs*.

44. Dixon-Mueller and Wasserheit, *Culture of Silence*; Wasserheit, "The Significance and Scope of Reproductive Tract Infections."

45. Over and Piot, "HIV and Other Sexually Transmitted Diseases"; Helen Saxenian, "Brazil: Women's Reproductive Health" (unpublished draft), World Bank paper, December 29, 1989.

46. I. Cohen et al., "Improved Pregnancy Outcome Following Successful Treatment of Chlamydial Infection," and J.M. Chow, "The Association Between Chlmaydia Trachomatis and Ectopic Pregnancy: A Matched-Pair, Case-Control Study," *Journal of the American Medical Association*, June 20, 1990; Sergi O. Aral and King K. Holmes, "Sexually Transmitted Diseases in the AIDS Era," *Scientific American*, February 1991.

47. Number of cervical cancers from Stanley et al., "Women and Cancer," and from Peter Piot, Professor of Microbiology at the Institute of Medicine, Antwerp, Belgium, private communication, May 8, 1991.

48. Dr. Nancy Kiviat, Attending Physician and Director of Pathology Department, Harborview Medical Center, Seattle, Wash., private communication, March 20, 1991; Saxenian, "Brazil: Women's Reproductive Health."

49. Deaths related to cervical cancer in the United States from National Center for Health Statistics, "Advance Report of Final Mortality Statistics, 1988," *Monthly Vital Statistics Report*, Vol. 39, No. 7, Supplement, 1990; David A. Grimes, "Deaths due to Sexually Transmitted Diseases: The Forgotten Component of Reproductive Mortality," *Journal of the American Medical Association*, April 4, 1986.

50. Angele Petros-Barvazian and Michael H. Merson, "Women and AIDS: A Challenge

for Humanity," *World Health*, November/December 1990.

51. International Planned Parenthood Federation (IPPF), "New IMAP Statement on the Acquired Immune Deficiency Syndrome," *IPPF Medical Bulletin*, December 1990; Over and Piot, "HIV Infection and Other Sexually Transmitted Diseases."

52. Mtimavalye and Belsey, *Infertility and Sexually Transmitted Disease*; Over and Piot, "HIV Infections and Other Sexually Transmitted Diseases"; D.G. Smith, "Thailand: AIDS Crisis Looms," *The Lancet*, March 31, 1990.

53. Over and Piot, "HIV Infections and Other Sexually Transmitted Diseases"; IPPF, "New IMAP Statement on the Acquired Immune Deficiency Syndrome"; Dixon-Mueller and Wasserheit, *Culture of Silence*.

54. Susheela Singh and Deidre Wulf, *Today's Adolescents, Tomorrow's Parents: A Portrait of the Americas* (New York: The Alan Guttmacher Institute, 1990); Center for Population Options (CPO), "The Facts: Teenage Pregnancy and Sexually Transmitted Diseases in Latin America," Washington, D.C., August 1990; CPO, "The Facts: Teenage Pregnancy in Africa," Washington, D.C., September 1990; Jodi L. Jacobson, *The Global Politics of Abortion*, Worldwatch Paper 97 (Washington, D.C.: Worldwatch Institute, July 1990); Wasserheit, "The Significance and Scope of Reproductive Tract Infections."

55. New rhetoric about the need to move beyond conventional family planning programs from author's observations during Office of Population, Agency for International Development, "Family Planning in the 21st Century," Seventh Cooperating Agencies Meeting, Washington, D.C., November 26–28, 1990.

56. For a discussion of contraceptive prevalence, see W. Parker Mauldin and Sheldon J. Segal, "Prevalence of Contraceptive Use: Trends and Issues," *Studies in Family Planning*, November/December 1988.

57. Charles Westoff, "Unmet Need for Family Planning in the Late 1980s," paper prepared for a briefing of the Congressional Coalition on Population and Development, May 18, 1990.

58. Total fertility rate for 1970 from Saxenian, "Brazil: Women's Reproductive Health," and for 1990 from Population Reference Bureau, *1990 World Population Data Sheet* (Washington, D.C.: 1990).

59. Saxenian, "Brazil: Women's Reproductive Health."

60. William D. Mosher and William F. Pratt, "Contraceptive Use in the United States, 1973–88," *Advance Data*, March 20, 1990; "Dominican Women Rely Heavily on Sterilization; But Many Use No Method," *International Family Planning Perspectives*, June 1985.

61. Adrienne Germaine and Peggy Antrobus, "New Partners in Reproductive Care," *Populi*, December 1989; for further discussions on women's reproductive health, see Adrienne Germaine, "Reproductive Health and Dignity," presented to the International Conference on Better Health for Women and Children Through Family Planning, Nairobi, Kenya, October 1987, available from the International Women's Health Coalition, New York.

62. For a discussion of traditional measures of unmet need, see Charles F. Westoff and Luis Hernando Ochoa, "Unmet Need and the Demand for Family Planning," *Demographic and Health Surveys Comparative Studies Number 5*, April 1991, and Charles Westoff, "The Potential Demand for Family Planning: A New Measure of Unmet Need and Estimates for Five Latin American Countries," *International Family Planning Perspectives*, June 1988.

63. Worldwatch Institute estimate based on the estimated increase in maternal deaths

to 600,00 per year, according to Walsh et al., "Maternal and Perinatal Health," on data for AIDS deaths and various reproductive tract infections and other STDs from Petros-Barvazian and Merson, "Women and AIDS," on Over and Piot, "HIV Infection and Other Sexually Transmitted Diseases," on IPPF, "New IMAP Statement on the Acquired Immune Deficiency Syndrome," and on private communications with Drs. Nancy Kiviat, Peter Piot, and Judith Wasserheit.

64. Married women who lack access to contraception from Craig Lasher, Population Crisis Committee, Washington, D.C., private communication, June 4, 1991; Deborah Maine et al., "Prevention of Maternal Mortality in Developing Countries; Program Options and Practical Considerations," presented at the International Safe Motherhood Conference, Nairobi, Kenya, February 10–13, 1987.

65. Anne Tinker, "Safe Motherhood: How Much Does It Cost?" World Bank draft paper presented at the Conference on Safe Motherhood for the SADCC countries, Harare, Zimbabwe, October 29-November 1, 1990.

66. SEWA information based on author's observations during travel in India, September 15-October 27, 1990; other information on birth attendant training programs can be found in Jodi L. Jacobson, "Midwife Crisis," *World Watch*, July/August 1991, and in WHO/FIGO, *Traditional Birth Attendants*.

67. Wasserheit, "The Significance and Scope of Reproductive Tract Infections"; Kiviat, private communication; Meheus quoted in Wasserheit, "Reproductive Tract Infections."

68. Charles C. Griffin, "The Need to Change Health Care Priorities in LDCs," *Finance and Development*, March 1991.

## Chapter 7. Mining the Earth

1. U.S. Library of Congress, Congressional Research Service, *Are We Running Out? A*

*Perspective on Resource Scarcity* (Washington, D.C.: U.S. Government Printing Office, 1978).

2. Rex Bosson and Bension Varon, *The Mining Industry and the Developing Countries* (New York: Oxford University Press, 1977).

3. Increase in iron, copper, and zinc production derived from historical data in Bosson and Varon, *The Mining Industry*, and from 1990 production figures in U.S. Bureau of Mines (USBM), *Mineral Commodity Summaries 1991* (Washington, D.C.: 1991); history of aluminum from John A. Wolfe, *Mineral Resources: A World Review* (New York: Chapman and Hall, 1984); aluminum production from USBM, *Mineral Commodity Summaries*.

4. Uranium is a metal, but is classed here with the fossil fuels for the sake of analysis.

5. Information on uses from USBM, *Mineral Commodity Summaries*.

6. Aluminum and steel prices and use of metals in steelmaking from USBM, *Mineral Commodity Summaries*; estimated relative value of world metals sales is a Worldwatch estimate, based on data in ibid.

7. 1988 consumption figures derived from data in World Resources Institute (WRI), *World Resources 1990–91* (New York: Oxford University Press, 1990); industrial nations' historical shares of steel and other metals consumption from Olivier Bomsel et al., *Mining and Metallurgy Investment in the Third World: The End of Large Projects?* (Paris: Organisation for Economic Co-operation and Development (OECD), 1990).

8. Minerals demand from Bomsel et al., *Mining and Metallurgy Investment*.

9. For more on the materials use trends discussed in this section, see Bomsel et al., *Mining and Metallurgy Investment*; Marc H. Ross and Robert H. Williams, *Our Energy: Regaining Control* (New York: McGraw-Hill, 1981); Eric D. Larson et al., "Materials, Af-

fluence, and Industrial Energy Use," *Annual Review of Energy, Vol. 12* (Palo Alto, Calif.: 1987); Peter F. Drucker, "The Changed World Economy," *Foreign Affairs*, Spring 1986; and Robert U. Ayres, "Industrial Metabolism," and Robert Herman et al., "Dematerialization," in Jesse H. Ausubel and Hedy E. Sladovich, eds., *Technology and Environment* (Washington, D.C.: National Academy Press, 1989).

10. Lead and iron and steel recycling are Worldwatch Institute estimates based on data in USBM, *Mineral Commodity Summaries*; aluminum from U.N. Environment Programme, *Environmental Data Report 1989/90* (Cambridge, Mass.: Basil Blackwell, 1989).

11. Bomsel et al., *Mining and Metallurgy Investment*.

12. USBM, *Mineral Commodity Summaries*.

13. Import dependence of Japan and Western Europe from Bosson and Varon, *The Mining Industry*, and from Faysal Yachir, *Mining in Africa Today* (London: Zed Books, 1988); United States from USBM, *Mineral Commodity Summaries*.

14. Yachir, *Mining in Africa Today*.

15. Reserve figures from WRI, *World Resources 1990–91*; growth of reserves from "Human Factors Influencing Resource Availability and Use: Group Report," in Digby J. McLaren and Brian J. Skinner, eds., *Resources and World Development* (London: John Wiley and Sons, 1987).

16. Reserves from USBM, *Mineral Commodity Summaries*; István Dobozi, "Perestroika and the End of the Cold War: Possible Mineral Trade Implications for the USSR and Eastern Europe," presentation at annual meeting of the American Association for the Advancement of Science, Washington, D.C., February 17, 1991.

17. Georgius Agricola, *De Re Metallica* (New York: Dover Publications, 1950).

18. Trucks and shovels from Bosson and Varon, *The Mining Industry*.

19. The sources for Table 7–3 are: Julio Díaz Palacios, "Environmental Destruction in Southern Peru," *Earth Island Journal*, Summer 1989; Nauru from "Who Will Clean Up Paradise," *Asiaweek*, January 4, 1991, and from Martin Weston, Nauru Government Office, London, letter to the editor, *Economist*, February 23, 1991; Philip M. Fearnside, "The Charcoal of Carajás: A Threat to the Forests of Brazil's Eastern Amazon Region," *Ambio*, Vol. 18, No. 2, 1989; Severonikel from Valeriy E. Berlin, "Conservation Efforts in Kola Peninsula's Lapland Preserve Detailed," *JPRS Reports*, June 17, 1991; "Sabah Mining Pollution - Part One: Villagers Demand US $6 Million Compensation," APPEN (Asia-Pacific Peoples Environment Network) Features, Penang, Malaysia, 1990; David Cleary, *Anatomy of the Amazon Gold Rush* (Iowa City: University of Iowa Press, 1990). Superfund sites from Steve Hoffman, U.S. Environmental Protection Agency (EPA), Washington, D.C., private communication, November 5, 1991; EPA and Montana Department of Health and Environmental Sciences (MDHES), *Clark Fork Superfund Master Plan* (Helena, Mont.: 1988); Peter Nielsen and Bruce Farling, "Hazardous Wastes Endanger Water, Wildlife, Land: Mining Catastrophe in Clark Fork," *Clementine* (Mineral Policy Center, Washington, D.C.), Autumn 1991.

20. EPA and MDHES, *Clark Fork Superfund*; Nielsen and Farling, "Mining Catastrophe in Clark Fork"; Peter Nielsen, Executive Director, Clark Fork Coalition, Missoula, Mont., private communication, October 16, 1991; Cabinet Mountains from "Shame on Montana" (videotape), World Wide Film Expedition, Missoula, Mont., 1991.

21. USBM, *1988 Minerals Yearbook* (Washington, D.C.: U.S. Government Printing Office, 1989).

22. Share of metal ore discarded as tailings, metal contaminants in tailings, and tail-

ings pond examples from Johnnie N. Moore and Samuel N. Luoma, "Large-Scale Environmental Impacts: Mining's Hazardous Waste," *Clementine* (Mineral Policy Center, Washington, D.C.), Spring 1991; sulfur content of metal ores from Martyn Kelly, *Mining and the Freshwater Environment* (London: Elsevier Science Publishers, 1988); organic contaminants from Christopher G. Down and John Stocks, *Environmental Impact of Mining* (New York: John Wiley and Sons, 1977); toluene use in concentrators from Daniel M. Horowitz, "Mining and Right-to-Know," *Clementine*, Winter 1990; health effects of toluene from Eric P. Jorgenson, ed., *The Poisoned Well: New Strategies for Groundwater Protection* (Washington, D.C.: Island Press, 1989).

23. Michael C. Howard, *Mining, Politics, and Development in the South Pacific* (Boulder, Colo.: Westview Press, 1991); David Hyndman, "Digging the Mines in Melanesia," *Cultural Survival Quarterly*, Vol. 15, No. 2, 1991; David Clark Scott, "Rebels Keep Papua New Guinea Mine Closed," *Christian Science Monitor*, July 7, 1989; "A Mine of Controversy," *South*, June/July 1991; Moore and Luoma, "Mining's Hazardous Waste."

24. Detlev Möller, "Estimation of the Global Man-Made Sulphur Emission," *Atmospheric Environment*, Vol. 18, No. 1, 1984; effects of fluoride emissions from Paul R. Ehrlich et al., *Ecoscience: Population, Resources, Environment* (San Francisco, Calif.: W.H. Freeman, 1977).

25. Dead zones from Moore and Luoma, "Mining's Hazardous Waste," except for Sudbury fish kills and Trail smelter pollution, from Down and Stocks, *Environmental Impact of Mining*.

26. Berlin, "Conservation Efforts in Kola Peninsula's Lapland Preserve Detailed"; Chilean and U.S. smelter emissions from United Nations, Economic Commission for Latin American and the Caribbean, *Sustainable Development: Changing Production Patterns, Social Equity and the Environment* (Santiago, Chile: 1991).

27. Historical grade of copper ore from Bosson and Varon, *The Mining Industry*; estimate of copper ore mined based on data and estimates of copper grades in various countries from Janice Jolly, USBM, Washington, D.C., private communication, October 18, 1991.

28. Scale of Bingham Canyon mine from Andrew Goudie, *The Human Impact on the Natural Environment* (Cambridge, Mass.: MIT Press, 1990); Kennecott toxics report from Horowitz, "Mining and Right-to-Know."

29. Goldstrike from Kenneth Gooding, "American Barrick's Glittering Run of Luck Continues," *Financial Times*, October 4, 1991; Amazon mining from Cleary, *Anatomy of the Amazon Gold Rush*.

30. Gold price and mercury in Amazon from Cleary, *Anatomy of the Amazon Gold Rush*; Indonesia from Alexander Gurov, "Gold Rush in Kalimantan," *Asia and Africa Today*, No. 2, 1990; Zimbabwe from Paul Jourdan, Institute of Mining Research, Harare, Zimbabwe, private communication, April 12, 1991; other nations from Melvyn Westlake and Robin Stainer, "Rising Gold Fever," *South*, March 1989.

31. "Heavy Rains Burst South Carolina Dam: Major Cyanide Spill," *Clementine* (Mineral Policy Center, Washington, D.C.), Winter 1990; bird kills from Alyson Warhurst, "Environmental Degradation from Mining and Mineral Processing in Developing Countries: Corporate Responses and National Policies," draft discussion document for meeting of the Mining and Environment Research Network, Steyning, U.K., April 10–13, 1991.

32. Total world mineral extraction is a Worldwatch Institute estimate, based on data in USBM, *Mineral Commodity Summaries*; the estimated sediment load in the world's rivers is 16.5 billion tons per year, according to J.D. Milliman and R.H. Meade, cited in Brian J.

Skinner, "Resources in the 21st Century: Can Supplies Meet Needs?" *Episodes*, December 1989.

33. Area mined is a Worldwatch Institute estimate, derived by multiplying world production data by 1980 U.S. land use/production ratios; world production from USBM, *Mineral Commodity Summaries*; ratios derived from Wilton Johnson and James Paone, "Land Utilization and Reclamation in the Mining Industry, 1930–80," Bureau of Mines Information Circular 8862, Washington, D.C., 1982; Elizabeth Dore, "Open Wounds," *NACLA Report on the Americas*, September 1991.

34. Sussex from Down and Stocks, *Environmental Impact of Mining*; Comstock Lode and observations in 1877 by William Wright from Duane A. Smith, *Mining America: The Industry and the Environment, 1800–1980* (Lawrence: University Press of Kansas, 1987).

35. Fearnside, "The Charcoal of Carajás."

36. Grande Carajás from Dore, "Open Wounds"; Albrás from Bomsel et al., *Mining and Metallurgy Investment*; share of Tucuruí electricity consumed by Albrás is a Worldwatch estimate based on energy use and aluminum output figures from ibid. and from "Power Failure: A Month to Assess Albrás Damage," *Gazeta Mecantil*, March 18, 1991, and on estimate of the dam's annual output from Robert Goodland, *Environmental Assessment of the Tucuruí Hydro Project* (Brasilia: Eletronorte, S.A., 1978); for information on the destructive nature of the Tucuruí dam, see Barbara J. Cummings, *Dam the Rivers, Damn the People* (London: Earthscan, 1990).

37. Energy requirements of aluminum smelting from U.S. Congress, Office of Technology Assessment (OTA), *Nonferrous Metals: Industry Structure—Background Paper* (Washington, D.C.: U.S. Government Printing Office, 1990); requirements for mining, beneficiation, and alumina refining from Martin Brown and Bruce McKern, *Aluminium, Copper, and Steel in Developing Countries* (Paris:

OECD, 1987); total energy consumption in aluminum production is a Worldwatch Institute estimate derived from these sources and from 1990 production estimate in USBM, *Mineral Commodity Summaries*; electricity use in smelting converted into Btu. assuming a 64/36 percent mix of fossil and nonfossil electricity generation (while a large portion of aluminum smelting is powered by hydroelectric sources, much of that energy could be directed into other uses now dependent on fossil energy sources); low electricity rates from Ronald Graham, *The Aluminium Industry and the Third World* (London: Zed Books, 1982).

38. Energy use in copper production is a Worldwatch Institute estimate derived from 1990 production estimate in USBM, *Mineral Commodity Summaries*, and from estimates of energy requirements per ton of copper in Brown and McKern, *Aluminium, Copper, and Steel*, and in Bernard A. Gelb and Jeffrey Pliskin, *Energy Use in Mining: Patterns and Prospects* (Cambridge, Mass.: Ballinger Publishing, 1979); energy use in steelmaking is from Department of Energy, Energy Information Administration, *Manufacturing Energy Consumption Survey: Consumption of Energy 1988* (Washington, D.C.: 1991); figure includes some energy used in fabrication as well as crude production, but does not include that used in mining and ore concentration.

39. OTA, *Nonferrous Metals*; Brown and McKern, *Aluminium, Copper, and Steel*; declining grade of copper ore from Bosson and Varon, *The Mining Industry*.

40. Warhurst, "Environmental Degradation from Mining"; Ok Tedi from Howard, *Mining, Politics, and Development*.

41. Projected additional minerals price decline from International Monetary Fund, "Primary Commodities: Market Developments and Outlook," World Economic and Financial Surveys, Washington, D.C., July 1990.

42. U.S. miners' deductions must not exceed half the operation's taxable income; taxation of mineral industries from John J. Schanz, Jr., *The Subsidization of Non-Fuel Mineral Production at Home and Abroad* (Washington, D.C.: Congressional Research Service, 1987), from Talbot Page, *Conservation and Economic Efficiency, An Approach to Materials Policy* (Baltimore, Md.: Johns Hopkins University Press, 1977), and from National Commission on Supplies and Shortages, *Government and the Nation's Resources* (Washington, D.C.: U.S. Government Printing Office, 1976); special tax provisions for minerals are spelled out in United States Code, Vol. 26, sections 611–617; depletion allowances for various minerals are also listed in USBM, *Mineral Commodity Summaries*.

43. Tax subsidy to the mining industry from Executive Office of the President, *Budget of the United States Government* and *Special Analyses: Budget of the United States Government* (Washington, D.C.: U.S. Government Printing Office, various years); U.S. Congress, Joint Committee on Taxation, "Estimates of Federal Tax Expenditures for Fiscal Years 1992–1996," Washington, D.C., U.S. Government Printing Office, April 1991.

44. For General Mining Act, see "Mining Reform Alternatives Compared: Point-by-Point," *Clementine* (Mineral Policy Center, Washington, D.C.), Spring/Summer 1990, and U.S. General Accounting Office (GAO), *Federal Land Management: The Mining Law of 1872 Needs Revision* (Washington, D.C.: 1989); lack of revenue and value of mineral production on federal land from James Duffus III, Director, Natural Resources Management Issues, GAO, testimony before the Subcommittee on Mining and Natural Resources, Committee on Interior and Insular Affairs, U.S. House of Representatives, Washington, D.C., September 6, 1990.

45. W.C.J. van Rensburg, *Strategic Minerals* (Englewood Cliffs, N.J.: Prentice-Hall, 1986).

46. Ibid.; GAO, "Federal Encouragement of Mining Investment in Developing Countries for Strategic and Critical Materials Has Been Only Marginally Effective," Washington, D.C., 1982.

47. British/German arms race from Paul Kennedy, *The Rise and Fall of the Great Powers* (New York: Random House, 1987); for the influence of military demand on the evolution of the aluminum industry, see Graham, *The Aluminium Industry*; quote from Harry N. Holmes, *Strategic Minerals and National Strength* (New York: MacMillan, 1942).

48. Page, *Conservation and Economic Efficiency*.

49. World Bank, *World Debt Tables 1989–90* (Washington, D.C.: 1989).

50. Economic decline in Zambia from Jane Perlez, "Rainy Days in Zambia (Price an Umbrella!)" *New York Times*, June 5, 1990, and from Tony Hodges, "Zambia's Autonomous Adjustment," *Africa Recovery* (United Nations, New York), December 1988; child deaths from Alan B. Durning, *Poverty and the Environment: Reversing the Downward Spiral*, Worldwatch Paper 92 (Washington, D.C.: Worldwatch Institute, November 1989).

51. Bomsel et al., *Mining and Metallurgy Investment*.

52. Nationalization in Guinea from Graham, *The Aluminium Industry*; all others from Bosson and Varon, *The Mining Industry*; cartels from ibid.

53. The mineral-centered development strategy described here is thoroughly laid out in Bosson and Varon, *The Mining Industry*; World Bank lending for minerals projects from World Bank, *Annual Report* (Washington, D.C.; various years) (figure includes International Development Association commitments); World Bank price forecasts and Guelbs project from Bomsel et al., *Mining and Metallurgy Investment*.

54. Les Guelbs from Bomsel et al., *Mining and Metallurgy Investment*; GDP of Mauritania from World Bank, *World Development Report*

*1981* (New York: Oxford University Press, 1981).

55. Bomsel et al., *Mining and Metallurgy Investment*; USBM, *Minerals Yearbook* (various years).

56. Bomsel et al., *Mining and Metallurgy Investment*.

57. Howard, *Mining, Politics, and Development*; Hyndman, "Digging the Mines in Melanesia"; Scott, "Rebels Keep Papua New Guinea Mine Closed"; "A Mine of Controversy."

58. American Anthropological Association (AAA), "Report of the Special Commission to Investigate the Situation of the Brazilian Yanomami," Washington, D.C., 1991.

59. Quote from Richard Barnet, *The Lean Years: Politics in the Age of Scarcity* (New York: Simon and Schuster, 1980); AAA, "Report of the Special Commission"; decree from Comissão Pela Criação do Parque Yanomami, "Diario Oficial Publica Delimitação de Terra Indigena Yanomami em Area Continua," news bulletin, São Paulo, July 26, 1991.

60. Agricola, *De Re Metallica*.

61. Lewis Mumford, *Technics and Civilization* (New York: Harcourt Brace Jovanovich, 1963).

62. Warhurst, "Environmental Degradation from Mining."

63. Minerals use trends from Bomsel et al., *Mining and Metallurgy Investment*; Ross and Williams, *Our Energy*; Larson et al., "Materials, Affluence, and Industrial Energy Use"; Drucker, "The Changed World Economy"; Ayres, "Industrial Metabolism"; Herman et al., "Dematerialization."

64. OTA, *Technical Options for Conservation of Metals: Case Studies of Selected Metals and Products* (Washington, D.C.: U.S. Government Printing Office, 1979).

65. "Old Cars Get a New Lease on Life," *Financial Times*, September 3, 1991; Bill Siuru, "Car Recycling in Germany," *Resource Recycling*, February 1991; "Peugeot Developing Facility to Recycle Junk Automobiles," *Multinational Environmental Outlook*, March 5, 1991; "Volvo Announces Plans to Recycle Cars as Part of Environmental Impact Scheme," *International Environment Reporter*, September 11, 1991; Krystal Miller, "On the Road Again and Again: Auto Makers Try to Build Recyclable Car," *Wall Street Journal*, April 30, 1991; "Daimler Has 10% of Recycler," *New York Times*, March 29, 1991; Stuart Marshall, "Green Scrapyards," *Financial Times*, March 23, 1991.

66. Share of world living in developing countries from Population Reference Bureau, *1991 World Population Data Sheet* (Washington, D.C.: 1991).

## Chapter 8. Shaping Cities

1. Leonardo Benevolo, *The History of the City* (Cambridge, Mass.: MIT Press, 1980).

2. Annual rate of urban land conversion in Bangkok for 1974–84 from David E. Dowall, "The Land Market Assessment: A New Tool for Urban Management," paper prepared for the Urban Management Program of United Nations Center for Human Settlements (UNCHS), World Bank, and United Nations Development Programme (UNDP), University of California, Berkeley, March 1991; the area of Manhattan (5,817 hectares) from *Encyclopaedia Britannica*, 15th ed.; Bruce Babbitt, "Age-Old Challenge: Water and the West," *National Geographic*, June 1991; Cairo from Robert L. Schiffer, "The Exploding City," *Populi*, Vol. 15, No. 2, 1988; Benevolo, *The History of the City*.

3. United Nations, *World Urbanization Prospects 1990* (New York: 1991).

4. Nigerian remark cited in Christopher Alexander, *A Pattern Language: Towns, Build-*

*ings, Construction* (New York: Oxford University Press, 1977).

5. Peter Hall, "Three Systems, Three Separate Paths," *APA Journal*, Winter 1991; Motor Vehicle Manufacturers Association, *Facts and Figures '91* (Detroit, Mich.: 1991).

6. Kevin Kasowski, "Sprawl: Can it Be Stopped?" *Developments* (National Growth Management Leadership Project), Summer 1991; Howard LaFranchi, "Brussels: Europe's Unofficial Capital Builds for the Future," *Christian Science Monitor*, May 1, 1991; Peter Hall, "Population and the Planning of Large Cities in the Developed Countries," paper prepared for the International Conference on Population and the Urban Future, Barcelona, Spain, May 19–22, 1986 (hereinafter cited as Population and Urban Future Conference).

7. John Pucher, "Capitalism, Socialism, and Urban Transportation: Policies and Travel Behavior in the East and West," *APA Journal*, Summer 1990; Jürgen Friedrichs, "Large Cities in Eastern Europe," in Mattei Dogan and John D. Kasarda, eds., *The Metropolis Era, Vol. 1: A World of Giant Cities* (Newbury Park, Calif.: Sage Publications, 1988); Hilary F. French, *Green Revolutions: Environmental Reconstruction in Eastern Europe and the Soviet Union*, Worldwatch Paper 99 (Washington, D.C.: Worldwatch Institute, November 1990).

8. U.S. House of Representatives, Committee on Banking, Finance, and Urban Affairs, *Compact Cities: Energy Saving Strategies for the Eighties* (Washington, D.C.: U.S. Government Printing Office, 1980).

9. Regional Plan Association, *Regional Plan Association—1990* (Annual Report) (New York: 1989).

10. A.K. Jain, *The Making of a Metropolis: Planning and Growth of Delhi* (Delhi: National Book Organization, 1990); Aderanti Adepoju, "Population and the Planning of Large Cities in Africa," paper prepared for the Population and Urban Future Conference.

11. Wraith quoted in Adepoju, "Population and the Planning of Large Cities in Africa."

12. Jorge E. Hardoy and David Satterthwaite, *Squatter Citizen: Life in the Urban Third World* (London: Earthscan Publications, 1989); UNDP, *Human Development Report 1990* (New York: 1990).

13. Campaign for New Transportation Priorities, *Urban and Suburban Transportation: Programs and Policies for More Livable Cities*, Policy Paper 1 (Washington, D.C.: 1991).

14. Kevin Kasowski, "Bridging the Gap," *Developments* (National Growth Management Leadership Project), Spring/Summer 1990.

15. Ricardo Jordan Squella, *Population and the Planning of Large Cities in Latin America*, paper prepared for the Population and Urban Future Conference; Jain, *The Making of a Metropolis*; UNCHS, *Transportation Strategies for Human Settlements in Developing Countries* (Nairobi: 1984).

16. Boris S. Pushkarev and Jeffrey M. Zupan, *Public Transportation and Land Use Policy* (Bloomington: Indiana University Press, 1977).

17. Francis Violich and Robert Daughters, *Urban Planning For Latin America: The Challenge of Metropolitan Growth* (Boston: Oelgeschlager, Gunn & Hain, 1987).

18. Martin Gellen, *Accessory Apartments in Single-Family Housing* (New Brunswick, N.J.: Center for Urban Policy Research, 1985); David E. Dowall, *The Suburban Squeeze* (Berkeley: University of California Press, 1984).

19. Peter Newman and Jeffrey Kenworthy, *Cities and Automobile Dependence: An International Sourcebook* (Aldershot, U.K.: Gower, 1989).

20. Ibid.; the murder rate in Hong Kong was 1.5 per 100,000 people; Population Cri-

sis Committee, *Cities: Life in the World's 100 Largest Metropolitan Areas* (Washington, D.C.: 1990).

21. Newman and Kenworthy, *Cities and Automobile Dependence*.

22. Dirk H. ten Grotenhuis, "The Delft Cycle Plan: Characteristics of the Concept," *Velo City 87 International Congress: Planning for the Urban Cyclist*, proceedings of the Third International Velo City Congress, Groningen, the Netherlands, September 22–26, 1987.

23. Timothy Egan, "A Stroll in the Country for City Dwellers, Starting Downtown," *New York Times*, June 24, 1991; Noel Grove, "Greenways: Paths to the Future," *National Geographic*, June 1990; Marion Shoard, *This Land is Our Land* (London: Paladin Grafton Books, 1987).

24. Elizabeth Deakin, "The United States," in Jean-Philippe Barde and Kenneth Button, *Transport Policy and the Environment: Six Case Studies* (London: Earthscan Publications, 1990); Jain, *The Making of a Metropolis*; UNCHS, *Transportation Strategies for Human Settlements in Developing Countries*.

25. Tim Elkin and Duncan McLaren with Mayer Hillman, *Reviving the City: Towards Sustainable Urban Development* (London: Friends of the Earth, 1991); John Roberts, *User-Friendly Cities: What Britain Can Learn from Mainland Europe*, Rees Jeffreys Discussion Paper (London: Transport and Environmental Studies of London, 1989); Jens Rorbech, "Eliminating Cars from City Centers," *Alternative Transportation Network*, March/April 1990.

26. Gordon Oliver, "Portland Goes for Broke," *Planning*, February 1989; Kasowski, "Sprawl: Can it Be Stopped?"

27. "Do Higher Densities Produce Affordable Housing?" *Developments* (National Growth Management Leadership Project), December 1990; "Town Planning: Where it

Works," *The Economist*, September 1990; Kasowski, "Bridging the Gap"; Jessica Mathews, "The Costs of Unplanned Urban Sprawl," *Washington Post*, January 13, 1991.

28. Pam Dunham, Tri-Met Transit Authority, Portland, Oreg., private communication, February 15, 1991; Kasowski, "Bridging the Gap."

29. Oregon Department of Land Conservation and Development, "Transportation Planning Rule," Salem, Oreg., April 26, 1991; Oliver, "Portland Goes for Broke."

30. Charles L. Wright, "A Characteristics Analysis of Non-Motorized Transport," *UMTRI Research Review* (University of Michigan Transportation Research Institute), March/April 1990.

31. Michael Philips, *Energy Conservation Activities in Latin America and the Caribbean* (Washington, D.C.: International Institute for Energy Conservation (IIEC), 1990); Jaime Lerner, *The Curitiba Mass Transit System* (Washington, D.C.: IIEC, 1989).

32. Lerner, *The Curitiba Mass Transit System*.

33. Paul Niebanck, "Growth Controls and the Production of Inequality," in David J. Brower et al., *Understanding Growth Management: Critical Issues and a Research Agenda* (Washington, D.C.: The Urban Land Institute, 1989); Advisory Commission on Regulatory Barriers to Affordable Housing, *"Not In My Backyard": Removing Barriers to Affordable Housing* (Washington, D.C.: U.S. Department of Housing and Urban Development, 1991). Of course, the lack of available, inexpensive housing is not the only obstacle low-income people face; the very poor cannot afford even the cheapest available shelter, and therefore need financial assistance (from the government, private organizations, and public-private partnerships) to obtain decent housing.

34. Advisory Commission on Regulatory Barriers to Affordable Housing, *"Not In My Backyard"*.

35. 1000 Friends of Oregon and The Home Builders Association of Metropolitan Portland, "Managing Growth to Promote Affordable Housing: Revisiting Oregon's Goal 10," unpublished draft, Portland, Oreg., April 15, 1991.

36. John D. Kasarda, "Economic Restructuring and America's Urban Dilemma," in Dogan and Kasarda, *The Metropolis Era, Vol. 1*; Lucia Mouat, "Employers Open New Routes for Workers Commuting to Suburbs," *Christian Science Monitor*, February 7, 1991.

37. Hernando de Soto, *The Other Path: The Invisible Revolution in the Third World* (New York: Harper & Row, 1989).

38. Hardoy and Satterthwaite, *Squatter Citizen*; de Soto, *The Other Path*.

39. Akhtar Badshah, "The Shape of Things to Come," *Development Network* (Aga Khan Development Institutions), no date; UNDP, *Human Development Report 1990*.

40. Norman Krumholz and John Forester, *Making Equity Planning Work: Leadership in the Public Sector* (Philadelphia: Temple University Press, 1990); John D. Edwards, *Land Bank and Land Prices* (Ottawa: Ministry of State for Urban Affairs, 1974).

41. Jain, *The Making of a Metropolis*.

42. William A. Doebele, "Land Policy," in Lloyd Rodwin, ed., *Shelter, Settlement, and Development: An Overview* (Boston: Allen and Unwin, 1987).

43. Ibid.; Yong Hyo Cho and Young Sup Kim, "Land Tax Policy in Korea" in Frank J. Costa et al., *Urbanization in Asia: Spatial Dimensions and Policy Issues* (Honolulu: University of Hawaii Press, 1989); discussion of accurate property assessment from U.S. House of Representatives, Committee on Banking, Finance, and Urban Affairs, *Compact Cities*, which notes that in the United States, laws or constitutions in most states require assessing land and improvements uniformly, based on

market value. These requirements are routinely violated, however.

44. Walter Rybeck, "Pennsylvania's Experiments in Property Tax Modernization," *NTA Forum* (National Tax Association), Spring 1991; U.S. House of Representatives, Committee on Banking, Finance, and Urban Affairs, *Compact Cities*.

45. Altshuler quote from the introduction to Krumholz and Forester, *Making Equity Planning Work*.

46. London Council cited in Barde and Button, *Transport Policy and the Environment*; Friends of the Earth, *An Illustrated Guide to Traffic Calming: The Future Way of Managing Traffic* (London: 1990); John Roberts, "Traffic Calming," presentation at the Bicycle Federation of America Pro Bike 90 Conference, Washington, D.C., September 12–16, 1990.

47. Bob Smyth, "Britain's 'Green Revolution': Bringing Nature Back to the City," *UNESCO Sources*, July/August 1990.

48. Elkin and McLaren, *Reviving the City*; Will Nixon, "The Greening of the Big Apple," *E Magazine*, September/October 1991; Rick Bonlender, "Cabbages and Camaraderie," *Utne Reader*, May/June 1991.

49. David Katz, "Metropolitan Food Systems and the Sustainable City," in Sim Van der Ryn and Peter Calthorpe, *Sustainable Communities: A New Design Synthesis for Cities, Suburbs, and Towns* (San Francisco: Sierra Club Books, 1986).

50. William H. Whyte, *City: Rediscovering the Center* (New York: Doubleday, 1988).

51. Jane Jacobs, *The Death and Life of Great American Cities* (New York: Random House, 1961).

52. Whyte, *City: Rediscovering the Center*.

53. Anthony Downs, *Neighborhoods and Urban Development* (Washington, D.C.: Brookings Institution, 1981); Joyce Leviton, Man-

ager, Community Planning Division, Baltimore City Planning Department, Baltimore, Md., private communication, October 17, 1991.

54. Lloyd Rodwin and Bishwapriya Sanyal, "Introduction," in Rodwin, *Shelter, Settlement, and Development*.

55. Matrix Book Group, *Making Space: Women and the Man-Made Environment* (London: Pluto Press, 1984); Dolores Hayden, *Redesigning the American Dream: The Future of Housing, Work, and Family Life* (New York: W.W. Norton, 1984).

56. Population Reference Bureau, *1991 World Population Data Sheet* (Washington, D.C.: 1991); United Nations, *World Urbanization Prospects 1990*.

57. Hardoy and Satterthwaite, *Squatter Citizen*.

58. Richard E. Stren and Rodney R. White, eds., *African Cities in Crisis: Managing Rapid Urban Growth* (Boulder, Colo.: Westview Press, 1989); Adepoju, "Population and the Planning of Large Cities in Africa"; William A. Doebele, "Land Availability and Urban Future in Developing Countries," *Ekistics*, September/October 1986.

59. Roberts, "Traffic Calming"; Peter Tautfest, "Clearing Up the Euro-Jam," *World Monitor*, March 1991.

60. Charles C. Whiting, "Twin Cities Metro Council: Heading for a Fall?" *Planning*, March 1984. Metropolitan Toronto has a similar property tax-base sharing system, according to councillor Dale Martin, Municipality of Metropolitan Toronto, press release, October 1990.

61. Mathews, "The Costs of Unplanned Urban Sprawl"; Deborah A. Howe, "Review of Growth Management Strategies Used in Other States," report prepared for the Oregon Department of Land Conservation and Development, Salem, Oreg., February 1991; Kevin Kasowski, "Land Use Planning

Myths," *Journal of Soil and Water Conservation*, March/April 1991.

62. To illustrate the primacy of some Third World megacities, Bangkok's population is six times as great as that of Thailand's 12 next-largest cities combined, according to United Nations, *Population Growth and Policies in Mega-Cities: Bangkok*, Population Policy Paper No. 10 (New York: 1987); Metropolitan Manila produces one third of the Philippines' gross national product, according to World Commission on Environment and Development, *Our Common Future* (New York: Oxford University Press, 1987).

63. Bob Yuhnke, "The Amendments to Reform Transportation Planning in the Clean Air Amendments of 1990," paper presented at the NAMVECC 90 Motor Vehicle Emissions Control Conference, Tampa, Fla., December 11–14, 1990; Kevin Kasowski, "America's Transportation Future: Bold Senate Reform Bill Challenges Bush Administration's Status Quo," *Developments* (National Growth Management Leadership Project), Summer 1991.

64. Oath of the Athenian city-state cited in James A. Clapp, *The City: A Dictionary of Quotable Thought on Cities and Urban Life* (New Brunswick, N.J.: Rutgers University Center for Urban Policy Research, 1984).

## Chapter 9. Creating Sustainable Jobs in Industrial Countries

1. Organisation for Economic Co-operation and Development (OECD), *Historical Statistics 1960–1988* (Paris: 1990).

2. Herman E. Daly and John B. Cobb, Jr., *For the Common Good: Redirecting the Economy Toward Community, the Environment, and a Sustainable Future* (Boston: Beacon Press, 1989).

3. Lucinda Wykle et al., *Worker Empowerment in a Changing Economy* (New York: Apex Press, 1991); Richard Kazis and Richard H. Grossman, *Fear at Work: Job Blackmail, Labor*

*and the Environment* (Philadelphia: New Society Publishers, 1991).

4. Report of the Task Force on Environment, "Our Children's World: Steelworkers and the Environment," in United Steelworkers of America, *Report of the Committee on Future Directions of the Union*, 25th Constitutional Convention, Toronto, Canada, August 27–31, 1990.

5. The term "industry" here includes manufacturing, mining, transportation, and electric utilities; manufacturing's share declined from 26 to 21 percent between 1960 and 1988, see OECD, *Historical Statistics 1960–1988*; changes within the industrial sector from OECD, *The State of the Environment* (Paris: 1991).

6. *Economic Report of the President* (Washington, D.C.: U.S. Government Printing Office, 1989).

7. Barry Commoner, *The Poverty of Power* (New York: Bantam Books, 1976).

8. U.S. Department of Labor, Bureau of Labor Statistics (BLS), "Multifactor Productivity in U.S. Manufacturing and in 20 Manufacturing Industries, 1949–1986," unpublished database, April 1989.

9. Environmental Protection Agency (EPA), Office of Air Quality Planning and Standards, *National Air Pollutant Emission Estimates 1940–1989* (Research Triangle Park, N.C.: 1991); Chemical Manufacturers Association, *U.S. Chemical Industry Statistical Handbook 1990* (Washington, D.C.: 1990). Although patterns of industrialization vary from country to country, the same basic picture arises outside the United States as well; see OECD, *The State of the Environment*, and Wolfgang Benkert and Martin Gornig, "Umweltschutz, Wirtschaftsstruktur und Arbeitsmarkt in Nordrhein-Westfalen," in Joke Frerichs et al. (eds.), *Jahrbuch Arbeit und Technik in Nordrhein-Westfalen 1988* (Bonn: Verlag Neue Gesellschaft, 1988).

10. Share of energy and chemical industry employment calculated from "Energy Workers Worldwide," *Global Warming Watch*, July 1990, and from International Labour Office (ILO), *Yearbook of Labour Statistics 1989–90* (Geneva: 1990); refining industry from Keith Schneider, "Petrochemical Disasters Raise Alarm in Industry," *New York Times*, June 19, 1991; coal industry from U.S. Department of Energy, Energy Information Administration, *Coal Production 1988* (Washington, D.C.: U.S. Government Printing Office, 1989), and from U.S. Department of Commerce, Bureau of the Census, *Statistical Abstract of the United States 1990* (Washington, D.C.: U.S. Government Printing Office, 1990); coal employment forecast from ICF Resources Inc., "Comparison of the Economic Impacts of the Acid Rain Provisions of the Senate Bill (S. 1630) and the House Bill (H.R. 1630)," prepared for EPA, Fairfax, Va., July 1990; comparable European data from "Environment Statistics," Theme 8, Series C (Statistical Office of the European Communities (Eurostat)), 1989.

11. Management Information Services Inc. (MISI), "Simulation of the Economic Impact of Pollution Abatement and Control Investment: Methodology, Data Base, and Detailed Estimates," Washington, D.C., May 1986; U.S. Department of Commerce, Bureau of the Census, *Manufacturers' Pollution Abatement Capital Expenditures and Operating Costs: Final Report for 1988* (Washington, D.C.: U.S. Government Printing Office, 1990); Ken Geiser, "The Greening of Industry. Making the Transition to a Sustainable Economy," *Technology Review*, August/September 1991; job creation estimates from MISI, "Numbers of PABCO Jobs Created in 1988," unpublished draft, Washington, D.C., May 1990, and from Directorate-General Employment, Industrial Relations and Social Affairs, Commission of the European Communities, *Employment in Europe 1990* (Luxembourg: Office for Official Publications of the European Communities, 1990).

12. For a critique of the pollution control approach, see Christian Leipert, *Die Heimlichen Kosten des Fortschritts. Wie Umweltzerstörung das Wirtschaftswachstum Fördert* (Frankfurt: Fischer Verlag, 1989), and Barry Commoner, *Making Peace with the Planet* (New York: Pantheon Books, 1990).

13. Geiser, "The Greening of Industry"; Amal Kumar Naj, "Some Companies Cut Pollution by Altering Production Methods," *Wall Street Journal*, December 24, 1990; Scott McMurray, "Chemical Firms Find that it Pays to Reduce Pollution at Source," *Wall Street Journal*, June 11, 1991.

14. Electronics industry example from Andrew Pollack, "Moving Fast to Protect Ozone Layer," *New York Times*, May 15, 1991. The United Nations Industrial Development Organization (UNIDO) furnishes additional examples in electroplating, waste-paper processing, printed circuit-board manufacturing, corrosion protection, textile printing, and other areas; UNIDO, *Industry and Development: Global Report 1990/91* (Vienna: 1990).

15. John E. Young, *Discarding the Throwaway Society*, Worldwatch Paper 101 (Washington, D.C.: Worldwatch Institute, January 1991); energy use in car manufacturing calculated from Mary C. Holcomb et al., *Transportation Energy Data Book: Edition 9* (Oak Ridge, Tenn.: Oak Ridge National Laboratory, 1987).

16. Packaging share of paper production from Sandra Postel and John C. Ryan, "Reforming Forestry," in Lester R. Brown et al., *State of the World 1991* (New York: W.W. Norton & Co., 1991); Anita Glazer Sadun et al., "Breaking Down the Degradable Plastics Scam," Center for the Biology of Natural Systems (CBNS), Queens College, City University of New York, report prepared for Greenpeace, 1990.

17. Christopher Flavin, *Slowing Global Warming: A Worldwide Strategy*, Worldwatch Paper 91 (Washington, D.C.: Worldwatch Institute, October 1989); Hilary F. French, *Clearing the Air: A Global Agenda*, Worldwatch Paper 94 (Washington, D.C.: Worldwatch Institute, January 1990); Christopher Flavin and Alan B. Durning, *Building on Success: The Age of Energy Efficiency*, Worldwatch Paper 82 (Washington, D.C.: Worldwatch Institute, March 1988).

18. Capital requirements from Statement of Leonard S. Rodberg before the Subcommittee on Energy Conservation and Power, Committee on Energy and Commerce, U.S. House of Representatives, June 28, 1983; Christopher Flavin and Nicholas Lenssen, *Beyond the Petroleum Age: Designing a Solar Economy*, Worldwatch Paper 100 (Washington, D.C.: Worldwatch Institute, December 1990).

19. Skip Laitner, Economic Research Associates, Eugene, Oreg., "Designing Energy Strategies to Incorporate External Costs into Public Policy: Where LES is More," paper presented to the National Regulatory Research Institute's Annual Conference, Columbus, Ohio, September 1988.

20. Paul L. Montgomery, "Heavy Energy Tax is Proposed to Curb Emissions in Europe," *New York Times*, September 26, 1991.

21. Steve Colt, University of Alaska, Anchorage, "Income and Employment Impacts of Alaska's Low-Income Weatherization Program," ISER Working Paper 89.2, prepared for Second Annual Rural Energy Conference, Anchorage, October 12, 1989.

22. Holger M. Eisl et al., "Investing in the Future: An Economic Analysis of the New York State Weatherization Assistance Program," CBNS, Final Report, Prepared for New York State Department of State, Division of Economic Opportunity, April 5, 1991.

23. Worldwatch Institute calculations, based on Eisl et al., "Investing in the Future."

24. Leonard Rodberg, *Employment Impact of the Solar Transition*, a study prepared for the

use of the Joint Economic Committee, Congress of the United States (Washington, D.C.: U.S. Government Printing Office, 1979).

25. Employment Research Associates, "Biomass Resources: Generating Jobs and Energy," report prepared for the Great Lakes Regional Biomass Energy Program, Council of Great Lakes Governors, Lansing, Mich., November 1985. The biomass sources assessed included alcohol fuel, energy from wood and from municipal waste, recovery of landfill methane gas, and recovery of methane produced at wastewater treatment plants.

26. The technologies included were residential building insulation, district heating, heat exchangers, heat pumps, domestic solar hot-water systems, and biogas plants. Given considerable methodological problems that the authors themselves point to, the results should only be seen as indicating the order of magnitude of job effects. See Olav Hohmeyer et al., Fraunhofer Institute for Systems and Innovation Research, *Employment Effects of Energy Conservation Investments in EC Countries*, prepared for Commission of the European Communities (Luxembourg: Office for Official Publications of the European Communities, 1985).

27. H. Craig Petersen, "Sector-Specific Output and Employment Impacts of a Solar Space and Water Heating Industry," Utah State University, Logan, December 1977.

28. Quote is from Rodberg, *Employment Impact of the Solar Transition*; Rodberg, Statement before the Subcommittee on Energy Conservation and Power. Solar collectors that circulate liquids as a heat transfer medium require relatively more plumbing skills in installation, while air circulating systems rely more on duct work and represent a better opportunity for sheet metal workers. See Petersen, "Sector-Specific Output and Employment Impacts of a Solar Space and Water Heating Industry."

29. A Minnesota study found that a dollar spent on petroleum products creates a demand for $1.49 of goods and services in the national economy, but only 64¢ in the state economy because the state relies on imported oil. A dollar spent on renewables, by contrast, has a net local economic effect of $2.33–$2.92 because of higher local supplies. See Richard R. Lancaster, "Economic Impact of Alternative Energy Development in Minnesota," a report to the Legislative Commission on Minnesota Resources, Minnesota Department of Energy, Planning and Development, Energy Division, June 1983. For petroleum exporters' dependence on oil revenues, see Michael G. Renner, "Stabilizing the World Oil Market," *OPEC Review*, Spring 1988.

30. Lack of R&D support from Michael G. Renner, "Hot Air on Global Warming," *World Watch*, May/June 1990; solar employment from Rodberg, Statement before the Subcommittee on Energy Conservation and Power; future prospects from *Photovoltaic Insider Report*, June 1991, and from Christopher Flavin and Rick Piltz, *Sustainable Energy* (Washington, D.C.: Renew America, 1989).

31. "Automobile Workers Worldwide," *Global Warming Watch*, October 1990/January 1991; Motor Vehicle Manufacturers Association (MVMA), *Facts and Figures '90* (Detroit, Mich.: 1990); Markus Hesse and Rainer Lucas, *Die Beschäftigungspolitische Bedeutung der Verkehrswirtschaft in Nordrhein-Westfalen*, Forschungsprojekt im Auftrag des Instituts für Landes- und Stadtentwicklungsforschung (Berlin/Wuppertal: Institut für Ökologische Wirtschaftsforschung, 1990).

32. Hesse and Lucas, *Die Beschäftigungspolitische Bedeutung der Verkehrswirtschaft in Nordrhein-Westfalen*; East German railway jobs from "Wettbewerbsnachteile der Bundesbahn Vermindern Chancen einer Ökologischen Trendwende in der Verkehrspolitik," *Ökologische Briefe*, June 12, 1991; personnel shortage and overtime from Rainer Graichen, "Das Öffentliche Transportunterneh-

men Deutsche Bundesbahn als Instrument Beschäftigungssichernder Verkehrs- und Umweltpolitik," *WSI Mitteilungen*, No. 6, 1988.

33. Hesse and Lucas, *Die Beschäftigungspolitische Bedeutung der Verkehrswirtschaft in Nordrhein-Westfalen*; Markus Hesse and Rainer Lucas, *Verkehrswende. Ökologische und Soziale Orientierungen für die Verkehrswirtschaft*, Schriftenreihe des IÖW 39/90 (Berlin and Wuppertal: Institut für Ökologische Wirtschaftsforschung, 1990).

34. Hesse and Lucas, *Die Beschäftigungspolitische Bedeutung der Verkehrswirtschaft in Nordrhein-Westfalen*; Shawn Tully, "Comeback Ahead for Railroads," *Fortune*, June 17, 1991.

35. German data include direct, indirect, and induced jobs, and are taken from Hesse and Lucas, *Verkehrswende*, from Graichen, "Das Öffentliche Transportunternehmen Deutsche Bundesbahn," and from Martin Junkernheinrich, "Beschäftigungswirksamkeit von Verkehrswegeinvestitionen. Eine Explorative Studie am Beispiel Nordrhein-Westfalen," unpublished manuscript, Institut für Ökologische Wirtschaftsforschung, Bochum, Germany, 1991.

36. Hesse and Lucas, *Die Beschäftigungspolitische Bedeutung der Verkehrswirtschaft in Nordrhein-Westfalen*; Hesse and Lucas, *Verkehrswende*. The developmental and production-related know-how of car manufacturers can easily be applied to chassis construction for light rail vehicles, for example. See Hinrich Krey, "Denkbare Alternative Produktionsansätze in der Automobilindustrie," in Die Grünen im Bundestag (eds.), *Welche Freiheit Brauchen Wir? Zur Psychology der AutoMobilen Gesellschaft* (Berlin: Verlag für Ausbildung und Studium, 1989). Comparison of highway and bike path construction from Junkernheinrich, "Beschäftigungswirksamkeit von Verkehrswegeinvestitionen."

37. Improved fuel economy does not imply any fundamental job effects in the motor vehicle industry itself. Still, to the extent that car manufacturers improve fuel efficiency by incorporating more light-weight plastic and aluminum components instead of steel, indirect employment shifts occur among supplier companies. The motor vehicle industry consumes a large share of the total volume of these materials produced every year. Between 1977 and 1989, the amount of steel per car manufactured in the United States declined by 22 percent, while plastics and aluminum grew by 34 and 60 percent, respectively. See MVMA, *Facts and Figures '90*. Worldwide, automotive demand for aluminum is expected to quadruple by the year 2000; "Vorfahrt für Aluminium im Autobau," *Süddeutsche Zeitung*, June 1/2, 1991.

38. Bureau of the Census, *Statistical Abstract of the United States 1990*; Young, *Discarding the Throwaway Society*.

39. Jim Quigley, "Employment Impact of Recycling," *BioCycle*, March 1988; EPA, Office of Solid Waste and Emergency Response, *Characterization of Municipal Solid Waste in the United States: 1990 Update* (Washington, D.C.: 1990).

40. ALCOA from U.S. Congress, Office of Technology Assessment, *Facing America's Trash: What Next for Municipal Solid Waste?* (Washington, D.C.: U.S. Government Printing Office, 1989); employment in primary aluminum industry from Bureau of the Census, *Statistical Abstract of the United States 1990*; Quigley, "Employment Impact of Recycling."

41. The data are for a variety of facilities of different capacities. Recycling depots receive and process materials from drop-off centers and curbside programs, and rely on manual separation and labor-intensive processing. Materials Recovery Facilities are larger plants with automated separation and processing technologies. All numbers are based on the assumption that capacities are fully utilized. Vermont and New York City data are

a Worldwatch Institute calculation based on Tellus Institute and Wehran Engineering, *Analysis of Solid Waste System Costs for the State of Vermont*, report submitted to the Vermont Interregional Solid Waste Management Committee, Boston, Mass,, and Burlington, Vt., July 1990, and on Jim Meyer, Deputy Director, Policy Planning, New York City Department of Sanitation, private communication, July 12, 1991.

42. Barry Commoner, "Why Dump Recycling?" (op-ed), *New York Times*, May 29, 1991.

43. Quigley, "Employment Impact of Recycling"; Rudolf Hickel, "Wirtschaften ohne Naturzerstörung—Strategien einer Ökologisch-ökonomischen Strukturpolitik," in Frerichs et al., *Jahrbuch Arbeit und Technik in Nordrhein-Westfalen 1988*.

44. David S. Wilcove and Jeffrey T. Olson, The Wilderness Society, "Biological Diversity and Conservation of Ancient Forests of the Pacific Northwest," paper presented at the annual meeting of the American Association for the Advancement of Science, Washington, D.C., February 18, 1991; job loss claims by timber industry and Thomas report estimates from John Lancaster and Rick Atkinson, "Saving Owl May Cost 20,000 Jobs," *Washington Post*, September 7, 1990; Tom Hamilton et al., "Economic Effects of Implementing a Conservation Strategy for the Northern Spotted Owl," U.S. Department of Agriculture, Forest Service, and U.S. Department of the Interior, Bureau of Land Management (BLM), Washington, D.C., May 1, 1990.

45. Northwest forest loss from Wilcove and Olson, "Biological Diversity and Conservation of Ancient Forests"; Adams from "The Future of Forests," *The Economist*, June 22, 1991; leveraged buyouts from John C. Ryan, "Wall Street Goes Wild," *World Watch*, November/December 1989.

46. Wilcove and Olson, "Biological Diversity and Conservation of Ancient Forests";

Jeff DeBonis, "Timber Industry's Claims," *Journal of Forestry*, July 1989.

47. Export share and profitability from Catherine Caufield, "The Ancient Forest," *The New Yorker*, May 14, 1990; Olson from Valjean McLenighan, *Sustainable Manufacturing. Saving Jobs, Saving the Environment* (Chicago: Center for Neighborhood Technology, 1990). The Forest Service/BLM report identifies additional options to save or generate several thousand jobs, including boosting the net wood supplies through greater harvesting efficiency, enhancing recreational or commercial fisheries, gathering needed ecological data, and monitoring of forests; see "Plan to Save Jobs Suppressed," *Inner Voice*, Summer 1991. Proponents of the "Forests Forever" initiative in California to ban clearcutting claim that 40,000 timber jobs could be gained by curtailing the export of unprocessed trees; Wykle et al., *Worker Empowerment in a Changing Economy*.

48. Wilcove and Olson, "Biological Diversity and Conservation of Ancient Forests"; DeBonis, "Timber Industry's Claims."

49. For example, it has been estimated that some 1,500 jobs may be lost due to efforts to preserve the Tongass National Forest in Alaska. But the Forest Service subsidizes logging there to the tune of $40 million a year, a sum that could be used to pay each logger income support during a transition period. See Wykle et al., *Worker Empowerment in a Changing Economy*. Bush administration position from Brad Knickerbocker, "An Endangered Human Species," *Christian Science Monitor*, June 6, 1991.

50. Redwood program from Kazis and Grossman, *Fear at Work*.

51. Phyllis Cribby, "Working with a Union to Create Jobs and a Sustainable Economy," *Journal of Pesticide Reform*, Fall 1990; Bill Resnick, "Proposal—A Feasibility Study and Resource Identification for Transforming Oregon's Forest Products Industry," Labor-Environmental Solidarity Network Research

Committee, Eugene, Oreg., unpublished draft, 1991.

52. Resnick, "A Feasibility Study and Resource Identification"; Elliott A. Norse, "What Good Are Ancient Forests?" *The Amicus Journal*, Winter 1990; The Wilderness Society, "Ancient Forests of the Pacific Northwest," Fact Sheet, Washington, D.C., undated.

53. Eric Mann, "Environmentalism in the Corporate Climate," *Tikkun*, March/April 1990; Wykle et al., *Worker Empowerment in a Changing Economy*; right to call for an investigation from Kazis and Grossman, *Fear at Work*. The European Community proposed the establishment of eco-audits, but watered them down after encountering industry opposition; instead of a mandatory framework, the revised proposal would make companies' participation voluntary, and does not provide for the work force to be consulted during an audit; see David Thomas, "Brussels Backs Down on 'Eco-Audit,' " *Financial Times*, April 5, 1991, and "Öko-Audit: EG-Vorschlag für Betriebliche Umwelt-Kontrolle," *Ökologische Briefe*, June 5, 1991. A number of agreements have recently been concluded in the German chemical industry that give worker representatives greater access to relevant information concerning their company's operations; see "IG Chemie-Papier-Keramik Schließt Umweltschutz-Betriebsvereinbarung bei den Leuna-Werken ab," *Arbeit und Ökologie*, July 3, 1991.

54. Arthur Braunschweig, "Energieabgabe und Rentenversicherung. Überlegungen und Berechnungen für die Bundesrepublik Deutschland," in Hans G. Nutzinger and Angelika Zahrnt (eds.), *Für eine Ökologische Steuerreform. Energiesteuern als Instrumente der Umweltpolitik* (Frankfurt: Fischer Verlag, 1990).

55. John Gever et al., *Beyond Oil* (Cambridge, Mass.: Ballinger, 1987); Lawrence Mishel and David M. Frankel, *The State of Working America, 1990–91 Edition* (Armonk, N.Y.: M.E. Sharpe, Inc., 1991).

56. Reduced retraining funds from Robert Reich, "Who Champions the Working Class?" (op-ed), *New York Times*, May 26, 1991; funds as share of gross domestic product from Nancy J. Perry, "The Workers of the Future," *Fortune*, Special Issue: The New American Century, Spring/Summer 1991.

57. Wykle et al., *Worker Empowerment in a Changing Economy*.

58. Proposed benefits for coal miners from Wykle et al., *Worker Empowerment in a Changing Economy*; "Owl Ruling Seen Keeping Lumber Out of Market," *Journal of Commerce*, May 28, 1991.

59. The German unions in particular have been pushing for introduction of the 35-hour week as a means of job creation; see Gerhard Bosch, "From 40 to 35 Hours: Reduction and Flexibilisation of the Working Week in the Federal Republic of Germany," *International Labour Review*, Vol. 129, No. 5, 1990.

60. Lloyd Jeffry Dumas, *The Overburdened Economy* (Berkeley, Calif.: University of California Press, 1986).

## Chapter 10. Strengthening Global Environmental Governance

1. "Biodiversity: A Progress Report on the Convention and the Strategy," *Global Environmental Change Report*, August 16, 1991; Center for Global Change, "International Negotiations on Climate Change," a briefing paper prepared for the Climate Action Network U.S., Washington, D.C., January 30, 1991; "U.S. Rejects Targets in Forest Negotiations," *Earth Summit Update* (Environmental and Energy Study Institute (EESI), Washington, D.C.), September 1991; "PrepCom III Ends, Next is New York," *Network '92* (The Centre for Our Common Future, Geneva), September 1991; Maurice F. Strong, "Preparing for the UN Conference

on Environment and Development," *Environment*, June 1991; Debora MacKenzie, "Strong Words to Save the Planet," *New Scientist*, August 10, 1991.

2. Lynton K. Caldwell, "Beyond Environmental Diplomacy: The Changing Institutional Structure of International Cooperation," in John E. Carroll, ed., *International Environmental Diplomacy* (New York: Cambridge University Press, 1988); number of treaties from U.N. Environment Programme (UNEP), *Register of International Treaties and Other Agreements in the Field of the Environment* (Nairobi: 1991), and from U.S. International Trade Commission (ITC), *International Agreements to Protect the Environment and Wildlife* (Washington, D.C.: 1991); Table 10–1 based on UNEP, *Register of International Treaties*, on ITC, *International Agreements*, on Christer Ågren, "Easier May Mean Harder," *Acid News*, June 1991, on "Delegates of More Than 40 Nations Pledge to End Marine Dumping of Industrial Waste," *International Environment Reporter*, November 21, 1990, on "London Dumping Convention Sets 1994 Ban on Incineration at Sea of Toxic Wastes," *International Environment Reporter*, November 1988, on Madeleine Cheslow, legal assistant, Treaty Section, Office of Legal Affairs, United Nations, New York, private communication, November 6, 1991, on Lee Kimball, *Southern Exposure: Deciding Antarctica's Future* (Washington, D.C.: World Resources Institute (WRI), 1990), and on Alan Riding, "Pact Bans Oil Exploration in Antarctica," *New York Times*, October 5, 1991.

3. UNEP, "UNEP Profile," Nairobi, July 1990; Lloyd Timberlake, "Action on the Environment: the Role of the United Nations," International Institute for Environment and Development in cooperation with UNEP, London and Nairobi, 1989.

4. For a discussion of traditional conceptions of national sovereignty, see Gordon C. Schloming, *Power and Principle in International Affairs* (New York: Harcourt Brace Jovanovich, 1991).

5. Maurice Strong, "Beyond Foreign Aid—Toward a New World System," address to International Development Conference, Washington, D.C., March 19, 1987.

6. Garrett Hardin, "The Tragedy of the Commons," *Science*, December 13, 1968.

7. Elisabeth Mann Borgese, "The Law of the Sea," *Scientific American*, March 1983.

8. Ibid.; United Nations, *A Quiet Revolution: The United Nations Convention on the Law of the Sea* (New York: U.N. Department of Public Information, 1984); Ann L. Hollick, "Managing the Oceans," *Wilson Quarterly*, Summer 1984.

9. Douglas M. Johnston, "Marine Pollution Agreements: Successes and Problems," in Carroll, *International Environmental Diplomacy*.

10. Borgese, "The Law of the Sea"; U.N. Office for Ocean Affairs and the Law of the Sea, "International Institutions and Legal Instruments," UNCED Research Paper No. 10, U.N. Conference on Environment and Development (UNCED), July 1991; "Marine Pollution: Policy Options for the 1992 Conference on Environment and Development," U.S. Government paper submitted to Second UNCED Preparatory Committee meeting, Geneva, March 18, 1991; Miranda Wecker, Center for International Environmental Law (CIEL)–U.S., Washington, D.C., private communication, October 4, 1991; Johnson, "Marine Pollution Agreements," and David Edwards, "Review of the Status of Implementation and Development of Regional Arrangements on Cooperation in Combatting Marine Pollution," both in Carroll, *International Environmental Diplomacy*.

11. Borgese, "Law of the Sea"; Kimball, *Southern Exposure*.

12. Borgese, "The Law of the Sea."

13. Hollick, "Managing the Oceans"; Leigh Ratimer, "The Law of the Sea: A

Crossroads for American Foreign Policy," *Foreign Affairs*, Summer 1982.

14. Cheslow, private communication, October 22, 1991; Wecker, private communication; Council on Ocean Law, "The United States and the 1982 UN Convention on the Law of the Sea: A Synopsis of the Treaty and Its Expanded Role in the World Today," Washington, D.C., 1989.

15. World Commission on Environment and Development, *Our Common Future* (New York: Oxford University Press, 1987); Jeffrey Laurenti and Francesca Lyman, *One Earth, Many Nations: The International System and Problems of the Global Environment* (New York: United Nations Association of the United States (UNA-USA), 1990).

16. Borgese, "The Law of the Sea"; Lee A. Kimball, "International Law and Institutions: The Oceans and Beyond," *Ocean Development and International Law*, Vol. 20, 1989.

17. Cynthia Pollock Shea, *Protecting Life on Earth: Steps to Save the Ozone Layer*, Worldwatch Paper 87 (Washington, D.C.: Worldwatch Institute, December 1988); Douglas G. Cogan, *Stones in a Glass House: CFCs and Ozone Depletion* (Washington, D.C.: Investor Responsibility Research Center, 1988); "Vienna Convention for the Protection of the Ozone Layer, Final Act," UNEP, Nairobi, 1985.

18. "Montreal Protocol on Substances That Deplete the Ozone Layer, Final Act," UNEP, Nairobi, 1987; Environmental Protection Agency (EPA) estimate cited in John Gliedman, "The Ozone Follies: Is the Pact Too Little, Too Late?" *The Nation*, October 10, 1987.

19. Richard Elliot Benedick, *Ozone Diplomacy* (Cambridge, Mass.: Harvard University Press, 1991).

20. Ibid.

21. Benedick, *Ozone Diplomacy*; Malcolm W. Browne, "93 Nations Agree to Ban Chemicals that Harm Ozone Layer," *New York Times*, June 30, 1990; "Montreal Protocol Parties to Study Earlier Phaseout Date for CFCs, Halons," *International Environment Reporter*, July 3, 1991; "Montreal Protocol Ratification Status," *Atmosphere* (Friends of the Earth, Washington, D.C.), June 1991; Cheslow, private communication.

22. Benedick, *Ozone Diplomacy*.

23. Armin Rosencranz and Reina Milligan, "CFC Abatement: The Needs of Developing Countries," *Ambio*, October 1990; Cogan, *Stones in a Glass House*; Donald M. Goldberg, "Technological Cooperation and the Montreal Protocol Multilateral Fund: A Brief Description," CIEL-U.S., Washington, D.C., June 1991; ozone fund commitments from Interim Multilateral Fund for the Implementation of the Montreal Protocol, Montreal, Que., Canada, private communication, October 31, 1991.

24. William K. Stevens, "Ozone Loss Over the U.S. is Found to be Twice as Bad as Predicted," *New York Times*, April 5, 1991; Liz Cook, Friends of the Earth, Report on the Third Meeting of the Parties to the Montreal Protocol on Substances That Deplete the Ozone Layer, Nairobi, June 19–21, 1991; Liz Cook, Friends of the Earth, Testimony before the Environmental Protection Subcommittee, Committee on Environment and Public Works, U.S. Senate, Washington, D.C., July 30, 1991; "Montreal Protocol Parties to Study Earlier Phase-out"; Martha Hamilton, "The Costly Race to Replace CFCs," *Washington Post*, September 29, 1991; Elizabeth Barratt-Brown, "Building a Monitoring and Compliance Regime Under the Montreal Protocol," *Yale Journal of International Law*, Vol. 16, No. 2, 1991.

25. Peter S. Thacher, "Focussing on the Near Term: Alternative Legal and Institutional Approaches to Global Change," in WRI, *Greenhouse Warming: Negotiating a Global Regime* (Washington, D.C.: 1991); Peter H. Sand, *Lessons Learned in Global Environmental Governance* (Washington, D.C.: WRI, 1990);

Gareth Porter and Janet Welsh Brown, *Global Environmental Politics* (Boulder, Colo.: West-view Press, 1991).

26. For various perspectives on this debate, see WRI, *Greenhouse Warming*; see also "Developments in the Law: International Environmental Law," *Harvard Law Review*, May 1991; Benedict, *Ozone Diplomacy*.

27. James MacNeill, "The Meshing of the World's Economy and the Earth's Ecology," in Steve Lerner, *Earth Summit: Conversations with Architects of an Ecologically Sustainable Future* (Bolinas, Calif.: Common Knowledge Press, 1991).

28. James K. Sebenius, "Designing Negotiations Toward a New Regime: The Case of Global Warming," *International Security*, Spring 1991.

29. Don Goldberg, "Procedures for Adopting and Amending Conventions and Protocols" (draft), CIEL-U.S., Washington, D.C., 1991; Thacher, "Focussing on the Near Term"; Kimball, "International Law and Institutions."

30. Sand, *Lessons Learned*; Abram Chayes and Antonia H. Chayes, "Adjustment and Compliance Processes in International Regulatory Regimes," in Jessica Tuchman Mathews, ed., *Preserving the Global Environment: The Challenge of Shared Leadership* (New York: W.W. Norton & Co., 1991); on the ILO, see James Avery Joyce, *World Labor Rights and Their Protection* (London: Croom Helm, 1980); Kimball, "International Law and Institutions"; Kimball, *Southern Exposure*.

31. Porter and Brown, *Global Environmental Politics*; Karen Schmidt, "Industrial Countries' Responses to Global Climate Change," *Environmental and Energy Study Institute Special Report*, Washington, D.C., July 1, 1991; Nigel Haigh, "The European Community and International Environmental Policy," Institute for European Environmental Policy, London, January 1991.

32. Porter and Brown, *Global Environmental Politics*.

33. Chayes and Chayes, "Adjustment and Compliance Processes"; Elizabeth P. Barratt-Brown, Natural Resources Defense Council, Testimony before the Subcommittee on Human Rights and International Organizations, Committee on Foreign Affairs, U.S. House of Representatives, Washington, D.C., October 3, 1991; Scott Hajost and Quinlan J. Shea, "An Overview of Enforcement and Compliance Mechanisms in International Environmental Agreements," presented to International Enforcement Workshop, Utrecht, the Netherlands, May 8–10, 1990.

34. Sand, *Lessons Learned*; Chayes and Chayes, "Adjustment and Compliance Processes"; Barratt-Brown, "Testimony"; Barratt-Brown, "Building a Monitoring and Compliance Regime"; Hajost and Shea, "An Overview of Enforcement and Compliance Mechanisms"; "Developments in the Law: International Environmental Law"; Benedick, *Ozone Diplomacy*; Porter and Brown, *Global Environmental Politics*; Kimball, *Southern Exposure*.

35. Barratt-Brown, "Building a Monitoring and Compliance Regime"; Sand, *Lessons Learned*; Chayes and Chayes, "Adjustment and Compliance Processes."

36. Alan Mager, U.S. National Marine Fisheries Service, private communication, Washington, D.C., October 23, 1991; Barratt-Brown, "Building a Monitoring and Compliance Regime"; John Simpson, "NPT Stronger after Iraq," *Bulletin of the Atomic Scientists*, October 1991; Chayes and Chayes, "Adjustment and Compliance Processes"; see also Owen Greene, University of Bradford, "Building a Global Warming Convention: Lessons from the Arms Control Experience?" in "Pledge and Review Processes: Possible Components of a Climate Convention," Royal Institute of International Affairs, London, report of a workshop held August 2,

1991, and Peter Grier, "On-Site Arms Control Verification Proceeds," *Christian Science Monitor*, September 25, 1991.

37. Sir Geoffrey Palmer, Former Prime Minister of New Zealand, "Toward a New International Law for the Environment" (draft), April 16, 1991; UNA-USA and the Sierra Club, *Uniting Nations for the Earth: An Environmental Agenda for the World Community* (New York: 1990); Pamela Leonard and Walter Hoffman, *Effective Global Environmental Protection: World Federalist Proposals to Strengthen the Role of the United Nations* (Washington, D.C.: World Federalist Association, 1990); Philippe Sands, "The Environment, Community, and International Law," *Harvard International Law Journal*, Spring 1989; "Developments in the Law: International Environmental Law"; Hilary F. French, "The EC—Environmental Proving Ground," *World Watch*, November/December 1991.

38. "U.S. Imposes Ban on Imports of Endangered Animals, Goods," *Washington Post*, July 19, 1991; ITC, *International Agreements*.

39. Charles Arden-Clarke, *The General Agreement on Tariffs and Trade, Environmental Protection and Sustainable Development* (Gland, Switzerland: World Wide Fund for Nature (WWF), 1991); General Agreement on Tariffs and Trade (GATT), "United States—Restrictions on Imports of Tuna: Report of the Panel," Geneva, September 3, 1991; "GATT Tuna Ruling Spawns Environmentalist, Congressional Backlash," *Inside U.S. Trade*, September 6, 1991; Keith Bradsher, "U.S. Ban on Mexico Tuna is Overruled," *New York Times*, August 23, 1991.

40. "Intellectual Property and Technology Transfer: An Uneasy Relationship," *Global Environmental Change Report*, September 28, 1990; "The Issue of Technology," *Network '92* (The Centre for Our Common Future, Geneva), August 1991; "Nordic Nations Offer Solution to Issue of Technology Transfer," *International Environment Reporter*, September 11, 1991.

41. "Intellectual Property and Technology Transfer"; "Biodiversity: A Progress Report"; see also Darrell Posey, "Effecting International Change," *Cultural Survival Quarterly*, Summer 1991; Walt Reid, WRI, Washington, D.C., private communication, October 22, 1991.

42. "Little Progress Seen in Talks on Biological Diversity Convention," *International Environment Reporter*, October 9, 1991; "All Mouth, Too Little Money," *ECO* (NGO Newsletter, Climate Change Negotiations, Nairobi), September 16, 1991; "PrepCom Makes No Progress on Financial Resources," *Earth Summit Update* (EESI, Washington, D.C.), September 1991; John Madeley, "Debt Problem Hampers Forestry Deal," *Financial Times*, August 21, 1991.

43. David Reed, *The Global Environmental Facility: Sharing Responsibility for the Biosphere* (Washington, D.C.: WWF-International, 1991); "First Round of Projects to be Funded Under Green Fund Announced by World Bank," *International Environment Reporter*, May 8, 1991; "The Global Environment Facility," *Our Planet* (UNEP), Vol. 3, No. 3, 1991; Frederick van Bolhuis, Global Environment Facility, Washington, D.C., private communication, November 5, 1991.

44. "Beijing Ministerial Declaration on Environment and Development," Ministerial Conference of Developing Countries on Environment and Development, Beijing, June 18–19, 1991; "Minister Vows to Vigorously Support Plan for a Third World 'Green' Fund," *International Environment Reporter*, July 17, 1991; van Bolhuis, private communication; "Global Environment Facility Remains an Empty Vessel," *ECO* (NGO Newsletter, Climate Change Negotiations), June 1991; "GEF Guidelines Criticized," *ECO*, September 18, 1991.

45. Alan Durning, *Poverty and the Environment: Reversing the Downward Spiral*, Worldwatch Paper 92 (Washington, D.C.: Worldwatch Institute, November 1989); Madeley,

"Debt Problem Hampers Forestry Deal"; Jim MacNeill, "The Greening of International Relations," *International Journal*, Winter 1989–90.

46. Hilary F. French, "A Most Deadly Trade," *World Watch*, July/August 1990; Greenpeace numbers, which include all wastes, not just those officially classified as hazardous, from Jim Vallette and Heather Spaulding, *The International Trade in Wastes: A Greenpeace Inventory* (Washington, D.C.: Greenpeace U.S.A., 1990), updated from Hal Kane with Linda Starke, *Time for Change* (Washington, D.C.: Island Press, in press); U.S. General Accounting Office, Report to the Chairman, Environment, Energy, and Natural Resources Subcommittee, Committee on Government Operations, House of Representatives, *Pesticides: Export of Unregistered Pesticides is Not Adequately Monitored by EPA* (Washington, D.C.: 1989).

47. French, "A Most Deadly Trade"; Vallette and Spaulding, *The International Trade in Wastes*; Marguerite Cusack, "International Law and the Transboundary Shipment of Hazardous Waste to the Third World: Will the Basel Convention Make a Difference?" *The American University Journal of International Law and Policy*, Winter 1990; "System to Warn Nations of Banned Chemicals Close to Implementation, U.S. Official Says," *International Environment Reporter*, June 5, 1991; "Africa Adopts Sweeping Measures to Protect Continent from Toxic Terrorism," *Greenpeace Waste Trade Update*, March 22, 1991.

48. Joseph LaDou, "Deadly Migration: Hazardous Industries' Flight to the Third World," *Technology Review*, July 1991; Barry Castleman, "Workplace Health Standards and Multinational Corporations in Developing Countries," in Charles S. Pearson, ed., *Multinational Corporations, Environment, and the Third World: Business Matters* (Durham, N.C.: Duke University Press in cooperation with WRI, 1987); French, "A Most Deadly Trade"; Porter and Brown, *Global Environmental Politics*.

49. H. Jeffrey Leonard, *Pollution and the Struggle for the World Product* (Cambridge, Mass.: Cambridge University Press, 1988); Ann Rappaport and Margaret Flaherty, "Multinational Corporations and the Environment: Context and Challenges," *International Environment Reporter*, May 8, 1991.

50. Meri McCoy-Thompson, "Sliding Slopes Break Thai Logjam," *World Watch*, September/October 1989; Richard A. Forrest, "Kogai to Gaiko: Japan and the World Environment," Masters Thesis, Asian Studies, University of Michigan, Ann Arbor, 1986; François Nectoux and Yoichi Kuroda, *Timber from the South Seas: An Analysis of Japan's Tropical Timber Trade and its Environmental Impact* (Gland, Switzerland: WWF-International, 1989).

51. La Dou, "Deadly Migration"; French, "A Most Deadly Trade"; Rappaport and Flaherty, "Multinational Corporations and the Environment"; "MITI Studies Plan to Require Firms Abroad to Comply with Domestic Pollution Standards," *International Environment Reporter*, July 31, 1991.

52. Arden-Clarke, *The General Agreement on Tariffs and Trade*; C. Raghavan, "Third World Cool to GATT Role in Environment," *Third World Economics*, March 1–15, 1991.

53. C. Ford Runge, "Trade Protectionism and Environmental Regulations: The New Nontariff Barriers," *Northwestern Journal of International Law and Business*, Spring 1990.

54. French, "The EC—Environmental Proving Ground"; *Environmental Policy in the European Community, Fourth Edition* (Luxembourg: Office for Official Publications of the European Communities, 1990).

55. The ruling was not a complete victory for the environment, as one element of the Danish law requiring that bottles be government-approved was overthrown by the Court as being "disproportionate" to the desired end. There had been some concern that this provision might reduce the number of re-

turned bottles that are actually refilled rather than merely recycled, but this does not appear to have materialized to any appreciable degree. "Landmark EEC Court Case on Returnable Bottles Gives Boost to Environment," *Ends Report*, September 1988; Club de Bruxelles, *EC Environmental Policy* (Brussels: 1990); "Commission of the European Communities v. Kingdom of Denmark - Case 302/86," *Report of Cases Before the Court, Vol. 8* (Luxembourg: Office for Official Publications of the European Communities, 1988).

56. John Maggs, "U.S. to Offer Environment Plan with Mexico Pact," *Journal of Commerce*, April 30, 1991; U.S. Environmental Protection Agency and Secretaria de Desarrollo Urbano y Ecología, "Integrated Environmental Plan for the Mexico-U.S. Border Area (First Stage, 1992–1994)," Working Draft, Washington, D.C., and Mexico City, August 1, 1991; Keith Bradsher, "U.S. and Mexico Draft Plan to Fight Pollution," *New York Times*, August 2, 1991; "Environmental Enforcement Provisions Must be Set Out in Trade Accord, U.S. Told," *International Environment Reporter*, October 9, 1991.

57. Statement of Senator Max Baucus, Chairman, International Trade Subcommittee, U.S. Senate Finance Committee, "Trade and the Environment," September 17, 1991; John Zarocosta, "Group Appeals to UN for Global Ecology Code," *Journal of Commerce*, September 5, 1991; Nancy Dunne, "U.S. Calls for a GATT Code on Environment," *Financial Times*, September 18, 1991; William Dullforce, "Gatt Revives its Working Group on Environment," *Financial Times*, October 9, 1991; Raghavan, "Third World Cool to GATT Role in Environment"; C. Raghaval, "North-South Divide Over GATT Involvement in Environment," *Third World Economics*, April 1–15, 1991; Information and Media Relations, "General Agreement on Tariffs and Trade (GATT): What it Is, What it Does," (Geneva: GATT, 1990).

58. The Centre for Our Common Future, Background information on the Hague Dec-

laration," press release (includes a copy of the declaration from conference held March 10–11, 1989), Geneva, undated; Gro Harlem Brundtland, Prime Minister of Norway and Chairman of the World Commission on Environment and Development, "Global Change and Our Common Future," The Benjamin Franklin Lecture, National Academy of Sciences, Washington, D.C., May 2, 1989.

59. Sands, "The Environment, Community, and International Law"; Durwood Zaelke and James Cameron, CIEL-U.S., "Global Warming and Climate Change–An Overview of the International Legal Process," *The American University Journal of International Law and Policy*, Winter 1990; Palmer, "Toward a New International Law."

60. MacNeill, "The Greening of International Relations"; Porter and Brown, *Global Environmental Politics*.

61. Patricia A. Bliss-Guest, U.S. Council on Environmental Quality, "Proposals for Institutional Reform of the UN System to Promote Sustainable Development Policies," presented at Twentieth Annual American Bar Association Conference on the Environment, Warrenton, Va., May 18, 1991; "Progress Report on Institutions," UNCED Preparatory Committee, January 31, 1991, and July 25, 1991, Geneva; Maurice Strong, "Statement to the Second Session of the Preparatory Committee for the United Nations Conference on Environment and Development," Geneva, April 2, 1991.

62. UNEP, *UNEP Profile*; UNEP, "Proceedings of the Governing Council at its Sixteenth Session," Nairobi, June 30, 1991; "The National Wildlife Federation," information sheets, Washington, D.C., May 10, 1991; UNA-USA and Sierra Club, *Uniting Nations for the Earth*; Leonard and Hoffman, *Effective Global Environmental Protection*.

63. Bliss-Guest, "Proposals for Institutional Reform"; UNEP, *UNEP Profile*; UNEP, "Proceedings of the Governing Council at its Sixteenth Session"; "UNEP Governing

Council Agrees to Expand Units Handling Industry, Environmental Law," *International Environment Reporter*, June 5, 1991.

64. "Statement by the U.S. Delegation on Institutional Issues," submitted to third UNCED Preparatory Committee, Geneva, August 22, 1991; "Report of the Aspen Institute Working Group on International Environment and Development Policy," Aspen, Colo., July 25, 1991.

65. Peter S. Thacher, "Short Discussion Paper on International Institutional Adjustments at 'Earth Summit,' " prepared for the Aspen Institute Working Group on International Environment and Development Policy, Aspen, Colo., July 18–25, 1991; The Stockholm Initiative on Global Security and Governance, "Common Responsibility in the 1990s," Prime Minister's Office, Stockholm, April 22, 1991; Lucia Mouat, "Global Commission Urges Reform of United Nations," *Christian Science Monitor*, May 30, 1991.

66. Stockholm Initiative, "Common Responsibility in the 1990s"; Bliss-Guest, "Proposals for Institutional Reform"; Mouat, "Global Commission Urges Reform"; Gerry Gray, "Italy Urges Sweeping Structural Changes at U.N.," *New York Times*, September 28, 1991; see also Helena Cobban, "Let's Rethink the Security Council," *Christian Science Monitor*, July 9, 1991.

67. Stockholm Initiative, "Common Responsibility in the 1990s"; UNA-USA and Sierra Club, *Uniting Nations for the Earth*.

68. Bliss-Guest, "Proposals for Institutional Reform"; Mouat, "Global Commission Urges Reform"; Brian Urquhart and Erskine Childers, *A World in Need of Leadership: Tomorrow's United Nations* (New York and Uppsala: Ford Foundation and Dag Hammerskjöld Foundation, 1990); John M. Goshko, "World's Diplomats Begin Jockeying to Pick New U.N. Secretary General," *Washington Post*, August 4, 1991.

69. Sands, "The Environment, Community, and International Law"; Liz Barratt-Brown, Natural Resources Defense Council, "Working Paper on Reform of Global Environmental Institutions," prepared for Consortium for Action to Protect the Earth, Washington, D.C., June 10, 1991; "PrepCom Opens its Process to Participation," *Network '92* (The Centre for Our Common Future, Geneva), October 1990; Victoria Dompka, "No Frivolity Please, We're British!," *ECO* (NGO Newsletter, Climate Change Negotiations, Nairobi), September 17, 1991.

70. Porter and Brown, *Global Environmental Politics*.

## Chapter 11. Launching the Environmental Revolution

1. E. Curtis Bohlen, Head of U.S. Delegation to Preparatory Committee for U.N. Conference on Environment and Development, at State Department briefing for nongovernmental organizations, Washington, D.C., August 6, 1991; Warren H. Lindner, Centre for Our Common Future and International Facilitating Committee, Geneva, private communication, October 14, 1991.

2. Roger Detels et al., "The UCLA Population Studies of CORD: X. A Cohort Study of Changes in Respiratory Function Associated with Chronic Exposure to $SO_x$, $NO_x$, and Hydrocarbons," *American Journal of Public Health*, March 1991; Judy Pasternak, "Long-Term Lung Damage Linked to Air Pollution," *Los Angeles Times*, March 29, 1991; "New Chernobyl Data Released," *Wall Street Journal*, April 19, 1991; William K. Reilly, "Statement on Ozone Depletion," U.S. Environmental Protection Agency, Washington, D.C., April 4, 1991.

3. U.S. Department of Agriculture, Economic Research Service, *World Grain Database* (unpublished printouts) (Washington, D.C.: 1991); World Bank, *World Development Report 1991* (New York: Oxford University Press, 1991).

4. World Bank, *World Development Report*.

5. U.N. Population Division, *Long-range World Population Projections: Two Centuries of Population Growth, 1950–2150* (New York: 1991).

6. T. Patrick Culbert and Don S. Rice, eds., *Precolumbian Population History in the Maya Lowlands* (Albuquerque: University of New Mexico Press, 1990); Schele quoted in David Roberts, "The Decipherment of Ancient Maya," *Atlantic Monthly*, September 1991.

7. Joseph C. Farman et al., "Large Losses of Total Ozone in Antarctica Reveal Seasonal $ClO_x/NO_x$ Interaction," *Nature*, May 16, 1985; Malcolm W. Browne, "93 Nations Agree to Ban Chemicals That Harm Ozone Layer," *New York Times*, June 30, 1990.

8. Douglas G. Cogan, *Stones in a Glass House: CFCs and Ozone Depletion* (Washington, D.C.: Investor Responsibility Research Center, 1988).

9. Christopher Flavin, *Reassessing Nuclear Power: The Fallout From Chernobyl*, Worldwatch Paper 75 (Washington,D.C.: Worldwatch Institute, March 1987).

10. Ernst von Weizsacher, speech at the launching of Worldwatch Institute Europe, Paris, September 24, 1991.

11. "Battle Looming Over Energy Tax Commission Expected to Propose This Month," *International Environment Reporter*, September 11, 1991; Ripa di Meana quoted in Howard LaFranchi, "EC Pushes to Adopt Model 'Sin Tax' on Energy Users," *Christian Science Monitor*, September 26, 1991.

12. "Germany Raises Energy Taxes," *European Energy Report*, March 8, 1991; "Bonn Brings in Major Oil Tax Rises to Fund East German Development," *European Energy Report*, May 31, 1991; "Germany's Ruling Parties Agree to Raise Gasoline Tax," *Global Environmental Change Report*, March 15, 1991; Karen Treanton, Statistics Department, International Energy Agency, Paris, private communication and printout, November 2, 1990.

13. Central Intelligence Agency, Directorate of Intelligence, *Handbook of Economic Statistics, 1990* (Washington, D.C.: National Technical Information Service, 1990); World Health Organization/U.N. Environment Programme Working Group, *Public Health Impact of Pesticides Used in Agriculture* (Geneva and Nairobi: 1989); Asian Development Bank, *Handbook on the Use of Pesticides in Asia-Pacific Region* (Manila, Philippines: 1987); Richard E. Rice, *National Forests: Policies for the Future, Volume 5, The Uncounted Costs of Logging* (Washington, D.C.: The Wilderness Society, August 1989).

14. California population and size of economy from *Information Please Almanac 1991* (Boston: Houghton Mifflin Co., 1991); Karen Griffin, *1990 Electricity Report* (Sacramento, Calif.: California Energy Commission, October 1990).

15. Matthew L. Wald, "E.P.A. Urging Electricity Efficiency," *New York Times*, January 16, 1991.

16. "The Carbon Club," *Atmosphere* (Friends of the Earth, Washington, D.C.), June 1991.

17. U.N. Department of International Economic and Social Affairs, *Review of Recent National Demographic Target Setting*, Population Studies No. 108 (New York: 1989); current fertility rate from Population Reference Bureau (PRB), *1991 World Population Data Sheet* (Washington, D.C.: 1991); Mexico's goal from President Carlos Salinas de Gortari, private communication, September 6, 1991.

18. Tellus Institute, *CSG/Tellus Packaging Study: Literature and Public Policy Review* (Boston: 1990).

19. Marcia D. Lowe, *The Bicycle: Vehicle for a Small Planet*, Worldwatch Paper 90 (Washington, D.C.: Worldwatch Institute, Septem-

ber 1989); automobiles from Motor Vehicle Manufacturers Association, *Facts and Figures '90* (Detroit, Mich.: 1990).

20. Robert J.L. Hawke, Prime Minister of Australia, "Speech by the Prime Minister: Launch of Statement on the Environment," Wentworth, N.S.W., Australia, July 20, 1989; Ministry of Housing, Physical Planning and Environment, *To Choose or To Lose: National Environmental Policy Plan* (The Hague: 1989); Ministry of the Environment, *Environment and Development: Programme for Norway's Follow-Up of the Report of the World Commission on Environment and Development*, Report to the Storting No. 46, 1988–89 (Oslo: Government of Norway, 1989); The Swedish Government, *A Living Environment: Main Proposals*, Bill 1990/91: 90 (Stockholm: 1991), translation by Linda Schenk and Michael Johns.

21. Ministry of Housing, Physical Planning and Environment, *To Choose or To Lose*; Ministry of Housing, Physical Planning and Environment, *National Environmental Policy Plan Plus* (The Hague: 1990).

22. Barber Conable, annual speech to the Board of Governors, World Bank, Washington, D.C., September 25, 1990.

23. Robert S. McNamara, "Reducing Military Expenditures in the Third World," *Finance & Development*, September 1991; Paul Blustein, "World Bank, IMF to Press Defense Cuts," *Washington Post*, October 18, 1991.

24. *Constitution of the Republic of Costa Rica 1949 (As Amended)* from the office of Ambassador Gonzalo J. Facio, Embassy of Costa Rica, Washington, D.C., October 22, 1991; PRB, *1991 World Population Data Sheet*.

25. For details of fourfold increase in global economy, see Lester R. Brown, "The New World Order," in Lester R. Brown et al., *State of the World 1991* (New York: W.W. Norton & Co., 1991).

26. Robert L. Simison, "European Electric-Car Firm, Supported By Los Angeles, Plans Late '92 Output," *Wall Street Journal*, September 10, 1991.

27. David Pimentel, Cornell University, Ithaca, N.Y., private communication, February 22, 1991.

28. Richard L. Ottinger and Nicholas M. Ward-Willis, Pace University, Pleasantville, N.Y., "Incorporating Environmental Externalities Through Pollution Taxes," September 27, 1991, presented at the World Clean Energy Conference, Geneva, Switzerland, November 4–7, 1991.

29. Peter Weber, "Green Seals of Approval Heading to Market," *World Watch*, July/August 1990.

30. Meri McCoy-Thompson, "Environmental Seal of Approval," *World Watch*, May/June 1989.

31. AT&T, "A Clean and Healthy Planet: AT&T Environment & Safety Report on Activities 1990," public relations document, Basking Ridge, N.J., undated; Barbara Baklarz, AT&T, Media Relations Manager, Environment & Safety, Basking Ridge, N.J., private communication, May 23, 1991.

32. Susan Williams and Kevin Porter, *Power Plays: Profiles of America's Independent Renewable Electricity Developers* (Washington, D.C.: Investor Responsibility Research Center, 1989); U.S. Department of Energy/Energy Information Administration, *International Energy Annual 1989* (Washington, D.C.: 1991).

33. Laura Zinn, "Whales, Human Rights, Rain Forests—And the Heady Smell of Profits," *Business Week*, July 15, 1991.

34. Ibid.

35. *Turning Values into Value: Ben & Jerry's 1990 Annual Report* (Waterbury, Vt.: Ben & Jerry's Homemade, Inc., 1991); Ben Cohen, chairperson of the board, Ben & Jerry's Homemade, Inc., before the Windstar Foundation Business Meeting, Aspen, Colo., Au-

gust 31, 1991; Rob Michalak, Public Relations Manager, Ben & Jerry's Homemade, Inc., Waterbury, Vt., private communication, October 22, 1991.

36. Ottinger and Ward-Willis, "Incorporating Environmental Externalities."

37. Janine Moore, Greenpeace International, Amsterdam, The Netherlands, private communication, October 1, 1991; Alan B. Durning, *Action at the Grassroots: Fighting Poverty and Environmental Decline*, Worldwatch Paper 88 (Washington, D.C.: Worldwatch Institute, January 1989); Hilary F. French, *Green Revolutions: Environmental Reconstruction in Eastern Europe and the Soviet Union*, Worldwatch Paper 99 (Washington, D.C.: Worldwatch Institute, November 1990).

38. Edward O. Wilson, *The Diversity of Life* (Cambridge, Mass: Harvard University Press, forthcoming).

39. Carbon dioxide emissions based on Gregg Marland et al., *Estimates of $CO_2$ Emissions from Fossil Fuel Burning and Cement Manufacturing, Based on the United Nations Energy Statistics U.S. Bureau of Mines Cement Manufacturing Data* (Oak Ridge, Tenn.: Oak Ridge National Laboratory, 1989), and on Thomas A. Boden et al., *Trends '91* (Oak Ridge, Tenn.: Oak Ridge National Laboratory, in press); Lester R. Brown and Edward C. Wolf, *Soil Erosion: Quiet Crisis in the World Economy*, Worldwatch Paper 60 (Washington, D.C.: Worldwatch Institute, September 1984).

40. Brown, "New World Order"; U.N. Population Divison, *Long-range World Population Projections*.

41. Jennifer Reese, "The Billionaires: More Than Ever in 1991," *Fortune*, September 9, 1991; millionaires estimated from Edmund Faltermayer, "Who are the Rich," *Fortune*, December 17, 1990.

42. Ivan Fallon, "The Jolly Green Giant," (London) *Sunday Times*, October 21, 1990; Nicholas Schoon and Virginia Myers, "Goldsmith to Fund Green Alliance," (London) *The Independent*, May 6, 1991.

43. Charles McCoy, "California Legislature Passes Timber Bill That Sharply Restricts Logging Practices," *Wall Street Journal*, September 16, 1991; Andrew Pollack, "Logging Regulation Bill Vetoed in California," *Washington Post*, October 13, 1991.

44. Peter Matthiessen, "The 'Madman' of Chernobyl" (op ed), *New York Times*, October 14, 1991.

45. Nicholas Lenssen, Worldwatch Institute, work with Father Polo as Peace Corps volunteer, May 1984–May 1987, and visit, November 26, 1990.

# Index